Tools
for
Building

Fine Homebuilding®

BUILDER'S LIBRARY

Tools for Building

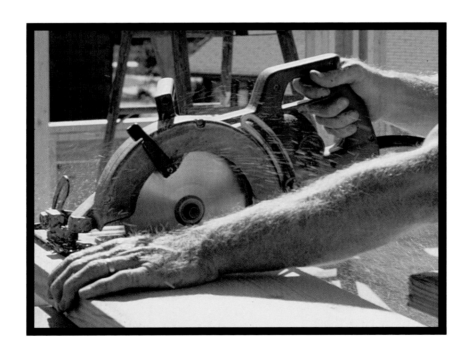

The Taunton Press

Cover photo by Stephen G. Pace

First printing: October 1988
Second printing: August 1990
International Standard Book Number: 0-942391-10-1
Library of Congress Catalog Card Number: 88-50565
Printed in the United States of America

A FINE HOMEBUILDING Book

FINE HOMEBUILDING is a trademark of The Taunton Press, Inc.,
registered in the U.S. Patent and Trademark Office.

The Taunton Press
63 South Main Street
Box 5506
Newtown, Connecticut 06470-5506

CONTENTS

There's something more to tools than their ability to transform raw materials into finished work. They somehow transform the workman too, and collectively have a way of becoming integral to his identity as a craftsman. This is why tools, aside from their great value as useful objects, are purchased and kept with unusual care.

In this book we've assembled 41 articles about tools and tool use from the back issues of FINE HOMEBUILDING magazine.* Here you'll find detailed information on most of the tools needed in residential construction—from T-squares and mason's twine to powder-actuated fasteners and oversize circular saws for cutting big beams. If you're interested in learning all you can about selecting and buying tools or about using them safely and effectively, the articles in this collection will add substantially to your store of information.

—*John Lively, editor*

*A footnote with each article tells when it was originally published. Product availability, suppliers' addresses, and prices may have changed since then.

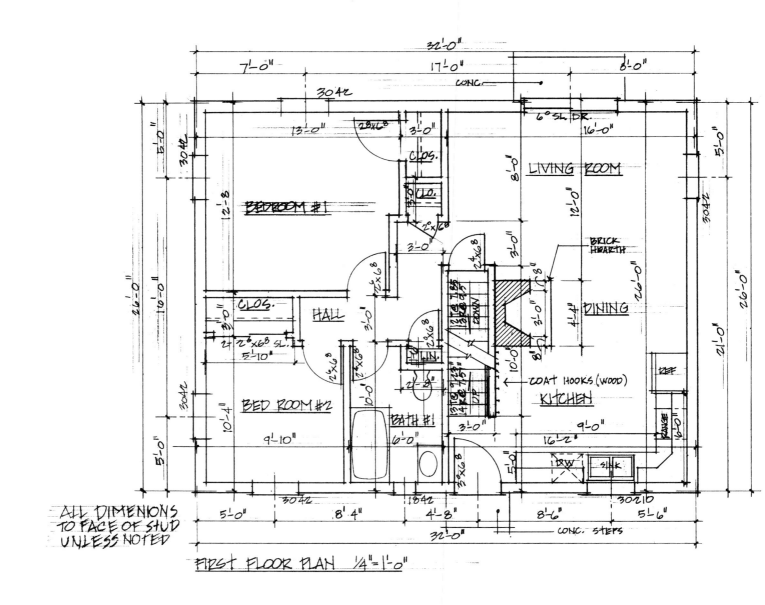

FIRST FLOOR PLAN ¼"=1'-0"

BOB SYVANEN HOUSE BREWSTER, MASS. DRAWN BY BOB SYVAN

ALL DIMENSIONS
TO FACE OF STUD
UNLESS NOTED

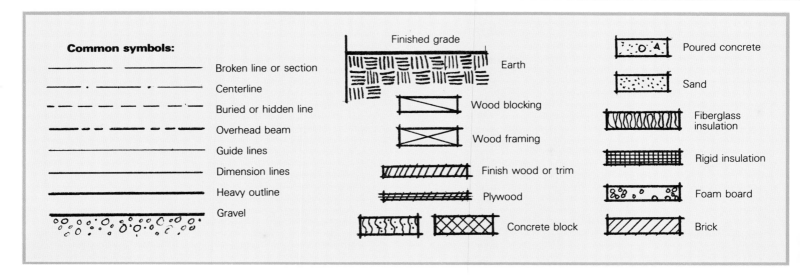

Common symbols:

Symbol	Name
———	Broken line or section
—·—·—	Centerline
— — —	Buried or hidden line
▬▬▬	Overhead beam
———	Guide lines
———	Dimension lines
━━━	Heavy outline
°o°o°	Gravel

Finished grade — Earth
Wood blocking
Wood framing
Finish wood or trim
Plywood
Concrete block

Poured concrete
Sand
Fiberglass insulation
Rigid insulation
Foam board
Brick

Drafting Basics
How one builder draws his own plans and elevations

ROOFING
ROOF SHEATH.
2X4 STUDS
2XU RAFT.
2X4 (CONT.)

RAKE BDS.
WALL SHEATH.

DET. @ RAKE 1½"=1'-0"

Note: Although drawn at ¼-in. scale, these plans have been reduced to fit in this book.

1987   SHEET 1 OF 5

by Bob Syvanen

Builders have a tremendous potential for drawing house plans. After all, they know how a house is built, they know the code and they know what a set of plans has to include. Builders also know that drawings don't have to be works of art to work.

Drawings for a complicated house design should be turned over to an architect. But simple plans for a house, garage or addition can be drawn readily enough by the builder. Thirty years ago, I built my first house and drew the plans myself with only high-school drafting experience and one summer as a carpenter's helper. Since then I've drawn plans for and learned much from some good architects and builders.

I have simplified my plans, particularly those drawn for skilled builders, and in what follows I will describe how I draw house plans that meet the building department's requirements, make the carpenter's job easier and satisfy the client.

Tools—My drawing board is a 33-in. by 36-in. piece of a solid-core door, with a sheet-vinyl drafting surface. I've long since replaced my T-square with a 36-in. parallel rule. I use a .5mm micro-lead mechanical pencil with H leads for all but the heavy lettering and line work (heavy hands might find the harder 2H lead better for layout work). Heavy lettering and line work I do with the standard 2mm mechanical pencil. I wouldn't be without an adjustable triangle, but mostly I use a 10-in. 45° triangle. I also have a 10-in. 30°/60° triangle and a 4-in. lettering-guide triangle. I use a circle template to show door swings—it beats a compass. Changes and mistakes are inevitable, so an eraser and erasing shield are a must. An architect's scale and a brush complete my list of tools (for more on drafting tools, see pp. 14-18).

Getting started—I do my drawings on tracing paper and cut all the sheets I'll need before I start drawing (typically at least four). Once I start, I don't like to break the continuity to cut more paper.

Building departments usually require a set of drawings that includes floor plans, a foundation plan, a section through the building and elevations. I turn over any unusual structural details to an engineer to work out. The cost for this service is minimal, and the peace of mind is worth it. The engineer's drawings must be stamped, signed and submitted to the building department along with the construction drawings.

Most small houses, additions and garages will fit on 11-in. by 17-in. sheets. I like this size because I can make photocopies of it. I can also make a copy of a copy (great for job-site changes signed by the client). And too, the 11-in. by 17-in. size is easy to work with on the job site. For 11-in. by 17-in. drawings, I make the paper 12 in. by 18 in., which is easily cut from 24-in. by 36-in. sheets, or from 24-in. or 36-in. wide rolls. The extra ½ in. all around allows room for taping the sheets down without interfering with the drawing.

After taping the first sheet of tracing paper to the board, I draw the 11-in. by 17-in. sheet size, making the line weight medium-heavy so that it can be traced easily later on (the 11-in. by 17-in. frame won't need to be measured again). Then I lay out the perimeter of the house (in the example we are using, a rectangle 26 ft. by 32 ft.) at ¼-in. scale, which is standard for floor plans. I leave 2 in. at the top for dimensions, 2½ in. to 3 in. at the bottom for dimensions and titles, and 3 in. on the left side for dimensions and binding. Any extra space on the right can be used for details.

These layout lines should be light, but not so light that they are difficult to see. The H lead is just right for me, as I have a light touch. I stroke with the pencil held at about 60° from horizontal, maintaining that angle from start to finish. It's an arm stroke, not a wrist stroke, that provides even pressure the full length of the line.

After drawing the exterior perimeter, I draw the interior perimeter lines to establish the thickness of the outside walls. The interior partitions come next, and I draw all the partitions to the approximate scale of their real thickness. For 2x6 stud walls, I use 6 in.; for 2x4 stud walls, I use 4 in. At ¼-in. scale, there isn't much difference between 3½ in. and 4 in. However, there is a noticeable difference between 6 in. and 4 in. I make sure a 2x6 stud wall looks fatter than a 2x4 stud wall.

When drawing house plans, keep in mind that no matter what the drawing itself measures, it's the dimensions indicated that the tradespeople on the site will use for construction. Therefore, the numbers must be right. If the drawing is also precisely scaled, so much the better.

Adding the elements—Exterior doors and windows are located and dimensioned to their centerlines. However, at this stage of the drawing they are just visual locations that will be dimensioned later. I locate the exterior doors and windows for layout purposes by measuring with

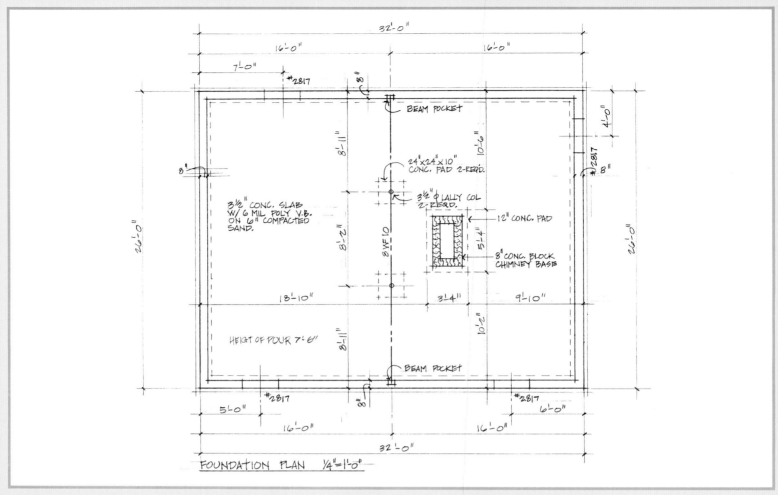

FOUNDATION PLAN ¼"=1'-0"

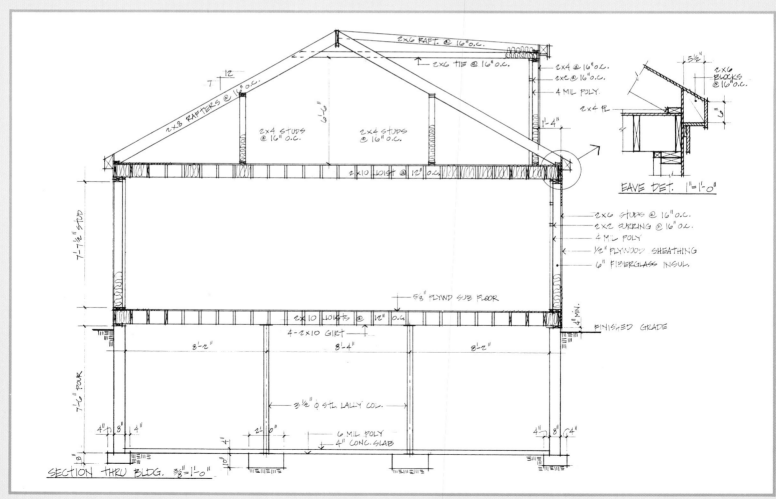

EAVE DET. 1"=1'-0"

SECTION THRU BLDG. ⅜"=1'-0"

a scale. I try to stay with full-foot or half-foot measurements. It is easy to dimension that way, and I've found that a plan that draws easily builds easily as well.

Interior doors are best located opening against a wall. The hinge side should be at least 4 in. from the wall to allow for framing and casing.

Our Massachusetts code requires that stairways be at least 3 ft. wide. The minimum headroom is 6 ft. 8 in. (6 ft. 6 in. for basement stairs), the minimum tread is 9 in., and the maximum riser is 8¼ in. There are other requirements, but those are the basics for stairway design.

Multiplying the number of treads (13 in this case) by the tread dimension (9½ in.) establishes the run or length of stairway to be 10 ft. 3½ in. So the space I must allow for the stairway on the floor plan is 3 ft. (minimum by code) by 10 ft. 3½ in.

For fireplace layout, I use the code and the style of the fireplace to determine the exterior masonry dimensions. My favorite fireplace, for both efficiency and looks, is a modified Rumford style with a 36-in. wide fireplace opening. The exterior masonry dimensions work out to 36 in. by 60 in. With the addition of the 20-in. by 64-in. front hearth, the total floor space required is 56 in. by 64 in.

Layout for kitchen cabinets is just a matter of deciding where they go. Base cabinets are 24 in. deep, and wall cabinets are 12 in. deep. I draw all the cabinet lines first and then locate the various appliances within them—range, dishwasher and refrigerator.

Bathrooms are fairly straightforward. The toilet is placed 15 in. from its centerline to a wall. An enclosed tub/shower is 5 ft. long. The sink is usually installed in an 18-in., 21-in. or 24-in. deep counter.

Once you're satisfied that everything is where you want it, darken the lines so that the drawing is easier to read. A medium-weight line with the layout pencil (H lead for me) will do for now. Changes will be easier, and you'll minimize smudges, if you leave the final punching up of the line work until later.

Dimension lines—The dimension lines come next, and they should be lighter in the finished drawing than the partition lines. The walls want to jump out at you, but the dimension lines just need to be clear.

Any dimension that will help the carpenters should be noted on the drawing. The dimensions outside the building should include the overall dimension, breaks in the overall dimension (such as in an L or U-shaped house), along with window and door centerlines. The carpenters need the centerlines of windows and doors for their layout. They know what the rough openings should be from the sizes specified in the manufacturer's catalogs. The dimensions inside the building should include partition locations, door locations (when a specific distance from a wall is desired), cabinets and counter sizes, fireplace location and size, and stair location and size (including tread and riser).

The first dimension line I make, ½ in. from the outside face of the exterior walls, is the window and door dimension line. The ½-in. space leaves

room for notes at windows and doors. The next dimension line is ⅜ in. out from the window dimension line. This line is for the breaks in the total dimension. The third line, ⅜ in. out from the second, is for the overall dimension. These spacings make the drawing easy to read.

Keep interior dimension lines near the walls to allow space for labeling rooms and to prevent lines from running through the dimension callout. Dimensions read best when they are positioned at the midpoint of a dimension line.

To terminate dimension lines, I favor a small 45° slash, drawn freehand. It is quick and easy to draw, and very clear to read. Wherever lines meet, whether they're dimension, partition or detail-drawing lines, they look best and read clearest when they extend past or cross each other. It is also easier to draw this way.

I end my dimension lines at the face of a partition because it is an easy way to dimension drawings accurately. However, mistakes can be made in the field by laying out to the wrong side of the partition (setting a wall on the wrong side of a line). Dimensioning to both sides of the partition is a way to prevent this.

Dimensioning this way introduces a ½-in. fraction to the dimensions because most interior studs are 3½ in. This is a bothersome addition, and so some draftsmen round off 3½ in. to 4 in. The carpenter, knowing what the draftsman has done, lays out the partitions using the 4-in. dimensions and then adjusts the half-inch at each partition. Since I make all dimensions read to the face of the studs (as opposed to the center), I put this note on all my floor plans: "All Dimensions to Face of Stud Unless Noted Otherwise."

It is easier for the draftsman and the carpenter to work with even numbers. I never use a dimension less than ⅛ in. anywhere on the plans. After all, I'm drawing a house, not a cabinet. It's better to stay with ¼ in. for a minimum dimension. Whatever system is used for dimensioning, the sum of the inside dimensions must equal the total exterior dimension. Always check this.

I put in all the guide lines for dimension callouts and the lettering at the same time. The lettering-guide triangle is the tool to use for this. It allows you to draw parallel lines quickly at various spacings. My dimension guide lines and note guide lines are spaced ³⁄₃₂ in. apart. Room labels and drawing labels are ³⁄₁₆ in. apart. The title box, with the owner's name, house address, draftsman's name, date and sheet number get the heaviest lettering on the page. To keep the drawings clean, I do the heavy lettering last.

Dimension callouts are placed above horizontal dimension lines and to the left of vertical dimension lines, reading parallel to the line. For the vertical dimensions and lettering, don't turn the sheet on the board; instead, turn your body 90° counterclockwise.

The simplest way to call out doors is to note the size at each opening. Windows similarly can be called out at the openings using the manufacturer's model number.

Second-floor plan—When the first-floor plan is finished, I tape a sheet of tracing paper over it and trace the 11-in. by 17-in. sheet size. All the

features from the first floor that show up on the second floor—exterior walls, stairs, chimney—I trace onto the new page. Then I proceed through the same steps that I followed for drawing the first-floor plan.

Foundation plan—The foundation plan is the easiest to draw, because it's the simplest—there are no partitions and few openings. It is also the most critical drawing, for this is the part of a house that is literally "cast in stone." I have seen floor plans changed because of mistakes in the foundation pour.

The first step is the same as for drawing the second-floor plan, I trace the outside of the floor plan and draw the inside of the foundation wall to show an 8-in., 10-in. or 12-in. thickness, as shown in the top drawing on the facing page. I then trace the chimney base, which will be the same size as the masonry dimensions of the fireplace above. Next I trace the stair location. For the girder size and the spacing of columns, I turn to my building-code handbook, which shows girder and column sizes (wood and steel) and spacings for columns (with footing size) for most conditions.

Footings are usually twice as wide as the foundation wall. For an 8-in. wall, I draw the footing as a solid line 4 in. outside the wall and a broken line 4 in. inside the wall, indicating that it lies under the basement floor slab.

I dimension windows to their centerline (the frames are usually cast in place), but I draw the doors and other openings to the masonry-opening size, which is determined by the door size and how it is to be trimmed.

Garage-door openings can be a problem area. I like the masonry opening to be 3 in. wider than the door. This additional width makes room for 2x jamb stock. I also call for the foundation wall to be thinned, at the opening, to the thickness of the stud wall. This allows the overhead door track and its 2x6 mounting board to extend to the floor.

I draw all openings and holes at this time; for instance, a beam pocket for a dropped girder (a beam with the floor joists resting on top of it, instead of butting into it). I call out "Beam Pocket" at each end of the girder with an arrow to the location. If the septic line, water line or power line must go through the foundation wall in specified places, those locations should be indicated on the foundation plan. More often the holes are punched through after the pour.

Notes—I call out door opening sizes in basement walls and label them "M.O." (masonry opening) for the benefit of the concrete contractor. I put the dimension line locating the center of the girder outside the foundation. When this dimension is drawn inside, it's not always clear whether the dimension reads to the inside face or outside face of the concrete wall.

Column footings are located and dimensioned to their centerline. But I draw in the perimeter of the chimney footing. For an average chimney, the code requires that the footing be 12 in. thick and 6 in. wider, all around, than the chimney base. This base is usually concrete block, so I size it to the block module that is close to the

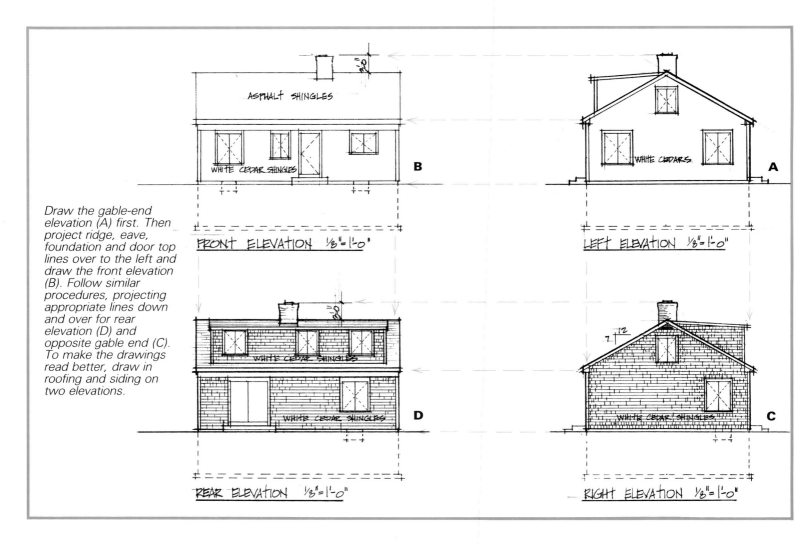

Draw the gable-end elevation (A) first. Then project ridge, eave, foundation and door top lines over to the left and draw the front elevation (B). Follow similar procedures, projecting appropriate lines down and over for rear elevation (D) and opposite gable end (C). To make the drawings read better, draw in roofing and siding on two elevations.

ASPHALT SHINGLES

WHITE CEDAR SHINGLES

B

FRONT ELEVATION ⅛"=1'-0"

WHITE CEDARS

A

LEFT ELEVATION ⅛"=1'-0"

WHITE CEDAR SHINGLES

WHITE CEDAR SHINGLES

D

REAR ELEVATION ⅛"=1'-0"

7 | 12

WHITE CEDAR SHINGLES

C

RIGHT ELEVATION ⅛"=1'-0"

fireplace masonry dimensions. I then make the footing 6 in. wider at the sides and locate it relative to the foundation walls. As with the foundation footings, I draw the chimney footings with broken lines.

To keep from confusing the concrete contractor, the foundation plan should stay as simple as possible. Too many dimensions and notes on a plan can cause dimensions to be missed or transposed. I like notes to be bold, boxed or underlined so that they jump out at the reader. I call out the floor condition with a note located within the walls of the foundation. A basement slab note would read: "3½-in. Concrete Slab With 6-mil Polyethylene Vapor Barrier Under on Compacted Sand." The garage-slab note would be: "4-in. Concrete Slab With 6x6 #10 Wire Mesh Over Compacted Sand."

One of the most important notes to go on the foundation plan indicates the height of the pour. Standard foundation forms are 8 ft. high, and since they are never filled to the top, I call for a 7-ft. 8-in. pour, or if I have to stretch it, I call for a 7-ft. 10-in. pour. I label the girder (4-2x10s, 6x12, 8W10) and call out posts or Lally columns with a note and arrow pointing to only one column. The note would read: "3½-in. Lally column, 4 required." All nailers should be pressure treated and so noted at each location (usually an exterior door). As with the other drawings, the last step is to darken the foundation-wall lines and the chimney base so that they jump out at the reader.

Section—The section through the building shows the foundation, the first-floor framing, the second-floor framing, the rafters and the stud walls. Then I make a note on the floor plan that indicates where the section is taken from. Section drawings are commonly done at a scale of ½ in. = 1 ft., but when space is limited, I often use ⅜ in. = 1 ft. For a simple house, garage or addition, I usually draw only half of the house in section. If the house is complex, I draw a full section and any unusual framing sections.

I start this drawing at the footing and progress upward as if I were building the house (bottom drawing, p. 10). On top of the footings, I draw the foundation walls with the mudsill on top. Next come the floor joists, girder, Lally columns and subfloor. The stud length can be figured once the floor-to-ceiling height is established, or vice versa. I draw the rafter next, locating the ridge and outlining the eaves. Nearby, I like to make a blown-up section of the eave detail at ¾-in. scale.

The adjustable triangle—This is the tool to use for drawing rafters and eave details. I draw a quick diagram of the roof pitch, 7 in 12 for example, and then set the adjustable triangle to the angle drawn so it will be ready whenever a 7-in-12 pitch is needed.

I draw the ceiling framing next, and if there is a dormer, I include it on this drawing as well. This means setting the adjustable triangle for the dormer-roof pitch. When the layout is done and

no changes are anticipated, I darken the line work to medium-heavy. I also put the conventional symbols on the various members—wiggly lines for insulation, X for cut-through framing members, and crosshatching for the earth (bottom drawing, p. 8).

Dimensions and labels—The features I dimension on the section sheet are footing size, foundation-wall height and thickness, concrete-slab thickness, floor-to-ceiling heights, and the distance from top of the foundation wall to the finished grade (on a sloped lot the grade dimension reads: "Varies").

It's important to place labels for members and materials for easy reading. When there is space, I label directly on the member. Otherwise I place the label to the side and draw an arrow to it.

For a material, I always place the label to the side and draw an arrow to it. I try to keep the labeling on the outside of the exterior wall (about ½ in. or so), lined up on a left margin. I draw the arrow lines, using the parallel rule, from the label to the material. Some labeling works better on the inside of the exterior wall, and some arrow lines have to be angled to get to the material being called out. The main objective is to make the information easy to read, and to provide enough information for the builder to build the house.

After the dimensioning and labeling is done and all corrections and changes have been made, I darken the line work. For this heavy line work, I prefer a 2mm H lead. I make the heaviest lines on members that are cut through by the section. Those members would be foundation, mudsill, headers, beams, ridge, eave trim and finished grade line.

Details—Detail drawings are necessary only for conditions that require special attention. They are just small sections at a larger scale. I do details at ¾-in. scale, but when the detail is complicated, I use a larger scale, sometimes even full scale (provided it fits on the paper).

Graph paper is nice for details because you just count squares and draw. Again, the drawing does not have to be a great work of art (a lot of details are drawn at the job site on wood scraps), but it must clearly show what the materials are and how they go together.

Elevations—Elevation drawings are head-on views of facades, and are typically done at ¼-in. scale. But I like to draw them at ⅛-in. scale so they'll fit on an 11-in. by 17-in. sheet. I can draw them faster at this smaller scale, and they still do the job of showing what the house will look like. The elevations usually required are front, rear, right and left. They illustrate siding, roofing, chimneys, windows, doors, roof pitch, roof trim, finished grade, foundations and any other exterior features.

I lay out a gable-end elevation first, in the upper right-hand corner of the sheet. I draw in the footing lines, followed by the top of the foundation wall. These features are the easiest to locate—8 in. for the footing thickness, and a 7-ft. 8-in. high poured concrete wall on top of it. I pick off the location of the various features (ridge, eaves, doors and windows) by measuring or calculating from the section drawing. For accurate drawings, these features can be mathematically calculated, but at ⅛-in. scale, I find measuring works fine. It's then a simple matter of drawing the side-elevation outline.

I use the dimensions on the floor plan to locate the windows, doors and chimneys. I indicate the finished floor with a light dashed line, scaled about 12 in. above the top of the foundation wall (for 2x10 floor joists). I locate the door tops at 6 ft. 8 in. from the finished floor. The tops of windows are usually the same height as the doors.

After the gable-end elevation is laid out, I project the ridge, eave, foundation and door-top lines over to the left and lay out the front elevation in the same manner as the gable-end elevation (drawing, facing page). I lay out the other gable-end elevation below the first one by projecting the ridge and exterior wall lines downward. I lay out the rear elevation by projecting down from the front elevation and projecting over from the second gable-end elevation.

Filling in—I detail the windows to show how they open (awning, casement, double-hung or fixed glass) and to indicate glass panes. At ⅛-in. scale I use single lines to separate panes, but I use double lines to show thickness for the frames and sill. Some window manufacturers have scale drawings of their different models available for tracing. To use these, I tape the scale window

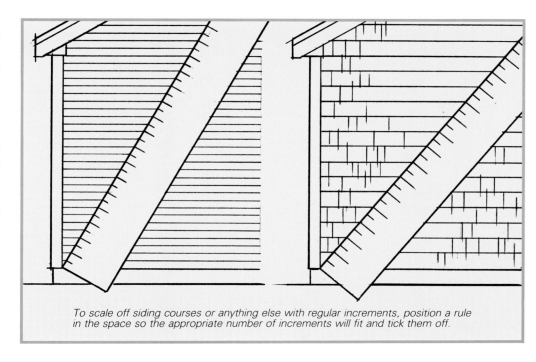

To scale off siding courses or anything else with regular increments, position a rule in the space so the appropriate number of increments will fit and tick them off.

drawing to a longish piece of paper and then slide the whole business under the elevation drawing. This allows me to position the window precisely where I want it for tracing without lifting the elevation sheet.

I indicate the window swing (casement, awning, hopper) with two dashed lines that start at the middle of the hinge side of the window and terminate on the opposite edge of the sash, each line to an opposing corner. I show sliding windows with an arrow on the movable sash, indicating the direction of the slide. Fixed glass is called out as such. I draw window and door casings last.

The final steps—After the elevations have been labeled and the line work has been darkened, nothing else needs to be done to make the drawing work. However, to make the elevations read better—more realistically—I draw in the siding and roofing on at least two view of the house.

For the roofing I like closely spaced (about ⅟₁₆-in.) broken parallel lines. The lines extend from gable to gable, parallel to the ridge. I prefer to stagger the lengths as I progress down the roof, starting at about ⅓ of the roof length and ending up with full-length lines at the eave. The result looks like a sunlit shingled roof.

I draw siding using the exposure of the siding material for spacing the line work. Shingle courses would be 5 in.; clapboards, 4 in., 5 in. or 10 in.; and vertical or diagonal siding would be 4 in. to 10 in. To locate the course lines on the drawing, I angle a scale in the space to be divided until the scale fits the right number of increments for the number of courses, as shown in the drawing above. It works for horizontal, vertical and diagonal siding. The line work can be continuous from corner to corner or broken similar to the roof. For shingles I add vertical lines to simulate individual shingles. This is not a necessity, but it does show at a glance what the siding is, and it dresses up a drawing.

I use a triangle against the parallel rule when

drawing shingle lines. I accent the corners, doors, windows, eaves and bottom courses by using more vertical lines in those areas. I use medium-heavy lines to show textures so as not to overpower the drawing.

After the texture and labeling are finished, I darken the line work. I do heavy lines with a 2mm H lead. Windows doors and trim are drawn heavy first, the outline of the house (including chimney and dormer) is heavier, and then the finished grade is drawn heaviest.

Titles—I put the titles on each sheet after all the plans are finished. This way the titles are consistent and more quickly done. I place titles on one line at the bottom of the sheet. I start with the client's name drawn heaviest, followed by the address a tad smaller and the draftsman's name and date the smallest. After the date, I leave 2 in. for revision dates, and in the corner, I put a bold sheet number followed by the number of sheets ("Sheet 1 of 5"). To highlight the title I draw a heavy line under it. I underline all titles, such as Bath, Kitchen, First-Floor Plan, Section Through, and Detail, on all sheets.

Finished drawings should be handled with care. Water is very destructive, and fingers smudge pencil lines. It's best to use photocopies for discussion and keep the original drawings in a safe place. If they must be rolled, drawings are best protected inside a tube. If I don't have one, I roll the drawings up and cover the roll with a piece of typing paper. I keep the roll together with tape rather than a rubber band, which tends to crease the drawing. □

Bob Syvanen is a consulting editor for Fine Homebuilding *and a builder in Brewster, Mass. His book* Drafting: Tips and Tricks on Drawing and Designing House Plans *is available for $8.95 from Globe Pequot Press Inc. (Old Chester Rd., Chester Conn. 06412). A three-part video, "Drawing House Plans with Bob Syvanen," is available for $104.85 from SVEL, 179 Underpass Rd., Brewster, Mass. 02631.*

Drafting Tools

It doesn't take a big investment to gear up for drawing your own plans

by Eric Rekdahl

My dad's drafting board was a fixture in my house while I was growing up, and I took my first drafting class in 7th grade. As an architect-builder, I spend countless hours working out designs at my own board, so I am sometimes amazed when my friends who are builders assign a kind of mystery to the tools and the procedures used to produce architectural drawings.

Scribbling on a scrap of 2x4 appears to be a long way from drafting a full set of architectural drawings. But the method of communication is the same. Drafting just allows you to be more precise and to visualize things more completely.

The entire building industry is geared to drawings, from your local building inspector to your plumbing sub who needs to remind you that you haven't left enough room for that 36-in. fiberglass shower stall. Drawing your own plans can save you money, prevent critical delays and contribute substantially to your understanding of how the building will go together and how well it will work. When completed, the drawings will represent your total knowledge of the project, and will serve as a touchstone in the communications among everyone involved.

Drafting is a craft if not an art, and that means that it requires both knowledge and practice. There are lots of books that can introduce you to drafting symbols, techniques and approaches. After that, it's a matter of practice. I'm not going to attempt to teach drafting here. Instead, I'll make a survey of the tools that will help you draw plans that are clear and accurate.

Drafting tools are quite simple, and a lot less expensive than the kind used to build houses. Unlike most construction tools, drafting tools are often manufactured by local concerns. Some national brands known for quality are J. S. Staedtler (1 Mars Court, Montville, N. J. 07045), Faber-Castell Corp. (4 Century Dr., Parsippany, N. J. 07054), Koh-I-Noor Rapidograph Inc. (100 North St., Bloomsbury, N. J. 08804), K & E (Keuffel & Esser, 20 Whippany Rd., Morristown, N. J. 07960), Dietzgen Corp. (250 Wille Rd., Des Plains, Ill. 60018) and Berol USA (Eagle Rd., Danbury, Conn. 06810), to name just a few. But you don't have to shop name brands to do well. The quality of a tool is generally evident from the quality of the materials used, and from the price. If you are in doubt, you can buy the nationally known brand or use it for comparison.

Lead and lead holders—Most architectural drawings are done in pencil lead. You can use either a wood-clad pencil or a lead holder,

which is the simplest kind of mechanical pencil (inset photo, facing page). Since you will have to sharpen the lead (called *pointing*) every 10 to 20 strokes, one of the critical factors in choosing a pencil is how you're going to sharpen it. Wood-clad pencils (Mars-Staedtler by J. S. Staedtler, Eagle Turquoise by Berol, and Castell by Faber-Castell are good examples) are cheap at about 50¢ to 60¢ apiece, but they are difficult to keep sharp since you have to remove all the wood to get to the lead. There are special kinds of sharpeners that remove just the wood and

leave the lead to be sharpened separately, but why bother?

There are two kinds of lead holders: the standard 2mm holder, and a variety of thin-lead holders. Some well-known brands of lead holders are Koh-I-Noor, K & E and Pentel. A standard lead holder uses 2mm-dia. leads and costs between $2 and $7. The holder generally has a push-button top controlling the clamping jaws near the point. This lets you expose just the correct amount of lead for pointing.

Pointers come in a variety of shapes and sizes, and run between $4.50 and $12.95. Some use a slightly conical sandpaper drum to sharpen the lead, some have blades, and some use an abrasive metal wheel. Whatever your choice, the idea is to sharpen only the lead. The softer the lead, the more often you'll have to sharpen it.

The advantage of thin lead holders, which are available in a variety of lead diameters (.3mm, .5mm, .7mm and .9mm) is that the lead usually doesn't require pointing. I've been using a .5mm lead holder almost exclusively for the past ten years. I have found that my line weight is more consistent, and the only sharpening I need to do is to chisel-point the lead (chamfer the lead up near the point) on a piece of scratch paper as I'm lettering.

Lead comes in a wide variety of hardnesses:

9H 8H 7H 6H 5H 4H 3H 2H H F HB B 2B 3B 4B 5B 6B

Hardest ⟵———— Medium ————⟶ Softest

The hardness you use is largely a matter of personal preference and is generally a measure of how complete the drawing is. Preliminary layout lines are drawn very lightly with harder leads than the lead that's used for lettering or borders toward the completion of the drawing. Leads for 2mm holders run the full range of hardness and cost around $5 a dozen, while thin leads are available from 6H through 2B and run less than $1 a dozen. You're not going to need the entire range. I have never used any harder than 3H or any softer than 2B. A good selection to start with would be 3H, H, HB and 2B.

Paper—You can draw on almost any type of paper. I often work out my preliminary details on 8½-in. by 11-in. graph paper, but most of my work is done on tracing paper for two reasons. First, the most economical method of reproduction for any sheet greater than 11 in. by 17 in. is a diazo process. This requires light to shine through the drawing paper to a light sensitive emulsion on the print paper, which is then developed by exposure to ammonia vapor (for

From *Fine Homebuilding* magazine (April 1985) 26:58-62

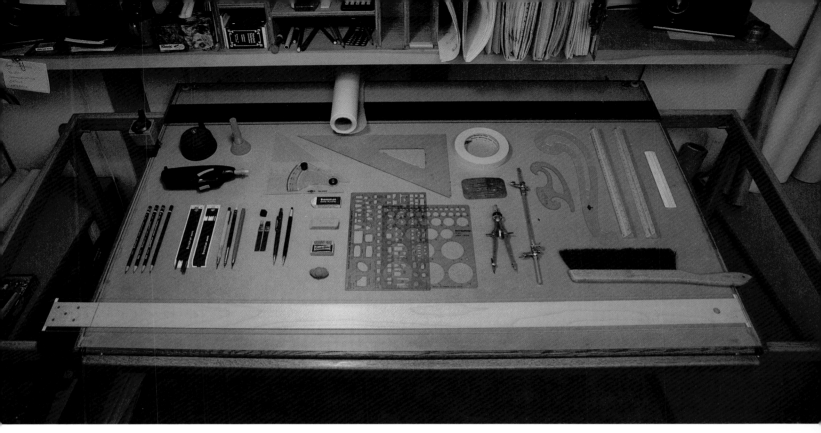

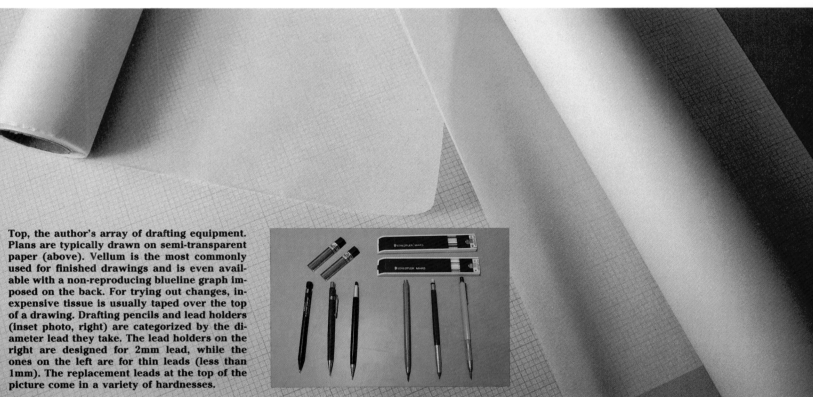

Top, the author's array of drafting equipment. Plans are typically drawn on semi-transparent paper (above). Vellum is the most commonly used for finished drawings and is even available with a non-reproducing blueline graph imposed on the back. For trying out changes, inexpensive tissue is usually taped over the top of a drawing. Drafting pencils and lead holders (inset photo, right) are categorized by the diameter lead they take. The lead holders on the right are designed for 2mm lead, while the ones on the left are for thin leads (less than 1mm). The replacement leads at the top of the picture come in a variety of hardnesses.

more on reproduction techniques, see p. 18). Second and most important, is the ability it gives me to trace over a previous drawing. Frequently, the first drawing I do is the floor plan. This is followed by successive layers—the second-floor plan, and foundation, framing and roof plans.

The most common type of tracing paper is vellum. Vellum comes in various qualities and thicknesses, and is available in rolls (a 36-in. wide roll 20 yd. long runs about $20), and in sheets that are multiples of 8½x11 or 9x12 (50 sheets of 18x24 also cost about $20). You can also get vellum that has a blue (non-reproducing) grid printed on the back side.

Another common type of tracing paper is much thinner and available only in rolls. It is variously referred to as "sketch paper," "tissue," "flimsy," "bum wad," or whatever, depending on where you are. As these names imply, it is not intended for permanent drawings but is torn to size using a straightedge and hurriedly placed over the permanent drawing to try out an alternative layout or arrangement. A 50-yard roll 12 in. wide costs only about $3. Because it is very thin, erasing is risky. But you can't beat it for preliminary planning and sketching since many layers of tissue can be built up before obscuring the one on the bottom.

More permanent transparent materials such as plastic film and linen are also used for drawing, but they are expensive and I use them only for big projects. Mylar is the most used plastic. It is textured to give some "tooth" for the lead to grab onto, but sometimes only on one side (drawing on the back is often very useful for things that aren't going to change, like structural

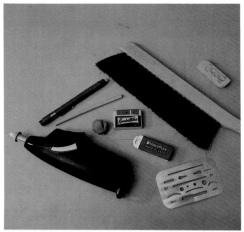

Erasers. Erasing isn't just for beginners—it's used more to improve a drawing than to correct mistakes. Abrasive, vinyl and kneadable erasers are shown here with an erasing shield (for protecting the lines that are to remain), an electric eraser and a drafting brush. The pencil-like tool holds a long, thin abrasive eraser.

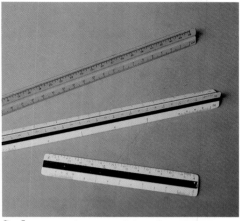

Scales come in several lengths, shapes and varieties. The one at the top of the photo is a triangular 12-in. engineer's scale that divides an inch into 10, 20, 30, 40, 50 and 60 parts. The more familiar architect's scales are represented by a 12-in. triangular model that has a ruler and ten commonly used scales, and a 6-in. model with eight different scales.

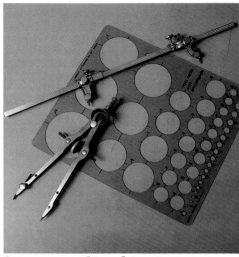

Compasses and templates. There are lots of ways to draw circles. A 12-in. beam compass can make circles with very large radii, but the 6-in. bow compass will usually suffice. Even simpler and less expensive is a circle template.

grid lines, etc.). On the textured side, repeated erasures tend to smooth the tooth, which changes the line weight somewhat.

Linen is the nicest surface I have drawn on. Unlike Mylar, the tooth is very durable so you can make a lot of changes (or mistakes) without worry. Linen's most serious liability is that a drop of water or coffee will dissolve the gel that is added to the fabric in manufacturing to give it transparency and rigidity. This will leave a spot when the drawing is reproduced.

Taping the paper to the board is essential if you're using a parallel rule or drafting machine. I use masking tape (½ in. or ¾ in.) because it is stickier than drafting tape since I like to stretch my paper tight when I put it down. Drafting tape, on the other hand, doesn't tear the paper as masking tape tends to do. Make sure that the top or bottom of the paper is parallel to your straightedge before taping it down. Move the straightedge down to the center of the paper and apply pressure with your forearm. Tape one of the top corners first, and without releasing pressure on the straightedge, stretch the paper across the board until it is tight and you can secure the tape on the other top corner. Repeat this procedure for the bottom corners by stretching the paper down and away at each corner. Make sure that the pieces of tape overlap the corner of the paper completely so that the straightedge won't catch the tape and roll it right off the paper.

After taping a sheet of paper to the board for the first time, draw a register mark at each vertical edge of the sheet using the straightedge. Make sure that you don't move the straightedge until you've marked both sides. The marks you are making will let you re-attach the sheet perfectly square to the straightedge just by positioning the paper underneath it so that the index marks show above the line of the straightedge.

Erasers—Erasers are important not so much for correcting mistakes as for inevitable changes of mind. Drawing plans requires you to think through each connection, and that allows you to

make corrections and even major changes throughout the process. There are three types of erasers: abrasive, non-abrasive and kneadable (photo above left). Each costs about 45¢. Abrasive erasers like the familiar Pink Pearl sand away part of the paper. They come in a wide variety of colors and shapes including a slender rod form that can be be used either in a tool that looks like a lead holder, or in an electric erasing machine.

The non-abrasive eraser was developed for plastic films to prevent tooth loss. These are generally made of a white or translucent vinyl. They erase by peeling up the graphite particles from the paper, which form little worm-like threads with the eraser residue. However, because they are not quite as thorough as the abrasive type, I sometimes start with the plastic and finish with the pink.

A kneadable eraser is really more like a lump of putty than an eraser. By working it back and forth in your hands, you bring fresh material to the surface. Pressing this on the paper will lift off the image, in offset fashion. I use it frequently to lighten a line or texture that got too dark. By varying the amount you scrub and the pressure, you can control how much is lifted off—within limits. It cannot scrub as clean as the abrasive, but because it can be shaped and molded to a point, it is good for removing smudges from the hard-to-get-at corners.

An erasing shield is a thin sheet of stainless steel with several odd-shaped holes punched in it. Placed over the drawing, it masks out what is to remain while allowing room to scrub clean within the hole. If you don't use the shield, an eraser will inevitably smudge the end of the lines that are to remain. A large shield costs about $2, a small one about 45¢. They can be hard to pick up from a flat surface until you bend them into a slight curve, which will give you an edge to grab.

Wiping away the erasure residue with the edge of your hand will smear the drawing. Blowing it away will just leave you hyperventilated and the paper moist. A better alternative is a

drafting brush. A horsehair version will run you less than $5. Also use it to give your board a clean sweep before you tape down a new sheet of paper. There's nothing more frustrating than trying to letter over a bump.

Scales—There are two general types: the architect's scale and the engineer's scale. The engineer's scale breaks the inch into 10, 20, 30, 40, 50 or 60 parts. Most often this translates to 1 in. = 20 ft. or 1 in. = 50 ft. More useful is the architect's scale, which represents feet in different fractions of an inch (such as ³⁄₃₂, ⅛, ³⁄₁₆, ⅜, ½, ¾, 1, 1½, and 3 in. to a foot).

Architect's scales are triangular or flat (photo above center). The 12-in. triangular cross section offers the most options. It has six edges for scales instead of four for the flat scale. Because the 10 architect's scales listed above can be paired up with multiples of each other (one reading right to left, the other reading left to right), only five edges are needed, so the sixth edge is a 12-in. ruler. These run from $2.25 to $25; I usually go for the midrange.

If you aren't familiar with this kind of scale, you will soon catch on to the fact that half of the numbers along one face of the scale belong to the scale that begins at the left, and that the other half of the numbers apply to the scale that begins on the right. Each of these scales is also broken down into scaled inches to the outside of its respective 0. Any length line can be drawn or measured in feet and inches by placing the nearest whole-unit increment at one end of the line and then measuring the other end of the line in inches where it extends beyond the 0.

Flat scales, which come in both 12-in. and 6-in. lengths, omit the seldom used ³⁄₃₂-in. and ³⁄₁₆-in. scales and the ruler. The 6-incher will cost you anywhere from $2 to $10. It is almost as useful, but far less cumbersome and frustrating when you're struggling to find the right scale. A good balance for me is to have a 12-in. triangular architect's scale and a 6-in. (pocket-sized) flat architect's scale.

I should pass on the admonition of every

drafting instructor I've ever had: "A scale is not a straightedge. It is used to measure only." That's good advice, but it's hard to follow when you're working out details on graph paper.

Triangles and templates—The best straightedge for vertical and angled lines is the triangle. Manufactured in various sizes and three different shapes, it is the inseparable companion of the T-square or parallel rule. Triangles are generally made of clear plastic about ⅛ in. thick, and are fixed or adjustable. Fixed triangles come in 30°-60°-90° and 45°-45°-90°. A fairly large fixed triangle such as the 14-in. 30°-60°-90° I use costs about $4. The adjustable triangle is essentially a right triangle with the hypotenuse attached so it can pivot. This lets you reproduce any angle. An 8-in. adjustable costs about $11 or $12.

You'll also need to draw circles occasionally, and this requires either a compass or a template. A compass has the advantage of being adjustable to different radii. The maximum radius a compass will draw, though, has a lot do with its size and design. A 12-in. beam compass at $15 to $22 is capable of much larger radii than the standard (6-in.) bow compass (which ranges from $9 to $22), but you won't often need to make circles that big. For drawing small circles, the seldom-used drop-bow compass works best. I find that I use a circle template (Berol's Rapidesign, a good one, costs around $4) most of the time simply because it's easier and it doesn't leave a hole in the paper. Compasses and templates are shown in the photo facing page, right .

Templates are also available for ellipses, triangles, squares, people, trees, furniture—almost anything imaginable. To get started, I would suggest a plumbing-fixture template at ⅛-in. and ¼-in. scale at $3 to $5. It is very useful when drawing floor plans. Also get a couple of French curves (one for long curves, one for tight curves), which will cost you from $1.50 to $6 depending on the size. They are invaluable for drawing a meandering walkway on the site plan or any other oddly curved line.

Straightedges—Equipped with the tools I've already talked about, you could make a respectable drawing sitting right at the kitchen table. But if you are going to be drawing even once a month, your efficiency will increase measurably with the addition of a straightedge and a drawing board of some kind.

Before you decide how far you're going to go in making or purchasing a drawing board, you should make a decision about the type of straightedge you're going to use.

A T-square is certainly the least expensive of your options, but constant diligence is required to make sure it is snug to the side of the drawing board (using a metal edge that clamps onto the side of your board gives you the most positive

Reproducing your drawings

The term blueprint originally referred to a photographic duplicating process that produced a negative image of white lines on a deep blue background. Technological advances in the last two decades have rendered this process archaic, but the term lingers on. Today's blueprints are produced by what is called a diazo process.

Diazo process—This method works by shining ultraviolet light through the transparent drawing onto a light-sensitive emulsion on the print paper. This will produce blue, black or brown lines, depending on the kind of emulsion the paper is coated with. The standard medium-weight paper gives you a choice of either blue or black, while the heavier-weight presentation-quality paper reproduces in either black or brown. My favorite is the sepia-brown tone that is produced on the lightest-weight paper because of the flexibility it offers.

The first advantage is that a sepia-tone diazo print can be used to produce a blueline or blackline diazo of itself because the lightweight paper it's printed on is transparent enough to let the ultraviolet light through.

Second, you can make changes on a sepia-tone print by using an eradicating solution to eliminate lines and then draw in any corrections. A blueline print made from this corrected sepia-tone print will record both the remaining sepia information and the new information. This is very useful when you need another floor plan, for instance, to indicate where electrical outlets should be installed. In fact, after I draw a floor plan for a complex job that will require lots of supplementary drawings, I sometimes get a couple of extra sepias made before I add notes and dimensions just in case I need them later.

Another option available from the diazo process is an ammonia Mylar print. This has all the advantages of the sepia, and because Mylar is virtually indestructible, it will put up with many more corrections. The process is more expensive, however.

Other processes—The technology of xeroxing has been changing almost as rapidly as the seasons, and could eventually replace the diazo process as the most economical way to reproduce technical drawings. So far, the greatest limitation to photocopying plans yourself is size. You have to draw on a greater number of smaller sheets (8½ in. by 11 in., or 11 in. by 17 in.).

Photography can be useful in some situations—copying old, fragile original prints, for instance. Almost anything can be copied photographically if you're willing to pay the added expense. My advice, however, is to take your copying problem to the local blueprint shop and let them advise you on the best, most economical method given their equipment. —E. R.

contact between board and square). This isn't a huge problem when you're drawing horizontal lines, but by the time you add a triangle for drawing vertical lines, you can sometimes need a third hand. T-squares can be made entirely of acrylic, of maple and acrylic, or of aluminum or stainless steel, in ascending order of durability and precision. They also come in standard lengths of 18 in., 24 in., 30 in., 36 in., 42 in. and 48 in. A square costs from $7 up to about $40, depending on its length and quality.

The parallel rule is more expensive (between $45 and $93), but it eliminates having to hold the straightedge tight to the board because its permanently attached cables keep it square at all times. These cables appear to pass through the end of the rule, but they actually run the entire length of the rule twice and cross each other in the process. The Mayline (619 North Commerce St., Sheboygan, Wis. 53081) parallel rule I use (photo previous page) has a series of roller bearings on the bottom that allow it to travel smoothly up and down the board.

The last option, which is even more expensive, is a drafting machine (Vemco Corp., 766 South Fair Oaks Ave., Pasadena, Calif., 91105 makes some excellent machines). Most machines use a drafting head that carries a protractor and two flat, metal, ruler-like projections that are set at 90° to each other—they look like a small framing square. These are actually straightedges printed with a scale, and they can be changed when you change scales during the drawing process. Whether these blades sit vertical and horizontal or at another angle on the paper is determined by rotating the knob at the center of the protractor.

This angle is maintained no matter where on the board the drafting head is moved. This is accomplished either with a system of arms and pivots that is somewhat like an adjustable drafting light, or with a vertical and horizontal track system that reminds me of a radial saw. The pivot system comes in arm lengths of 16 in., 18 in., 20 in., 22 in., 24 in., 30 in. and 36 in., and runs from $136 to $300. The interchangeable blades or scales cost between $10 and $24. A drafting machine that uses the tracking system runs between $312 and $575. It is possible to find good deals on used equipment.

Drafting boards—There are many ready-made drafting tables and boards available at moderate to high cost. You can also make your own. Almost anything works. When I was in school, many of us used a hollow-core door propped on a couple of 4x4 blocks for tilt. The one I'm using now I made from a sheet of ¾-in. plywood. It is 30 in. by 48 in., faced with a drawing-board cover of green vinyl (which cost about $25) and edged with oak. I backed the plywood with some 1x2s to counter warping and mounted the drawing-board cover with double-faced tape along its edges.

One addition worth considering is some form of drawing protector at the bottom of the board. Either a leaning bar or a Spiroll drawing protector (Spiroll International, 326 Springside Ave., Pittsfield, Mass. 01201) will do nicely to protect the bottom of a large tracing when only the top

is on the board. The leaning bar will also keep your pencil from rolling off on to the floor.

The tilt of the board is a matter of personal preference. I keep mine at about 10° because any steeper sends reference books and pencils sliding toward the floor. If you have the discipline to keep your board free of everything including your house cat, then you can tilt yours more, which will keep you from straining your back as you bend over to draw.

One way to keep your board just for drawing is to have a layout space next to it. It should be at least the size of your board, and will accommodate all your drawings in progress, reference materials and other necessary items. Pigeonhole storage for your drafting tools is also a nice convenience; in fact it becomes a virtual necessity if you are using a parallel straightedge, which sweeps the entire sheet and can't be lifted over implements. Pigeonholes are also useful for storing rolled-up original tracings if you don't have too many. For a lot of drawings, flat files work even better, but they're very expensive.

Good lighting is important, and a combination of fluorescent and incandescent is best. I prefer a good general lighting background of warm fluorescent tubes with an adjustable-arm incandescent drafting light for task lighting and to even out the fluorescent flicker.

A proper seat has become increasingly important for me with each passing year. Support in the right places and being able to change positions really determine how long you can spend at the board. The chair or stool has a lot to do with the height of your board. You have a couple of choices here: desk height of 29 in. to 31 in. or a standing height of 39 in. to 42 in. I have worked extensively at both heights, and have settled on putting my board at standing height. This way I can use a pneumatic high stool for sitting or get rid of the stool and stand. It feels good to be able to move around a little as I work. And the instant adjustability of the pneumatic stool allows me to leave the tracing in the same place on the board for either position.

Buying—I think the best place to start is the Yellow Pages of your phone book. Local suppliers of drafting tools are likely to be listed under headings such as Architects' Supplies, Artist Materials, Blue Printers, Copying and Duplicating Service, Drafting-Room Equipment, Drawing Materials, Engineering Equipment and Supplies, Graphic-Arts Materials, Photocopying, or Reproduction Service. By carefully comparing what suppliers are listed under these headings, you can get a feel for how comprehensive their selection is. Most large drafting and art-supply houses will carry a wide selection of tools from national manufacturers as well as a line or two of their own. Pick out a few likely prospects and visit them if you can. If not, phone and ask them if they have a catalog of their supplies. This may cost you a buck or two, but it's worth it if they can mail-order or deliver the tools to you. Your local blueprinter is also a good source when you don't have time to shop around. □

Eric Rekdahl's drawing board is located in Berkeley, Calif.

Job-Site Safety

The caliber of your work may have a lot to do with the future of your fingers

by Mark Feirer

If you're a builder or a contractor, you'd be safer working in a munitions factory. Building construction is one of the most dangerous occupations, ranking second only to mining in terms of risk. And despite regulation by agencies such as OSHA (the Occupational Safety and Health Administration), your chances of avoiding death or injury on the job aren't getting much better (see the sidebar on the next page). Accidental injury isn't the only risk you have to contend with. Health problems—cumulative injuries, if you will—are an insidious form of risk, since their effects can take years to show up. From "carpenter's wrist" to "carpet-layer's knee," silicosis to carcinoma, we're gradually learning more about the immediate and long-term health hazards of construction. We'll talk about health issues in a future article; in this one, the focus is on accidental injury.

Risks at the job site—Because it's difficult to find dependable, timely statistics on the exact nature of injuries in the building trades, it's useful to look at insurance rates as a rough guide to the degree of risk involved in various trades. Roofing is rated as the most dangerous house-building job, and not surprisingly, the most common accident involves a fall. A builder who has a medium-sized company in northern Florida told me that his worker's compensation payments amount to 32% of wages for the roofers on his payroll—if the roofer makes $15,000 a year, it takes an additional $4,800 a year to insure him. To put this in perspective, a secretary at the same company can be insured for about $37.50 per year—about ¼% of her $15,000 wage.

The same builder pays about 20% of a mason's wages into worker's compensation. Health-related risks are a big problem for masons, with the dusts generated by mixing, sawing or grinding leading to respiratory disease. But injury is also a significant risk. A California study found that over 80% of all safety and health claims by masons involve injuries from either strain and overexertion (the improper handling of loads, heat stress), falls, or being

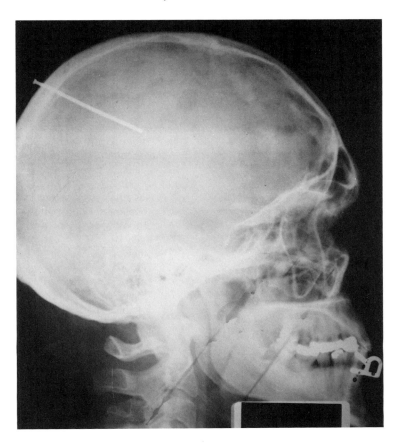

struck by something, like a brick falling from a scaffold or a stone chip hitting an eye.

Carpenters have a *relatively* good safety record at the construction job site, and their worker's compensation payments amount to only about 9% of their wage. Carpenters are most likely to lose time from their work as a result of back injury. Most back injuries (88%) are due to muscle strain or sprain from lifting improperly or too much. Falls are another major cause of injury for carpenters.

Some of the most dramatic accidents are caused by the misuse—and abuse—of tools. According to one manufacturer of woodworking machinery, table saws are by far the most dangerous (see the sidebar on p. 21). Ask a carpenter how he feels about the guard on his table

---

'**E**very carpenter thinks it will never happen to him.'

---

saw and you're likely to find the reason. He considers it a nuisance and removes it.

If you think that only electric power tools maim carpenters, however, consider the following incident. A construction company in Florida had suffered only one serious accident involving an employee in 13 years. It happened to one of their most experienced carpenters, and it happened with a hammer. Joe was working setting blocking in a confined space where visibility was poor. With a tap he started a 16d nail, not seeing that it was near a knot. When he struck the nail to drive it home, it skidded off the knot, spun into a nearby duct and ricocheted into his eye, penetrating the eyeball and nearly severing the optic nerve. There's a permanent hole in Joe's iris, though he's lucky: his vision is impaired, not lost.

Other tradespeople on the job site risk injury to lesser degrees, and the specific danger varies from trade to trade. The most common hazards to drywallers are cuts from knives, saws and metals, and electric shocks (see the sidebar on p. 22) as electric cords are abraded by sharp materials. Plasterers often suffer from skin irritation and respiratory problems, and also run the risk of eye injuries related to the use of pneumatic equipment. People who install insulation have to cope with various respiratory problems and heat stress, along with scratches of the eyeball from fiberglass.

Some people are more likely to suffer injuries than others. In 1985, an OSHA report linked the following factors to a disproportionate share of injuries and illnesses at the construction site:

Younger workers have higher accident rates than older workers. There are probably several reasons for this—differences of experience, a process of elimination that weeds out accident-prone workers over time, and the slower pace of older workers. Several contractors I talked to, in fact, stressed a steady, careful pace as being crucial in avoiding injury on their crews. One builder said he fires hot-shot carpenters who work at a pace too frenzied for safety.

New employees have a higher accident rate than long-time employees. They're less familiar with the work habits of their co-workers and with the style and pace of work that are required by their employer.

Medium-sized firms have higher accident rates than small or large firms. Large firms can afford to send supervisors to safety-training classes. In small firms, the level of teamwork is generally high, and because fewer people are on the job, it's easier for workers to keep track of what's going on around them.

Using hazardous substances increases risks considerably. Frequent contact with materials like asbestos or with chemicals, such as wood preservatives or concrete-cleaning acids, increases the danger of developing health problems, particularly over time.

Human error and injury—At some point in nearly every coffee-break discussion of job-site safety, a debate will flare around the question of who's at fault. In a number of conversations with builders and contractors, nearly everyone told me that injuries begin more often with the worker than with the tool being used. Figuring out why isn't easy.

Studies of why and how people take risks have shown that when the task is easy—low risk—the tendency is to underestimate your ability (be conservative). As the task becomes more difficult, the tendency is to overestimate your ability (take more risks). So it seems that we're not very good at estimating the probability of success when the task is either relatively easy or relatively hazardous.

Another reason for human error is fatigue—working after hours to meet a deadline. One carpenter who rolled into our office (he's on crutches now, and glad to be rid of his wheelchair) swore that he'd never work tired again. He had been staying overnight at the site of a major remodeling project in order to save himself a long drive home. After a quick dinner, the evening looked long and dull so he decided to work on a few details on the second floor. While reaching to close a window shutter, he leaned against another shutter that he thought was bolted—it wasn't. When he hit the cobblestones below, he fractured both heels. "It was carelessness bred of fatigue. At eight in the morning I would've tested the shutter before I put all my weight on it, but I was tired, and just wasn't playing with a full deck." Next time, he says he won't push himself so hard. "Even if you don't damage your body by working late, you don't do great work anyway."

Researchers have tried to figure out what causes accidents. One theory presumes that some people are just accident prone because of certain personality traits. A second blames management systems that push people to work fast-

Regulating safety

Construction safety laws and standards aren't new. In about 2200 B.C., the Code of Hammurabi called for the death penalty for any builder who, through carelessness, built a house that caused the death of its owner. In 1912, a group of corporations formed the National Safety Council in response to escalating accident rates. The NSC uses a voluntary process to encourage industrial safety, and now includes about 95% of the 500 largest U. S. corporations, along with medium and small-size businesses, government agencies, trade associations, insurance companies, and labor organizations.

In 1918, another group of U. S. companies formed what is now known as the American National Standards Institute. The ANSI of today is composed primarily of manufacturers and trade associations. It has developed hundreds of product standards, most of which cover such things as the pitches for screw threads. But a few are directed at occupational safety and health, like the standard for safety glasses. These standards are voluntary, arrived at through a consensus decision-making process. Just because ANSI has a standard for hard hats, manufacturers don't have to make them to that standard.

OSHA—In 1970, Congress passed the Occupational Safety and Health Act (OSHAct), which placed legal responsibility on employers to prevent injury and illness. A common misconception among residential builders is that this act covers only the largest construction businesses. It in fact covers *all* employers and employees in the U. S., with few exceptions (self-employed people, operators of family farms, and workplaces already protected by other federal agencies). The OSHAct is summed up by its general-duty clause:

"Each employer shall furnish to each of his employees employment and a place of employment which are free from recognized hazards that are causing or are likely to cause death or serious physical harm."

As a part of the OSHAct, Congress created one federal agency to supply the brains, another to wield a club and a third to keep the second from getting out of line. The National Institute of Occupational Safety and Health (NIOSH), under the Department of Health and Human Services, supplies basic research. The Occupational Safety and Health Administration (OSHA), under the Department of Labor, develops regulations based on NIOSH research, makes them law and enforces them by inspecting job sites and levying penalties against employers. Finally, the Occupational Safety and Health Review Commission (OSHRC) was created as an independent, quasi-judicial agency to field complaints about OSHA inspections. Any employer, employee or union can contest an OSHA action before the OSHRC.

To give OSHA a head start on regulating the workplace, Congress gave it the right to adopt safety and health regulations from other organizations without having to wait for NIOSH to get rolling, and without having to test the regulations. About 90% of the standards OSHA started out with came from ANSI, while the rest came from trade associations or other governmental agencies. This means that most OSHA standards were developed not by a federal agency but by private organizations.

There are a lot of OSHA regulations and standards (the 1985 book of construction standards runs 450 pages), and most have been criticized by nearly everybody. Labor berates them as insufficient to protect workers, while business figures they're too costly, stringent and inflexible. All OSHA regulations have to pass a cost-benefit test, but that doesn't always make them easier to swallow.

For builders, there's a pocket-sized version of the construction-standards book (with a safety orange cover, of course). It's called the "OSHA Safety and Health Standards Digest—Construction Industry" (furnished free by OSHA), and should be a fixture in the toolbox of everyone on the job site.

Dealing with inspections—Builders I've talked to about OSHA inspections recently have been blunt: "I think they should stay out of residential construction!" OSHA "compliance officers," while less than popular, have the legal right to enter and inspect any construction site without delay or harassment, and with very few exceptions, inspections are made without advance notice. The Supreme Court determined that OSHA can't conduct such "warrantless" inspections without an employer's approval. But if there's evidence of a safety violation, OSHA can get a search warrant and inspect anyway.

Under the OSHAct, every employer must inform employees of OSHA standards that apply to their job, so if you don't know what they are, ask. And any employee has the right to request an inspection if he feels there's something at the job site that may cause physical harm.

Trying to spend dollars where they will do the most good, OSHA has begun to target specific industries where the risk of injury is high, and building construction is in their sights. In 1973, about 27% of all OSHA inspections were at construction sites. In 1984, however, nearly 60% (about 94,000) of all inspections were at construction sites, making construction the only industry showing an increase in inspections over this period.

What happens if compliance officers show up at your job site? First of all, check their identification against the picture ID card that all officers must carry. The purpose of the inspection should be explained to you right away, and you can accompany the officers if you want. They can go anywhere and talk to anyone, though interruptions of work should be minimal. Any violations discovered during the tour and corrected immediately may still figure in a citation later on.

After the inspection, the officer will report findings to an OSHA area director, who will determine what citations, if any, will be issued. A fine of from $60 to $1,000 may be assessed for each violation, and if a subsequent inspection finds a repeat of an earlier violation, the fine might

er or harder than they should; piecework systems are often cited, and unions agree. A third theory figures that poor "fits" between worker and environment lead to accidents, and would redesign tools and the workplace for a better match between worker abilities and attitudes (the Swedes take this approach, and they've had some success with it). But no single theory tells the whole story, and despite all the safety regulations, experienced home-building professionals still get hurt.

I talked to an experienced carpenter from Maine who lost the end of his left ring finger to a table saw. He said that until the accident, he didn't think much of safety: "Every carpenter thinks it will never happen to him." Since the accident he's become a lot more concerned. Personal experience is indeed a good teacher, but where safety is concerned it's a rather painful and costly way to learn, and the lesson

go to $10,000. If an employer knowingly or intentionally commits a violation (if he knows, for example, that an open stairwell exists and makes no reasonable effort to guard it), the penalty for each violation might reach $10,000. And for willful violations resulting in the death of an employee, a six-month prison term might be added to the maximum fine.

But like a toothless dog, OSHA's bark promises more than its bite delivers. The fines actually imposed are small—the average penalty for violations that threaten "death or serious physical harm" is less than $200. In fact, the amount of the fine is usually less than the cost of providing the safety, so it's not surprising that OSHA hasn't been very effective.

Builders and contractors might be more inclined to accept OSHA if the agency could prove that it was saving lives at the workplace. A 1985 study by the Office of Technology Assessment, a federal agency, couldn't find much that would support this claim. Several researchers have found favorable but generally small changes in job-site accident rates, while others have not found any significant correlation between OSHA activity and workplace injuries. OSHA points with pride to injury rates that have been declining since 1981 (eleven years after passage of the OSHAct), but the OTA study suggests that OSHA can't take the credit. It concluded that the economic recessions and resulting high unemployment, along with a shift away from smokestack industries, are the most likely reasons for this decline. —*M. F.*

comes a little late. The best bet is to learn from the mistakes of others.

Case histories—A cabinetmaker/builder in Idaho got the call at 2 a.m.: a trailer loaded with satellite dishes had crashed through the front wall of a nearby gun shop, and the damage had to be repaired immediately. Ordinarily he would have worked with his own crew, but he was paired instead with an experienced carpenter he had never met. By mid-morning the damage was repaired and the two were finishing up trim work on the facade. As the carpenter was backing down a ladder, nail gun in hand and finger on the trigger, he bumped the gun into the cabinetmaker, who was tacking up some trim at the bottom of the ladder.

The nail gun fired, sinking a 10d nail in the cabinetmaker's skull: "The impact knocked me unconscious, and when I came to 10 minutes later, my head felt like it was lodged between the jaws of a Jorgensen clamp." After a rush to the hospital, surgeons extracted the nail. It had been traveling on a path from the back of the cabinetmaker's skull to his right eye—until the nailhead was snagged by his baseball cap. The Xray on p. 19 tells the tale.

Look in just about any listing of safety rules for pneumatic tools and you'll see a caution against carrying tools with your finger on the trigger. The cabinetmaker (who suffered no permanent damage) saw another danger: neither man knew what the other was working on, or where. He had some other observations about safety, too. "Experience in a trade doesn't have too much to do with avoiding accidents, and may in fact add to the problem because experienced tradesmen sometimes think they're infallible. Almost daily on jobs I'll see people abuse the table saw by cutting with the blade too high. A blade 1/8 in. above the stock won't do nearly as much damage as when it's 2 in. above—a blade can't tell the difference between wood and meat. Part of my own awareness of dangers on the job site comes from teaching industrial education. I got used to seeing lots of beginners around tools, and catching dangerous techniques before they turned into injuries."

A builder now working in New England had only one major accident in 15 years as a framing carpenter. "I wedged back the guard on my circular saw so I could follow a cut line and keep one hand on the lumber. I finished the cut but forgot the guard was up, and rested the saw against my knee. It took three dozen stitches to close me up." If you want to pep up a flagging conversation with a group of carpenters, ask them about saw guards. Most find the devices awkward on occasion, and sometimes a nuisance. Here's how one California contractor sees it: "I block the guard up when I have to cut a slight bit off the end of a board and sometimes when I'm cutting an angle across a board, because the guard can get hung up as it gets pinched between the saw and the edge. You sure have to concentrate on what you're doing, though. I got used to working with an open blade when I did timber framing with a chainsaw. One time the chainsaw backed out of the log I was working on and caught me at the in-

Preventing kickback

"The block was in the street before I knew it, and my hand was in the blade..." It's a classic description of table-saw kickback. The carpenter I was talking to had been more used to circular saws than table saws, and he lost the end joint of one finger learning about their differences. Kickback doesn't always result in mangled fingers, but since this carpenter was working so close to the blade, when the block shot toward the street his hand was there to take its place. You won't see it happening either—only the results.

According to the Power Tool Institute, table-saw kickback happens for several reasons. Sometimes the kerf in whatever you're cutting will close up and pinch the rear of the blade. Or the material can get wedged between the fence and the rear of the sawblade, as when the fence and the blade aren't parallel to each other. And if you start off with a crooked cut, the wood can bind against the side of the blade. Splitters help to keep the kerf open, and anti-kickback pawls can stop the workpiece before it becomes a projectile headed your way. Never tilt the sawblade toward the fence; if you do, the wood will be trapped between them and you'll be in trouble.

Kickback with a circular saw offers slightly different but equally grim results. It, too, can be caused by pinched blades and wedged wood. But instead of the stock kicking back at you, the saw may spin your way, and an uncontrolled circular saw is real trouble. Whenever you feel the need to force the saw through the cut, something's wrong. Shut off the saw and find the problem.

Frequently, builders and contractors I talked to prefaced the description of their accident with something like: "Funny thing is, I *knew* it was dumb when I started, but I just went ahead anyway..." Most of them could distinctly remember a split second of decision, and an internal "bell" or "small voice" that warned of danger ahead. And all of them wished they had listened.

On a radial-arm saw, kickback occurs when the stock binds between the back of the blade and the fence. Stock will be ejected toward the rear, or the saw may "climb" the work and race toward you. Always keep your body, particularly hands and arms, away from the line the saw would take if this happened. When you crosscut, pull the saw forward only enough to cut the stock; if you pull too far, the blade may catch the stock on the return trip and throw it.

On any of these saws, a dull or dirty blade can increase the chances of kickback; a buildup of pitch, for example, increases friction on the blade's surface and makes it more susceptible to binding. A warped blade is real trouble. Be sure that the set of the blade's teeth is adequate to provide clearance in the saw cut, otherwise the blade is likely to bind. And it really is time well spent to read the directions enclosed with your tools. —*M. F.*

Electrical safety

His shirt was still wet from perspiration when they found him in a crawl space beneath the house, dead. A journeyman electrician, he had been working with a double-insulated drill plugged into a droplight, which in turn had been plugged into a receptacle upstairs. From the severe burns that seared his back, it was easy to see what had happened. When he rolled over on his back to get a better angle on the holes he was drilling, a length of cord became pinned between his body and the ground. When he lifted the drill above his head, the drill plug separated slightly from the droplight and made contact with his damp shirt. When investigators unplugged the droplight cord upstairs, they saw that the grounding prong was missing.

It doesn't take much electricity to snuff out a life on the job site, particularly since the presence of moisture can turn a poor conductor into a very good one. Dry wood, for example, has a high resistance to the flow of electricity, but when saturated with water it becomes a pretty good conductor. The same is true of dry and wet skin. And shirts.

Electricity travels in closed circuits, flowing from and returning to a point of origin through some conductor. You become a part of this loop when you touch both wires of the circuit, or when you touch the hot wire and the ground (electricity will flow through you to the ground, and back to the source). You will also get a shock if the metal case of the tool you're using comes in contact with the hot wire of the circuit.

The plastic housing of double-insulated tools acts as an insulator for any short circuit within the tool, but it doesn't eliminate all danger of shock. So it's still crucial to maintain the integrity of the grounding system. If you or the tool ever become part of the hot circuit, electricity will flow through the ground wire, not through you. Any break in the grounding system renders it useless—and puts you at risk.

Mechanical devices, like fuses and circuit breakers, are another way to protect against shock, but they're intended primarily to protect wires and equipment from an excess of electricity that could damage them. They work by breaking the circuit when it's overloaded. A ground-fault circuit interrupter (GFCI) is a fast-acting circuit breaker that's better at protecting people. It senses imbalances in the flow of electricity through a circuit, and when the amount of electricity going into a protected system is greater than the amount coming out, the GFCI assumes that current is leaking somewhere and quickly breaks the circuit. The idea is to eliminate any leak that might allow electricity to course through a person.

At the job site, safety demands that ground-fault circuit interrupters be provided for all 15-amp or 20-amp circuits that are not a part of any permanent wiring.
—M. F.

step. The doctor lost count at 50 stitches, but I was back on the job in two weeks.''

Most builders and contractors get the job done without disabling the blade guard. The idea is to plan the work to avoid awkward situations that might tempt you to block back the guard. It takes a little forethought, but it's done all the time by experts.

Safety, speed and quality—Many builders see an inverse relationship between speed and safety. As the builder in New England puts it: "One of the reasons our crew has had a reasonably good safety record over the years is that we emphasize care and quality on our jobs, not speed. When I was working on production framing jobs in Alaska where speed was of the essence, there were frequent minor accidents, mostly with nail guns. I think safety is the incidental benefit of care and quality."

From a builder in Massachusetts I heard some similar comments: "I've had no major accidents in over 30 years working in the trades. The most important safety skill is anticipation, thinking one step ahead, and having your mind entirely on the job. I know very well that the radial saw can take a finger quickly, and so I'm always a little bit apprehensive about the tool, enough to respect its power. My message to apprentices is this: if you work for a safe boss, you're likely to develop safe habits. But if you see the boss doing things you know aren't safe, your first safety action should be to leave the job. Speed often leads to safety problems, so learn to work at a proper, consistent pace. Take a break if things get too frantic."

Others I talked to made a connection between the quality of their work and the safety of their workplace. A carpenter's coffee break may be much maligned, but it has probably saved more than a few fingers. If you're running a crew, take a lesson from basketball coaches who call time out when they see signs of frustration and fatigue.

"There are five people in my company," said another carpenter in Maine. "We've had some relatively minor incidents with jointers and routers, but no major accidents in six years. We've had most of our problems with hand tools, I think, because we let our guard down and don't expect the degree of danger found in our power tools. People get into safety trouble when they're preoccupied with something off the job, or overtired."

A woodworker in Connecticut who was trained in Japan reported that he never had a major accident. "I was originally trained to use hand tools only, and there the dangers are relatively minor. So I'm careful in the extreme with power tools, and always wear hearing protection and goggles. I guess I'm particularly careful with my eyes and head, because if I lost an arm or a leg, I could at least transmit my craft by telling someone else what I wanted and what to do. But if I lost my capacity to think or my eyesight, I would lose my craft entirely, and it's all that I have."

I've never seen it on a job, but this woodworker is so concerned about his eyes that he doesn't use carbide blades on a table saw be-

cause of the danger of carbide bits loosening and flying toward the operator at high speed—he saw it happen to an apprentice. Carbide blades on radial-arm or portable circular saws, he feels, aren't a danger because the rotation of the blade is away from the operator.

Aids to safety—Though a proper attitude may be the most valuable safety device you take to the job site, many contractors are more aware of safety glasses, hard hats and the like. These things help to minimize injuries and are definitely worth using, but they can't be relied upon entirely to keep you out of harm's way. The federal Office of Technology Assessment, in a survey of workplace safety, concluded that the effectiveness of many safety devices hasn't been demonstrated, particularly under job-site conditions: "Laboratory test results tend to exaggerate the effectiveness of personal protective devices." OSHA hasn't expressed a lot of confidence in such devices, either. It has a priority list of techniques for preventing accidental injuries, and the use of personal protective devices is at the bottom of it. In order of preference and effectiveness, OSHA would rather *eliminate hazards* from machines, methods or materials; *control the hazard* by enclosing it or isolating its source; *educate workers* to follow safe procedures; or *prescribe personal protective equipment* to shield them from the hazard. In this policy, OSHA is in agreement with other safety organizations. A major reason why larger-scale, more expensive solutions are preferred is that workers usually won't voluntarily wear safety devices. For a list of suppliers of safety devices, see the sidebar on the facing page.

Tool safety—The other half of the who's-at-fault debate pins the blame for injuries on unsafe tools. The issue of responsibility for accidents is not just academic—it comes up every time a liability suit is brought against a tool manufacturer. There has been a spectacular growth in the number of product-liability cases during the past few years, and in their costs. Plaintiffs are increasingly likely to name in the suit anyone who can be remotely tied to the cause of the accident. In a recent case involving a table-saw accident, nine separate parties were named as defendants, including the manufacturers and distributors of the table saw, the dado blades and the special blade guard, which wasn't even being used at the time of the accident. Of course, each party had to be represented by a separate attorney.

Prudence requires that manufacturers reduce the hazards of tool use in order to avoid costly suits, though only about 1% of product-liability suits ever go to trial. The rest are dropped or settled out of court. The increase in the number of suits may be due to the greater variety and number of tools available, or to new laws that require tool manufacturers to anticipate misuse of the tools and guard against it. It may also have something to do with Worker's Compensation insurance.

Early in this century, it was very difficult for employees to sue their employers for damages if an accident occurred. During the Progressive

For more information about job-site safety, the following sources are recommended.

OSHA Publication Distribution
Room S-2403
U. S. Department of Labor
Washington, D. C. 20210

OSHA publications are free. "OSHA Safety and Health Standards Digest-Construction Industry" is the best way to get an idea of what regulations affect you. "Personal Protective Equipment" will tell you what to look for in safety devices. "All About OSHA" offers most of what you need to know about how the agency operates, including detailed information about your rights and responsibilities.

National Institute for Occupational Safety and Health
Department of Health and Human Services
5600 Fishers Lane
Rockville, Md. 20857

NIOSH is primarily a research organization, but will provide free information on the dangers of substances at the construction job site.

United Brotherhood of Carpenters & Joiners of America
101 Constitution Ave. N.W.
Washington, D. C. 20001

The Occupational Safety and Health office at the UBC provides information to its members about safety and health, and its publications are available to members and non-members alike. Their volume "Health & Safety Hazard Identification Program" ($20.00) is a fairly complete collection of what the dangers are and how to avoid them.

Power Tool Institute
501 W. Algonquin Rd.
Arlington Heights, Ill. 60005-4411

The Institute is a trade association of power-tool manufacturers, and they have some of the most readable safety guides around. The best is "Safety is Specific" ($1.50; more than 20 copies, $1.00 each)

Klein Tools
7200 McCormick Rd.
Chicago, Ill. 60645

The booklet "Proper Use and Care of Hand Tools, Pliers, Screwdrivers, Wrenches, Striking & Struck Tools" (86 pp.) is full of tips and techniques.

There are many manufacturers and distributors of safety equipment, but the ones following have comprehensive or unusual product lines. Only toll-free phone numbers are given.

Bilsom International, Inc.
11800 Sunrise Valley Drive
Reston, Va. 22091

An informative catalog of hearing, eye, head and face protection.

H. L. Bouton Company
P.O. Box G
Buzzards Bay, Mass. 02532

Safety spectacles and goggles.

Direct Safety Co.
7815 South 46th St.
Phoenix, Ariz. 85044-5399

Safety cones, fire extinguishers, first-aid kits and other safety products.

HTC Products
120 E. Hudson
Royal Oak, Mich. 48067

Feed tables and work supports.

Industrial Products Company
21 Cabot Blvd.
Langhorne, Pa. 19047
(800) 523-3944
(800) 562-3305 (in Pennsylvania)

Comprehensive distributor of safety equipment.

Kenco Safety Products
78 Glasco Turnpike
PO Box 385
Woodstock, N. Y. 12498

Eye protection.

Magid Glove & Safety Manufacturing Co.
2060 North Kolmar Ave.
Chicago, Ill. 60639

Safety clothing and gloves.

Shophelper
P.O. Box 238
Tulare, Calif. 93275

Anti-kickback stock feeders for table saws and shapers.

SINCO Products Inc.
Hog Hill Road
P.O. Box 361
East Hampton, Conn. 06424
(800) 243-6753

Nets, safety belts, lifelines.

---

era, laws were passed to remedy this, and courts began to hit employers with costly judgments. So it was manufacturers who pressed for passage of Worker's Compensation laws. Under this system, workers are compensated for medical expenses and lost wages, but employers can't be sued except when they've willfully violated safety standards. By 1948, all states had Worker's Compensation laws. Because an injured worker can't sue his employer, he might instead aim the suit at the manufacturer of the tool that injured him in order to recover damages in excess of what worker's comp pays.

Tool manufacturers can be held liable for accidents caused by very old tools. If a worker in 1975 was injured on a tool built 40 years earlier, the manufacturer of the tool could be called to account for the accident, even if the tool hadn't been produced for many years. But between 1979 and 1981, laws were enacted in a number of states that set limits on liability of from five to twelve years. Some of these "statutes of repose" have been ruled unconstitutional, however, and legislation is pending in Congress to establish a national statute of repose. Until then, manufacturers may still have to defend outmoded tools.

Because of the rapidly escalating costs of product-liability suits over the past two years, tool manufacturers are spending more time and effort to ensure that their products are safe. To get an idea of what they do, I headed for Pittsburgh to visit Delta Manufacturing Corporation. Mat Ros, claims manager, told me that Delta uses one of three methods for safety-checking its tools. The most exhaustive method is called failure modes-and-effects analysis, and is used during the development of an altogether new tool. During this process, each part of the product prototype, down to the last nut and screw, is examined. For each part, an analysis is made of the possibilities of failure, the effect of failure on other parts and the likely result of such a failure in terms of operator safety and tool operation. An estimate of effect—from negligible to catastrophic—is assigned, and so is an estimate of frequency. Finally, a preventive measure is determined and costed out. All these bits of information are then factored into a simple equation and formulated into an "action priority," which tells Delta how important it is to make a change. Since a typical power tool can have 300 to 500 parts, it isn't surprising that this analysis method is used only for new, unproven tools. As we talked one afternoon in his office, Ros pushed a 200-page tome across his desk—it was the analysis of Delta's 10-in. radial saw.

To study new tools that are "evolutionary"—a new model of an existing table saw, for example—project managers at Delta can use one of two other analysis methods. Fault-tree analysis involves the construction of a logical, branching network of events that could lead to accident. The method used more often is called "hazard analysis." It's based on a checklist, filled out by the project engineer, and provides a systematic examination of possible safety problems. Can chips or dust ejected cause injury? Can the machine be inadvertently turned on? Are potential pinch points guarded?

On the floor of his office, Lou Brickner, Delta's director of product development, gave me the engineering view of product development and safety. He unfurled a product-development PERT (project evaluation and review technique) chart that stretched from his door to the opposite wall—and it's not a small office. A typical Delta product takes about two years from inception to production in a 14-stage process. While safety is an early consideration, it doesn't show up formally until the fourth development state—about six months into the project.

Later on, I asked Brickner about saw guards. He told me that one of the problems in designing them for a table saw is that the tool is so versatile, and what works perfectly in a ripping operation isn't ideal when the saw is set up for dadoing. "Any guard can be defeated, particularly on mobile tools like a circular saw," he said. "Guards are just added weight to contractors—until they hurt themselves."

Unique dangers—What sets the construction job site apart from most others in terms of safety is that what is built can cause as much injury as the tools and techniques used to build it. Earlier this year in Florida, the trusses of an unfinished roof, supported by a single brace that snapped, fell to the deck and killed a building inspector. And during the torrential rains last February in California, a man whose name is familiar to many was crushed to death when the experimental building he was sleeping in collapsed. Ken Kern died in his own construction of bark, mud, plastic pipe and concrete. He was the author of *The Owner-Built Home* and other books. □

Plumb Bobs, String and Chalkboxes

Working with string and the tools that hang from it

by Trey Loy

Building, it will surprise no one, is based on geometry and trigonometry. Points are established by measuring, these are connected to form lines, the lines are grouped to form planes, and these planes join to form a solid. Great—in theory. But this whole process relies on establishing straight lines with the right relationship to each other, and keeping them that way as you fill in the outline.

Levels and straightedges are good for short lines. But for long spans, a length of string, whether it is stretched between two nails, suspended by a weight on a plumb line, or coated with chalk and snapped against something, is indispensable. String can be used for many things: to plumb and level your work, to define points in midair, to tell you what's straight and what isn't, to establish grades, to align walls and floors, to make a circle or project its center up or down in space, and to mark your work for cutting or assembly. And if things aren't going well, you can always use the first 100 feet or so to go fishing.

String—String, or twine, is thicker than thread and thinner than cord. Twine is made from natural hard-leaf fibers such as sisal and manila, or from cotton or synthetic fibers like nylon, Dacron and polypropylene. The fibers are drawn into slivers, counted, and spun into threads that are twisted or braided.

Coarse cotton line is ideal for chalkboxes and will do for a plumb bob. Cotton fibers stretch very little, but they rot and mildew around water and cement products, and are easily abraded. Nylon, on the other hand, doesn't absorb water readily and is alkali resistant. Nylon string is also elastic, which is an advantage in stringing a line because you can get it very taut.

Nylon twine is either twisted or braided, and comes in twenty-some sizes ranging from a thin #3 to a thick #120. In carpentry and masonry, you'll be fine with one of two sizes: #15, which measures a skinny 1/16 in. in diameter, and has a breaking strength of 120 lb.; and #18, which measures a fat 1/16 in. and will withstand a 170-lb. force. The twisted version of either of these sizes of nylon line is pretty inexpensive, costing around $3 for a 350-ft. roll, and is adequate for laying out foundations and lining walls. It will stretch up to 8% of its length, and return to normal when released.

Braided nylon twine is a favorite with masons, because it's more durable and easier to work with than twisted line. It costs about twice as

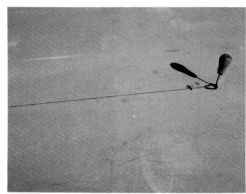

String is pretty basic stuff, but there is no end to the little tricks that make using it easier. If you're cutting gable gypboard or laying out walls, try a small, sharp scratch awl instead of a nail for holding one end of the snapline.

much, but it stretches less. One kind of braided string is even heat set for minimum stretch.

Nylon string comes in three colors: white, yellow and green. Green is hard to spot in a background of grass or shrubs, but it is the best color if you've got fishing on your mind. White is very popular, but I like yellow for its high visibility. All three colors are sold in lengths of 250 ft., 350 ft., 500 ft. and 1,000 ft.

One last kind of braided nylon worth mentioning is bonded nylon line. It is woven with an extra thread that is usually a different color and fiber. This bonded thread contributes strength and durability, and gives the twine a flecked appearance that makes it more visible than a solid color. It is treated to make it less slippery, and costs slightly more than braided line.

There are two other synthetics used in construction. For big commercial sites and highway layout, braided Dacron line is often used. It runs about $16 per 500 ft. Dacron has twice the breaking strength of nylon, but isn't elastic. Polypropylene is also very strong, but it's slippery and stiff, and doesn't hold knots well. Like Dacron, poly won't stretch. But it will float.

Securing a line—Knowing how to tie a variety of knots is important to me as a carpenter, yet I notice that many of the people I work with aren't sure how to proceed, and use knots that only hinder their effort. A good knot is not only simple to tie, but also easy to untie. One of the first places you'll need one is when you form a loop at the end of the string. A common knot for this is the *bowline*, which is shown at the top of the facing page (A). The resulting loop can be slipped over a nail or an awl. You can also slip the standing part of the line (the string back

down the line from the knot) through the bowline to create a simple slip knot.

String lines aren't much good unless they are taut, and using an elastic line like nylon makes that possible. The knot that holds the tension can't slip, but you should be able to release it without much fumbling and you shouldn't have to cut the string to tie it. A *twist knot* is the knot generally used by carpenters. It's formed by looping the string around your outstretched fingers once, and then twisting the loop three or four times (B). Place this loop over the nail, and stretch the string tightly with one hand, while pulling the excess through the twists with the other. Keep up this routine—heave and pull in the slack—until the line is singing. Sometimes it helps for your partner to pull from the middle of the span. Secure the knot by pulling the free end of the string back toward the nail. This will cause the twists to bunch up next to the nail, overlap themselves and create lots of friction. A lot of carpenters tie a couple of *half hitches* around the nail for security, but these are hard to loosen later. Instead, pass the standing part of the line around the nail once, making sure that it is sitting under the twists—this will provide all the friction needed to keep the string taut.

There's another simple knot that will keep a string tight. I call it a *tension hitch* (C), and I use it when I'm stringing lines between posts or stakes. Just take two wraps around the stake, making sure that the part of the line under tension is laid over the two turns. This combines the elasticity of nylon with the friction between layers of string to hold the hitch.

If you are stringing multiple lines, as you would laying out a foundation, don't cut the string, but take the spool to the next batter board, paying the line out as you go. Use a *clove hitch* (E) to secure it to the next nail, since it will cinch down no matter which end of the line you pull. You tie it by forming two consecutive underhand loops in the line, and laying the second loop on top of the first. The combined loops should then be slipped over the nail, and the ends pulled taut in opposite directions.

Although there isn't any reason to cut the string after making any of these knots, you will sometimes have to join two pieces of string. This is most easily done with a *surgeon's knot* (D). This is merely a square knot with an extra turn taken in the first overhand knot.

Once all of the knots have been untied, a lot of string still gets thrown away, because it's such an effort to wind it up in an orderly way. You

From *Fine Homebuilding* magazine (February 1985) 25:64-69

A. Bowline—*The best knot for forming an end loop that won't slip.*

1. Make a loop near end of line.

2. Pass free end up through loop.

3. Pass the free end around the standing string and back down through the loop.

B. Twist knot—*The knotless knot for making lines taut and securing them around a nail.*

1. Form a loop, twist it around your outstretched fingers three or four times, and lay it over the nail.

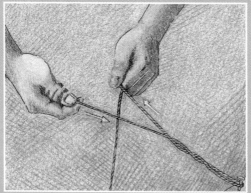

2. Tighten the line and retrieve the slack through the knot.

3. Pull the free end of the string back toward the nail and finish off the knot by pulling the free end back under the twists.

C. Tension hitch—*An easy knot to hold an elastic string like nylon taut between posts or stakes.*

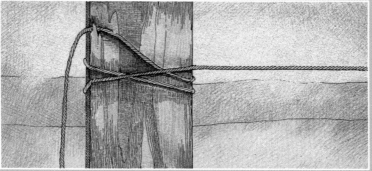

1. Make two wraps around the stake. Recover the slack so the line is taut. Make sure that the end of the line that is under tension crosses over the top of the two wraps.

D. Surgeon's knot—*Used for joining two pieces of string in line. Simply a square knot with an extra turn in the first overhand knot.*

E. Clove or builder's hitch—*Used to fasten the middle of a string so that tension can be brought from either end.*

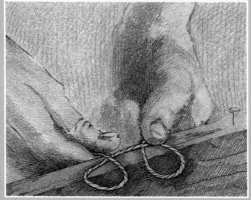

1. Form two consecutive underhand loops in the standing part of the line.

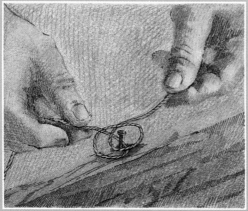

2. Lay the second loop on top of the first.

3. When slipped over the nail and tightened, the first loop should cross over the standing part of the line and the other one pass under.

Illustrations: Elizabeth Eaton

Mason's hardware for string

Since the mortar trade relies on string to keep courses level and wall faces plumb and even, lots of hardware has evolved to keep lines taut and yet easily raised for future courses. **Line pins** *drive into mortar joints, providing something to tie off to.* **Line blocks** *of either wood or plastic, which are held in place on corners by the tension of the string, are more versatile.* **Line stretchers** *actually straddle the masonry wall and are sized appropriately, and a* **line twig** *can be used in the middle of a string line to correct for sag.*

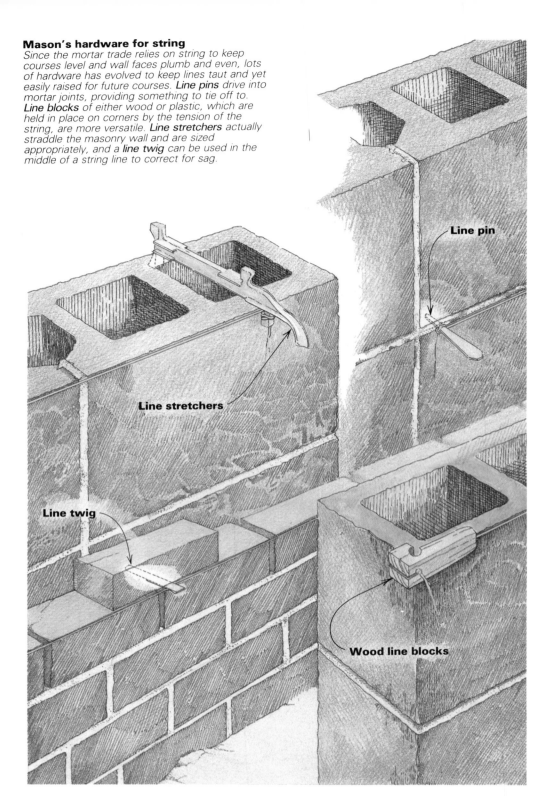

Line stretchers

Line twig

Wood line blocks

Line pin

can buy plastic winders that look like the letter H or make one out of a 1x4, but I was taught to use a 1x2 or a piece of pipe about 10 in. long. With it, you can imitate machine-winding, although your figure-eights aren't going to lay in quite so nicely. After building up a small core of string on the stick, hold it loosely in the middle and twirl the top of the stick in the direction of the string line so that it wraps around once, and then twist the top away so that the bottom gets a wrap. If you rotate the stick in your fingers at the same time you are twirling it in the air, you'll be able to distribute the wraps all along the stick so that you don't get one big ball in the center. When you're finished, secure the loose end by tying it to a nail and sticking it in the string.

Hardware—Masons rely on string to keep their courses straight and level, and they use a variety of fasteners to keep it taut and in place (drawing, left). But unlike most of the string lines that carpenters run, a mason's line has to move up every few courses. One method of securing the line is to use *line pins*. These are steel wedges (tempered ones are best) about 4 in. long that are driven directly into the mortar joint of a built-up corner, and used for tying off the string.

With block and brick, most masons use *line blocks*. These are small blocks of wood or plastic rabbeted on one side to form a heel that fits around a corner block or batter board. They are used in pairs, and the tension of the string between them keeps the blocks in place. A void in the inside corner of the block allows you to secure the string without affecting the block's grip, and a lateral groove on the inside face holds the tensioned string in place. Wood blocks grip the wall best and cost about 50¢ apiece. Plastic ones last longer but cost four times as much.

Line stretchers can also be used for block. These are made of steel or aluminum bar and have knobs on both top and bottom spaced so the stretcher will fit tightly across walls of two widths. The knob that fits over the front face of the wall is notched to hold the string. Line stretchers run about $7 a pair and come in several sizes. Adjustable models cost a bit more.

Even an elastic line like nylon will sag in the middle from its own weight on long walls despite heroic attempts to tighten it. This is where *line twigs* come in. These are flat metal line-supports that clip around the string like hairpins. Once attached to the string, the blade of the twig can then be set on top of a brick or block that has been laid to the working height in the middle of a wall. A loose block or brick can be stacked on top of the twig to hold it in place. Long walls may require more than one twig; they cost about 20¢ apiece.

A lot of masons use manufactured metal corner poles that can be set at the beginning of the job and left until the last course is laid. They combine the advantages of line blocks and story

A line level doesn't give a highly accurate reading because of the sag it creates even in the tautest string lines, but it's a useful tool for rough layouts and grading. This aluminum-clad version runs about $3.

poles. The strings are moved up the pole in course increments as the work progresses. Corner poles are available with attachments for both inside and outside corners, and in free-standing models or with telescoping braces. The cost of these aluminum or steel guides is prohibitive unless you do a lot of masonry.

Most of the time, I rely on a builder's level or tubular water level to set my level lines (I make sure that my batter boards are exactly level before I ever get the string out), but for very rough layouts a *line level* (photo facing page) will suffice. It is a lightweight aluminum tube about 3 in. long that is fitted with a level vial. Little hooks project from the tube so that it can be hung from the string. Line levels run about $3. Remember that the line sags somewhat of its own weight, and slightly more with the level, so the reading will only be approximate.

Strings for laying out—I use string the most when I'm laying out foundations. In this process, the strings form a full-scale drawing of the foundation plan. Begin by building batter boards just back from what will be the corners of the building. They should all be level with each other. Then run string lines between the batter boards, and adjust them until the dimensions of the building are correct, and the strings are square to each other (to check, measure the diagonals with a tape to be sure they're the same). You should set up additional batter boards to line up piers, post brackets or any other hardware that needs accurate placement.

By plumbing down from the perimeter strings, you can establish footing lines with loose chalk. Before removing the strings from the batter boards for the backhoe, clearly mark their final position with a single nail or saw kerf. After the trenching is completed, the lines can easily be replaced for forming.

String is also helpful when you're grading fill for a concrete slab. I run lines 4 ft. or 5 ft. apart just above the ground at finished concrete height, measuring down the thickness of the slab to check the level of the aggregate. A handy gauge for grading this way is to use an eyelet on your workboot that is the correct height to the string from the top of the gravel.

Gauging straightness—Strings that are used to line walls or to check an existing structure require some kind of offset where the string is attached at each end. This will allow the line to run parallel to what's being aligned without actually touching it, so that deviations in the material won't get in the way of the string. It's best to use a standard increment for this offset. Framers usually use a 1x or 2x scrap at each end, and then gauge along the string with a third block of the same thickness.

When lumber comes out of the sawmill it is square and straight, but it's a long way from there to the job site. If you suspect a high joist (you did crown them, didn't you?), use a string before you put the plywood down. This will show you how much to plane off if you have to. The same goes for setting big ridge and purlin beams. What gets sold as "minimum crown" in a huge beam can cause you a lot of problems

once the rafters are up, and it doesn't take long to run a string to find out how bad the hump is, so that you can either ignore it or correct it.

Figuring with string—String is also a good medium for puzzling out how things fit together. Those odd rafters—the ones that aren't in the book or that you can't work out on the square—can be defined with string line. An adjustable T-bevel and a level can then be used to gauge the angles off the string line. If you are doing this, make sure that your string really does represent the top edge of the rafter. It's easy to get in a hurry and stretch the string from the ridge down to the outside edge of the double top plate of a wall.

To get the height of the lower end of the string right, I usually tack a block to the top of the double top plate. It should be the same height as the distance from the seat cut to the top of the rafter. The top end of the string should be stretched over the ridgeboard unless the rafters require a seat cut at the top for a ridge beam or high wall. In that case, cut an appropriately sized block and tack it in place.

Plumb lines—Using a plumb bob is based on the fact that if you suspend a string and weight it at the bottom, it will be vertical and perpendicular to any level plane it passes through. Building projects as impressive as the Pyramids relied solely on plumb bobs to get true vertical. Flooding an irrigation ditch with water gave these builders a gauge of what was level. With these resources they achieved impressive accuracy. Modern builders have more sophisticated tools—transits and spirit levels—for establishing plumb, but there are lots of times when none of these is the right tool, and a plumb bob is.

Plumb bobs can do two basic things: provide a reference for true vertical, and project points up or down. Foundations are a good example of the latter. In this case the string layout hovers above the ground at least a few feet. Superimposing that layout on the ground—first for the backhoe and later for squaring the forms—requires plumbing down from the strings. Provided you didn't do too much celebrating the night before and a gale isn't building, a plumb bob is a very accurate way to do this.

Transferring the corner points to the ground is done by holding the plumb-bob string tight to the 90° intersection of batter-board strings without actually touching them. You should set your legs apart in a secure, comfortable stance, brace your arms against your body and lean directly over the plumb bob. In this case you will have to make sure that you are clear of the batter-board strings, but you'll be using this same position whenever you project a point from above. Hold the bob a fraction of an inch off the ground and concentrate on the intersection of strings above. Once you're satisfied with the position of the string, let it slip from your hand so that the point

Using a plumb bob to project the corner of a building down to grade or the top of the forms from intersecting batter-board strings requires a surprising degree of steadiness, but it's by far the most accurate and practical method.

hits the ground. If greater accuracy is needed, spot a nail in the dirt where the point hit and plumb it again, making sure that the point centers on the nail head.

To find a point along the line you've established, you will need to use a tape measure in combination with a plumb bob. This requires two people. Your helper should "burn a foot" of the tape (hold it on the 1-ft. mark), or use a leather thong to get a good grip while holding the tape accurately over the intersecting strings. A solid stance allows your helper to sight down on the tape and to brace against the tension that you'll be exerting on it. On the smart end of things, lay the plumb-bob string directly over the tape on the correct dimension. Make sure that you are paralleling the batter-board string, which is level and square to the rest of the layout, and then keep the tape taut while you pay attention to the bob itself.

Another common use of a plumb line is projecting an established point up in the air, such as lining up the face of a beam with the layout on the floor. It saves time to use two people here—one on the plumb-bob point at the floor and the other up on the beam.

A plumb bob also makes good sense when you need to establish a true vertical line but the distance is too great to be checked with a level. High walls, posts and very tall door and window jambs are good examples. When you use a plumb line this way, it's necessary to offset the string from the work to allow the plumb bob to hang free. When this offset measurement is constant along the entire height of the string, then the object is plumb.

Because a plumb line is absolutely vertical, it's also indispensable for laying out chimney flues

Figure-eight bend—*A stopper knot used either at the end of string to prevent unraveling, or inside the threaded cap of a plumb bob.*

Maybe the most common use of a plumb bob is to project a point up or down in space. Here, the author checks a layout point (represented by the duplex nail driven into the top of the stake) by using the plumb bob together with a tape measure. This requires a braced stance and steady nerves if the tape is going to be stretched tight enough for an accurate measurement from the original benchmark.

and stovepipes, and for figuring out where a light fixture goes in a sloped ceiling.

Almost any type of string will work to suspend a plumb bob, but braided nylon has no natural twist, so it doesn't spin in one direction and then in the other like a confused top. The line should be attached through the hole in the bob's threaded cap and tied off with a figure eight or stopper knot (drawing, facing page). When it's not in use, the string can be wrapped around the plumb bob or a spool. (Nail spool to the wall's top plate and drop the string over the spool's edge; the wall is plumb when the bob hangs a spool's width from bottom plate.)

Steel plumb bobs are the cheapest. Henry L. Hanson, Inc. (220 Brooks St., Worcester, Mass. 01606) makes a bullet-shaped, hexagonal bob that I see a lot, but there are many other manufacturers. Popular weights are 5 oz. and 8 oz., and they run well under $10. These are fine for short drops, but for anything a story high or more, you should use a heavier version. Solid brass plumb bobs in a teardrop shape are the most popular. General Hardware Mfg. (80 White St., New York, N. Y. 10013) makes them with replaceable steel tips in 6-oz., 8-oz., 10-oz., 12-oz., 16-oz., 24-oz. and 32-oz. weights. They range in price from $8 to $28. Stanley (Stanley Tools, 600 Myrtle St., New Britain, Conn. 06050) makes a painted cast-metal version in 6-oz., 8-oz. and 12-oz. weights for a bit less money.

The heavier the bob, the better chance that you'll be able to get a good reading when there's a breeze. But large plumb bobs are pretty cumbersome to carry around in your nail bags. The ideal setup is a small bob for most work, and a 16-oz. or 24-oz. bob for long drops where the wind is a bigger factor.

There are two other types of plumb bobs that you will occasionally see. The first is the old-fashioned squat type. These are made of iron, but because of their shape it is very difficult to see a mark beneath them. The other kind is the small-diameter, bullet-shaped steel plumb bobs that have been bored and filled with mercury to get a low center of gravity and lots of weight for their size. L. S. Starrett Co. (Athol, Mass. 01331) makes a 12-oz. plumb bob that is only 6 in. long and ⅞ in. in diameter.

Chalklines—Being able to connect two points at considerable distance from each other with a straight line that is highly visible by simply plucking a string is a gift from the gods that a builder couldn't live without. There's no end to the applications. Carpenters of the 19th and early 20th centuries had to chalk their lines by running the string over a hemisphere of solid chalk. A chalkbox is a lot easier.

There are a number of brands on the market priced under $10. The most popular are Stanley's, Evans' (The Evans Rule Co., 768 Freling-

huysen Ave., Newark, N. J. 07114) and Irwin's (The Irwin Co., 92 Grant St., Wilmington, Ohio 45177). Stanley and Evans chalkboxes have aluminum die-cast cases (Stanley also makes a less expensive polypropylene model) that you can fill through a threaded cap. All of these boxes are available in 50-ft. and 100-ft. models (you're better off paying the extra dollar for the extra length). Evans' best model, which runs under $7, has a crank that can be stored completely flush with the case, and will release the string from this position. A slide mechanism allows you to lock down on the string. The Irwin Strait-Line box is an aluminum alloy, but is filled from a nylon sliding window on the side. It costs about half as much as the other two.

There are also geared chalkline reels in ABS plastic (Keson Industries, Inc., 5 South 475 Frontenac Rd., Naperville, Ill. 60540) and aluminum (B & S Patent Developing Corp., Box 1392, Riverside, Calif. 92502) that will recover the string at up to four times the pace of a direct-drive box. This can be a real advantage when you're laying out large spaces. They run about $5 to $7. On the E-Z Fastline, you can disengage the gears, which lets the string free-spool out of the box, by keeping the top of the crank depressed. This is a nice feature, since with some boxes you have to cope with the handle spinning around in your hand as the string is released. Unfortunately, the geared boxes are quite large and take up a lot of room in your nailbags. I also haven't been impressed with their quality—the cranks on the ones I've seen are quite flimsy, and the plastic cover for the filler hole looks like it wouldn't survive an assault by 16d nails in the bottom of a nailbag.

Most chalkboxes are outfitted with cotton line to which a small metal hook/loop combination is attached. Cotton is used because it doesn't stretch, it leaves a crisp line, and the rough natural fiber retains the chalk well. It does, however, abrade easily. Although cotton replacement line is available for less than a dollar, I experimented with braided nylon for its toughness but I didn't have much luck. The line wouldn't hold much chalk, and what chalk did adhere was thrown every which way with the snap. Also, because nylon is elastic, it vibrated after the pluck, leaving a thick line.

Powdered chalk comes in four colors: red, blue, yellow and white. It is packaged in plastic

containers holding 1 oz., 4 oz. or 8 oz. of chalk, and a 1-gal. size weighing 5 lb. I keep an 8-oz. bottle in the toolbox, refilling it from the less expensive gallon jug. It pays to have a couple of different chalkboxes so that you can use contrasting colors when you want to overstrike a mistake or distinguish between two things in a complicated layout.

There aren't too many tricks to using a chalkbox. If it was recently filled, pluck the line in the air a time or two to shake off the excess chalk. But even if the string is really loaded at first, two to four snaps and you won't be able to produce a visible line. You could then rewind the string, but it's faster if you just have another few snaps to do to pull out more string instead.

You will often see carpenters automatically rap their chalkboxes on the floor or against their thighs before attaching the free end of the line. This merely redistributes the remaining chalk in a partially filled box so that the string will come out with a full coating.

The universal hook that comes on the end of all chalkboxes will work on the edge of almost anything but a concrete slab (the edging trowel usually has a larger radius than the hook can accommodate). In this case, you're best off getting a helper. On plywood or lumber, drive an 8d nail and lower the hook onto it or use a scratch awl. For shorter snaps, you can hold one end down with your foot. In a pinch, you can snap a line that is less than 18 in. or so by using your thumbs to hold the ends, and using your little finger to make the snap. This can be useful when you've got to cut a series of jogs in plywood siding, for instance. If you practice this a few times you'll find it faster than taking your combination square apart to connect the lines.

No matter how long the line, it must be quite taut to get a good snap. The pluck must be perpendicular to the surface to be marked, or you'll get a curved line. Lift the line just enough for the ends to clear and let it go. Take time to get it right the first time, because a second snap usually makes a mess. On long runs the line must be lifted so high that you run a real danger of not being able to pull straight up on the string. Solve this by holding the string down in the center and snapping each side individually. □

Trey Loy is a carpenter and contractor in Little River, Calif.

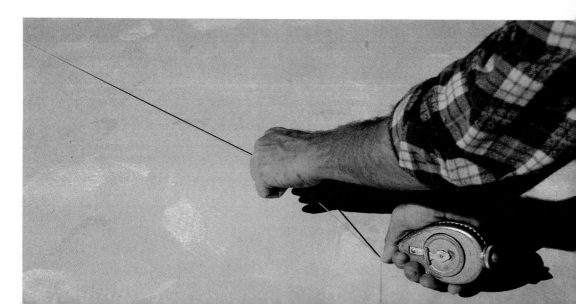

The Rafter Square

Laying out a roof with this basic tool and a new generation of accessories

by Jud Peake

Few carpenters would neglect to include a steel square when packing their toolboxes for a job. Yet, when pressed, quite a few good builders will abashedly admit that they generally use the square just for scribing a cut-off line on stock too large for their combination square. The steel square can serve a variety of functions, from stairbuilding to making simple checks for right angles, but it's especially useful for laying out rafters and other roof-frame members. With a little instruction, anyone can lay out cuts for common rafters, valleys, hips, jacks and gable ends. This doesn't require a knowledge of trigonometry, just a simple understanding of the geometry involved.

The rafter square—This versatile tool consists of two parts—the body, or blade, and the tongue (drawing, facing page). These two meet at the heel. The body is 24 in. long and 2 in. wide, and usually represents the level line, or run, in laying out rafters. Plumb, or rise, is represented by the tongue, which is 16 in. long and 1½ in. wide. The face and back of the square are usually imprinted with edge scales and math tables. The latter distinguish a rafter square from a framing square.

Squares are made of steel, usually painted black, or aluminum. Aluminum squares are typically more expensive, but lighter and less liable to bring second-degree burns to your palms on hot summer days. The best squares have their numbers stamped deeply into the metal rather than painted on. Most of them come with instruction books that are a handy toolbox reference.

The use of the rafter square is based on the geometry of right triangles. All right triangles have a 90° angle, which can be used to describe the intersection of a plumb and level line—the intersection of the tongue and the body of a framing square. Right triangles also share another quality: when the rise and run of a right triangle are increased proportionally, the hypotenuse lengthens proportionally, too, although its slope or pitch remains constant. A stair with a rise of $6\frac{11}{16}$ in. and a 10-in. tread has the same pitch as an 8-in-12 roof because the proportion between rise and run for each of them is the same. Since rafters are nothing more than the sloping side of the triangle, the rafter square acts as an infinitely expanding intersection of plumb and level, allowing you to use the rafter stock as the hypotenuse. More information on how the proportional nature of

the rafter square can come in handy will be presented later.

A useful quality of right triangles, discovered by Pythagoras, is that the sum of the square of the sides equals the square of the hypotenuse ($a^2 + b^2 = c^2$). To the roof framer this means that if the rise (a) and run (b) of the roof are known, then the length of the rafter (c) can be easily calculated.

Scales and tables—On the face side of the square, the side with the maker's stamp on it, inches are broken into eighths and sixteenths. On the back, the outside edge of both the body and the tongue shows twelfths of an inch. This is useful for scaling inches to feet. The inside edge of the tongue is laid out in tenths, and the face of the heel usually has a hundredths scale. By holding your tape measure against these last two scales, you can easily convert back and forth from decimal inches to sixteenths.

Different manufacturers of squares give slightly different information in the tables on the face of the square. Usually, the first line gives in decimal inches the lengths of common rafters per foot of run; the second line does the same for regular hip and valley rafters. These figures are listed in the tables by their unit rise. Units of run are always 12 in. The inch markings on the outside face of the body double as unit-rise headings under which unit rafter lengths can be found. None of the tables that give rafter lengths makes allowance for the thickness of the framing members that they butt. This allowance, referred to as reduction or shortening, is a factor I'll talk about later.

The next two lines in the tables give the actual difference in the lengths of jack rafters in inches and fractions. The first of these lines gives the common difference for jacks on 16-in. centers, and the second line for those on 24-in. centers. Most squares then show two lines of side cuts for hips, valleys and their jacks. Some squares have a seventh line, which gives the angle at which sheathing should be cut where it meets hips and valleys.

Unit measurement—The square can be used in two ways to determine the length of rafters. The first method is unit measurement. As shown in the drawing, top of facing page, this technique uses the proportional qualities of the right triangle, and expresses rise and run as a ratio. For common rafters, unit run is always 12 in., and the unit rise is the rise per foot of

run. The pitch triangle seen in most plans is a representation of unit measurement; so are the rafter tables on the square. For example, if you need the unit length of a common rafter on a 4-in-12 roof, look in the first line of the tables, length of common rafters per foot of run, under the 4-in. mark, the unit rise, on the outside of the body. The number given is 12 65. This means that for every foot of run with a rise of 4 in., the rafter will have to be 12.65 in. long. Check this figure by measuring diagonally with your tape between the 4 and the 12 on the square. You should get slightly more than $12\frac{5}{8}$ in., or 12.65 in. The drawing, right, shows how holding the rise and run of the square determines the unit length of the hypotenuse, which, for the purposes of framing a roof, is the edge of a rafter.

Once you have found the unit length of the rafter in the tables for a given rise and run, multiply this figure by the actual run (usually half the width of the building) to get the theoretical, or unadjusted, length. This measurement begins with a plumb cut at the top of the rafter and ends with the plumb cut of the bird's mouth, the 90° cutout where the rafter sits on the top plate of the exterior wall. You will have to add the length of the rafter tail, and subtract half the thickness of the ridgeboard.

Stepping off—The second method for finding an unadjusted rafter length is called stepping off. To step off, lay the square on the rafter with the tongue and body reading the pitch, and repeat this procedure as many times as there are feet in the total run (drawing, bottom of facing page). For example, if the actual run of a rafter on a 4-in-12 roof were 13 ft., you would have to mark the rafter 13 consecutive times to lay out the length of the body of the rafter. You would do this by setting the square on the rafter stock, crown side away from you, so that the heel of the square is toward you and the tongue is on your right. Align the 4-in. mark on the outside of the tongue, representing the rise, and the 12-in. mark on the body, representing the run, on the edge of the rafter. Now scribe a line on the outside of the body at the edge of the rafter, and slide the square along until the outside of the tongue, held on the edge of the rafter at the 4-in. mark, lines up with the scribed line, and scribe again.

Move the square and scribe in the same attitude twelve times from the original position. The plumb cut of the bird's mouth will intersect

From *Fine Homebuilding* magazine (August 1982) 10:56-61

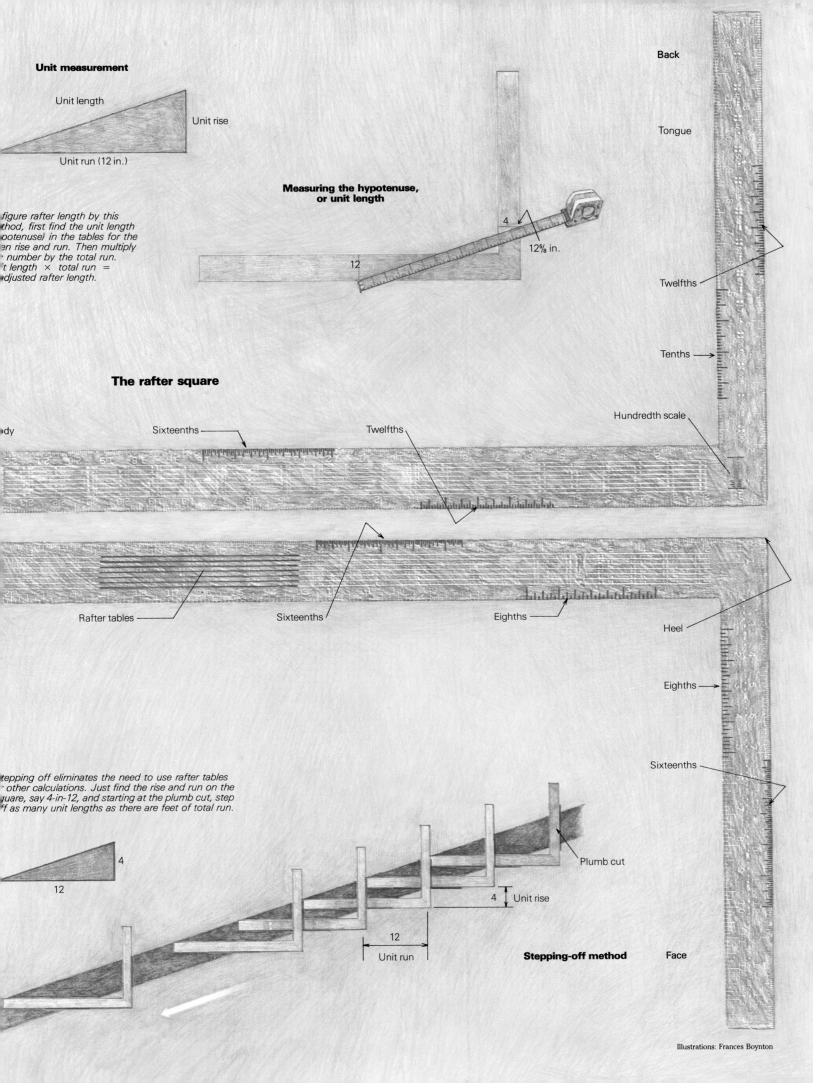

Unit measurement

Unit length

Unit rise

Unit run (12 in.)

figure rafter length by this
thod, first find the unit length
ootenuse) in the tables for the
en rise and run. Then multiply
number by the total run.
t length × total run =
djusted rafter length.

**Measuring the hypotenuse,
or unit length**

4

12⅝ in.

12

Back

Tongue

Twelfths

Tenths

Hundredth scale

The rafter square

Sixteenths

Twelfths

dy

Rafter tables

Sixteenths

Eighths

Heel

Eighths

Sixteenths

tepping off eliminates the need to use rafter tables
other calculations. Just find the rise and run on the
uare, say 4-in-12, and starting at the plumb cut, step
f as many unit lengths as there are feet of total run.

4

12

Plumb cut

4   Unit rise

12
Unit run

Stepping-off method

Face

Illustrations: Frances Boynton

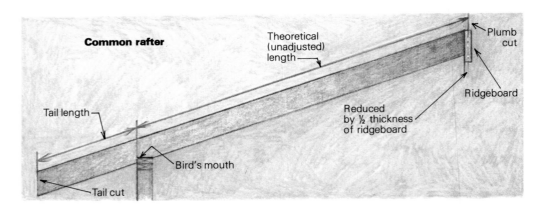

Common rafter

Tail length

Tail cut

Bird's mouth

Theoretical (unadjusted) length

Reduced by ½ thickness of ridgeboard

Plumb cut

Ridgeboard

the edge of the rafter at the thirteenth scribed line. This is the unadjusted, or theoretical, length of the rafter. Stepping off won't tell you its length in inches and feet. You'll have to measure it later.

When the run is not in whole feet, the remaining inches are measured along the level line of the body. This mark is brought back to the edge of the rafter by lining up the tongue with this mark and scribing a plumb line, while still holding the rise and run on the square along the edge of the material. The stepping-off method also requires reduction. As with unit measurement, you'll have to subtract half the thickness of the ridge, and add the length of any overhang. Stepping off must be done carefully because of the danger of accumulated error. It also doesn't give you the precise length of rafter stock at the outset.

Laying out a common rafter—The object of all of these tedious calculations is to cut a rafter pattern, which can then be used to lay out the remainder of the roof without any further headscratching. If you think of a rafter pattern as the only obstacle between you and the goal of calculating an entire roof plane, it will lighten the burden a little.

The first task is to lay out the plumb (top) cut of the rafter, as shown above. This cut will rest against the ridgeboard when installed. Lay it out by setting the square on the rafter stock just as you would for stepping off. Align the inch

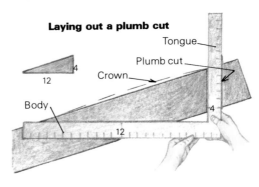

Laying out a plumb cut

Tongue

Plumb cut

Crown

Body

marks that correspond with rise and run on the outside of the tongue and body on the side of the stock nearest you (drawing, above). Remember to use the tongue for the unit rise, and the body for the unit run. Set your pencil against the outside of the tongue and draw the plumb line. This line represents the very center of the span, as if the rafters from each side were butting together without a ridgeboard. Because

this line doesn't take the ridgeboard into account, you must measure along the body of the square (a level line) half the thickness of the ridgeboard and draw a new line parallel to the original plumb line for the actual cut. For a 2x ridgeboard, you would measure ¾ in. perpendicular to the plumb line—not along the edge of the rafter—to get the shortening line.

Determine the unadjusted length of the rafter either by stepping off or by unit measurement. Measure from the plumb line (not the reduced cut-line) to the plumb line of the bird's mouth, known as the heel cut. This is the part of the bird's mouth that hooks over the outside of the wall (drawing, below).

To lay out the bird's mouth, make a mark 1½ in. up from the bottom of the heel cut. Begin measuring from the rafter edge nearest

Bird's-mouth layout

Heel cut (plumb cut)

Seat cut (level cut)

Heel cut-line

Seat cut-line

Tail

Bird's mouth

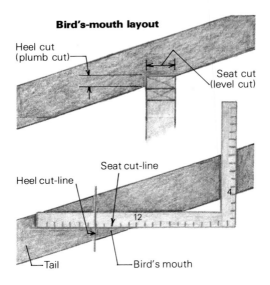

you. Now slide the square, still holding it at the correct rise and run, along the rafter toward the top plumb cut. When the body of the square intersects the 1½-in. mark on the heel cut, scribe along the body from the 1½-in. mark across to the edge of the rafter. This is a level mark; the heel (plumb) cut and the seat (level) cut make the bird's mouth. The 1½-in. depth of the bird's mouth is arbitrary, but it shouldn't be cut so deep that it weakens the rafter tails. The depth of this cut doesn't affect the roof's slope, but does affect the absolute height of the ridge. If you deepen the seat cut by 1 in. the ridge will be lowered by 1 in. This usually doesn't matter unless you already have high walls, purlins or a ridge beam in place.

You can now add the length of the tail, or

overhang. Beginning with the heel cut of the bird's mouth, measure down along the rafter (or step it off) and mark the tail cut. Standard tails can be cut square (perpendicular to the line of the rafter), cut level or cut plumb.

Laying out a regular hip or valley—Hips and valleys are different from common rafters because they take a diagonal path across the building. The run of regular hips and valleys angles across the plan at 45°, completing an isosceles right triangle with the run of the last common rafter and the top plate. This means that the run is longer than that of the common rafter, although the rise remains the same. The drawing below shows the relationship of the run of common rafters and hips. By applying the Pythagorean theorem, or by measuring diagonally between the 12-in. marks on the square, the unit run of the hip figures out to be about 17 in. for every 12 in. of common run. This means that each time you would use the

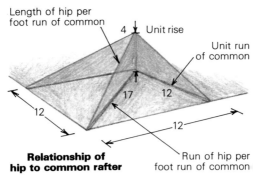

Length of hip per foot run of common

Unit rise

Unit run of common

Run of hip per foot run of common

Relationship of hip to common rafter

12-in. mark on the body of your square to find the cuts and lengths of common rafters, you use the 17-in. mark to work with hips and valleys. However, you still use the same rise figure and, in stepping off, take the same number of steps as you would with a common.

The adjustments for hip and valley rafters are more complicated than they are for commons. Because a hip intersects both the ridge and the common rafter at the top, each side requires a vertical 45° bevel to form the plumb cut. This is known as a double cheek or double side cut. The drawing below shows the reductions that

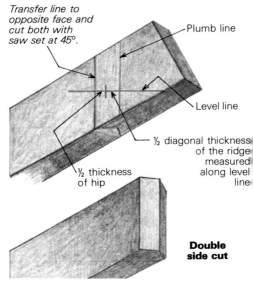

Transfer line to opposite face and cut both with saw set at 45°.

Plumb line

Level line

½ diagonal thickness of the ridge measured along level line

½ thickness of hip

Double side cut

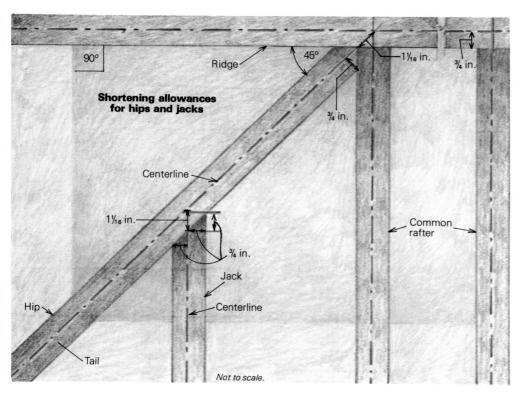

Shortening allowances for hips and jacks

90°

Ridge

45°

1¹/₁₆ in.

¾ in.

Centerline

¾ in.

1¹/₁₆ in.

¾ in.

Jack

Hip

Centerline

Tail

Common rafter

Not to scale.

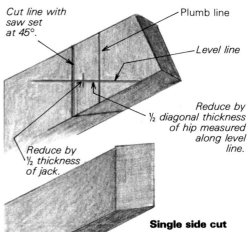

Cut line with saw set at 45°.

Plumb line

Level line

Reduce by ½ diagonal thickness of hip measured along level line.

Reduce by ½ thickness of jack.

Single side cut

are necessary for double side cuts. With the common rafters we deduct one-half the ridge thickness, measured level, on the side of the rafter. With a hip we have to deduct one-half the diagonal measure of the ridge thickness and again lay this out level on the side of the rafter. To move to the side of the rafter, you have to deduct another ¾ in. (for a 2x hip), again measured level, to account for the difference between the long point of the double bevel at the center of the hip and the short point on the side, as shown above.

These cuts can be made easily and accurately with a circular saw set at 45° because at any pitch, regular hips and valleys intersect common rafters at 45°. If you draw the correct double side cut on the top edge of the rafter, it won't appear as a 45° angle because the edge of the rafter is not a level line when installed. However, for a good fit using a circular saw on regular hips and valleys, the only mark you'll need is the plumb line.

In the tables, determine the lengths of regular hips and valleys the same way you find them for commons. Just make sure to look under the heading "length of hips and valley per foot of run." The bird's mouths are also similar except you have to use the 17-in. mark on the body for the level line, and the depth of the heel cut will be different. Hip and valley rafters are usually of wider stock than commons; so to make sure the tails are level, hip and valley bird's mouths have to be deeper, leaving the same amount of uncut rafter above them as you did on the commons. After adding length for the overhang you can lay out and cut the tail. If you are planning on a surrounding fascia, the tail cut has to be a double side cut.

The rafter tail is a good place to practice stepping off inches. For an example, assume that a 4-in-12 roof requires a 1-ft. 6½-in. tail. Step off the first foot of run as you did with the com-

mon, except with the hip, use 4 and 17. Draw a level line. Just as 17 (the diagonal measure of 12 and 12) gives you the first foot of run, the diagonal measure of 6½ and 6½ will give you the remainder of the run. Stretching a tape measure between these marks on the square gives a measurement of 9³/₁₆ in. Measure along the level line on the rafter tail 9³/₁₆ in., and the overhang will be correct.

Laying out a jack—A jack rafter is a common rafter that intersects a hip or valley before it reaches the ridge or plate. The only way that it differs from a common is its length and the bevel of its plumb cut. This is a single side cut, and in 2x material I make it with a circular saw set at 45°.

Once you have established the plumb line on the jack rafter, make the hip or valley reduction (one-half the diagonal thickness) along a

level line as shown in the illustration, above right. With a 2x hip or valley, this measures 1¹/₁₆ in. To reach the short point of the side cut, make a further reduction along the level line for one-half the thickness of the jack itself. This measures ¾ in. The jack reduction is necessary because you are laying out the side cut on the side of the rafter, rather than on the centerline of the top edge.

As with hip or valley rafters, using a saw with a shoe that pivots allows you to cut any regular hip or valley jack correctly by following the reduced plumb line with the saw set at 45°.

Big beams require the angle of the side cut to be laid out on the top edge of the rafter because a circular saw won't handle the depth of cut. Use a rafter book or the rafter tables for the co-ordinates on the square. If two figures appear under each rise, find the first figure on the body of the square, and set it on the edge of the rafter stock. Next find the second number on the tongue and place it on the same edge of the rafter. Check instructions for your square or book for which leg of the square to scribe against. If there is only one figure listed, then use it on the body, use 12 on the tongue, and make your mark along the tongue.

Once you have determined the length of the first jack, the rest are merely multiples. This is called the common difference, and can be seen in the framing diagram (drawing, below). Find

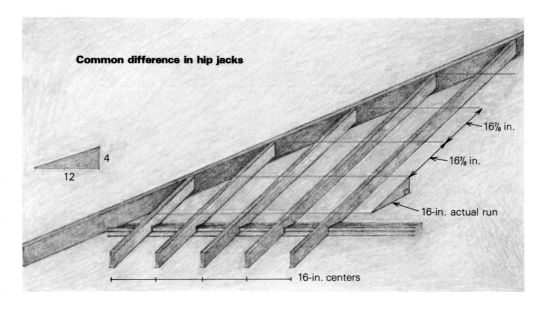

Common difference in hip jacks

4

12

16⅞ in.

16⅞ in.

16-in. actual run

16-in. centers

the appropriate table on your square (16-in. spacing or 24-in. spacing) and look up the pitch of your roof. The figure you see listed is the length of the first jack, excluding the length of the tail, and also the increase in the length of each subsequent jack.

Notice that the relationship that regular hips and valleys have with common rafters and plates is the same one that exists between jacks and their hip or valley rafter. This is an isosceles right triangle in plan, and means that the actual run of the first jack will be the same as its spacing. If the first jack is 16 in. away from the seat cut of the hip, it will have an actual run of 16 in.; if it's 24 in. along the plate, the actual run will be 24 in. This is an actual run, not a unit run.

Solving proportion problems—With a rafter square, you can easily determine the wall height under a shed roof. For example, if a 4-in-12 roof is supported by an 8-ft. wall on the low side, then what is the height of the supporting wall 13 ft. away on the high side? Use the twelfths scale. Lay the 4-in. mark of the tongue and the 12-in. mark of the body on a straightedge, as shown below. Draw a line against the

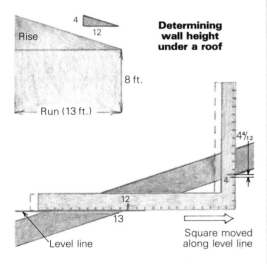

Determining wall height under a roof

body representing a level line. Then move the square along this line until 13, representing the actual run, lines up with the edge of the material. The answer, 4⁴⁄₁₂, reads on the tongue of the square where it first comes in contact with the wood. This figure (4 ft. 4 in., when multiplied from unit dimensions to actual dimensions) represents the rise of the wall above the established 8-ft. mark. The height of the other wall is then 12 ft. 4 in.

Determining the length of gable-end studs is another proportion problem, and can be solved in the same way as determining wall heights under a roof. Like jack rafters, the length of the first gable stud is equal to the difference in the lengths of the other studs. The length of the first stud can be determined by the proportional method, with a calculator, or by measurement. To use the square, follow the directions for finding wall heights. In this case the spacing of your studs, typically 16 in. or 24 in., is the actual run. □

Jud Peake is a carpenter and contractor in Oakland Calif.

Other tools that help

The rafter square is still king. Despite challenges from quite a number of patented devices, few roofs get framed without the use of a rafter square. It remains the best choice because of its accuracy, durability and variety of necessary data. Still, there are several other useful tools that can simplify the job. Most of these are used in conjunction with a rafter square.

Rafter books. These guides give listings of rafter lengths for common, hip, valley and jack rafters referenced by span, and are typically organized by pitch from ½-in-12 to 24-in-12. The pitch angle is given, as well as the corresponding layout numbers on the steel square for all cuts and bevels. Although quick and accurate, these guides will leave you in the dark if you're working on an irregular or polygonal roof. One widely used rafter book is *The Full Length Roof Framer* (A.F. Riechers,

Box 405, Palo Alto, Calif. 94302). It lists 48 different pitches and includes the cuts and bevels for gable and cornice moldings. It is pocket size, bound, and sells for about $6.

Squangle (Mayes Bros. Tool Mfg. Co., Box 1018, Johnson City, Tenn. 37601). This device is small enough to fit into your nail bag and can be used with one hand. It has some limited rafter tables on its tongue, although it's best used with a rafter book or the rafter tables on a square. Unlike a square, the Squangle can convert a unit rise and run into degrees. But once the tool is dropped from a roof, it may not work accurately. It sells for about $9.

Speed Square (The Swanson Tool Co., Box 434, Oak Lawn, Ill., 60453). This tool is also small enough to be carried on your tool belt. It comes with an instruction book and extensive, full-length rafter tables. A solid

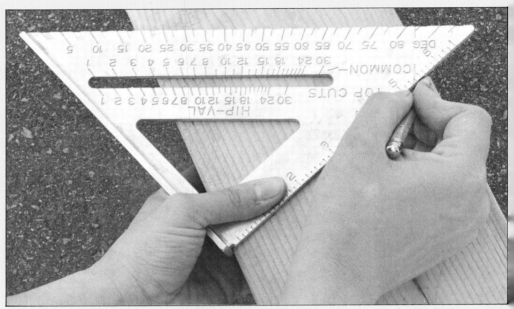

The Speed Square is an aluminum casting small enough to fit into nailbags. Angles in degrees are given on the face of the tool, and it comes with an instruction book and rafter tables.

The Squangle is one of the relatively new tools based on the rafter square. It has limited tables, but is smaller than the square and gives equivalent angles for roof pitches.

aluminum casting, the Speed Square won't bend or break, but because of its sharp points, you wouldn't want it hanging from your belt if you lost your balance and took a fall. Angles in degrees are also given on the face. It takes two hands to use it, and costs $8.35.

Two other squares that are nearly identical to the Speed Square are the Carpenter Handy Square for $7.49 (Macklanburg-Duncan Co., Box 25188, Oklahoma City, Okla. 73125), and the Angle Square at $7.67 (Johnson Level and Tool Mfg. Co., 2072 North Commerce St., Milwaukee, Wis. 53212).

Stair-gauge fixtures. These really help if you use the framing square. They are purchased in pairs, usually made of milled brass, and cost about $8. You fix them to the square by tightening a setscrew on each one. Attach these stops at the points on the square that define the pitch you are using (such as 4 and 12), and you can repeatedly set the square accurately on the rafter stock without having to read the numbers each time. If you are careful when you attach them to the square, they will improve your accuracy greatly, particularly if you are using the stepping-off method. As the name says, they are also very helpful in laying out stair stringers.

Layout tee. This is a roof-framing aid that you make on the job site. Tees are patterns, or templates, of the tail and bird's mouth, or the ridge cut of a rafter that is used to transfer the layout onto rafter stock. They are made of a short length of rafter with a 1x4 nailed to the edge as a fence to reference the tee to the rafter being marked.

Pitch board. This is simply a piece of plywood cut in the shape of a right triangle defined by the rise and run of the roof to be framed. It is used for stepping off rafters in the same manner as a framing square. It can also help mark cuts for gable-end studs and bird's mouths.

Calculator. One of the items you are likely to find in the toolbox of a canny roof framer these days is an extra battery. With the advent of the $10 pocket calculator, the framing square has a new companion. Because roof-framing calculations are based largely on the Pythagorean theorem, any calculator with a square-root key will do. Using a calculator is more accurate and less tedious than reading the tables on a framing square because you are able to deal directly with the equation and the variables involved.

It's important to decide what units you are using—inches, feet or decimal inches/feet—and remain consistent throughout the calculation. I find it easiest to enter measurements and take the answers in inches to save conversion steps, which are a common source of error. I use my calculator to determine pitch angles, rafter lengths, common difference in jacks, gable-end stud heights and other proportional problems, as explained below. —*Jud Peake*

Using a pocket calculator

Proportion. This is a useful calculation in determining wall heights, as in the example given (drawing, facing page) using the framing square. This is a matter of converting a unit rise and run to an actual rise, given an actual run. My calculator uses the algebraic operating system, so your keystrokes may be different; but the logic goes like this:

If $\dfrac{\text{unit rise}}{\text{unit run}} = \dfrac{\text{actual rise}}{\text{actual run}}$,

then actual rise $= \dfrac{\text{unit rise}}{\text{unit run}} \times$ actual run.

To find the actual rise of a 4-in-12 roof over a 13-ft. run:

$\dfrac{4}{12} = \dfrac{\text{actual rise}}{13 \text{ ft.}}$, and actual rise $= \dfrac{4}{12} \times 13$ ft.

This answer is in feet. On the calculator, the keystrokes are:

rise $\div$ run $\times$ actual run (ft.) $=$ actual rise (ft.).

Difference in the lengths of gable studs. The unadjusted length of the first gable stud is also the difference in the lengths of the gable studs. This is just another proportion problem:

$\dfrac{\text{difference in length of studs}}{\text{spacing of stud centers}} = \dfrac{\text{rise}}{\text{run}}$.

The keystrokes are:

rise $\div$ run $\times$ spacing (in.) $=$ difference in length (in.).

The formula is simplified for common stud centers. For studs 24 in. o.c.,

difference in length of studs $= 2 \times$ unit rise.

For 16-in. centers,

difference in length of studs $= 1.333 \times$ unit rise.

Lengths of common rafters. These are given in a general way by the Pythagorean theorem:

length of common $= \sqrt{\text{rise}^2 + \text{run}^2}$.

However, you need to be clear about which units of measure you are using. If you use the actual rise and run in feet, the answer will be the actual length of the common, expressed in feet. If you use the unit rise and run, the answer will be the unit length of the rafter. This is a length in inches for every 12 inches of run. The simplest formula uses the unit rise and run:

length of common rafter (in.) $= \sqrt{\text{rise}^2 + 144} \times$ actual run (ft.).

The keystrokes are:

rise x^2 $+$ 144 $=$ $\sqrt{}$ $\times$ actual run (ft.) $=$ length of common (in.).

This answer doesn't account for the thickness of the ridge. There is less chance of error if you make this allowance during the layout of the rafter.

Lengths of regular hips and valleys. Once you determine the run, you can find the length of a hip or valley. Because the run of a regular hip or valley is the diagonal of a square whose sides are runs of the common rafters, the run is the square root of twice the square of the common run.

Run of hip $= \sqrt{2 \times \text{run of common}^2}$, and

length of hip $= \sqrt{\text{run of hip}^2 + \text{rise}^2}$

$= \sqrt{2 \times \text{run of common}^2 + \text{rise}^2}$.

Or you can use unit rise, unit run, and the run of the common rafter:

hip length $= \sqrt{2 \times \text{unit run}^2 + \text{unit rise}^2} \times$ actual run of common.

Since the unit run is always 12, this becomes:

length of hip $= \sqrt{288 + \text{unit rise}^2} \times$ actual run of common.

The square root of 288 is $16^{31}\!/_{32}$, or almost 17, the same 17 that you use on the framing square for the run. The keystrokes for finding a regular hip or valley length with a calculator are:

rise x^2 $+$ 288 $=$ $\sqrt{}$ $\times$ actual run (ft.) $=$ unadjusted hip length (in.).

Again, it's useful to make the ridge reduction on the actual rafter. This time, though, the ridge thickness is a diagonal measure:

$\dfrac{\text{ridge thickness in inches}}{2} \times \sqrt{2} =$ diagonal of ½ ridge thickness.

In an isosceles right triangle, the square root of 2 multiplied by the side equals the hypotenuse.

Difference in the lengths of hip and valley jacks. The first jack has an actual run equal to the spacing of the jacks. The length of this jack, unadjusted, will be equal to the difference in the lengths of the jacks:

difference in length of jacks (in.) $= \sqrt{\left(\dfrac{\text{rise}}{\text{run}} \times \text{spacing}\right)^2 + \text{spacing}^2}$.

For jacks 16 in. o.c.:

difference $= \sqrt{(\text{rise} \times 1.333)^2 + 16^2}$.

For jacks 24 in. o.c.:

difference $= \sqrt{(\text{rise} \times 2)^2 + 24^2}$.

To adjust for thickness on the long point side, deduct the following:

thickness of hip $\times \sqrt{2} - \dfrac{\text{thickness of jack}}{2}$

Bevels and angles. Plumb, level and bevel cuts can be converted to degrees if your calculator has trig functions. The keystrokes are:

for angle A, rise $\div$ run $=$ $\boxed{\text{TAN}^{-1}}$

for angle B, run $\div$ rise $=$ $\boxed{\text{TAN}^{-1}}$

Scaffolding

What goes up mustn't come down accidentally

by Scott McBride

There are few subjects in construction with as little glamour or as much importance as scaffolding. Often erected in a hurry, abused by those who literally depend on it and torn down without ceremony, a scaffold is the ugly chrysalis whose removal reveals a butterfly.

Hard-earned knowledge of construction rigging is one of my most important resources as a builder. The ability to erect a safe, effective work platform is a skill that can be acquired only through thoughtful experimentation with the different systems available. There are nearly as many types of scaffolding as there are different types of jobs, and the ideal setup for a given situation is often a combination of several. As a result, I sometimes enjoy rigging a job more than I enjoy the job itself.

A word of caution is in order before I begin. The Occupational Safety and Health Administration (OSHA) has identified scaffolding as a leading cause of accidents in construction. OSHA's standards for the construction industry include 17 pages on scaffolding. While I mention some of these regulations in my discussion, it would be impossible, in this space, for me to list them all. Therefore, I recommend that everyone read the OSHA standards before setting up or using any type of scaffold. For more on OSHA and for information on how to get a copy of their *Construction Industry Standards*, see the sidebar on p. 39.

Planks—The basic scaffold consists of two parts: a pair of supports and a horizontal platform. Wood planking is the most common platform material. The standard scaffold plank available at lumberyards is a full 2-in. by 9-in. scaffold-grade roughsawn spruce plank. The rough texture provides a non-skid surface, and the extra thickness makes a more substantial platform than ordinary 2x dimension lumber. Thirteen feet is the standard length, providing for a 12-ft. span with 6 in. of overlap at each support. Some regulations insist on even shorter spans, dropping down to a 10-ft. maximum.

All planks should be inspected carefully for defects. Small knots and some checking on the ends of planks is okay. But long spike knots and short grain are dangerous because they break the continuity of the wood fibers. Large enclosed knots and splits should also be eyed with suspicion. All of these defects are aggravated by

Scott McBride is a carpenter and contractor in Irvington, N. Y.

water and dry rot, so planks should be stickered when not in use. Periodic application of wood preservative is also a good idea. If planks become the least bit punky, get rid of them.

Twist should also be considered a serious defect in scaffold planks. It can make the plank roll as you step from side to side. If this sudden shift is extreme, you can lose your balance and take a fall.

Two planks side by side (18 in.) are the minimum for safety on any scaffold. The planks should be cleated together so that they bend in unison. Nail a piece of plywood on the underside every 4 ft. along the planks. Nail the cleats only into the middle of each plank, to reduce the chances of their splitting with cross-grain movement and to make them easier to disassemble. Some people make do with just one plank for sit-down work like painting or shingling, but even here a second plank is best for safety and provides more room for tools and buckets. Be-

sides, a second plank is cheap insurance when you're risking a fall.

You can make up your own "plank" with two good Douglas fir 2x4s on edge and a 24-in. wide strip of ¾-in. plywood nailed over them. This composite plank is easily made from materials already on the job, and will stay nice and rigid under several hundred pounds.

An attractive but expensive alternative to wood planks is the extendable aluminum platform used by many contractors. These are straight, adjustable and can span longer distances than wood planks, so fewer supports are required. I have seen aluminum extension ladders used as platforms, but this is dangerous. Their rails aren't built heavy enough for this purpose and will bend.

It's a good idea to attach any scaffold platform to its supports so that it can't slip off accidentally. This is an OSHA requirement, but their standards say only that planking must be se-

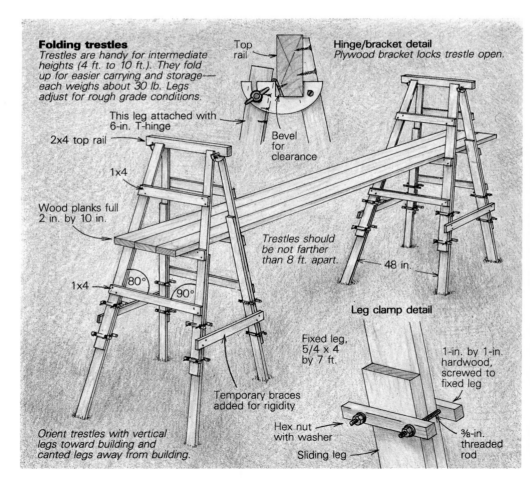

Folding trestles
Trestles are handy for intermediate heights (4 ft. to 10 ft.). They fold up for easier carrying and storage— each weighs about 30 lb. Legs adjust for rough grade conditions.

This leg attached with 6-in. T-hinge

2x4 top rail

1x4

Wood planks full 2 in. by 10 in.

1x4

1x4

80°

90°

Orient trestles with vertical legs toward building and canted legs away from building.

Top rail

Bevel for clearance

Hinge/bracket detail
Plywood bracket locks trestle open.

Trestles should be not farther than 8 ft. apart.

48 in.

Leg clamp detail

Fixed leg, 5/4 x 4 by 7 ft.

1-in. by 1-in. hardwood, screwed to fixed leg

Temporary braces added for rigidity

Hex nut with washer

Sliding leg

⅜-in. threaded rod

Drawings: Christopher Clapp

cured and don't suggest how to do it. Depending on the type of scaffold, I use clamps, ropes or nails. The first two will work with metal supports and platforms. They also offer the advantage of not damaging the equipment in any way. The advantage of nails is that they can be installed quickly and that a toenail on the edge of a plank is unlikely to trip anyone, as a rope or C-clamp might. On the other hand, a nail head sticking up on the face of a plank becomes a real hazard when it catches a boot heel.

The end of a plank should not extend more than 1 ft. beyond its support. If this rule is observed, a false step by a worker beyond the support is unlikely to flip an unsecured plank. Planks laid in a row should overlap directly above a support and should overlap by at least 12 in.

Sawhorses and trestles—The simplest support for scaffold planks is a good pair of sawhorses. A collection of sawhorses in various heights (2 ft., 3 ft. and 4 ft.) is a worthwhile investment for any contractor or serious do-it-yourselfer. Masons require a heavy horse with 2x4 legs, but the carpenter will generally find a lighter horse of 5/4 spruce to be handier. The spread of the legs should be just enough to provide stability, about 20° to 30°. Any more than this and the horses become bulky and awkward.

Drywall screws are the best fasteners for sawhorses because they resist the constant twisting strain that tends to work nails loose. If all the joints are gusseted with plywood, a very light and durable sawhorse can be made at little cost.

Some people use stepladders for scaffold supports. The stepladder is handy and adjustable, but its lack of spread parallel to its rungs makes it unstable. Also, it can accommodate the width of only one plank, and the portion of the stepladder above the plank gets in the way of the work. A better device for working in the 4-ft. to 10-ft. range is the wooden trestle.

The trestle is an overgrown version of the sawhorse, with extra bracing. It's useful where an intermediate height must be reached, or if pipe scaffolding isn't available.

The folding trestles that I developed for my own use have adjustable legs and a working range of 4 ft. to 10 ft. (drawing, facing page). When working above 7 ft., I nail temporary bracing between the opposing frames of each trestle. This rig works well under rough-grade conditions because the legs are independently adjustable. I use them on single-story work, where sawhorses won't quite reach and pump jacks are too much bother. The trestles are made of 5/4 clear pressure-treated yellow pine, and each unit weighs about 30 lb. They can be carried easily by one person, and when folded up will fit nicely in a van or station wagon.

Pipe scaffolding—Tubular welded frame scaffolding, called pipe scaffolding by most builders, is unsurpassed where a strong, freestanding work platform is needed (drawing, above right). It affords bountiful workspace when fully planked, and can be erected by one person. I was amazed and delighted the first time I set up a 24-ft. steel tower by myself in less than an hour with pipe scaffolding and planks. Pipe scaf-

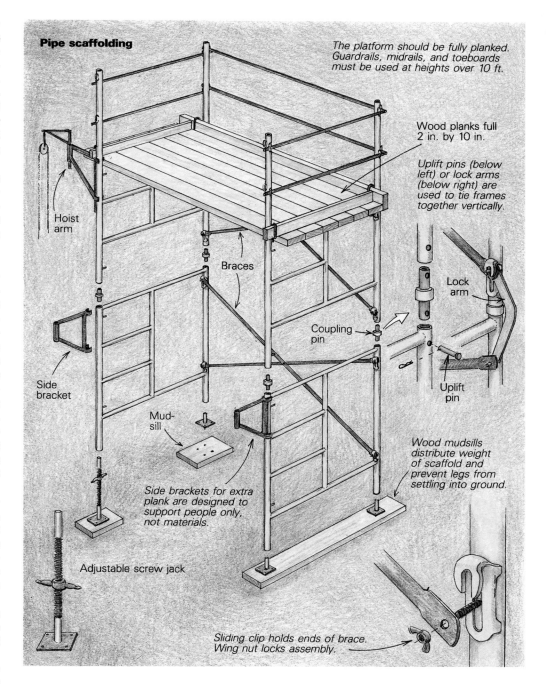

Pipe scaffolding

The platform should be fully planked. Guardrails, midrails, and toeboards must be used at heights over 10 ft.

Hoist arm

Wood planks full 2 in. by 10 in.

Uplift pins (below left) or lock arms (below right) are used to tie frames together vertically.

Braces

Lock arm

Coupling pin

Uplift pin

Side bracket

Mud-sill

Wood mudsills distribute weight of scaffold and prevent legs from settling into ground.

Side brackets for extra plank are designed to support people only, not materials.

Adjustable screw jack

Sliding clip holds ends of brace. Wing nut locks assembly.

folding is also just about the only system that can get you safely above the eaves and away from the roof at the same time, as required in chimney work.

Each unit consists of two rectangular frames and two pairs of diagonal braces. The units can be stacked vertically to considerable height, but must be attached to the building every 26 ft. Most units have a ladder as an integral part of the frame, but since it's difficult to climb straight up, I usually use an extension ladder to get up on the scaffold. Pipe scaffolding can be strung out horizontally as far as you like. When extending horizontally, it takes only one frame and two pairs of braces to yield one additional unit, since adjoining units share a common frame.

The frames are welded tubular steel, about 1¼-in. O. D., and the braces are either steel tubing or angle stock, with a rivet in the middle of each pair. Removable coupling pins lock the frames together when they're stacked on top of each other. The ends of the braces slip over

threaded studs on the frames, and are held in place by sliding clips. For extra rigidity, a nut is used to lock the brace on the stud.

The most common pipe-scaffold unit is about 6 ft. high by 5 ft. wide by 8 ft. long, but unfortunately there is no standardization of sizes among manufacturers. If you're going to buy used pipe scaffolding, set it up and make sure it all fits together before you buy it. Two identical-looking frames can have legs that differ by a maddening inch or two from center to center, or they can have legs of slightly different diameters. This makes it impossible to stack them.

In addition to the basic units, various accessories are available to adapt the system to different situations. For uneven ground, you can get adjustable screw jacks that fit up into the legs of the frames. These jacks can level a scaffold even after it's heavily loaded. Their range of adjustment is about 12 in. to 18 in.

You can get side and end brackets that serve as outboard supports for an extra plank. They can be hung at various heights on the scaffold's horizontal members. You can also buy hoist arms for lifting small loads. All of these attachments increase the risk of overturning the scaffold. When using them, you should always tie the scaffold frames together vertically with uplift pins or lock arms.

OSHA requires the use of guardrails, midrails and toeboards on all open sides of any scaffold over 10 ft. high. For pipe scaffolds, you can buy manufactured guardrails and gates that slip over the coupling pins.

In addition to its use as a work platform, the strength and stability of pipe scaffolding lends it to various other applications in construction. For instance, it makes an admirable alternative to the rickety wooden A-frame often used to hold up a steel beam until its supporting Lally column is cut and welded in place.

A tower of pipe scaffolding located just outside an attic dormer job provides a useful landing for the delivery of building materials and the removal of debris, leaving the household below less affected by construction traffic. Where attic staircases are narrow, an exterior landing may be the only way to get large items like plywood and drywall into the house. Pipe scaffolding is available through many rental outfits and lumberyards, as well as from specialized dealers listed in the Yellow Pages under "Scaffolding."

Pump jacks—Pump jacks are the pre-eminent scaffolding system for residential sidewall work, since they provide access to a maximum area with minimum rigging (drawing, below right). In addition, their adjustability lets you always work at the optimum height. The basic components of the pump-jack system are jacks, poles, metal brackets and diagonal wooden braces. One well-known brand of pump jacks is Hoitsma (Adjustable Scaffold Bracket Co., P.O. Box 595, Paterson, N. J. 07544). I paid about $50 for each set of one jack and one brace.

The jack mechanism employs a pair of spring-loaded clamps that alternately bind on a pole made of doubled 2x4s. While the lower clamp bites the pole, the upper clamp is raised with a foot pedal. The upper clamp then bites the pole, and the weight of the operator, amplified through leverage, raises the lower clamp and the entire platform several inches. Like a toy monkey the jack creeps up the pole, offering the operator an infinitely variable height adjustment. If you're working alone, you can raise one jack only a foot or two before you have to walk down and pump the other to bring the platform up to level again. To lower the platform, the bottom clamp is released by pressure from the operator's heel, and the upper clamp is rotated with a crank. Since this clamp is forged with a spiral twist, the rotation causes the clamp to roll gently down the pole, without actually losing its grip. Metal rollers prevent all parts of the jack except the clamps from binding on the pole.

Okay, that's the way pump jacks are supposed to work. In reality, pump jacks have been the object of much cussing. The problems begin with rust. Because the springs and rollers are made of steel, the springs start to lose their springiness and the rollers start to lose their rol-

liness after exposure on the job site. The clamps that are supposed to bind on the pole don't, and the parts that shouldn't bind do.

Various difficulties result, including ulcer-causing jam-ups, followed by heart-stopping free-falls of a foot or more. Then somebody discovers that rapping the jacks with a hammer here and there seems to help temporarily. But the pump jack suffers in the long run and eventually responds with ever-increasing orneriness.

An occasional treatment with penetrating oil will help immensely to prevent these problems, as will storing the jacks under shelter when not in use. Examine them regularly for signs of deterioration, paying special attention to the cotter pins (used to hold various parts in place), which are apt to rust through and fall out.

Select the best lumber you can get when choosing stock for your poles. Where I live, the choice is between Douglas fir and pressure-treated southern yellow pine. Although the fir is a little stronger than the plantation-grown yellow pine, I prefer the pine because it's less liable to decay. This danger is compounded by the rainwater that gets trapped between the 2x4s. I once had a 28-ft. pole snap in the middle while a helper and I were standing it up. It was dry on the outside, but rotten on the inside.

The poles should be spiked up using plenty of 10d nails, with joints staggered no closer than 4 ft. (6 ft. is better). Joints should be smoothed off, or they'll snag the pump jacks. Check the width of a new pole in several places before set-

ting it up—extra-wide 2x4s create problems. An aluminum version of the pump-jack pole is made by Alum-A-Pole Corp. (P.O. Box 66, Staten Island, N. Y. 10303). Although I have had no experience with these, they obviously offer the advantages of stability and immunity to decay.

The first step in setting up pump jacks is to attach the brackets to the building. You can do this from a ladder or while sitting on the roof, if the pitch is low enough. The bracket, a Y-shaped affair, is made of steel. A yoke at one end holds the pole, and small pieces of angle iron at the other two ends swivel for attachment to the roof or sidewall. Locate the brackets carefully, spacing them no farther than 10 ft. apart when using wooden scaffolding planks.

In general, the brackets should be attached only to sound framing lumber. When fastening to the roof, gently lift up a shingle and hunt underneath with hammer and nail until you find a rafter. If your probing brings you too close to the edge of the shingle, skip to the one below it. You can get a clue to the rafter locations by looking for nail heads in the soffit or fascia. After you find the rafter, drive a couple of 16d nails through the bracket and sheathing into the rafter itself. Bend the last inch of the nail over, or use a duplex nail, so you can remove it later.

If you have to fasten the brackets to the rake or fascia, make sure these trim boards are well nailed to the framing, and use drywall screws to attach the brackets.

Once the brackets are attached, slip the pump

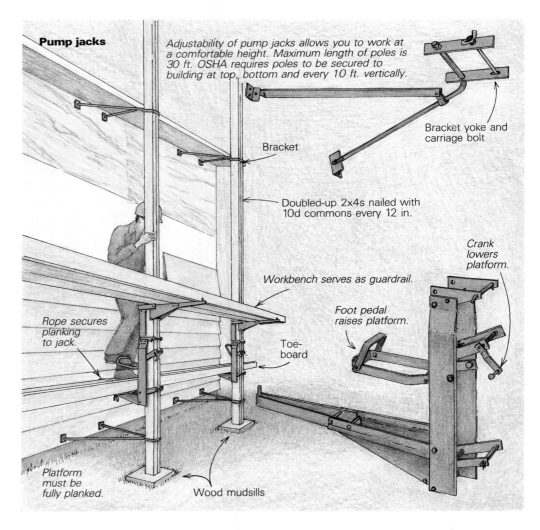

Pump jacks

Adjustability of pump jacks allows you to work at a comfortable height. Maximum length of poles is 30 ft. OSHA requires poles to be secured to building at top, bottom and every 10 ft. vertically.

Bracket

Bracket yoke and carriage bolt

Doubled-up 2x4s nailed with 10d commons every 12 in.

Crank lowers platform.

Workbench serves as guardrail.

Foot pedal raises platform.

Toe-board

Rope secures planking to jack.

Platform must be fully planked.

Wood mudsills

jacks over the ends of the poles. Disengage the bottom roller with your hand and pull the jack about 2 ft. up the pole. Now it's time to raise the poles, which you can do by walking them up from below, like a ladder. Or you can carry the top up a ladder, while someone else carries the bottom forward on the ground. A safer method is to hoist the pole up with a rope and a pulley.

Once the pole is standing up, remove the carriage bolt from the bracket yoke, slip the pole into the yoke, and replace the bolt. OSHA regulations require that you also attach the poles to the building at the bottom and every 10 ft. vertically, though many people don't bother. In any case, you should have several extra brackets.

Be sure to set each pole on a wide, stable footing to keep it from sinking into the ground. A length of 2x8 works well. The jacks can now be laid with planks and pumped up to the desired working height. When the scaffold gets up around 10 ft., it will start to sway from side to side more than is comfortable. At this point, diagonal braces should be nailed from the bottom of each pole to just below the jack on the neighboring pole, forming an X. OSHA doesn't require these braces, but I think they're a good idea. A nail where the two braces cross will further stiffen the setup. The braces can be 1x4s, but 2x4s are better if you need lengths of 16 ft. or more. On tall setups (over 20 ft. high), use at least one additional pair of braces. Thirty feet is the maximum length of poles allowed by OSHA, and that's really pushing it.

Ladder jacks—When you're working at just one height (doing cornice repair, for instance), ladder jacks are the easiest setup to use. These are heavy steel brackets that hook onto the rungs of an extension ladder (drawing, below). Some types are adaptable for use both under a ladder and above it. The distance from the hooks to the crossbars that carry the planks is adjustable to fit the angle of the ladder. I prefer to use ladder jacks above the ladder because this puts me at a more comfortable distance from the wall. Also, the ladder itself can get in the way when the jacks are hung underneath.

After attaching the hooks, you carry the scaffold planks up and lay them across the jacks. This is tough to do alone, but can be managed by first throwing a 2x4 between the jacks. The 2x4 will support one end of a plank as it is slid out from one ladder jack to the next. I use C-clamps to hold the planks firmly to the crossbars and to help to unify the rig.

To those accustomed to clinging to a ladder, this system is scary at first. In fact, it's a lot safer than working from a ladder, and is only a little harder to set up. Its chief disadvantage is a certain inflexibility of height adjustment, limited by the spacing of the ladder rungs. Also, where the sections of an extension ladder overlap, most ladder jacks cannot be used at all.

To work a long run of cornice, I sometimes set up a column of pipe scaffold in the middle, and run ladder jacks out to either side. The pipe scaffold provides a solid, roomy work island,

OSHA and residential construction

After looking at over 100 photographs and visiting several job sites, I gave up hope of finding a scaffold on a residential job that conformed to OSHA standards. For instance, the pump jacks I saw had their poles standing directly on the ground, the platforms usually consisted of one 10-in. plank, and there were no guardrails or toeboards. That's why no photos accompany this article. It's too bad OSHA regulations aren't more widely observed, but OSHA doesn't have the resources to inspect every construction site, so they concentrate on commercial jobs, where most accidents occur.

This doesn't mean that OSHA compliance officers never visit residential construction sites. Sometimes they do. And theoretically, their reports to the area office can lead to fines of up to $10,000 and to a shutdown of the job through a restraining order from a federal district judge. In reality, this almost never happens. If an OSHA compliance officer notices a violation on the site of a new home, he usually just tells the contractor to fix it. The contractor agrees to do so, and that's the end of it.

When I called OSHA's area office in Hartford, Conn., to ask about composite planks and homemade trestles, I was told that no regulations specifically prohibit them, and that compliance officers have the latitude to make judgment calls in such cases. Making judgment calls is just what carpenters do. But for the sake of expedience, they're usually willing to settle for something less than a scaffold that will support "four times the maximum intended load" that OSHA requires.

Safety on the job site is always a compromise between caution and expedience (see pp. 19-23). If it is not impossible, it would certainly be impractical to build a scaffold that was 100% safe. Even OSHA is limited by law to standards that are judged financially feasible and realistic. Unfortunately, not all contractors and carpenters agree with OSHA's definition of these terms.

As a carpenter, I never read OSHA's standards for scaffolding. As an editor preparing an article on scaffolding for publication, I had to read them. I will admit that they seem to call for extreme measures, requiring for compliance more time, effort and material than most tradespeople that I know would be willing to give. But they also make me aware that I've taken some foolish chances with scaffolding that I've built. Now that I've read OSHA's standards, I would build safer scaffolds, which is reason enough to encourage others to read them. Call the OSHA office in your state (listed in the Blue Pages under Labor Dept.) and ask for a copy of *Construction Industry Standards (#1926)*. It's free, and the information, though occasionally tough to wade through, could save your life. —*Kevin Ireton*

Ladder jacks
This type of ladder jack can be used above or below the ladder rungs. Jacks should not to be used at heights over 20 ft.

Platform width must be at least 18 in. When using wood planks, ladders must be no more than 10 ft. apart. The planks should overlap the bearing surface by 12 in.

Adjusts for different angles of ladder.

and the ladder jacks let me work the entire length of the side in one shot.

Wall brackets—The wall bracket, used primarily in rough carpentry, is a steel triangle that bolts into the frame of the house and supports scaffold planks (drawing, below). Since you have to drill a hole for the bolt, this system is unsuitable for siding installation unless you're able to work from the top down. As a result, wall brackets are used mostly to install sheathing. The advantages of wall brackets are speed of installation and their complete independence from grade conditions, which can be pretty miserable around a new house.

Wall brackets can be used safely, but you have to be careful about where you bolt them. I know of two carpenters who have "gone down" on these. In both cases the scaffold failed because it was bolted into a single bad stud that either broke or tore out. The lateral strain exerted by wall brackets is considerable. Wherever possible, bolt into double studs, double plates, or rim joists. If single studs are the only choice, the bolt should pass through a short piece of clear 2x4 horizontally spanning at least two good studs, as shown in the drawing.

I've seen wall brackets that use nails instead of bolts. Although these probably work okay, they make me nervous and I avoid them. The possibility that my own weight will pry the nails out seems too real.

Roof brackets—A cousin of the wall bracket is the roof bracket, an adjustable triangle with a tongue that's nailed under a roof shingle (drawing, bottom left). The roof bracket is much more secure than the wall bracket because the roof carries most of the weight. Also, the nails that hold them are subjected mostly to shear forces, as opposed to the withdrawal forces exerted on the nails or bolts of wall brackets. Still, you should be careful to nail only into rafters, and don't skimp on the nails either. Use three 10d or 16d commons. When lifting asphalt shingles, a putty knife will help to separate the ones that have become cemented down. After removing the brackets, be sure to drive the nail heads down, or they may work their way up through the shingle. If the shingle tears, apply a dab of roof cement under the damaged area.

There is no convenient way to install guardrails on a roof-bracket scaffold. On roofs with a pitch steeper than 4-in-12 or where the eaves are over 16 ft. from the ground, OSHA requires the installation of a "catch platform" below the working area or else the use of a safety belt and lifeline. A catch platform amounts to a complete scaffolding setup, including guardrails, midrails and toeboards, located just below and extending 2 ft. beyond the eaves.

Site-built scaffolding—The high price of lumber and the availability of manufactured scaffold systems has reduced the use of site-built wood scaffolding. In a pinch, however, the carpenter may have to put something together from materials already on the job. The guiding principles of wood-scaffold construction are to use plenty of nails (duplex nails come in handy here), and to triangulate everything for rigidity.

More common than complete wood scaffolds are localized rigs built on the spot to solve a particular problem. On Victorian houses especially, the overhangs create a nightmare for the sidewall mechanic. In such places, manufactured scaffolding often doesn't work, and you have to build your own.

A trick some carpenters use at window or door openings is a simple cantilevered beam. They nail a 2x4 across the rough opening to serve as a fulcrum, and then stick a long 2x10 or similar heavy beam on edge out the window. With one end well nailed to a partition inside the house, the other end becomes a scaffold support. As much length as possible is extended inside the house to counter the weight of the scaffold load. This type of scaffold is sometimes used where many windows are arranged together at a given height, such as the south wall of solar houses.

Improvisation—I have used suspension cables, window hooks, and a host of other devices to support a platform. A nearby tree has come in handy on occasion, as has the roof of my van. Imagination is important, but creativity must always be tempered with common sense. The final consideration, of course, must be safety. You owe this not only to yourself and your loved ones, but also to the other tradespeople who place their trust in your scaffold. Their lives depend on you. □

Wall brackets

Wherever possible bolt into double studs, double plates, or rim joists. Brackets must be fully planked.

OSHA requires guardrails, midrails, and toeboards at all open sides of platforms above 10 ft.

Bolt and nut secure wall bracket.

Rope secures planks to bracket.

Blocks distribute load.

When you must locate a bracket between studs, use a short piece of 2x4 to span adjoining studs.

Roof brackets

On roofs steeper than 4-in-12 or where the eaves are over 16 ft. from the ground, OSHA requires a catch platform or the use of a safety belt and lifeline.

Use three 10d or 16d common nails. Nail only into rafter.

Bracket adjusts for different roof pitches.

Nails in fascia indicate location of rafter.

On-Site Carpentry with a Circular Saw

Cutting in place saves time and trouble

by Jud Peake

The portable electric circular saw isn't just a labor-saving device. It's a tool that can do things which would be impossible with a handsaw. The circular saw is hazardous, and its electric cord tethers you to an outlet, so you've got to organize your work differently than you would if you were using a handsaw. But if you can develop the right habits, tricks and sequences for moving materials, nailing and cutting, you can work safely and also save time and energy.

I think worm-drive saws are best. They are better balanced, harder to stall and, most important, the blade is on the left, so a right-handed person can see the cut in progress. If I were left-handed, I would investigate sidewinder models with the blade on the other side.

Whenever wood binds on the blade, a circular saw will kick back toward the operator. Always support the workpiece in such a way that one part will fall away after the cut. Cut framing lumber near the floor, supported on your foot, as shown below, not on a sawhorse. A right-hander

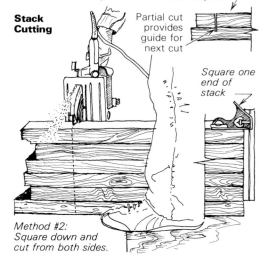

Supporting Lumber During a Cut

Right-handers brace wood with left hand, with wood supported on right foot.

should hold the wood with the left hand, supporting the end closest to the cut on the right foot, with the right hand a little to the right of the body. Make sure at least part of the foot of the saw is always resting on the work.

Cutting in place—If you set out to build a house you must realize you're going to have to move its entire weight from wherever the material is

dropped to the site. This consideration should dictate how the carpenter organizes his or her work. One of the first things you realize is that the circular saw is best used for cutting in place. In addition to reducing physical labor, cutting in place can reduce the necessity for measuring and marking on site and at the lumber pile.

Before you move anything, consider the stack of lumber as a convenient place to cut many pieces to the same length—say, 30 studs for a low wall. First square up one end of the stack by beating on the ends with a hammer and check-

Method #1: Cut top stud at full blade depth.

Stack Cutting

Partial cut provides guide for next cut

Square one end of stack

Method #2: Square down and cut from both sides.

ing with a square, then cut across the top or along the side at the uneven end (method #1, left). If you cut across the top of the stack, the depth of the blade will exceed the thickness of the wood enough to score a guide for cutting the next layer. Be sure your cut is square.

Another way (method #2, left) is to square down the side of the stack across the edges of the lumber. You must be able to get at both edges to complete the cut. This method means you'll have to move more material, but it is usually more accurate and faster in the long run.

Joists are usually lapped, but if they do require cutting (to fit between hangers, for example), lay them between the beams with one end resting on top of the hanger, as in the drawing below. Eyeball a cut along the top of the overlapped beam, allowing the blade to graze the corner of the beam. If the tool is new to you, set the blade depth $\frac{1}{8}$ in. deeper than the joist is thick. With a little practice, you'll be able to rest the toe of the

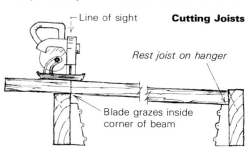

Line of sight **Cutting Joists**

Rest joist on hanger

Blade grazes inside corner of beam

COMMON BUILDING TERMS

Blocking—Short pieces cut to fit between framing members. Blocking is used structurally to prevent framing members from twisting, or to provide nailing surfaces for wall panels. Blocking is also used as a draft stop to keep fire from spreading within a building's concealed spaces.

Cripples—Framing members that support the ends of a header, also called trimmers.

Double plate—The plate at the top of a stud wall, doubled to allow overlapping plates at intersecting walls.

Eyeball—To gauge a cut by sighting, unaided by a line, string or square.

Hangover—The portion of the material that will be cut off in place later.

Kerf—The material lost to sawdust. You can't cut a piece 80½ in. long into two pieces 40¼ in. because you'll lose about ⅛ in. in the saw kerf.

Sidewinder—A saw in which the shaft of the motor is parallel to the spindle of the blade.

Skip-sheathing—1x material laid with large spaces between courses to allow the shingles or shakes they support to breathe.

Snap a line—To lay out a cut by making a line with a chalk box.

Staggers—Intersections of structural plywood sheathing should form a T, not a cross. In other words, three pieces of plywood—not four—comprise a correct intersection. This practice is called staggering the joints and requires some portion of a full sheet (usually half) to begin alternating courses of sheathing. These partial pieces are called staggers.

Tack—To nail only enough to hold in place. Used when the material might be removed, or nailed off later.

Tear-out—The splintering of wood fibers caused by a blade as it leaves the cut. Backing the workpiece with a scrap board will prevent tear-out.

Titch—A small cut or notch made as a guide for the main cut.

From *Fine Homebuilding* magazine (June 1981) 3:33-35

saw on the work and adjust the depth of your cut by pivoting the saw.

The subfloor provides another excellent opportunity to use the technique of cutting in place. Tack the plywood in position for half the area to be covered, allowing the ends to run wild over the perimeter of the building. Snap lines around the perimeter and cut. Use the large scraps as staggers for the second half, snap the rest of the perimeters and cut. If you are going to have a lot of hangovers 4 ft. long or more, it is a good idea to pre-cut them first on the plywood stack before spreading.

When you are framing walls, you should cut various cripples, jacks, blocking and double plates in place. Spread your pre-cut studs and plates and nail them together. Now spread your double plates across the studs near the top of the walls and position cripples with one end resting on the floor tight against the header; the long end extends over and beyond the bottom plate. Also spread lengths of material for head jacks, sill jacks, and atypical blocking. Cut all these components to length at one time. Don't interrupt the process to nail, measure or possibly snag the saw's cord on uncut material.

Cut double plates by eyeballing a square cut in line with the appropriate channel mark on the top plate. For cripples, eyeball along the top of the bottom plate, as in the drawing below. The

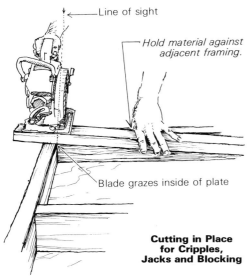

— Line of sight

— Hold material against adjacent framing.

Blade grazes inside of plate

Cutting in Place for Cripples, Jacks and Blocking

tight cut you need here will cause the blade to scratch the top flat side of the bottom plate and can cause the saw to kick, if you don't hold the cripple firmly enough. Keep your knee behind your elbow and your foot out of the line of the cut. Cut jacks and blocks in the same manner. If the material can't be well braced during a cut, make a slight titch, or nick, with the sawblade, as a reference point, then cut nearby with adequate support.

Pocket cuts—This trick has a wide range of applications. Start with only the toe of the saw's foot on the wood. Instead of pushing the saw along the line of cut, hinge the saw on its toe, hold the blade guard back with one hand (drawing, top of next column) while slowly lowering the blade into the work. This method allows cuts directly into the middle of the work, without access cuts from the side. It can be used to cut holes

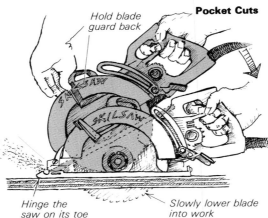

Hold blade guard back

Pocket Cuts

Hinge the saw on its toe

Slowly lower blade into work

in subfloors for toilet flanges, for example.

The diagonal let-in brace installation provides a test for both cutting in place and pocket cutting. Lay the 1x brace (a brace 1 in. by some other dimension) in position diagonally across the wall, carefully avoiding nails in its path. Cut off the bottom of the 1x at the angle formed by the bottom plate, as in the drawing below. The

Letting in a Brace

Hold diagonal brace with your foot. Make ¾-in. deep pocket cuts using edge as guide.

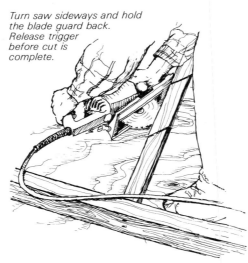

Turn saw sideways and hold the blade guard back. Release trigger before cut is complete.

brace needn't be tacked; hold it in place with your foot as you work. While resting the foot of the saw on the 1x and guiding the blade along its edge, lower the saw blade into the studs and plates the ¾ in. necessary to let in the brace. Next, kick the 1x out of the way, and turn the

saw sideways, so the plane of the blade is parallel to the plane of the floor. Hold the trigger handle with one hand and, with the other, grasp the blade guard flange and the top handle. Now lower the blade into the wood and keep your feet out of the way. Because you're holding the guard back, it's important to let off the trigger just before the end of the cut; the inertia of the blade will finish the cut and the blade will be dead by the time you're ready to take it out.

You can also use the pocket cut in conjunction with an improvised guide for trimming corners on existing shingled walls. Tack a length of scrap 1x over the shingles to coincide with the trim. Set the saw depth so the blade doesn't quite reach the tarpaper below the shingles and run the saw along the 1x guide. Break the shingles off the rest of the way and apply the trim. If the tarpaper should accidentally be cut, cover the slice with asphalt-base hydroseal before trimming. This method is an inexpensive alternative to weaving the shingles at both the inside and outside corners.

Cutting two at once—If you can cut single pieces in place, why not cut two? To cut skip-sheathing, lap both pieces over the rafter, making sure that each piece reaches center. Don't tack the material in your line of cut. After all the pieces are tacked in place, cut all the laps in one pass each, as shown. Plywood sheathing can be

Cutting Two at Once   Finished cut

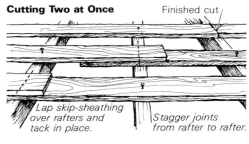

Lap skip-sheathing over rafters and tack in place.

Stagger joints from rafter to rafter.

cut in the same way, but instead of eyeballing, you will have to snap a line.

You can cut two boards at once to bisect any angle. For rough work, such as the intersection of plates, lap one piece over the other and eyeball a titch on the outside corner. Cut through both pieces, heading for the titch from the inside corner. The kerf left in the bottom piece will indicate the angle for completing the intersection. This trick is useful when the walls don't meet at 90° angles (drawing below). For more careful

Intersecting Plates

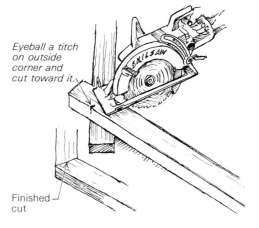

Eyeball a titch on outside corner and cut toward it.

Finished cut

work, you can square up on both of these corners and draw a connecting line. In this case, you will need to move the material together after the cut to make up for the saw kerf.

If, for some reason, you are unable to move the material ends together, you can always find a bevel at which to set the saw to hide the kerf. As you can see in the drawing, it is impractical to

Hiding the Kerf

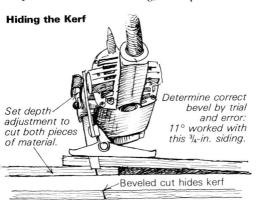

Set depth adjustment to cut both pieces of material.

Determine correct bevel by trial and error: 11° worked with this ¾-in. siding.

Beveled cut hides kerf

try to predict the exact angle. Trial and error works best. The beveled lap cut can sometimes be used when doing exterior trim or siding. Start from the bottom and cut laps in place as you go. Don't wait until it's all up to cut.

Cutting a bevel in thicker material can be difficult. The 45° bevel is easy to visualize; it bisects a right angle. But with a circular saw it can be hard to execute. Let's take an example from rough work. You've cantilevered some joists for a bay window that require 45° cuts, and snapped your lines. Square down the face of the joist, set the bevel on your saw, and cut. You find out soon you can't cut one side of the bay window from above; you usually can't reach it from below, either. Instead, square down from the long point and make a square cut, as in the drawing below;

Cutting a Bevel in Thick Material

1st cut

Snap line for finished bevel.

2nd cut

Square down at long point.

Continue blade down square edge.

then cut into the top edge of the joist along the snap-line mark until the blade has reached its full depth. Continue the cut by leading the front of the blade down the square end edge of the joist. I have found this method to be consistently more accurate than relying on the saw's beveling capabilities.

Trim work—It can be hard to use the circular saw here, but often it's the only power saw on hand. In this case, the best place to cut is on sawhorses. Cut from the backside of the material, so the tear-out is hidden. For outside miters you just have to cut carefully. Tilt the square up toward the saw, so that, instead of running over it, the saw runs against the edge of the square, which acts as a guide. If the material is wide and tends to get forced onto the untoothed portion of the blade where it binds, make relief cuts on the waste side. Don't try to make a pocket cut on a beveled miter.

For inside corners on trim of rectangular cross section, I think the butt joint is best. It's easiest, and, if the material cups or shrinks, it's much more difficult to see any gap in the joint. If a miter joint is used, any gap will be obvious to people as they walk by.

Sometimes you can get stuck cutting molded material for interior trim without a miter box; either you don't have one on hand or your material won't fit in the one you do have. You can make perfectly acceptable inside corners by first making a 45° bevel with a circular saw and then back-cutting the joint with a coping saw. A back-cut joint is cut at slightly less than 90° to allow the trim's visible edge complete contact with the adjacent trim. This is useful when joining trim with complex contours (drawing below). To in-

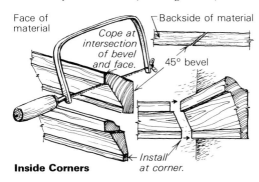

Face of material

Cope at intersection of bevel and face.

Backside of material

45° bevel

Install at corner.

Inside Corners

stall picture molding, for example, butt the material between the walls on one end of the room. Measure and cut the material for the adjoining side just as if you were going to miter the inside corner. Make this cut from the backside of the material with a circular saw and follow the line formed by the intersection of the face of the material and the end-grain bevel made by your circular saw cut with a coping saw. Make the piece ¹⁄₁₆ in. long, and the back-cut trim will dig into the adjoining piece and hide any errors.

Dimensions and notching—If you want to crosscut or rip something at 1½ in. or 3½ in., you don't have to measure and mark. The circular saw has these dimensions built in. From one side of the foot to the far side of the blade is about 3½ in.; from the other side of the foot to the near side of the blade is about 1½ in. Eyeball the ap-

propriate side of the foot along the edge of the material to get your cut. If you have some odd-sized rip to make that is not greater than 3½ in., and a rip fence isn't handy, make a mark on the toe of the foot at the correct distance from the blade and lead this mark down the edge of the material to be cut.

Notches around posts for exterior decking can be accomplished quickly by cutting from the backside. Start a saw cut into a scrap of the same material and stop just as the blade touches the lower corner, as in the drawing. Make a pencil

Notching Posts

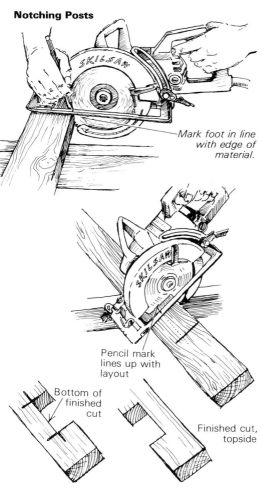

Mark foot in line with edge of material.

Pencil mark lines up with layout

Bottom of finished cut

Finished cut, topside

mark on the foot of the saw in line with the square edge of the wood (this mark won't be accurate if you change the depth adjustment of the saw or work with varying thicknesses of material). Lay out the notch on the backside of the work and cut past the intersecting lines until the pencil mark lines up with the layout; this hides tear-out and saves handsawing.

If you use the circular saw enough, someday it's going to kick back on you when you really don't expect it. That's why it's important to make your safety precautions habitual. Support the wood well, stand to the side of the line of cut, release the trigger before the end of the cut, and back up your elbow with your knee when possible. Eyeball your cuts square—the more you do it the better you'll get. Cut in place whenever practical and work your material—moving and nailing into a pattern with your cutting to save unnecessary movement. Don't use your tape measure unless you have to. □

Jud Peake is a contractor in Oakland, Calif..

Sawhorse

A traditional approach to the simple trestle

by Tom Law

When I was an apprentice, the old-timers I worked with referred to sawhorses as trestles or trestle benches, and many a new man on the job had his skill tested, and longevity determined, by the task of sawhorse making. I was given that test a time or two and had the results closely scrutinized by some good, but notoriously grumpy, old carpenters.

Spanned by a pair of sturdy planks, trestle benches can be used as work platforms (scaffolding), and as work tables when topped off with a plywood panel. The top members, sometimes called cross beams, and the legs can be made of thick stock when they're required to support heavy loads. When used for scaffolding, tops are usually made of on-edge 2x6s or 4x4s. If extra stability is needed, tops can be made of 2x8s flatwise, with 2x4 or 1x8 legs.

In most situations, lightness and portability are virtues, and I continue to make sawhorses the way I learned from my first textbook. These sawhorses, like the one in the drawing at right, are strong and fairly easy to move around. Detailed instructions for making them are not included in most new textbooks, but they used to be, and the old *Audels* even explained how to figure the length of the leg using trigonometry.

A sawhorse should be knee high, which is typically about 2 ft. In the old days, when most lumber was cut with a handsaw and the stock was held down with one knee, this was a good height to deliver the thrust from the saw. Some horses had a long slot in the top that was used for ripping. The material to be cut was fully supported by the top, and the saw would pass through the slot. These days most lumber is cut with circular saws, but 2 ft. continues to be a convenient height.

Sometimes I make horses with longer legs to use as scaffolding to reach high ceilings, and later cut the legs to normal height. Sometimes I cut the legs even shorter so the top is only about 12 in. high. A plank laid across low sawhorses will put me at the right height for working close to the ceiling for installing crown moldings or door and window trim.

It's also helpful to have a shelf in at least one horse. I use a length of 1x12 for the shelf and wedge it evenly between the legs. Then I add 1x2 strips along the sides (to keep tools from rolling off the shelf). The strips are screwed to the legs and to the edges of the shelf. Aside

Consulting Editor Tom Law is restoring an old house in Frizzelburg, Md.

from holding tools and materials, the shelf strengthens the horse by preventing the legs from spreading laterally. The only problem with a shelf is that it makes the horses harder to stack. I put the ones with shelves on the bottom and stack the others on top.

To make a stable work platform, the legs of a sawhorse must splay in two directions. To lay out these splay angles, I keep in mind two sets of figures for the framing square: 4 in 24 and

5¼ in 24. Setting the leg 4 in. from the end of the top and having it angle out so its bottom end is plumb with the end of the top is the basis for the 4-in-24 figure. It makes the horse very stable, and even the full weight of a worker standing right on the end of the cross beam won't cause the horse to tip over. The angle of splay across the width of the horse is 5¼ in 24.

I begin making a horse by preparing the cross beam. First I select a straight, clear piece of 2x4

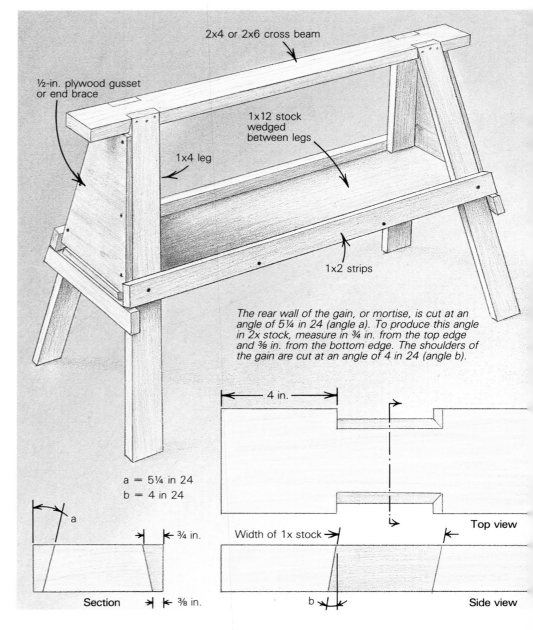

2x4 or 2x6 cross beam

½-in. plywood gusset or end brace

1x12 stock wedged between legs

1x4 leg

1x2 strips

The rear wall of the gain, or mortise, is cut at an angle of 5¼ in 24 (angle a). To produce this angle in 2x stock, measure in ¾ in. from the top edge and ⅜ in. from the bottom edge. The shoulders of the gain are cut at an angle of 4 in 24 (angle b).

a = 5¼ in 24
b = 4 in 24

4 in.

Top view

¾ in.

Width of 1x stock

a

Section   ⅜ in.

b   Side view

or 2x6 and cut it to a length of 42 in. The legs of a well-made trestle have to be let into the cross beam, so the next thing I do is lay out the four mortises, or gains, that will receive the tops of the legs. Because the legs splay in two directions, the shoulders of the gain slope in one direction and the rear wall of the gain in another (bottom drawing, facing page).

To locate the outer shoulder of the gain, I measure 4 in. in from the end and square a line across the top. Then I lay the framing square across the edge of the beam, hold the figures 4 on the tongue and 24 on the body (making sure the figures are on the same edge of the square) and mark the angle. All the succeeding angles could be laid out in this way, or once the first angles are marked, the rest of them can be reproduced with a sliding T-bevel (drawing below, top right). I use a piece of the leg stock to mark the width of the gain.

The depth of the gain is ¾ in. on the top surface and ⅜ in. on the beam's bottom. I use a combination square in depth-gauge mode to lay out these lines (drawing below, top left). After the layout is done, I make a series of sawcuts

spaced about ⅜ in. apart to the depth of gain (drawing, bottom left), then chip them out and clean up the gain with a chisel.

The cuts on the tops and bottoms of the legs are parallel and form a compound angle, 4 and 24 on the flat and 5¼ and 24 on the edge. Cutting this angle is a good exercise in the precise use of a handsaw, but the angle can be cut with any power saw with its shoe set to the proper bevel angle. Since the leg is angled, it has to be longer than 24 in. to make the top 24 in. high. If you work out the length mathematically, you'll find that it comes to about 24⅝ in. But when I'm making the legs I don't spend much time with math—I just cut them 26 in. long. The extra height suits my frame.

Next I secure the legs in their gains. The fit should be snug, but not so tight that you have to pound them in. I squirt glue on the rear wall of the gain, tap in the top of the leg and fasten it with three 8d nails (drawing, bottom right).

Before the glue has time to dry, I attach trapezoidal gussets, or end braces, made from scraps of ½-in. plywood. Their non-parallel sides are laid out and cut at the angle of 5¼ in 24. When

the braces are applied (I like to use glue and drywall screws here), the legs should be made to conform to their angle, since they may be out of line due to a miscut mortise. When the legs are attached and braced, the sawhorse should stand on a flat floor without wobbling.

As an aside, let me say that it's never a good idea to use drywall screws in load-bearing situations. Used in conjunction with glue in non-load-bearing applications, as in the gussets here, they will do just fine. But unlike nails, which are made of ductile steel, drywall screws are made of brittle, hardened steel, and they can snap off when loaded. Whenever you're building scaffolding or making structural connections in a frame, avoid the temptation to use drywall screws.

A sawhorse is a fairly simple tool, but one that eases the burden of building. It can be made in about an hour's time, and will last for years if given reasonable care. I sometimes cover the top of mine with a piece of scrap plywood to take the numerous sawcuts. If you do that you should glue the plywood on, not nail it. The probability of a new sawblade finding a nail is surprisingly high.   □

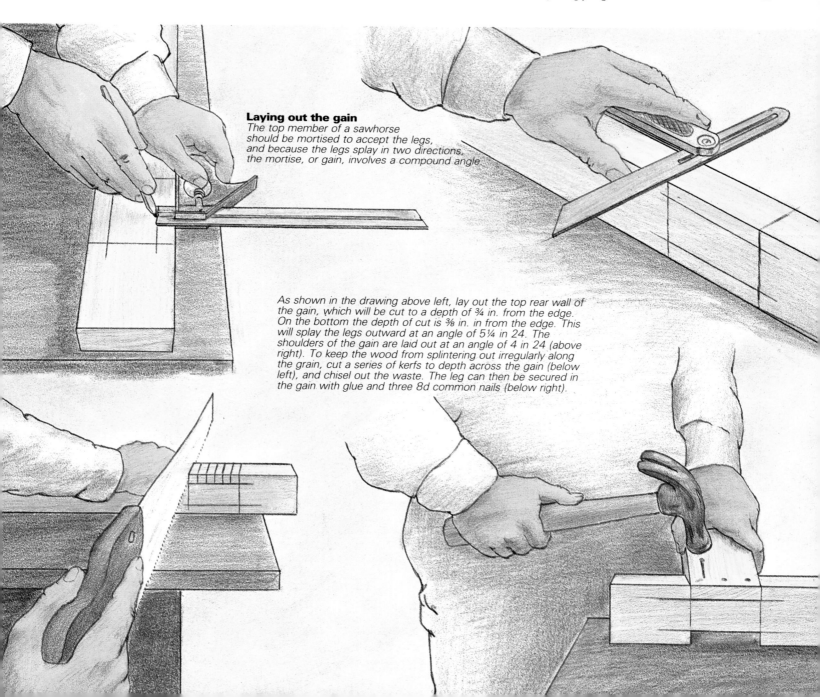

Laying out the gain
The top member of a sawhorse should be mortised to accept the legs, and because the legs splay in two directions, the mortise, or gain, involves a compound angle.

As shown in the drawing above left, lay out the top rear wall of the gain, which will be cut to a depth of ¾ in. from the edge. On the bottom the depth of cut is ⅜ in. in from the edge. This will splay the legs outward at an angle of 5¼ in 24. The shoulders of the gain are laid out at an angle of 4 in 24 (above right). To keep the wood from splintering out irregularly along the grain, cut a series of kerfs to depth across the gain (below left), and chisel out the waste. The leg can then be secured in the gain with glue and three 8d common nails (below right).

Handsaws

Care and use of a tool that gets little attention these days

by Tom Law

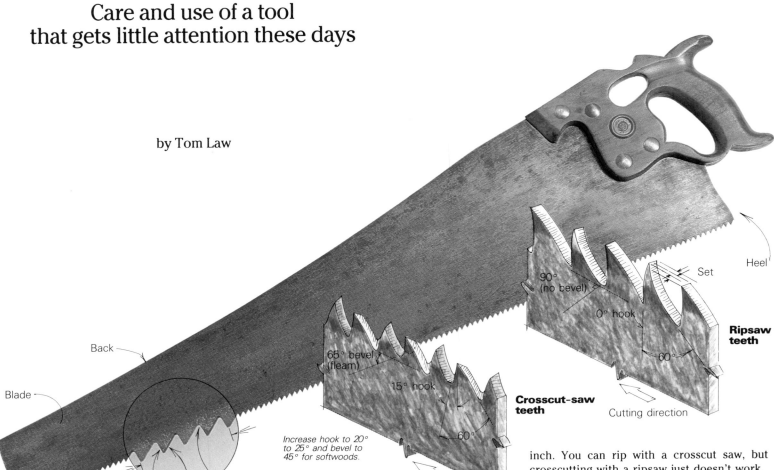

Back — **Blade** — **Toe** — 1 in. 5 points, 4 teeth — **Gullet** — **Back of tooth** — **Face of tooth**

65° bevel (fleam) — 15° hook — 60°
Increase hook to 20° to 25° and bevel to 45° for softwoods.
Cutting direction

90° (no bevel) — 0° hook — 60° — **Set** — **Heel** — **Ripsaw teeth**
Crosscut-saw teeth — Cutting direction

I have a special affection for handsaws. I was taught by carpenters who used handsaws almost exclusively. My first framing job as an apprentice was a highway bridge in a remote location with no electricity; all the cutting was done with handsaws. I learned to keep mine sharp, and ended up filing saws for the entire crew. In later years, I sharpened the saws for crews of more than 25 carpenters on large commercial projects.

Even though most of the cutting I do these days on the houses I build and remodel is with power saws, I still use my handsaws. It's surprising how often their slender profile, depth of cut, and lack of power cord make them handy. And the finest scribe-fitting I do almost always calls for a handsaw.

But because of the dominance of power saws today, few in the generation after me have learned handsaw skills. With incorrect technique and an inferior saw that is dull or badly sharpened, handsawing can be pure drudgery. But it doesn't need to be. The difference is in knowing how to pick out a good saw, how to joint, shape, set and sharpen the teeth, and how to use it once it's sharp.

Basics—Most handsaws are about 26 in. long. Shorter ones (24 in., 22 in. or less) are called bench saws or panel saws. The top edge of the saw, called the back, can be straight or skewed. Skew-backs taper from handle to toe in a gentle S-curve; they were favored in the first part of the century. Skewbacks are better at cutting a curved line, but I still prefer square-back saws. They make good medium-length straightedges, and you can even scratch a square line across the blade and use it as a framing or combination square. The front end of the saw is the toe; the rear, down below the handle, is the heel.

One of the first things to learn is the difference between a crosscut saw and a ripsaw. Crosscut saws are made to cut across the grain, and their teeth act like a row of knife points, severing the fibers as they cut. Crosscut saws come with 7, 8, 9, 10, 11 or 12 points per inch. The more points, the finer the cut. A 7-point, for example, is used for wet rough framing; an 11 or 12-point for fine trim work.

Ripsaws, like the Disston D-8 skew-back shown above, are made to cut along the grain. Their teeth act like a row of chisels and remove small chunks of wood as they go through the cut. Ripsaws have larger teeth and deeper gullets than crosscut saws, and 4½, 5, 5½ (the most common) or 6 points per inch. You can rip with a crosscut saw, but crosscutting with a ripsaw just doesn't work.

Points per inch and number of teeth per inch are not the same. As shown in the small drawing above left, a 5-point saw has 4 teeth per inch, a 10-point has 9 teeth, and so on.

Viewed from the side, each tooth on a handsaw forms a 60° angle. But how these cutters are tilted forward and aft (called pitch, or *hook*) is different for the two saw types. Still viewing the saw in profile, imagine a line that connects all the gullets. A line drawn down the face of the sawblade perpendicular to this represents zero hook. It is this lack of pitch that gives the teeth of a ripsaw their chisel-like quality. The tops of crosscut teeth, however, are pitched back from this perpendicular line (about 15° for cutting hardwoods).

Another angle to consider is the one across the tooth face. This *bevel,* or *fleam,* is determined by whether the file used in sharpening is held perpendicular to the sawblade or askew. Viewed from above, ripsaw teeth are filed at a right angle to the sawblade. Crosscut teeth are alternately beveled 65° to the face of the blade, producing a knife-like point on the leading edge of the tooth.

For crosscutting softwoods, the hook should be increased to 20° to 25°, and the bevel should be closer to 45°. This way the saw will cut the wood rather than tear it, which would cause the blade to bind in the kerf against the torn fibers.

One thing ripsaws and crosscut saws have in common is *set*—the alternate bending of

From *Fine Homebuilding* magazine (April 1984) 20:68-72

You can learn a lot about a saw by making it sing. The tone and its duration are good indicators of the quality of the steel and its thickness. To produce a note, the author has thumped the blade near the handle with his thumb to set the metal vibrating, and is varying the sound by increasing or decreasing the curve of the blade with finger pressure on the toe of the saw.

the top half of the teeth. Each tooth is bent either to the right or left of the body of the sawblade. Setting the teeth makes the cut, or kerf, wider than the blade thickness and reduces the friction of metal against wood. Good blades are also taper-ground; that is, the blade is thinner in section at the back than at the teeth. Taper-grinding improves the balance of the saw by lowering the blade's center of gravity, and works in the same way as set to reduce friction in the kerf to all but the teeth themselves. The thickest part of the blade goes into the new wood along the kerf, while the trailing metal is thinner.

A little history—Today I carry two saws—an 8-point crosscut for general work, and a 10-point crosscut for trim. The old-timers carried five or six saws in their own box. This "nest of saws" might include a 5½-point rip, a 7-point crosscut or an 8-point with wide set for wet lumber, an 8-point for general work, a 9-point for outside trim and a 10-point or 11-point for fine trim, and maybe an over-the-hill favorite for tight places or when there was danger of dulling against nails or masonry.

Turn-of-the-century saws were wider than saws made today; the extra metal added weight to help make the cut. Moderate-width blades called *lightweights* were also made. Saws of this period were generally good, but the quality of the steel was sometimes inconsistent. A single blade could have some very soft teeth, while others were so hard they would ruin a file. Too, the metal could be so brittle that the teeth would snap off when being set. The best use for one of these is to hang it proudly on the wall as old grandpa's.

One of the best blades I've seen (and owned) is a Disston D-15, with a "V" and "Proclaim Victory throughout the World" printed on the side; this type was made at least as early as 1921. Disston also made excellent saws into the 1950s. One of the best of these was the D-95, with its incongruous plastic handle. Atkins also produced excellent saws during this period.

While domestic manufacturers were going downhill in the 1960s, Sandvik of Sweden was producing strange-looking but marvelous saws. They came with plywood handles embossed with sea serpents. The best grade had a plastic handle—this at a time when quality was symbolized by walnut. The line of teeth was also peculiar; it was convex. The natural arc that is produced by the motion of sawing is the reason for the convex curve. When the saw is progressing toward the middle of the cut, the blade curves down to meet the increasing pressure most effectively.

The quality of American-made handsaws deteriorated rapidly during the 1960s and 1970s, as manufacturers responded to the market with lower quality and higher prices. Today's saws, wrapped in plastic and covered with promotional claims, are sad remembrances of what saws were 30 years ago.

Finding a good saw—My advice is not to get a new saw—buy an old one and fix it. Literally hundreds of saws have passed through my hands, and I can get a good idea of their quality just by filing a few teeth. The expression "They don't make them like they used to" is certainly true, but just because a saw is old doesn't necessarily mean it's good. If you have an old saw that is deeply pitted by rust or has sharp kinks in it, get rid of it. Although I've heard that slapping a saw on the surface of a body of water will straighten out a bend, you can't prove it by me. A kinked blade is damaged goods, and serious pitting means you're getting less steel than the original sawmaker thought you should have. But if a saw is only rusty, give it a few tests.

Take it by the handle and shake it back and forth; the front half should whip. If it moves very little, the metal is too thick and heavy, and the saw will be clumsy to use. If it moves so much that it's flimsy, it is cheap and too thin, and will be hard to control in the cut. If it moves just right, try this—pass your fingers through the hole in the handle and hold it by the cheeks; hold the toe end with your other hand, and bend the blade into an S-curve toe up, heel down (photo above). While starting the bend, thump the blade near the center of the handle with your thumb and it will emit a musical tone. The pitch and duration of the sound are indicators of the quality of the metal and balance of the blade. A dull sound of short duration indicates an unworthy blade; a high pitch of long duration indicates good quality and balance. There are some exceptions to this test. Some excellent old blades that are quite wide sound rather gutteral.

I've heard old-timers say that a good spring-steel blade should snap back straight after the toe has been passed through the hole in the handle. I think this goes a little far in inviting a brittle blade to snap, or even good steel to retain a bend, but you do want to flex the saw to check the quality of its steel.

If you've found an old blade, don't worry about the teeth—they can be recut. Clean off the rust by any method from sandblasting to hand sanding, and polish the blade bright with fine abrasive paper. Then make a new handle. Today's handles are just chunks of wood with scratches on the side, screwed onto the blade. Those scratches are barely recognizable as heads of wheat, an ancient symbol that proclaims the virtues of labor. Old handles were made to fit the hand and were scooped and curved in styles from graceful to grotesque. It may take a day or longer to make a nice handle, but that won't be much time if your grandchildren inherit the saw.

If the line of the teeth on your old blade is crooked or concave from toe to heel, it's because it has been improperly filed. Some old carpenters touched up their saws before they left the job each day, and filed only the dulled teeth. That practice has drawbacks. A sawblade doesn't get equal wear along its length as it moves through the cut. It's the center portion that gets the most work and wears the fastest, but it's a mistake to file only the teeth that are dull. This condition will disrupt the rhythm of each tooth contacting the wood when sawing and will give you a ragged cut.

Getting the teeth in shape—A saw with broken or very uneven teeth may have to be retoothed. This is best done by a saw shop,

Sharpening a handsaw

Jointing. A flat mill bastard file is used to joint (level and align) the tops of the teeth, left. This creates a line of saw points of equal height (or slightly convex on some saws) so that each one will be brought to bear on the wood when sawing. Here a simple L sawn from a pine block is used to hold the file perpendicular to the face of the sawblade. Manufactured metal jointers that clamp over the file and act as a guide on the blade give the same results. Even when the height of the saw teeth doesn't need correcting, the flattened tops of the teeth that result from a light jointing are a useful guide when shaping and sharpening the teeth.

Setting. A saw-set is used to bend the top half of the teeth alternately to the left and right. As shown above, the plunger pushes on the saw tooth, forcing it against the anvil each time the pistol grip of the handle is squeezed. All saw-sets are adjustable for width of set. A handsaw used mostly on wet lumber should get a wider set than one used mostly on dry wood to reduce friction on the blade and to evacuate the moist sawdust more easily.

Shaping and sharpening. Using a triangular taper file held at a 65° angle to the face of the blade, the author sharpens a crosscut saw (right). On a ripsaw, the angle is 90°—perpendicular to the sawblade. In both cases, the file cuts only on the push stroke. Unless the saw has been abused or sharpened badly, shaping the teeth can usually be a part of the sharpening process. Every other tooth is sharpened on the first run down the blade, and then the saw is turned around in the vise to get the remaining teeth. You'll have done the job well if the gullets are equally deep, and if none of the saw points reflects light. If any of them do, they either haven't been filed yet (below), or they need another stroke or two.

whose machines will punch or grind out a new line of teeth in minutes—something that would take hours by hand. But when it comes to sharpening the teeth of a saw that hasn't been badly abused, I like to do it myself.

Sharpening a saw involves four operations—*jointing,* which makes the teeth the same height; *shaping,* which evens out the size of the teeth and the depth of the gullets; *setting,* which bends the teeth alternately to either side of the blade; and *sharpening,* which gives each tooth its precise point. When saws are maintained in good condition, not all of these operations have to be performed each time. That's one of the problems with sending your saws out to be sharpened. Often, all you'll need is a light touchup with a file, but most saw shops have just one price—$3 to $7 for the full gamut of operations. And they'll end up keeping your saw for a week.

Also, sharpening machines that use a file will produce the same big-teeth little-teeth pattern as hand filing (sidebar, above right). Corrective filing for this condition is a matter of judgment, not what a machine is good at. Even a saw fresh out of its wrapper needs some hand work. It will have the right angles on the teeth, but they probably will not be very sharp. I don't like machine setting either, because it tends to push the whole tooth out rather than bending just the top half.

Learning to hand-file a saw takes some practice because the result has to be near perfect. But don't hesitate to try it. You can always correct your errors. After all, each time you file a saw, you are making new teeth.

Hand-filing a saw that is just slightly dull takes me about 15 minutes. No jointing, shaping or setting is required, just two or three lightly controlled strokes on each tooth. Lightly jointing, resetting and sharpening a saw take me about half an hour; reconditioning a misshapen saw takes me about two hours. But I've had a chance to practice some. When I was filing for a crew, I would average three saws an hour, or 24 a day. A 26-in., 8-point saw has 184 teeth; 24 saws a day is 4,992 teeth.

Before you begin filing, the first thing you need is good light; your eyes will be in close concentration for a long time. The best is natural sunlight on a bright but cloudy day. When I'm inside at my bench, I work under four 40-watt fluorescent lamps.

The next thing you need is a saw vise. You could make yourself a wooden one, but manufactured metal ones are more common. Most of these are about 12 in. long and hold the sawblade, teeth up, with an eccentric roller-bar or cam lock. Saw vises are short enough to be carried in the toolbox, but you have to keep sliding the saw along in the vise as your filing progresses. The vise I like best is a Lodi, made in California, but unfortunately, it's not being manufactured any longer. The jaws hold the saw along its entire length, with clamps at each end. In any case, the vise should be set up so that it's about 4 in. above your elbow.

With the exception of a flat mill-bastard file used for jointing, the tool that will be doing all

the cutting is an ordinary triangular taper file. These come in lengths from 5 in. to 8 in., and cross-sectional thicknesses called regular, slim, extra slim and double extra slim. Which one you use isn't critical, since all triangular files have equal 60° sides, but for most saws I use a 7-in. double-extra slim. The reason I use this thickness is that the apex of the triangle is sharper than on thicker files, and this serves to cut the gullet deeper. The narrow cross section also makes it easier to judge the angles on longer teeth. I like the longer files because I get more cutting per stroke.

Jointing is done to correct the line of teeth and make them all of equal height. This line should be either straight or convex. A saw in good shape won't need much jointing, but the resulting flat tops of the teeth will be useful later on in shaping and sharpening.

To joint, put the saw in the vise with the teeth up and about 2 in. of the blade showing. Using long strokes with a flat mill file, keep working the tops of the teeth, flattening the points until the top of each tooth has been struck (photo facing page, top). It's important that the file be perfectly perpendicular to the sawblade. You can make a simple wood block to ensure alignment, or buy a metal handsaw jointer that does the same thing.

Shaping corrects any teeth that have been deformed by bad sharpening or, more likely, contact with a nail. It ensures that the teeth are all of uniform size and spacing. If the saw is in good condition, some shaping can be done while sharpening. Hold the file at a 90° angle to the face of the sawblade, whether you are shaping a ripsaw, which will also be sharpened this way, or a crosscut saw that will get sharpened with alternating bevels. Sharpening will take a bit longer this way, but you'll be able to shape more accurately.

Place the saw in the vise with the handle to your right, letting the teeth show about ¼ in. If too much blade is out of the vise, the metal will bend when the file is in motion, causing the file to chatter and wear down quickly. Select the first tooth from the toe that is set toward you, and place the file in the gullet to the left of this tooth. Hold the file horizontally, an end in each hand, and push it straight across. As the file passes through the gullet, the left side is cutting the back side of one tooth and the right side is cutting the front side of another. File until one half of the flat top made by jointing is worn away, skip the next gullet and go to the next tooth set toward you. File it as before, and then move down the length, skipping every other gullet. When you've finished that side, turn the saw around and again select the first tooth from the toe that is set toward you. This will be the one you skipped the first time through. File this side the same as the other, using the flat tops as a guide—when the tooth comes to a point properly, the top will seem to disappear, as it will no longer reflect light. Check the depth of the gullets as you progress to make sure that they are the same.

Setting tends to distort the leading edge of the tooth and should always be done before

sharpening. It is done with a tool called a saw-set, which works on the principle of hammer and anvil, although the hammer is called the plunger and is activated by squeezing the pistol or plier-grip handle. The anvil is beveled and adjustable for different-size teeth, usually with a dial that adjusts for the saw's number of teeth per inch.

As with jointing and shaping, setting is not always required. Under average conditions, a saw can be sharpened about three times before it needs resetting. At this point, the teeth have been filed so much that the set near the middle of the tooth is eliminated. Wet lumber requires wide set, while dry wood requires little. Set also affects the smoothness of the cut—a 10-point saw with almost no set will make as fine a cut as an 11-point saw.

To use a saw-set, index the plunger with the top half of a tooth that is bent away from you and squeeze the handle (photo facing page, center left). The plunger will bend the tooth over against the anvil. Take it easy, though; too much pressure will cause the plunger to slip over the top of the tooth. Move down the blade, skipping every other tooth just as in filing, then reverse the saw and set the other half of the teeth.

Sharpening. I was taught to sharpen by placing the saw in the vise with its handle to my right and to work from the toe to the heel, so I'll explain it this way, although you can start wherever you like. Hold the saw just ¼ in. above the top of the vise. Start with the first tooth that's bent toward you, and place the file in the gullet to its left. For a crosscut saw (photo facing page, bottom right), hold the file horizontal, point the front of the file toward the handle of the saw at a 65° bevel to the face of the sawblade, and tilt the file for the hook to 15° away from vertical. For a sharper point, hold the handle of the file slightly lower than the tip. If you're cutting softwoods, change the bevel to 45°, the hook to 20° or 25° and keep the file handle lower.

File on the push stroke only, then lift slightly and return to start and stroke again. File until half of the flat top is removed if you are shaping and sharpening in one operation, or until half of a sharp point is produced if you are just sharpening. Once you're finished on this side, reclamp the saw so that the handle is on the left, begin again at the toe, and file the gullets that you deliberately skipped on your first run. When you have completed every other tooth with the saw in this position, examine the points for reflected light—sharp points will be invisible. Refile any that gleam.

Sharpening a ripsaw is considerably easier. In most cases, the file should be held horizontal, the bevel is 90° to the sawblade, and the there is no hook, which means holding the file face straight up and down. Some carpenters give the teeth an 8° hook so they can crosscut with their ripsaw if they have to.

Human eyes are not calibrating devices that display angles of bevel and hook on a scale, but when the eye and the mind form a partnership, you can make very fine judgments about consistency. The key here is practice, but as an aid in the beginning, crosshatch the top of your vise at the desired angle and hold the file parallel to these marks. There are commercial devices that hold the file at the correct angle, but I think these are a hindrance to learning the stroke freehand.

The final step in sharpening is side dressing. Old-timers did it to remove metal burrs from the sides of the teeth. Lay the saw flat on the bench or up high in the vise, and lightly run a file or oilstone down the side of the teeth, as shown in the photo below. Then repeat on the other side. I do this to reduce the set slightly.

When you have finished filing, hold the saw with the teeth up. They should feel sticky when touched with your fingertips. Sight down the line of teeth—it should be straight (or slightly convex), the points should look identical in shape and size, the gullets should form a straight line, and the set should be equal on each side. If the saw is filed and set correctly, a needle will slide down the valley formed by the set in the teeth. But the real test is how the saw cuts.

Take a flat piece of 1x6 and clamp it edgewise on a workbench. Mark a 45° line across the top, and a plumb line on the side. Start a cut across the board using long rhythmic strokes. Stop the saw in various positions and examine the kerf; you should be able to see the tiny V-cuts on each side, and they should be equally deep. If the points of the teeth are even, the saw will go right down the line with only a pushing-ahead motion. If the saw wanders and must be pushed to one side, the teeth are not even and it's back to the vise.

Using a handsaw—Hand-sawing is straightforward as long as you relax. Muscling the saw won't do you or the saw any good. With the stock laid on sawhorses, bring the saw to the cutline. Place the teeth on the waste side of the line, and brace the blade with the thumb of your free hand. Slowly draw the saw back, letting the teeth drag on the wood. This will start the cut. Push the saw lightly forward to cut a little deeper. Now move your thumb away; too much pressure on the first few strokes may cause the saw to jump out of the kerf, leaving you with some lifetime scars.

Now angle the saw about 45° above horizontal for crosscut saws and 60° above horizontal for ripsaws. Three or four moderate strokes should start a reasonable kerf so that you can begin using longer strokes. Most amateurs use short jabbing strokes. This wastes energy and sacrifices control. Instead, stand so that your shoulder, elbow and hand are in line, and the saw is an extension of the line. Use the full length of the blade with long rhythmic strokes. If the saw chatters on the return stroke, you are not pulling it straight back, or the blade is bent.

As you saw, the center portion of the blade does the most work. The toe end is just for starting and requires less pressure to keep it from jumping out of the kerf. Pressure is applied progressively toward the middle and then decreasingly until the heel is reached; then you lift and return for the next stroke. To me, this kind of motion feels more like slicing than sawing. The stroke motion is not a straight line, as it would seem. Because the elbow is lower at points than the hand and shoulder, the motion is actually a segment of an arc. Straight saws will have a barely perceptible rocking from toe to heel as they cut, while a convex line of teeth won't.

Generally, ⅛ in. is the shortest piece to cut off with a handsaw. When there is no resistance on one side of the blade, it will wander to that side. Backcutting is one alternative if you are fitting only one face of a board. The wood on the underside of the cut will provide the needed resistance. Another way is to block the end of the piece to be shortened. For example, if you have a piece of molding that is just one blade thickness too long, take a piece of the same molding and clamp or nail it in the miter box at the saw guide, butt the molding against the piece and saw through. The block provides the required resistance.

Some expert sawyers can saw square cuts and miters freehand without lines. The trick is to use the polished sides of the saw as a mirror. The reflected image in the sawblade tells you when the angle is right.

Base molding is more easily cut with a handsaw than by machine because you don't have to move the wood in and out of the box. Use a sawhorse with a 2x6 nailed onto the side of the top. Make a kerf in this 2x6 for a one-sided miter box. Then move the molding to the end of the sawhorse for any handsawn straight cuts, and finish the molded part with a coping saw. For flat moldings, perfect joints can be made by tacking a miter joint together and then sawing through the joint itself. □

Tom Law lives in Davidsonville, Md.

Side dressing. **Several quick strokes with an oilstone or file along each side of the blade remove any burrs produced by sharpening. It is also useful in reducing the set of a saw slightly.**

Site-Sharpening Saw Blades

It may not be a skill you use often, but it can sure come in handy

by Tom Law

It's bad enough when passersby suspect that there's a fire on your job site because of all the smoke in the air from your last skillsaw cut. But when you do finally dip into your sawbox for a sharp blade and discover that the blackened one you are using is the best you've got, you might want to overreact.

Jumping in your truck and driving all the way back to town for a case of throwaway blades isn't necessarily the answer. If you know the rudiments of sharpening a circular-saw blade, you can have your saw back in action in 20 minutes (less if you are just touching up the blade) and save yourself some money and a time-wasting trip into town.

I sharpen all of my own steel blades. Besides saving a few bucks and knowing that the blades will be consistently sharp, I get a kick out of filing as long as I can do them a few at a time during the evening. Hand-filing steel blades is not difficult, and it's not necessary to have memorized the textbook on tooth geometry to produce a better cutting blade.

Sharpening circular-saw blades is quite a bit like sharpening handsaws (see pages 46-50), except that in most cases the teeth are larger and more widely spaced, so they are easier to see and file. And since the blade is driven by

electricity and not your arm, getting the exact pitch and bevel angles right isn't critical if your goal is just to get the blade to cut.

Blade types—Carbide-toothed blades have become much more popular for table saws, radial-arm saws, power miter boxes and even for portable circular saws as the technology has improved and the price has come down over the last 20 years. The flats on carbide-tooth inserts can be touched up with diamond-dust stones, but once they reach the stage where they are burning through the work, they should be sent to a sharpening service for regrinding on a diamond wheel. Despite their popularity, I use carbide-tipped blades only for composition materials like particleboard, where the dulling action of the glue is best resisted by the harder teeth. I use high-speed steel blades for everything else because I don't have to rely on anyone else for sharpening. I make sure that the steel blades I buy are hard enough to hold an edge but not so hard that they destroy the file; this knowledge comes only with experience.

The types of steel blades most commonly used on portable power saws are rip, crosscut, combination and fine-tooth combination

blades. There are a number of specialty blades including *planer* (a smooth-cutting, hollow-ground finish blade), *plywood* (a blade with lots of evenly spaced teeth that leave a smooth edge with very little chipping of the surface veneer), and *metalcutting* (small teeth with negative hook for cutting thin sheet metals and extrusions). Many specialty blades are just as easy to touch up with a file as common steel blades.

Basically, woodcutting blades do only two things, rip and crosscut, and the teeth are designed to do one or the other. Ripping is done parallel to the fibers, and the teeth act as small chisels plowing out the kerf. Crosscutting is done perpendicular to the fibers, and the teeth act as knives slicing through them. A combination blade has teeth that are a compromise between rip and crosscut teeth, allowing it to do both tasks reasonably well. It is used primarily for framing. Fine-cutting combination blades, such as the master combination, are used primarily for trim work. They have two types of teeth—spurs and rakers. The spurs do the cutting while the rakers remove the sawdust. These teeth aren't all at the same height—since the rakers do no cutting, they are held slightly below the spur

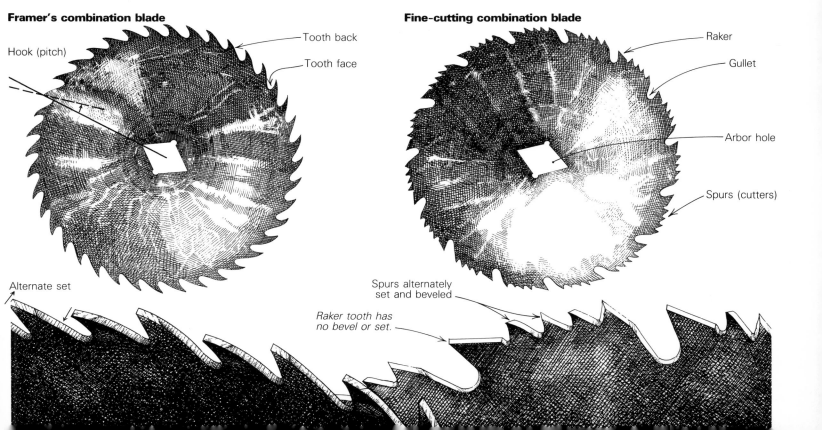

Framer's combination blade

Hook (pitch)

Tooth back

Tooth face

Alternate set

Fine-cutting combination blade

Raker

Gullet

Arbor hole

Spurs (cutters)

Spurs alternately set and beveled

Raker tooth has no bevel or set.

points. Spurs and rakers are usually arranged in segments with four spurs (set alternately) preceded by a raker. These segments are separated from each other by deep gullets.

The face of each tooth will be consistent with the others on the blade in pitch or hook angle, whether it be negative or positive (drawing, previous page). If the faces of the teeth are beveled, then these will alternate from side to side. With the exception of rakers, most circular-saw teeth also have some degree of set to reduce friction. On a planer blade, the teeth have no set, but the body of the blade is tapered toward the center (hollow ground).

Whether or not the backs of circular-saw teeth are beveled depends on the type of blade. In any case, the back of the tooth usually falls away rapidly in what's known as the clearance angle, which helps direct sawdust down into the gullet and out.

There are several reasons why circular-saw blades require attention. When teeth wear from wood cutting, the points become worn toward the center, leaving a sharper ridge on each side. Under magnification, the dulled area is blunt; the metal is rounded over rather than sharp. As teeth wear, their cutting action is slowed and more of a load is put on the saw motor. The accumulation of pitch on the side of blade can also cause a lot of friction; an all-purpose spray cleaner such as 409 or Fantastic is the easy solution for this. And then there's the enemy of any cutting edge—the hidden nail. When a blade strikes metal the points of the teeth can become severely distorted. Then as the blade turns in the wood, the jagged edges cause it to wobble and vibrate violently.

Several steps are required to sharpen such a blade. A full regimen would include jointing, setting, gumming (deepening the gullets), and shaping and repointing the teeth by filing their backs and faces. On a job site, you probably will only want to take the time to joint and repoint. But remember that repeating just these two procedures will eventually change the shape of the teeth.

Jointing—The first step in sharpening is to make sure that the teeth form a true circle that is concentric to the arbor hole. This way each tooth will be doing equal work. If you file only the teeth that have struck metal, for example, you may be making them shorter than the others, and they end up taking the day off.

I joint a circular-saw blade by removing it from the saw arbor and remounting it in the opposite direction of rotation. Then I place the saw's baseplate, in its lowest position, over an oilstone or sandpaper and slowly low-

Jointing. **With the blade mounted backwards in the saw and the shoe lowered all the way, the author just touches the edge of a sharpening stone with the blade at full speed. This guarantees a truly circular blade that is concentric with the arbor, and produces a flat spot on each tooth that acts as a sharpening guide.**

er the spinning blade (photo facing page). A light touch is critical. Too much pressure will gouge deep ruts in your stone, overheat the steel (possibly ruining its temper) and send chunks or grains of stone flying. Slowly lower the saw until the blade barely touches; when the sparks stop, lower it again. After doing this a few times, examine the teeth to make sure each one has a small flat spot on the top.

Jointing as an operation by itself can improve the cutting action of a blade that has just come into contact with a nail. When I'm cutting through old strip flooring (something I do often in remodeling), I expect to hit nails. Old floors were put together with cut nails—lots of them. I move the saw slowly along the cutline, and as soon as I hear the familiar screech of metal abusing metal, I lift the saw. Moving ahead slightly, I lower it again without trying to cut through the nail. When the blade will no longer cut I take it off, turn it around and joint it. This removes the flared burrs on the part of the tooth where the point used to be and restores the blade to round. Although I haven't really sharpened it, the blade will cut and I can finish the job, jointing whenever it's necessary. This trick allows me to use just one blade, and even if it is destroyed in the process, which is not likely, it's cheaper than sending a carbide blade out to be sharpened.

Repointing—Once you've jointed the blade and removed it from the saw, you're ready to repoint it. The blade has to be secured for this task. The handiest workbench on a framing job is a rough window sill. A scrap of 2x4 or 2x6 can be used for a saw vise. Drive a nail through the block and then through the arbor hole into the sill, sandwiching the blade. If you want to get a little fancier you can purchase a metal saw vise. The one I use is a small handsaw vise that clamps by means of an eccentric roller bar. The ideal height for filing the sawblade is about 4 in. below your armpit. Indirect sunlight is the best illumination for this.

When I file circular saws I do the whole tooth, trying to maintain the same shape each time. The idea is to reproduce the original configuration of the teeth as best you can. To get the best results, of course, you need specialized sharpening equipment and a knowledge of tooth geometry. But if you're just trying to turn a useless blade into a serviceable one, this method will work.

On rip or combination blades select a tooth that is set away from you, and file the face first. Although some larger-toothed blades will accommodate a mill file, the file I like best for this job is a crosscut. In section it is the shape of a teardrop with teeth all around, including the large round edge. Place a flat side of the file on the face (front side) of the tooth and cut only on the push stroke, two or three times (photo top right). If the file matches up in size with the gullet, you will be able to kill two birds with one stone with these strokes by gumming at the same time you're filing the face of the tooth. File straight across on the push stroke until half of the flat spot made by

Repointing. Using a crosscut file (right), which looks like a teardrop in section, you can often file the face of the tooth and deepen the gullets (gumming) at the same time. Two or three long, even forward strokes should be enough. Make sure to follow the already established hook and bevel. Repointing (middle right) is completed by removing the flat spot created by jointing on the back of the tooth. When the gullets are small, a chainsaw file can be used to deepen them (bottom right). Although you may not find yourself doing this on site, if the gullets get too shallow sawdust can begin to accumulate in the blade, causing increased friction.

jointing is worn away. On blades with a 90° tooth face (no bevel), such as rip blades and some framing combination blades, this stroke should be perpendicular to the body of the blade, but you'll find that holding the file at a very slight angle will reduce the drag on it considerably. If the tooth face is already beveled, duplicate the existing angle by eye.

Next, you're going to file the top of the tooth to bring it to a point (photo middle right). Whether or not this area is beveled depends on what kind of blade you are filing. Most cutting teeth (but not rakers) are beveled on top in the direction of their set. To reproduce this bevel, start the file in a horizontal position with its handle perpendicular to the blade itself. Then adjust the face of the file to the bevel by dropping the handle down and moving away from perpendicular. Continue with every tooth that is set away from you, and then reverse the blade and file the remaining half of the teeth.

For larger crosscut teeth or combination spurs and rakers, I use a cant file, which is triangular in section with angles of 30°, 120° and 30°. Adjust each segment in the vise vertically and file those spurs set away from you, keeping the hook and bevel correct. The rakers are filed straight across just 1/64 in. below the spur points. I always file the rakers on the first half no matter which side comes up first. Fine-tooth crosscut blades (including planer blades) should be done with a taper file, which is an equilateral triangle in section.

A few refinements—Circular-sawblade setting is normally done with a sawset just like handsaws. Although you are not likely to be doing this on the job site, you can revert to the traditional hammer-and-anvil method if one or two teeth are way out of line. Use the edge of a concrete slab, or even better, a heavy steel hardware flange or an I-beam for an anvil. It isn't necessary to gum the blade every time you sharpen its teeth, but making sure that the gullets are all the same depth is essential. To ensure good results, draw a pencil line around the face of the blade with a compass to indicate where to stop filing. Make sure that this circle is concentric with the outer one that is formed by the tooth points. Round bottom gullets can be filed with the round edge of a crosscut file, a round end-mill file or a chainsaw file (photo bottom right). □

Tom Law is a contractor in Columbia, Md.

Illustration p. 51: Elizabeth Eaton

The Worm-Drive Saw

How this powerful tool compares with a sidewinder saw

by Jim Picton

When I saw my first worm-drive saw on a job in Brattleboro, Vt., the foreman said it was a left-handed saw, and I carried that belief with me for many years. The sidewinder, or contractor's saw, is the preferred tool here in the East, so it wasn't until I moved to Anchorage, Alaska, that I really got to use a worm-drive saw and to see the advantages it offers.

I saw a lot of production framing in the West, where the worm-drive saw was used almost exclusively. I also built my share of expensive custom homes in the Chugach foothills near Anchorage, and the worm-drive saw was king there too. Before I moved back East, I bought one, and I still rely on this kind of saw for most of my cutting.

It's impossible to mistake a worm-drive saw for a sidewinder. The motor for the worm-drive saw is parallel to the blade, instead of perpendicular to it, and the blade is mounted on the left side of the body. The grips are also different. Worm-drive saws have a trigger switch mounted on the hand grip, which sits just behind the saw. There's another full-sized grip—angled slightly toward the user—right on top of the saw. In contrast, sidewinders have their handle and trigger switch at the two-o'clock position (Porter-Cable features a top-mounted handle that gives you a grip straight up, at twelve o'clock), and a sort of "saddle horn" at ten o'clock. But what really distinguishes the worm-drive saw from all of the others is the worm gear inside (sidebar, facing page).

Although my construction crew here in Connecticut claims that my worm-drive saws are ungainly and outpaced by their own light, tight Makita and Porter-Cable sidewinders, my spare worm-drive saw seems to get quite a lot of use when there's heavy work to do. Worm-drive saws do take some getting used to. General cutting should be approached in a surprisingly different manner, so you almost have to re-educate yourself about circular saws in order to use the worm-drive saw's full range of capabilities.

One of the fastest and safest ways to cut framing lumber with a worm-drive saw is to hold the work at an angle off the ground with your left foot. Your right foot should be well back. This way the saw is held out to the right of your body, and the weight of the saw literally makes the cut. In this position, the offcut falls only a few inches to the ground, and if the saw should kick back, it won't be into your body.

From *Fine Homebuilding* magazine (December 1984) 24:36-41

Sawing stance—What bothers people most about worm-drives is the weight: 15 lb. or more versus 11½ lb. or less for garden-variety sidewinders. There are some jobs for which a worm drive is just too heavy, but in most cases the extra weight is useful if you know how to take advantage of it.

The trick is to cut downhill. The position of the rear handle lets you stand above the work, the saw practically dangling in your hand with little or no pressure on your wrist. The left-mounted blade allows right-handers to see the line of cut clearly from as much as an arm's length away, so you can start the cut close and just gradually extend your arm. The saw's own weight moves it through the cut.

When right-handers operate a sidewinder they are positioned to the left of the saw, whose blade is mounted on the right. To watch the path of the blade directly in front of the cut, a right-hander must look over the top of the saw or lean forward to see in front of the motor. This means staying right on top of the saw with your elbow bent and your wrist crooked. It's a position you get used to, but if you try to assume this stance with a worm-drive saw, you wind up holding it in your left hand. This makes the slight angle of the top grip feel strange.

Instead, worm-drive saws are intended to be held with the right hand on the trigger grip. With this stance, you're on the same side of the saw as the blade, and your view of the cut is wide and clear.

You get used to using your body to support the work, as Jud Peake points out in his article on worm-drive techniques (see pp. 41-43). Setting up material so it that can be cut in a downhill direction would be a pain in the neck if it weren't for the well-documented fact that carpenters stand perpendicular to the horizon. This happy circumstance, combined with the rear grip and arm's length view of the blade, means you can eliminate the need for sawhorses or even flat areas to make your cuts—a real advantage in site work.

Carpenters who aren't used to worm-drive saws may consider this practice dangerous, but it's not, provided you keep a firm footing and don't walk into obvious traps. In general, you lean the work in front of you, and cut forward. Make sure the area behind you is clear, so if you need to step back you won't trip. You cut with the saw a comfortable distance away and to your right (photo facing page). This way, your eyes aren't so vulnerable to wood chips thrown by the saw, and if kickback occurs, you're not in the path of the blade.

Cutting techniques—For crosscutting anything from a 1x4 to a 2x12, I support the board on edge with my left foot, step back with my right, and drop the saw through the line. The offcut falls only a few inches, so it doesn't bounce or get damaged. Ripping boards is even easier. With one end on the ground and the other end supported on a window sill or bucket, I stand next to the saw, pushing ever so slightly as it rides downhill.

For single thicknesses of plywood, whether

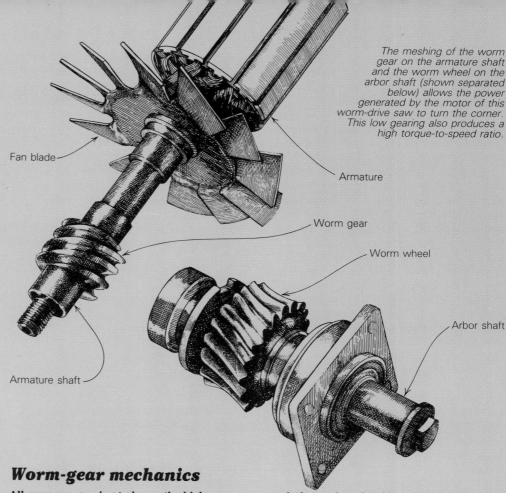

The meshing of the worm gear on the armature shaft and the worm wheel on the arbor shaft (shown separated below) allows the power generated by the motor of this worm-drive saw to turn the corner. This low gearing also produces a high torque-to-speed ratio.

Fan blade

Armature

Worm gear

Worm wheel

Arbor shaft

Armature shaft

Worm-gear mechanics

All saws use gearing to lower the high rpms of the motor before they are delivered to the blade. A worm-drive saw accomplishes this with two gears at right angles to each other, as shown above. The *worm gear* is about 1½ in. long and ¾ in. in diameter, and is attached directly to the splined armature shaft on the long axis of the saw. The armature shaft runs through a ball bearing to turn the worm gear, and the other end of the worm gear is supported by a ball bearing at the front of the saw. The threads of the worm gear engage the *worm wheel;* it is mounted on the arbor assembly, which runs across the saw, at right angles to the armature shaft. The arbor is supported by ball bearings on each side of the worm wheel, and runs out to the blade on the left side. This setup results in the saw's elongated shape. Since the mechanical energy "turns a corner" at the junction of the arbor and the worm gear, the motor sits behind the blade, not next to it.

But the worm gear's primary advantage isn't that it changes the shape of the saw. Instead, the worm gear is the key to the saw's power and durability. Gears can be cut to a number of different configurations that reduce relatively high motor speeds to acceptable rpm levels at the arbor. Some consumer tools just use straight-cut gears. The shoulders of these gears have very little support and can wear quickly and even shear off when subjected to the kind of shock load that comes with hitting a nail or making a pocket cut into a large knot. A helical gear—particularly the worm gear—is a great deal more durable because the teeth on the driving end are threads and so supported on all sides. But there is a trade-off here. Non-worm gears can be made from high-carbon alloy steel, which can be heat-treated for tremendous wear resistance. Worm gears are made from a less durable material, like bronze, that has a low coefficient of sliding friction. This is necessary to minimize the heat and wear caused by the peculiar meshing of these gears.

Even so, the worm gear takes a high motor rpm and delivers it to the arbor at a much slower speed and with greater torque. Each revolution of the worm on the armature shaft turns the worm wheel on the arbor by only a few notches. The unrestricted arbor speeds on worm-drive saws are 4,300 rpm for the Black and Decker Model #3051, and 4,400 rpm for Skil's Model #77 and Milwaukee's Model #6377, as opposed to an average of 5,400 to 5,800 rpm for most sidewinder saws. Given the size of the motors in worm-drive saws, this slower speed means an amazing amount of torque behind a given rpm.

In framing, you run into heavy work requirements like ripping through several thicknesses of plywood, cutting a stack of rafters, or ripping 2xs over 16-ft. lengths. Worm-drive saws practically walk right through this kind of work. The high torque-to-speed ratio of worm-drive saws means that as you load the tool down, the speed of the motor changes little, so you can push the saw just about as fast as the blade will cut.

Unlike worm-gear saws, the initially high rpms of most sidewinders come way down in heavy work. And while the worm-drive saw will continue to cut smoothly even if it's pushed hard enough to bring the motor down to half its usual pitch or less, the sidewinder at this point is ready to bind up in a full stop. This is a dangerous situation, because the torque of the blade against the wood as you ease off on the feeding pressure can result in kickback. At best, you get a bumpy ride when you bear down on a sidewinder, and the only alternative is to cut more slowly. — *J. P.*

Illustration: Elizabeth Eaton

it's a rip or a crosscut, I like to hold one end up with my left hand while the other end rests on the ground. I let the saw ride down the line as far as I can reach, then drop the work and finish the cut from the other side.

Despite the advantage of making the weight of a worm-drive saw work for you by cutting downhill, it's often better to work flat on finish work where you need more control. If you are finish-cutting plywood, you don't want to stop the cut and pick it up from the other side. Instead, lay the work on a level, well-supported surface, and climb right up onto it if you are cutting across a full 4 ft. The setup technique is the same as with a sidewinder saw. Although in this case the weight of the worm-drive ceases to be an advantage, you can use the rear-grip handle to advantage by locking your wrist. This way, your wrist can be used for fine course corrections, and the full force of your upper arm and shoulder is used to power the saw through the work. Locking your wrist like this can relieve a lot of the muscle fatigue in long, laborious cuts like sawing a stack of curved plates out of ¾-in. plywood. I sometimes lock my arm straight and just lean into the work, using my entire upper body to drive the saw.

For fine cutting, the full-sized upper handle on worm-drives gives you a secure and comfortable grip. It helps control direction when you're freehanding a scarf joint in fascia, mitering a soffit or making an in-place cut with the saw held sideways out in front of you (photo facing page, right). I don't have any objection to the horn-type grips on sidewinder saws, but a full hand-width handle suits me better. My brother's old Stanley worm-drive has a rear grip that wraps right around to form the top grip—like some chainsaws—and a horn grip at the front left corner to boot.

One of the toughest ways to cut with any kind of circular saw is straight up. Of course it's best not to get into spots like this, but more than once I've let a piece of fascia run wild on the end of a building, only to realize that I must now get below it to make the bevel cut required for the return. Actually, this is a good argument for having both a worm-drive saw and a cheap sidewinder knocking around among your tools. Because the blades of sidewinder saws and worm-drive saws are on opposite sides, their shoes tilt in opposite directions. A sidewinder saw would make the bevel cut on the fascia I was talking about from above—a real improvement over having to undercut a suspended board.

But for times when you have no choice, you will have to support the offcut end of the board and make the cut as fast as possible before the weight of the offcut collapses the kerf, binds the blade, and causes kickback. Although a lightweight saw seems like the best choice for overhead work, I worry about relying on the muscles in a bent wrist to power the saw through with no hangups. My choice is to get a straight arm locked behind a worm-drive, and press it.

If you can't cut downhill or support the weight of the saw on the work and push from

behind, you might as well set the worm-drive aside. I once stood on a steep roof steadying myself with my left hand to cut siding for an upper wall, with my right hand holding my worm-drive saw in front of me unsupported. If you want to sample the strain this puts on muscles and tendons, try picking up a suitcase and holding it out in front of you with your wrist bent at 90° to your arm for a few minutes. Handling my saw like this for a couple of hours put my wrist out of commission for a week. Next time, I'll use a sidewinder.

Safety—Everyone I know who works with tools for a living is vitally concerned with safety. Like professional athletes, tradespeople can't do their jobs without healthy bodies. Using any saw in a cavalier manner is foolish. If you are a novice builder or just unfamiliar with the saw you are using, you should start out slowly and as always, concentrate completely on what you are doing. You need to know the basic rules of saw safety listed in the owner's manual of any saw you use, and follow them. One oft ignored imperative, for instance, is unplugging your saw before changing the blade. Another common mistake is to burn through a cut with a dull blade instead of taking the time to change it.

But for me, safety sometimes goes beyond the usual admonitions, and this brings up the subject of blade guards. Worm-drive saws have a spring-return guard identical to the ones you find on sidewinders. The shape and operation of the guard are based on a set of design compromises that keep the blade covered when it's not buried in the work, and still allow it access to the work—most of the time. It is the exceptions that create truly unsafe situations. When you use any portable circular saw to cut an acute angle on the face of a board, the opening action of the guard is a lot less positive than when the shoe of the saw is perpendicular to the work. This often causes the saw to slide down the edge of the board before engaging. Also, if you are cutting with the shoe of the saw set at a bevel angle approaching 45°, the problem gets worse. At this point it's necessary to hold the guard up somehow in order to make the cut. This is also true if you are ripping or crosscutting less than ¼ in. from a board (the photo on p. 54 shows a board being trimmed by a sliver).

The procedure taught by experts in the field of safety is to hold the guard back with one hand while operating the trigger switch of the saw with the other. This requires two hands on the saw, which in turn means clamping the work to a horizontal surface before making a cut. This is something I do if I'm making a critical cut on a piece of finished woodwork, but I can't afford the time and frustration of getting out a C-clamp for every 2x4 I have to shorten. As a result, I block up the guard for the cuts I mentioned above. I know that doing this is a bone of fierce contention among safety experts, tradespeople and manufacturers. But I think that as an alert and well-informed operator, I am freer to give my full attention to the saw I am handling and the work beneath it

when I am not distracted by having to struggle with the guard. I have had too many near-accidents with saws that have hung up on the ends of boards because the guard didn't retract, or kicked back on me because the guard snagged on the work and made the saw veer off course. However, I want to stress that I have come to these conclusions only for myself after using professional-duty saws daily for nearly 15 years. This is not a procedure a novice should use.

There are lots of ways to keep the guard retracted, but I think that the safest is to use a small wedge or shim shingle between the lift lever for the retractable guard and the body of the fixed upper guard. This way, you can remove it easily after you've completed the cut. Then make sure that the saw is to the side of your body when you are cutting, and that your elbow remains locked until you have finished the cut and taken your finger off the trigger.

Some portable power tools now have automatic electric brakes, and in this situation, I think a brake would contribute to safety. I've used Black & Decker's Sawcat, which is equipped with a brake, but I don't know of any worm-drive saws with this feature.

Maintenance—Any good power tool has replaceable parts, and worm drives are no exception. There are over a hundred pieces to my Skil Model 77, all accessible with a screwdriver and pliers. Although I have taken saws apart myself, I find it more economical to send them into service through a dealer. They come back quickly and in perfect shape. In most cases, the repairs that I have ordered were for damage inflicted on the job site, and not for mechanical failures in the saws themselves. One day, I tried to cut overhead costs by using a motorcycle as a work vehicle. My worm-drive saw flew off the back at the first good bump, and I had to gather it up in a shopping bag over a quarter-mile stretch. I sent it into repair with dim hopes, but two weeks later it returned completely rebuilt, like new, for just over half the cost of a new saw.

To keep the worm gears in good condition, you are supposed to change the gear lubricant about four times a year. Most manufacturers sell a gooey kind of oil especially for this. It comes in something like a toothpaste tube, and you just unbolt the oil-fill plug, drain the old stuff, and squirt in the new. I confess I'm pretty bad at following this schedule. In fact, I haven't changed lubricant in more than four

Cutting techniques. A worm-drive saw has an advantage in ripping sheet stock because you don't have to lean over the blade. The rear-mounted trigger handle allows you to extend your arm—a safer stance that doesn't require constant repositioning as you rip long pieces (photo, facing page, top left). By using two hands on the rear of the saw and locking your wrists and elbows, you can actually push the saw with your upper body (bottom left). This lets you power through gang cuts or wet lumber without sacrificing control or fatiguing your arms. The top handle on a worm-drive saw can be useful for more than carrying when you're edge-cutting out in front of you (right).

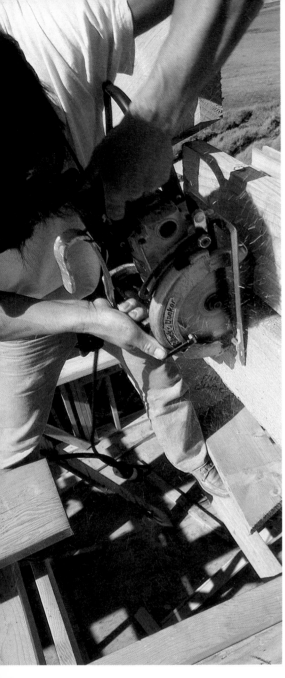

years. Nonetheless, our saws work fine winter and summer under daily use. A properly maintained worm-drive should last for decades.

Blades—The only other maintenance required on worm-drive saws is occasional replacement of the brushes—standard procedure for all electric motors—and, of course, changing blades. Some worm-drive saws have an integral positive stop to lock the blade while you loosen the arbor nut. It is a spring-loaded button located at the front of the saw, and you push it in and turn the blade until the stop clicks into place. An offset blade wrench supplied with the saw fits the arbor nut, which is reverse-threaded (photo bottom left).

To prevent blade slippage, the arbors on all the larger worm-drive saws are diamond-shaped in section rather than round. Blades that fit this arbor are readily available—they have a diamond-shaped knockout that has to be removed before the blade can be mounted. This diamond knockout feature is not universal, so check before making the purchase. It also makes sense to save one or two of those knockouts in one corner of your tool box—you'll need them to return to the round arbor fitting if you are going to use one of these blades on saws with round arbors.

Almost any kind of circular-saw blade will work in a worm-drive saw. I keep a carborundum blade for masonry and a planer blade for fine work. For general purposes, carbide-tipped blades work well, but they cut a pretty wide swath. Also, the cheapest ones still cost over $5, and they're ruined after two or three encounters with a nail. I buy "throw-away" combination blades in bulk for their finer cut, and they cost about $2.60 each. They can be resharpened, but the service costs as much as the blades themselves.

Models, brands and prices—My saws use a 7¼-in. blade, and this is the most common size. With the base retracted to its fullest, a new 7¼-in. blade will yield a depth of cut of a little less than 2½ in., depending on the brand of the saw. This depth is reduced by any bevel you may set on the saw. At 45°, most 7¼-in. saws can take a little more than 1⅞ in. of bite.

The other common sizes of worm-drive saws are 6½ in. and 8¼ in. The 6½-in. saw (both Skil and Black & Decker make one) has enough blade to cut through a 2x at 45°. This sounds like a good choice until you realize that it weighs only ½ lb. less than a 7¼-in. saw and takes up about the same amount of space. You can also go upscale with worm-drive saws to

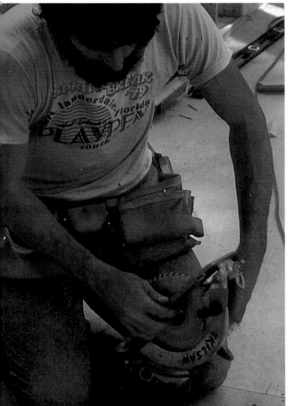

Using the weight. By cutting down on the work, both hands can be used for control in a deep pocket cut like the one on this exposed ridge beam, above left. The aluminum hook wired to the saw solves the problem of where to set it down when every surface within reach is at a pitch.

Changing blades. The blade lock makes this procedure easy. With the saw unplugged, left, unscrew the reverse-threaded arbor bolt to the right, and insert the blade with its teeth up.

an 8¼-in. blade size, but here you'd have to lug around four extra pounds that will buy you only another ½ in. in depth of cut. On the small end of things, Porter-Cable makes a trim and paneling (or siding) worm-drive saw that uses a 4½-in. blade. At 7 lb., this saw is a tough little alternative to the usual worm-drive saws for lightweight materials.

All the worm-drive saws I've used are good, and all of them are expensive. In my opinion, you can't buy a bad—or cheap—worm-drive (sidebar, facing page). With the exception of the little Porter-Cable, worm-drive saws are nearly identical in design. All of them have a wraparound shoe that measures 1½ in. to the blade from the edge on one side, and considerably wider on the other. The depth-of-cut adjustment is on the left rear of the saw, and is similar to most sidewinders. The rear of the shoe drops down to limit the blade exposure. The setting can be made quickly because it isn't geared or restrained in dovetail ways. Instead, a thumb lever operates an eccentric, which holds the adjustment by compression. The bevel adjustment is similar, only the shoe pivots from the front of the top blade guard. The angles stamped into the pivot guide are seldom reliable for accurate cuts.

My favorite worm-drive saw is the Skil Model 77, because its size (17 in. long) and weight (15¾ lb.) are about as conservative as you can get in a 7¼-in. worm-drive saw. I also give it high marks for good behavior and durability. This saw lists for $247, but it's not hard to get one for $180 to $200. I like to buy my gear from a dealer who specializes in contractors' supplies. By waiting for his promotional sale, I've been able to get a Model 77 for $150. I've seen lower prices, but I like the fact that my dealer does his own repair, and gives me the attention a regular customer deserves.

The 7¼-in. Milwaukee Model 6377 worm-drive lists for $230. At 17 lb., it is a bit heavier than the Skil, and it is also 1¼ in. longer. The differences are hardly noticeable in operation though, and the saw has an extra 2 amps of draw and the solid, well-built feel that's typical of Milwaukee tools. The closest thing to a Skil 77 in size, weight, and appearance is the Black & Decker model #3051. This 7½-in. worm-drive saw weighs 16½ lb. and is 17½ in. long. We have one that handled well through some rough treatment, but it was in for repairs twice, and it is the only worm-drive saw that ever completely stripped its gears on one of our jobs. The Black & Decker lists for $232.

We used to have a Rockwell worm-drive saw, but currently the only worm-drive saw made by Porter-Cable (Rockwell's successor) is the 4½-in. trim saw. None of the major Japanese tool manufacturers I know of makes a worm-drive either.

Whichever worm-drive saw you choose, you can be secure in the knowledge that it is one of the most reliable, well-constructed and repairable saws available today. Once you get used to it, you'll never want to switch. □

Jim Picton is a contractor who lives in Washington Depot, Conn.

Power saws: rating the ratings

Label reading has become a necessary sport for cost and quality-conscious buyers, and shopping for power tools is no exception. The serial-number plate on every portable circular saw lists electrical and speed ratings that should provide a basis for comparison between types of saws, and between the different brands within each category. Some manufacturers' catalogs list even more specs on their tools—things like horsepower and torque. But even after you read these figures, it's hard to know what you're getting.

The biggest problem is the proliferation of rating categories. Long ago, the marketing divisions of the major tool manufacturers discovered that the buying public was more impressed by hard numbers generated by engineers than they were with the war of superlatives waged by the advertising agencies. But since the different brands within each category often came in with similar numbers, new ratings (or the same general rating taken farther back on the power train or under a higher load) were used. As a result, ratings that described only a minor part of a tool's performance were often touted because they generated bigger comparison numbers than the rating the competition was featuring that year.

Recently, there has been a trend toward offering professional-duty power saws with less hype and fewer ratings. Manufacturers of worm-drive saws are beginning to list just the amperage and the arbor speed. To get a better idea of how these and other terms could be used reliably to determine saw power and quality, I talked to several engineers, service mechanics and a customer-service representative at the companies that make full-size, worm-drive saws. I began by asking what power or quality rating they would look for first in choosing a saw. Most replied that no single rating or any combination of ratings really speaks to the total quality of a saw, but that amperage, arbor speed, and to a lesser degree, horsepower, hold the greatest promise for describing what the saw will actually do.

Amperage—Since most of the portable power saws in the United States operate on 110-120 volts, one of the differences between saw motors will be evident in how many amps each draws. Although an inefficient electric motor or gearing system can take a large amperage draw and use it to generate more heat than power, generally the greater the amp rating, the more powerful the motor.

Taken by itself, a saw's amperage rating won't really tell you about how it cuts or about the quality of the components like gears and bearings. But the amperage rating can help you determine the general quality of a saw. Worm-drive saws in the 7¼-in. category are pretty closely grouped. Milwaukee's worm-geared workhorse draws 15 amps, while Skil's and Black & Decker's 7¼-in. worm-drive saws use 13 amps. These figures are higher than those for sidewinders generally. There are two reasons for this. The first is evident: worm-drive saws are designed in every way as professional-duty saws, and they have to be capable of heavy cutting. There is a much wider range of sidewinders, from low-amperage consumer saws to heavy-duty saws with about the same amperage draw as worm-drives. The second reason involves the action of the worm-drive itself. Because a worm gear slides rather than rolls like a spur or helical gear, its efficiency is reduced. In fact, the reason a worm-drive saw uses a bath-type lubrication is to minimize the effect of the heat produced in the gears.

Knowing the amperage rating of a electric tool is important in using it safely since it will determine the size drop cord you will need and the circuit you're going to tap into. Because the amperage figure is important in these ways, the methods for determining amperage are standardized and have to meet both government and private specifications. For instance, manufacturers applying for a U.L. listing are required to stamp the amperage rating right on the tool, and it must be a figure that is generated during continuous operation. The continuous-operating range of electrical tools in this kind of rating is defined by a maximum rise in temperature in the windings of 65°C during operation.

Arbor speed—The arbor speed of a saw is how fast the blade will turn measured in revolutions per minute (rpm). Generally, smoother cuts are produced by higher rpms. Most inexpensive power saws run at high speed, but they slow way down when their blades meet the work (remember that advertised arbor speed is a no-load measurement). At this point the advantage is lost. This is where amps need to be considered again. A high-amperage saw (13 to 15 amps) that is geared down to a low rpm (4,300 to 4,400 rpm) has the torque to maintain much of this speed even during heavy cutting. These qualities are particularly valuable in a saw that has to make long rips in green lumber or will be used in unsupported, freehand crosscutting where speed is of the essence and binding is much more likely—typical uses for worm-drive saws.

There are several professional-duty sidewinder saws, such as Black & Decker's Sawcat and Milwaukee's 7¼-in. contractor's saw, that draw similar amperage to the worm-drive saws, but turn at a high (5,800) rpm. An exception that is new to the market in the last year is Porter-Cable's 7¼-in. Speedtronic, which draws 14½ amps and operates at a constant 4,500 rpm, regulated by a microprocessor-based control.

Torque—One rating that in part measures the cutting ability of a power saw is *torque*. Although this term is often used interchangeably with power, they are not the same. Torque measures the turning force of the tool (this can be felt in the jerk a high-torque saw makes when you first pull the trigger), while *horsepower* (defined below) takes both torque and arbor speed into account.

Although torque sounds like a useful category for comparison because it's measured in concrete units—foot-pounds—it can be deceptive because of the different ways it can be measured. The first thing to distinguish when describing a saw using torque is whether work was actually being done when the rating was taken. *Stall torque* and *locked rotor torque* both measure the maximum torque that a motor can deliver, but the saw can't perform at these limits. Another much lower figure is *rated torque*, which unlike the other two, is measured at a more normal level of output, at which the tool can operate indefinitely. Unfortunately, many ratings aren't labeled as to which kind of torque they measure.

Horsepower—Few ratings have the reputation that this one does for certifying the power of a machine, but the difference between the way a gasoline engine and a universal-wound electric motor do their work is considerable. Electrical horsepower is based on a formula: output watts divided by 746. But there is more than one way to calculate horsepower, and many engineers use the following formula: $hp = torque$ (ft.-lb.) $\times rpm \times K$ (K, a constant, is $.1904 \times 10^{-3}$). This one sounds a little less abstract because it deals in terms (torque, rpm) that can be experienced.

Horsepower is actually measured with a dynamometer, which charts the complete output curve of the saw from zero to the maximum. Where the horsepower is measured and how high the saw is revving have everything to do with the number that is generated.

Motor horsepower is measured at the motor itself rather than at the arbor. It isn't very significant to the saw purchaser since it isn't an end-of-the-line number, but is measured back behind all the power transfer at the gears. A more useful figure is horsepower measured at the arbor at *operating speed*. For worm-drive saws, you'll get a rating of just over 1.0. This is *rated horsepower*, which is also confusingly called *full-load horsepower*. This is the actual horsepower you will be using since it's measured at a level where the tool can operate continuously. Rated horsepower is somewhere between 40% and 70% of *maximum horsepower*, which means that the saw is pushed to its very limits. When a saw is said to "develop" a certain horsepower, it is this maximum rating that is being used. Although you can use the maximum-horsepower figure for comparison, remember that your saw wouldn't be able to deal with this loading for more than a few seconds before its windings began to burn. Worm-drive saws (7¼ in.) develop between 2¼ and 2¾ hp at this level of operation.

Reputation and price—The best determiners of quality in a portable circular saw may be the tool's list price and its reputation among people who own one. Pick the most expensive saw you can afford, and then try to get it as cheaply as possible. A well-wound motor, solid castings and ball bearings are expensive, and the price of a good saw will reflect this. Price is a less important consideration when you are choosing within a category, such as full-size worm-drive saws, where all of the brands are similarly priced, and of correspondingly high quality.

A saw's reputation in the field also helps fill in information that isn't available elsewhere. Electrical and work ratings don't measure the durability of a tool; that's a matter of the quality of the parts and the craftsmanship used in putting them together. The reputation that a tool gets with rental yards and repair shops will give you a good insight. Convenience is something else that is best rated subjectively. And in this area there is no substitute for talking to people who already own the saw and use it for a living.

—*Paul Spring*

Power Miter Saws
Crosscutting trim with accuracy and speed

by Geoff Alexander

The best of the traditional miter boxes are beautiful and elegant tools. For generations, craftsmen have used a backsaw and miter box to trim out houses; and in skilled hands, these tools do nice work. But power miter saws have all but eliminated the miter box as a finish carpenter's tool. Sometimes called chop saws, power miter saws are faster, more accurate and better able to withstand job-site abuse than miter boxes. With a stiff-bodied, carbide-tipped blade, a power miter saw can shave a minute amount from a cut you just made to give you a precise fit. But with a traditional miter box, you've got to get your cut exactly right the first time, because a backsaw won't cut true if it's not supported on both sides by the wood.

There are several makes and models of power miter saws, but they all have the same basic setup—a table about 5 in. wide by 16 in. long and a vertical fence at the rear to position and hold the work. A sawblade and motor are mounted to a spring-loaded arm that terminates in a handle and trigger-switch. To make a cut, the arm assembly is pulled down so that the blade passes through the work. When downward pressure on the handle is released, the arm assembly returns to its rest position above the work. The entire arm assembly is pivot-mounted so that the blade can be set to cut any angle from 45° right to 45° left, or sometimes a little more.

Power miter saws find many applications on the construction site. Plumbers working with plastic pipe often use them to create fast, clean joints. Since non-ferrous metals can be cut safely on a power miter box fitted with a carbide blade, I frequently use mine to cut aluminum extrusions such as sliding-door tracks, shower-door parts and trim for a tub surround. For cutting exclusively non-ferrous metals, use a negative-hook carbide blade, wear safety glasses and cut slowly.

The power miter saw's intended function, and the job at which it is truly extraordinary, is cutting wood trim. Its portability and fast setup time, the ease of setting the angle of cut, and its ability to make tight-fitting joints quickly make it the best choice for cutting inside and outside miters, butt joints on baseboard, door and window casing, chair rails, crown molding and other pieces of wood trim.

Its chief virtue, however, is its ability to shave ⅟₃₂ in. off the end of a board, or to modify the angle of cut by a fraction of a degree,

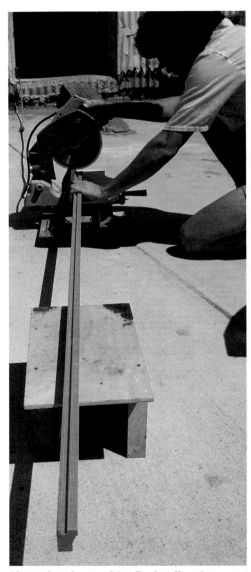

Alexander keeps his Rockwell miter saw mounted on a short 2x12, which makes it easier to carry and gives it a stable base. He made a pair of work-support tables whose tops are level with the saw table. Cutting long unsupported pieces is difficult and dangerous.

and to do these things without sacrificing any of the crispness or accuracy of the cut. When I began working as a carpenter in 1970, one of the first things I learned was that professionals make almost as many mistakes as amateurs. But professionals are very fast at fixing their mistakes. In this context, the power miter saw is truly a professional's tool. Its capability of correcting errors and still achieving a perfect joint with little wasted time or material justifies the saw's cost to anybody doing professional-calibre finish carpentry.

What's on the market—When I bought my first power miter saw in the early 1970s, I got a Rockwell 34-010 because it was the only one on the market. It has a 9-in. blade, a particleboard table and a manual blade brake. By the late 1970s, Black & Decker and Makita were each making a 10-in. saw. Makita made several noteworthy improvements, first with its 2400B (10 in.) and then its LS1400 (14 in.). Both Makitas have a slotted steel table that pivots along with the arm assembly when setting the angle. Both have an automatic electric brake, and a dust bag. Accessories include table extensions, an adjustable stop, and a vise for clamping the work in place.

The Black & Decker (#3090) also has an automatic brake, but the saw itself is of lightweight construction and has a particleboard table. Black & Decker is discontinuing model #3090 and replacing it with an upgraded 10-in. saw (model #3091) that has a pivoting table. Hitachi's current models (the C10FA 10-in. saw and the C15FA 15-in. saw) have an automatic brake; a dust bag, table extensions and a vise are standard equipment. These saws have something unique—a phenolic-resin fiberboard insert for the slot in the table, and a carrying handle.

In my estimation, Sears power tools are designed for the home owner rather than the tradesman (although that wasn't always true), and judging by look and feel alone, their power miter saw is meant for the consumer market. Of possible interest, however, is Sears' radial miter saw—a 7½-in. compromise between a power miter saw and a small radial-arm saw. I think its design has definite potential. Rockwell's portable frame-and-trim saw, the Sawbuck, is a much more fully realized and versatile version of the radial/miter saw concept. If the Sawbuck can withstand daily job-site use, it may well be as important an innovation as the original power miter saw.

The blade brake—At this point, all of the power miter saws except Rockwell's have an automatic brake on the blade. As soon as you release the trigger, the brake brings the blade to a stop within a few seconds. Rockwell's manual brake is operated by pushing a thumb button on the handle. The button actuates brake shoes that grip the spinning shaft. Having worn out three sets of brake shoes ($8 a whack if you replace them yourself, about $35 if the repair shop does it), I now try to mini-

From *Fine Homebuilding* magazine (February 1984) 19:42-45

mize my use of the brake. But since I often have to work near the blade right after cutting to remove scrap or to align the next cut, and since the saw is a real screamer (5,000 rpm under load), I use the brake a lot anyway. And that's why I prefer automatic brakes.

Pivoting vs. stationary tables—Because a pivoting table (actually it's a round baseplate insert in the center of the table) stays in the same relation to the blade whatever the setting, it can have a permanent slot cut into it to receive the blade. With a wooden table, the blade actually cuts into the table surface. The advantage of the wooden table is that the slot is exactly the width of the saw's kerf (when the table is new), so the workpiece is firmly supported on both sides of the cut. This minimizes splintering on the bottom of the work where the blade passes through. The disadvantage of the wooden or composition table is that each time you set the saw to a new angle and make a cut, a little bit more of the table gets eaten away. Also, any minor widening of the existing slots in the table lessens the support behind the cut and increases the likelihood of splintering. If the only angles you cut are 90° and 45°, a table can last a long time, but I usually end up making mincemeat out of mine on each major job. Frequent replacement or resurfacing of the wooden table helps keep the splintering under control.

With pivoting tables, you don't have to worry about the blade chewing up the surface. But because the slot in the rotating metal baseplate is wider than the blade, the workpiece doesn't get support where the blade exits, and so your wood can splinter out on the back side of the cut. Hitachi addresses this problem directly by filling the slot with a replaceable, phenolic-resin fiberboard insert. Since this is a new feature I've never used, I can't say how long each insert will last. You will certainly need to change inserts if you change to a thinner blade.

Setting the angle—Each saw manufacturer handles the angle setting a little bit differently. Rockwell put positive stops (plunger in slot) at 45° and 90°, and at 22½° on the new machines. To change from one detent to another, you can move the handle to about the right place and let the plunger fall into place. After many years of heavy use, the settings are still reliable on my saw. To set any other angle on the Rockwell, you pivot the arm to the right spot and tighten a thumbscrew down on the protractor scale. Unfortunately, the screw has a tendency to pull the whole arm assembly slightly to one side as it tightens. This throws off the setting. I often tighten the thumbscrew lightly to avoid changing the

angle, and then move very carefully to avoid bumping the saw and throwing off the setting. This strategy usually works if I'm making only one cut, but isn't always successful for making multiple cuts at the same setting.

The Makita saws (except the model 2401B) have no positive angle stops. Each angle setting must be locked in place by tightening the same handle with which you set the angle. It clamps horizontally against the side of the protractor scale, and does so with no shifting. When I first used the Makita, I thought that the lack of positive angle stops would be a nuisance, but I have found that not to be so. The handle lock works quickly and reliably, and the protractor scale is easy to read. Best of all, it's easy to set the saw for 44½°—a real problem on the Rockwell saw because the detent-and-thumbscrew arrangement almost always makes the setting drift. Most other power miter saws do have positive stops, but I have not used any of them enough on the job to know their idiosyncracies.

Size of the saw—All of the manufacturers except Rockwell make a 10-in. saw. For the purpose of comparison, Rockwell's 9-in. saw performs like the 10-in. saws. Hitachi's 15-in. saw (C15FA) and Makita's 14-in. saw (LS1400) are in a class by themselves, however. Substantially larger and heavier than the other saws, they can also cut much larger stock in a single pass. But for ordinary finish carpentry, I don't see much use for the big saws. And as we shall see, even the 9-in. Rockwell can be used to make square cuts on a 2x6, and can cut any type of miter on a 2x4.

Without removing the blade guard on the 14-in. Makita, the widest board you can cut is

8 in. The portability of the smaller saws is an advantage while doing finish work, both for moving from room to room and from job to job. Because of their size, beefier construction and slow blade speed, the big saws are best for gang-cutting green 2x4s or 2x6s, or for cutting 4x4s and 4x6s. But Makita and Hitachi use the same motor on their big saws as they do on their 10-in. saws, so don't expect to get extra cutting power.

Several saws have means to lock the pivoting arm in a safe down position, which makes carrying the tool a little easier. Hitachi is the first to have a separate carrying handle. I often carry my Rockwell by the main handle if the blade is locked down, but the Makita is hard to carry one-handed. The arm on the new Hitachi can be held down by a flimsy chain—an arrangement that seems inadequate to me. The table extensions on the Japanese saws are sometimes useful, but I almost always leave them off because they are in the way when moving the saw, and they are too short to be helpful when cutting long boards. The Makita and the Hitachi have a stop gauge that fastens onto the extension arms for repeat cuts. But most often the stock you're cutting is too long or too short for the stop gauge to be of any use.

Setting up the saw—On the job site, everything that is done is a compromise between the right way and the fast way; setting up the miter saw is no exception. In the "right-way" universe, the saw is at waist height, there's 6 ft. of solid auxiliary support on each side, the blade has just been sharpened, the floor's clean, and there's a cold beer waiting at the end of the day. Back in the real world, though,

If Alexander is going to be on site for an extended period, he brings his two tool-drawer units, which sit on either side of the saw and support the work. Note that the plywood saw table is shaped to prevent the kerf from breaking through the edge. This keeps the wood in one piece and makes a better surface to cut on.

we don't always have the time to set it up that way, so here are some techniques that should help ease the compromise.

One thing you should never do is cut a long board without supporting it at the far end. In the hustling pace of the job, it's tempting to try holding a long board to the saw table with nothing more than hand strength. About eight years ago, I tried to hold a 10-ft. piece of trim with no outrigger support. My fingers were curled around the fence to clamp the board down, which worked fine until I made the cut. Then, having lost the counterweight of the off-cut end, the piece started to fall, and in an attempt to save it, I grabbed the spinning saw-blade instead, and left a quarter inch of my middle finger behind in the sawdust.

When I'm moving from job to job, I always carry with me one or two little auxiliary tables with 6-in. by 10-in. plywood tops that are mounted on two lengths of 2x stock, as shown in the photo on p. 60. These tables are the same height as the miter-saw table, and let me use it anywhere I can find a continuous surface to work on (including the floor). My Rockwell saw has been mounted on a 2x12 for several years now. The board is easier to clamp down than the saw alone, and it lets me carry the saw on my right shoulder while I'm carrying the tables in my left hand. This way I can carry a basic setup on, off or around the job in one trip.

With the auxiliary tables, I can adjust to almost any situation. If there is a long, flat 2x12 and a pair of sawhorses available, it's fast to set the board across the horses and flop the saw down. Then, by positioning the auxiliary tables on either side of the saw, most lengths of stock can be handled easily. But if nothing springs to hand, and there aren't too many cuts to make, put the saw on the floor, get down on your knees, and get to work. By the time you make some elaborate setup, you probably could have finished all the cuts.

If I'm going to be on a job for a while, however, I want a comfortable setup. There are several ways to make one. When I'm really moving into a job, I have several sets of tool drawers with casters mounted on one side that I take along. Each one is about 2 ft. square and about 3 ft. tall. I also have a table built to the right height so that when the miter saw sits on the table, its cutting surface is the same height as the tops of the drawer units. This setup (photo previous page) supports the workpiece on both sides, and offers small work surfaces and drawers for tools, hardware and sandpaper.

Sears and Rockwell both sell steel stands as accessories for their saws, but it's easy to build your own out of wood. With the power miter saw sitting on a stand, the saw is at a comfortable working height, but unless you're building doll houses, you'll need a way to hold up the ends of long boards.

One contractor I know built a stand for his Makita 2400B, and then made two detachable wings. Each wing has an oak 1x6 for a table and an oak 1x2 for the fence. To fasten the wings to the saw, he bolted short lengths of angle iron to the saw itself, and then tapped the angle iron to receive flathead machine screws through the table of the wing. Each wing then had one leg of appropriate length hinged to its table so the leg would fold flat for storing and carrying.

If you screw the miter saw to the center of a long board (say a 10-ft. 2x12), and then fasten tables to the board on each side of the saw to get support at the correct height, you can create a stable work surface to which you can affix stop blocks for making repeat cuts. While this system does require sawhorses to set the board on, and it takes up a fair amount of space, it offers a solid work surface. Biesemeyer, Inc. (216 South Alma School Rd., Suite 3, Mesa, Ariz. 85202) makes an outrigger support with an integral stop gauge called the T-Square Miter Saw Stop System.

Choosing a blade—All of the power miter saws come with an ordinary steel blade. The first thing you should do is take it off and put on a carbide-tipped blade. The teeth on car-bide blades are accurately aligned so they make cleaner, more precise cuts, and the tooth form stays practically the same after each sharpening. Carbide-tipped blades can cut aluminum, and some other non-ferrous metals and plastics, as well as other abrasive woods and wood products like particleboard. They stay sharp about 40 times longer than steel-tooth blades. If you plan to cut only wood, the alternate top bevel (ATB) is a good choice of tooth design, but if you expect to use the saw periodically for aluminum or plastic pipe, the triple-chip tooth design is stronger and more durable. With either style, a 9-in. or 10-in. sawblade with 40 to 60 teeth will give good results. Expect to spend $1 per tooth or more for a good carbide blade. Some cheap blades have improperly tensioned plates, or teeth that are poorly fastened to the blade. There should be at least ⅛ in. of carbide on each tooth of a 40-tooth saw. The price, the warranty and the manufacturer's reputation are the best indications of quality.

Making cuts—Keep the table clean. Watch out for sawdust accumulating where the table and the fence meet. Even a little dust here can cause your workpiece to misalign and give you a bad cut. Take special care to keep small offcuts out of the blade's path. If the blade catches a loose scrap, it can hurl it like shrapnel in almost any direction.

Mark your cut on the workpiece where the saw will enter the work. If you're cutting a 1x4 laid flat, the saw will enter the middle of the board; if you're cutting a board positioned on edge, you'll have to mark the cut on the top edge. As long as your pencil mark is near where the blade first enters the stock, there is no need to square it across the entire board. Make sure that the work is in good contact with the table and the fence, and that it is solidly supported at the end. To align the cut, I usually start the saw and then sight along the spinning blade as I pull it toward the work. As the blade enters the work, I move my head to the left so that the flying sawdust will miss my

Casing a window

In an ideal world, two 45° angles add up to 90°, but in the real world of construction, it doesn't always work out so neatly. Walls, ceilings and floors may all be out of square or out of plumb. One job that often reveals framing inaccuracies is casing a door or window opening, especially if the casing is a wide or complex molding. I correct the inaccuracies as I go, without wasting time or material. I always work from the bottom up. If the casing goes around all four sides of a window, picture-frame style (instead of sitting on top of a window stool), I cut and nail the bottom first, leaving a constant reveal between the casing and window frame. Then, for each side, I make a trial cut at 45° and test-fit it, holding it with the same reveal and snug to the wall and jamb. If it fits perfectly, I mark the length and cut another true 45° at the top.

If the angle isn't perfect, I recut the miter, leaving the saw at the 45° setting, but shimming the material at the fence. To help me gauge the thickness of the shim, I compare the length of the miter cut to the length of the fence on the miter saw, and adjust accordingly.

For example, let's assume I'm using my Rockwell to cut 1x4 trim. The length of the miter cut is about 4⅞ in. The length of the fence to the left of the sawblade is 8¼ in. Assume that the original cut left a gap at the heel of the miter that I eyeballed to be ⅟₃₂ in.. Then, since the left-hand fence is roughly twice as long as the miter, I'd want to use a shim that was about ⅟₁₆ in. thick placed against the fence right next to the sawblade. This would change the angle of the cut slightly, just enough to shave the toe of the miter to close the gap at the heel and get a good fit. I very seldom measure any of these things. Eyeballing becomes much more accurate with practice.

If the angle looks correct, but the miter gaps open on the face side of the trim, I correct it by elevating the board with a shim placed on the table near the blade. Then I recut the miter—in effect, back-beveling the cut, taking care not to change the edge where the original cut meets the face of the trim. If the casing has a deep molded shape, I back-bevel with great care to avoid changing the shape of the face edge of the cut.

Once I've got both lower miters fitting properly, I cut the side casings to length using a true 45° cut, squirt a little glue into the joints, and nail them in place. I usually leave the top third of the trim unnailed until I have cut and fit the head casing, and then always put at least one nail across the miter itself. To fit the head casing, I cut one miter to a perfect fit first, then make the length cut and any necessary adjustments to the second miter. Then I glue the miters and nail the trim in place. —G. A.

face. Then I check the accuracy of the cut, and make an adjustment if needed. In any case, the blade guard is almost always in my line of sight, an issue I will discuss below.

If you're doing rough work, you can feed the blade through the wood as fast as you can go without taxing the motor. But if the appearance of the cut is important, it's better to use a slow, steady stroke. The blade can pull splinters out of the top of the cut on the up-stroke, so if that's a concern, hold the blade at the bottom of the cut for a moment and pull the stock away from the blade before you let the blade come back up.

Sometimes, no matter how smoothly you cut, the bottom of the cut will splinter. The best way to minimize the splintering is to put a smooth piece of wood on top of the saw's table as an auxiliary table and place your work on that, show side up. For my Rockwell, I make up several auxiliary tables at a time, in a shape that allows the wood of the table to extend beyond the saw cuts.

Pushing the limits—The blade does not achieve maximum cutting width at table height. But adding an auxiliary table that's about 2 in. thick greatly increases the cutting width (photo top right). Rockwell claims a crosscutting capacity of 2½ in. deep by 4 in. wide, but by raising the table 2 in., you can cut a board 2½ in. by 5 in. wide; or with a thicker table, 1½ in. by 6 in. wide. But if you have only a few wide cuts to make, you can bury the saw in the work and then lift the front edge of the board up into the saw until the cut is complete. Or you can cut to full depth from one side of the board and then flip the board over, eyeball the kerf straight across, and finish the cut from the other edge.

If you're working on edge, there are two advantages to be gained by putting a spacer between your work and the fence. If you come out about 3 in. from the fence, you can fit a wider board under the saw when the saw is in its uppermost position. The very deepest cuts can be made with the stock positioned so that the arbor washer just clears the inside of the work (middle photo at right). The spacer must be a uniform thickness so it will be precisely parallel to the fence, and high enough to support the work on its back side.

Using the miter saw to work on the edge of a board, you can cut fairly intricate shapes. Say you've got to fit a piece of 1x4 to the base of a round lighting fixture, and your client, eager to help with the job, has just broken your last saber-saw blade. To make the cut on the miter saw, space the work away from the fence so the blade cuts horizontally at the deepest part of the cut. Then make repeat cuts just shy of the line on the face of the work (bottom photo at right). After removing most of the stock, you can sculpt the wood by using one hand to raise and lower the saw while the other hand slides the work back and forth along the auxiliary fence. Working this way, it's best to remove only about 1/16 in. of wood at a time.

One year, I did so many latticework jobs

The saw's width of cut can be increased by shimming the work up from the top surface of the table. This means wide trim can be cut in one motion, without having to be flipped over to finish the cut from the other side.

The saw's depth-of-cut capacity for working with thick pieces and framing members can be increased by spacing the work out from the saw's fence. The spacer should be sized to position the work so that the arbor washer just clears its back edge. The spacer should be a uniform thickness for an accurate cut.

Notching the edge of a board on a power miter saw can be done by making a number of downward cuts to a scribed line. The cut is cleaned up by raking off small amounts of wood with the blade.

that I wrote charts of lath-lengths on the top of one of my miter-saw work tables. It's easy to stack six or seven lengths of lath on top of each other and cut them all at once, and so I could just sit at the saw and make "kits" while somebody else nailed them off. It's a good idea to cut the very short pieces from longer pieces so you don't have to hold the wood too close to the saw.

Safety—For me, the thorniest safety issue concerning power miter saws is whether or not to use the blade guard. All the saws come from the factory with a blade guard that in some manner shields the blade. But in order to make accurate cuts, you must have a clear view of the blade at the moment it enters the wood. Unfortunately, most of the blade guards get in the way. On my Rockwell, the original guard was made of yellow translucent plastic. When it was new, it was very hard to see through, and after a few months of use, it was so dinged up that I took it off, and eventually threw it away. Rockwell's new guards are transparent, but even so, the visibility diminishes rapidly as you use the saw because fine sawdust clings to the plastic.

Even after shortening my finger on a saw without a guard, I still prefer working without one. Had I been using the blade guard at the time, it would not have interceded on my finger's behalf.

The blade guard is still on my Makita, but I keep a piece of wire handy to tie it back. One has to make one's own peace with guards. They probably have prevented some accidents, and perhaps caused as many by obscuring the blade. I don't like them, and I suspect that the things I do in order to see around them are at least as dangerous as working without them. But I wouldn't recommend removing a guard to a novice.

When the saw is cutting at 45°, it has a tendency to pull the work into the blade. If the blade is dull, the pull is even stronger. If you're cutting short pieces, and have to hold the work in the acute angle the blade makes with the fence, get out the vise if your saw has one. If it doesn't, find a way to clamp the work to the table or fence. □

Geoff Alexander is a carpenter and woodworker in Berkeley, Calif.

Jigsaws

There are more blades than ever, and the tools are getting more powerful

by Craig Savage

My first jigsaw was a beautiful chrome beast made by Sears, and I got it when I was 13 years old. I guess my father decided I couldn't do too much damage to myself or the house with it. I used it to cut circular holes in some cabinet doors so I could mount speakers in them. The weight of the speakers soon ruined the hinges on the doors, but it was my first jigsaw project.

Now that I'm a contractor who relies on tools to make a living, I have lots of saws. I have two sizes of worm-drive circular saws, a 10-in. table saw, a bandsaw, innumerable handsaws, a chainsaw, a large reciprocating saw and a jigsaw. I need each one for different operations, but I use the jigsaw for the greatest variety of functions.

The hand-held jigsaw does few jobs really well. It doesn't cut curves as well as a bandsaw, or make cuts as true and as fast as a table saw. So why would anybody want one? The answer is that it can make an adequate cut through just about any material you're likely to find on a job site. This includes wood, metals, plastics, cardboard, rubber, linoleum, slate, silicones, epoxies, clay, stone and laminates.

I use my jigsaw to make back-beveled rips and notches in siding, and bird's mouths and decorative cuts in rafter tails. I use it to cut bolts,

file metal and slice foam insulation. I also use the jigsaw to make cutouts for sinks, vents, electrical outlets and plumbing fixtures. The jigsaw finishes blind cuts made with the circular saw, and does the rough-out work on complicated scribe fits. It rarely makes the finished cuts, but as a finish carpenter I can't work without one.

Some of the new jigsaws are so powerful that in certain instances carpenters prefer them to circular saws because they are more maneuverable. One builder I know uses his Porter-Cable #7648 along with a 4-in., 6-tooth blade to make all his rough cuts for concrete forms.

The basic jigsaw—A jigsaw is a small reciprocating saw that is known variously as a scrollsaw, a bayonet saw, hand jig or just plain jigsaw. The saw's cutting action comes from a motor-driven shaft that moves up and down, usually perpendicular to the plane of the material that's

A versatile tool. **A jigsaw's narrow blade allows it to cut quick and accurate circles in plywood or composition board, especially when you use a circle-cutting attachment (photo top). This Bosch jigsaw has a baseplate that can be tilted from side to side, allowing the saw to make bevel cuts.**

being cut. Typically, the shaft passes through self-lubricating bronze bushings. The best bushings, however, are made of powdered steel with oil forced into it. The blade attaches to the end of the shaft and protrudes through a base that slides over the work. Jigsaws used to have a ¾-in. throw, but in the new generation of saws it has been increased to 1 in. This makes for faster cutting and increased blade life.

On most jigsaws, the rear edge of the blade is backed by a bearing guide, which helps to keep the blade from twisting and bowing when you're cutting tight curves. The new Porter-Cable jigsaw #7648 has three guide bearings, one on each side of the blade, as well as one behind. These do an excellent job of stabilizing the blade (top photo, facing page).

There are two kinds of jigsaw switches: fixed speed and variable speed. If you are buying your saw for a specific production or assembly-line job, a single or two-speed saw is what you need. Single-speed saws run at full speed, developing maximum power with optimum cooling. Their switches are simple and reliable.

Single-speed switches can be a trigger, paddle or sliding button. These switches operate on AC current, and they are either on or off. The trigger is the most common and probably the safest of the three. It's hard (but not impossible) to turn on the saw by accident when you pick it up. This is possible with a saw with a paddle switch unless a safety is built into it. The sliding-button switch can be dangerous if you need to stop the saw quickly.

Trigger-controlled variable speed—As you look for more applications for your jigsaw, you'll want to consider variable speed. This feature gives you more control for all kinds of cuts. It lets you cut slowly into brittle ceramic tile, or quickly through a 2x4.

Jigsaws are powered by universal motors. These small, powerful, high-speed motors can operate on either AC or DC current. Variable-speed switches regulate the amount of current delivered to the motor, thereby controlling its speed. Motor speeds can range from 0 to 3,200 rpm—some saws start at 0 rpm, others start at 300 or 500 rpm. The trigger-type variable-speed switch makes use of a silicon-controlled rectifier (SCR), which works as a diode to deliver DC current to the universal motor. More DC current is applied with increased trigger pressure. This gives more power to the tool, and its speed increases.

At about 70% top speed, a bypass switch is closed and AC current is applied. The motor jumps to full speed. The speed setting is determined by the trigger position only. This means that loading the tool will decrease its speed unless the trigger is depressed further. This is called non-feedback speed control.

The newest saws feature electronic speed controls with feedback. These saws use microelectronics to sense the speed changes and maintain blade speed at all loads. Full torque is delivered at all speeds.

Some trigger switches have a screw that limits the power delivered to the motor, which governs the speed of the blade. I don't like these switches because they limit your ability to control the saw based on the sound it makes under load. Another configuration controls the speed with a separate dial, usually numbered, that is preset before you pull the trigger. Changing speeds while running this type of saw is difficult, if not impossible. However, once you know your material and pick a speed, this feature is handy.

Double insulation—This is now the U. L. standard, and it means that an electric tool has to have a primary and a secondary layer of protective insulation between you and the parts carrying electric current. Also, it must not have a ground wire, and the primary and secondary handles must be electrically non-conductive. The U. L. standard recognizes that people are tempted to break off that third prong that makes the grounding connection, or to use an adaptor without adequate grounding.

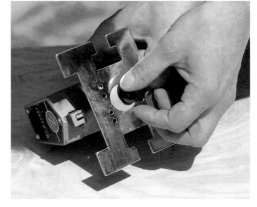

The Porter-Cable #7648 barrel-grip jigsaw (top left) has three guide bearings to stabilize the blade. When the saw is in orbital mode, the bearing in the middle moves in and out along the back edge of the blade. This action moves the blade into the work on the cutting stroke, and away from it on the down stroke. The saw's fixed baseplate is very stable but doesn't allow bevel cutting. The baseplate on Milwaukee's #6287 (middle and bottom left) can be secured in three positions, allowing it to cut close to walls while maintaining a wide, stable base. The head of the saw tilts at 45°, which lets it make angled cuts while the tool remains upright.

Orbital action—Many saws on the market today have a four-stage orbital action. You select your setting by moving a lever from 0 to 3. When you're on 0, the blade moves straight up and down. This mode is best suited to cutting thick metal, ceramic tile or very hard wood.

Setting number 1 designates the smallest orbit. As the blade moves up and down, the guide nudges the blade back and forth—toward the work on the up stroke, away from it on the down stroke. This helps in several ways. The blade can cool when it's not in contact with the work, and the chips can clear the kerf. This setting is good for tight scroll cutting and cutting hardboard.

Number 2, the medium orbit, works well on plastics because instead of blade friction melting the material, chips are ejected without heat build-up. Light metals can be cut without lubrication.

Setting number 3 has the most aggressive orbital action. I find that if I put more pressure on the toe of the saw, the saw seems to self-feed. Bounce and chatter are eliminated, plunge cuts are easier and scroll cuts are faster.

The only bad thing I can say about orbital action is that it adds moving parts to the simple action of the jigsaw. On the plus side, the orbital action reduces blade wear, turns in a very sharp radius, and it cuts in a hurry.

Baseplates—Jigsaws have two common baseplate styles. One is the narrow, thin-gauge metal base with a rolled-up edge. The other is a thicker, wider square-edged plate. You can't have both. Narrow baseplates are more maneuverable, and they usually tilt 45° in both directions, allowing you to make beveled cuts. The thick, square-edged plate comes on saws that don't have the tilting feature, but it provides a more solid contact with the work, which translates into more accurate cuts.

There is one saw that is an exception to this rule, and it is my personal favorite. The Milwaukee model #6287 has a heavy-duty, asymmetrical baseplate that can be positioned to suit particular kinds of cuts (middle photo), and the entire head of the tool tilts to allow 45° cuts (bottom photo). Unfortunately, at a $312 list price this tool couldn't compete with lower-priced models, so it has recently been discontinued. Those who want one might still find them in stock, but not for long.

Some baseplates accept anti-splintering inserts. These plastic devices fill in the gap in the baseplate around the blade, leaving a narrow slot for the blade to do its work. The insert acts as a chipbreaker, holding down the wood and reducing splintering along the cut line.

Blades—There used to be one type of blade called a universal blade. It fit all the jigsaws. Then Rockwell (now Porter-Cable) introduced its Bayonet hook, which was supposed to hold the blade better, make blade changes easier and sell more Rockwell blades. Then Bosch came out with its version of a bayonet lock. It works marvelously, and it helps sell Bosch blades.

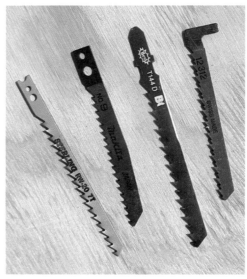

Both of the newer blades claim to be stronger than the universal type (top photo at right). They have more metal at the blade's shank, which should mean greater durability, and my experience bears this out. Universal blades break more frequently than the Bosch or Rockwell blades when I'm doing bevel or plunge cuts, because these cuts place a great deal of strain on the blade's shank. Since universal blades have holes in their shanks, they can snap under the strain.

Blade variety and availability are important considerations when you're deciding what saw to buy. The universal blades come in a myriad of styles, some of which cannot be found in the other configurations. For instance, there is a universal blade that allows you to cut flush up to a wall; it's shown in the bottom photo at right. Porter-Cable and Bosch both offer a wide variety of blades, but finding them can be tough unless you live near a well-stocked supplier. Hardware stores will have universal blades, but probably will not carry Bosch or Porter-Cable blades.

Most blades are made of high-speed steel, but some are bimetal blades constructed with a hard cutting steel welded to a softer, shock-absorbing, flex alloy. These blades last longer.

The material you are cutting and speed at which you cut it determine which blade to use. Woodworkers have the largest selection of blades. For instance, Black & Decker makes a 5-tooth-per-inch, skip-tooth blade that sails through rough cuts in plywood. At the opposite end of the spectrum are the blades with 36 teeth per inch. These blades make slow, smooth cuts in hard or brittle materials like metal, cultured marble, fiberglass and extremely hard woods. There are also blades with carbide teeth that are meant to cut through nails in old work, narrow blades with a very thin

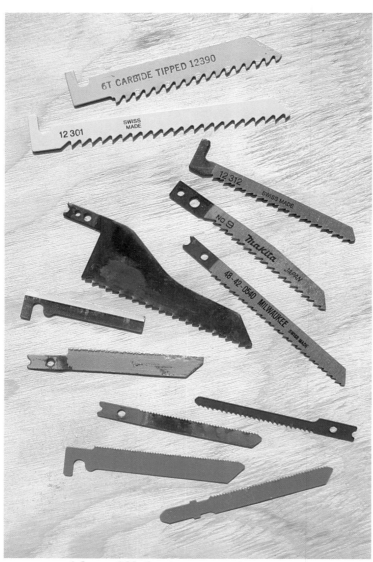

A bevy of blades. Styles range from big carbide teeth for cutting in nail-embedded wood to knife edges for cleaving soft stuff (above). The big blade in the middle allows you to cut flush to a wall because its extra width brings it in line with the toe of the baseplate. From left to right in the top photo, the universal jigsaw blade and a Makita blade. These are both affixed to their shafts with a locking pin and a setscrew. Next is a Bosch blade and one for a Porter-Cable jigsaw. These two are locked to their reciprocating shafts by means of the bayonet tabs at the top of the blades.

profile for tight scroll cutting, and extra-long blades for deeper cuts.

Like other sawblades, jigsaw blades have set, which makes the saw cut, or kerf, wider than the thickness of the blade so that the blade may move freely, remove chips and avoid overheating. Set is achieved by alternately bending the teeth, or by hollow-grinding behind the cutting edge to improve blade clearance. Another style is the "wavy set." It's a gentle, sine-wave curve in the blade, and it makes for an efficient cut, with noticeably longer blade life. Many fine-toothed metal-cutting blades have wavy set.

Although most blades are designed to cut wood or metal, there are specialty blades for other materials. If you need to work tile, slate or other ceramic or masonry materials, you can use a blade coated with Carborundum. Bosch makes three rasps—flat, round and triangular—that can shape edges smooth and clean hard-to-reach corners. Sawblades evolve into serrated knives when the teeth get very small. Knife blades can cut soft materials like leather, foam, paper, cloth or sponge rubber.

Cutting with the jigsaw—Using a jigsaw is no mystery. Finding the right combination of cutting speed and blade type is a trial-and-error process. As a rule of thumb, the larger the saw tooth, the faster you will cut the material. If you've got an orbital saw, follow the general guidelines already mentioned for the settings.

Hold the base down hard against the work, start the cut slowly, and feel the blade doing its work. It will cut smoothest and straightest with steady, moderate pressure.

Unless you use a down-cut blade, you are going to have some splintering on the upstroke of the cut. You can overcome this problem by first scoring the line of cut with a sharp knife or by pressing tape over the cut and marking on that. As an alternative, you can clamp two finish faces together and cut through both at the same time. Hollow-ground blades with no set in their teeth splinter wood less. I have even used wavy-set metal blades to get splinter-free cuts in hardwood.

Plunge cuts—Plunge cutting is a handy way to start cuts in the center of a panel. Start by tilting the saw forward and resting the front of the base on the work, as shown in the photo on the facing page. With the saw angled this way, turn the blade on but don't let it touch the work. Now very slowly, and with a good two-hand grip on the saw, begin to pivot the saw downward so that the blade just touches the work. The blade will start a slot that angles its way into the material, and eventually through it. When it pene-

Jigsaw race contestants

Brand name	Model no.	Speed	Stroke	Orbit	Switch	Amp	Blade type	Blade mount	Base type	Suggested price
Black & Decker	3159-10	2100, 3100	1 in.	4 settings	2-speed paddle	4.5	Universal	Allen-head setscrew	0°-45° stamped metal	$183.00
Bosch	1581 VS	500-3100	1 in.	4 settings	Electronic trigger	4.33	Bosch	Slotted setscrew	0°-45° stamped metal	$225.00
Makita	4301 BV	0-3100	1 in.	4 settings	Electronic trigger	3.5	Makita & universal	Allen-head setscrew	0°-45° stamped metal	$208.00
Milwaukee	6255	0-3100	1 in.	0	Trigger	3.8	Universal	Slotted setscrew	0°-45° stamped metal	$199.00
Porter-Cable	7648	500-3200	1 in.	4 settings	Electronic trigger	4.8	Porter-Cable	Allen-head setscrew	Fixed flat base	$199.50
Ryobi	JSE 60	1000-2700	1 in.	4 settings	Electronic trigger	3.5	Universal	Phillips setscrew	0°-45° stamped metal	$198.00

trates the wood, set the saw on its baseplate and begin to cut.

Plunge cutting is tricky until you get used to it. Make sure the work is secure and can't vibrate. Make the plunge in a slow, steady motion. Orbital action makes it easier. The blade has to be straight, and a short stiff one is better than a long one for this cut. If you are working on a finished surface, cushion the tips of the base with tape or a piece of scrap to keep it from marring the surface.

Bevel cuts come in handy when you are scribing wood trim. I make a bevel cut at 3° off perpendicular, keeping the blade to the outside of my scribe line. This gives me a thin edge of material to remove to get the perfect fit. The maximum bevel you can make with a jigsaw is 45°. At 45°, 30% of the depth of the cut is lost, which means that it is impractical to bevel-cut stock over 1 in. thick. Also the blade tends to wander off the straight line when bevel cutting. Wide bases and good blade guides help bevel cuts stay straight.

Accessories—Jigsaw companies make a variety of accessories that make the tools more versatile. While ripping is not really the best use of the jigsaw, most manufacturers do offer a rip guide. A typical rip guide usually consists of a steel guide rod and an adjustable fence that's at 90° to the rod. The rod slides into the base and is held with a setscrew. The fence follows along the edge of the board, cutting a constant distance from the edge. As an alternative you can

Sometimes you need to start a cut in the middle of the workpiece. Here the author demonstrates a plunge cut using the Bosch 1581 VS jigsaw. This cut begins with the tool tilted forward on the toe of the baseplate, with the blade above the work. With both hands on the saw and the blade at speed, Savage slowly pivots the saw downward so that the blade engages the work, as shown in the photo. The blade will cut an angled slot through the work until it penetrates fully and the baseplate presses flat against the work surface.

clamp a straightedge to the workpiece to guide the base of the saw.

A circle-cutting guide can come in handy if you need to cut round holes in panels (photo p. 64). It has a trammel point or pin, attached to one end of the guide rod. The pin is driven into the center point of the circle to be cut. The other end attaches to the base of the saw. Starting in a hole drilled on the circumference, the jigsaw travels along a circular path.

For cutting metal efficiently, Bosch offers an automatic blade lubricator that allows you to operate on orbital action without metal buildup on your blades. Bosch also makes a special foot that replaces the base to follow the curves on corrugated metals.

Several companies sell tables that accept jigsaws. With their bases securely fastened under the table, the hand jigsaw turns into a lightweight stationary jigsaw. These tables provide support for delicate scrollwork or precise filing.

Some saws blow air on the blade to clear the dust and help you to see the cut line. This is an advantage unless you want lubricant to stay on the cut line. Then you might want to switch off the air to the blade.

Two companies—Black & Decker and Sears—make a jigsaw with a scrolling head. These two saws allow you to turn the blade without turning the saw body. Carpenters frequently find themselves cutting out countertops or floor vents, usually next to a wall. The scrolling head allows them to cut right up to the wall, turn the scrolling head, and then continue with the body of the saw traveling sideways to the cut.

Cordless saws—Black & Decker has just come out with a cordless jigsaw that is really a wonderful tool. It accepts their standard battery pack, which charges in a separate DC converter from the wall or car lighter. To go up on a roof and cut shingles, to crawl under a floor and trim some stubborn floor joist without having to drag a cord along, or to scroll away without getting wound up in a cord is just heaven. The flat, sturdy base of this tool has the distances from the blade edge to the base edge engraved in it. This allows quick setup to a straightedge. Finally, it has a blade-storage space in the saw body.

The North Idaho jigsaw time trials—Cutting speed is important if you use your jigsaw a lot. When carpenters first used the Bosch 1581 VS orbital jigsaw, they were amazed. The saw, which appears to have set the standard for the current generation of jigsaws (1-in. stroke, 0 to 3 orbital settings, directed air stream) seemed to sail across a 2x4. That was before the other manufacturers hit the market with their own versions of professional-grade jigsaws.

I decided to test several saws in the most subjective test I could devise. This was a test of crude speed—the six-second dash. The six contestants were the Bosch 1581 VS, the Porter-Cable 7648, the Makita 4301 BV, the Black & Decker 3159-10, the Ryobi JSE 60 and the Milwaukee 6255. I put each one of these tools into the hands of an experienced carpenter and got out my stopwatch. That's my kind of science.

Our racetrack was a sheet of ¾-in. plywood, and I wanted to see how far each saw would go in a straight line in six seconds. The saws were all set at high speed and each had a new, six-tooth "saw set" blade. All the saws tested except the Milwaukee 6255 have orbital action. If the saw had orbital action, it was set at full.

Our results showed that while some saws were definitely faster than others, speed alone wasn't a significant enough factor to influence a carpenter's choice of a favorite saw. Our opinions follow.

Black & Decker 3159-10. This saw (photo third from top) surprised the whole crew. Its 4.5-amp motor had plenty of power. It ran neck-and-neck with the Bosch and Porter-Cable. It cut straight and didn't wander. The paddle switch and barrel grip seemed to be a disadvantage in this speed-at-any-cost race. The barrel grip doesn't let you get leverage the way the overhead handle does. (You can't put both hands to advantageous use). But this goes both ways—the barrel-grip gives good control over accurate cuts, and the act of gripping puts you in position to look at the line. This saw has a

The rest of the contestants. Top to bottom: the Milwaukee 6255, the Makita 4301 BV, the Black & Decker 3159-10 and the Ryobi JSE 60.

sturdy flat baseplate, a decent blade-attachment system and it is lightweight and easy to grip.

Porter-Cable 7648. This was the tiger of the saws tested. Its 4.8-amp motor never had to come up for air. It has a large barrel (almost too large for small hands), and its three ball-bearing blade-guide system allowed the most amazingly tight radius cuts. (Radius cutting was a side event, considered only after we knew that we had enough blades for the primary race.) The air directed at the cut was more than adequate to remove chips, and the base is large and flat and allows easy view of the cut line.

This saw has an on-off button switch located slightly offset, at the position of the right thumb. This was a new way to turn on a tool and took some getting used to. Its speed control, on the rear of the barrel, must be set before cutting.

The Makita 4301 BV had a sturdy and well-balanced feel. Its motor is a 3.5-amp high-tech (electronic switching) type, and its orbital action seemed smooth and vibration free.

The Makita (photo second from top) was the fastest in the race, but you can be sure we were all surprised when it broke five blades in six runs. Makita's blades fit only their saws, so we changed to universal blades to see if that was the problem. It wasn't—we broke them too.

The Ryobi JSE 60 (bottom photo) ran last. Although its design and feel were first class, its 3.5-amp motor just didn't have the beef. Its Phillips-screw blade attachment wouldn't last long, and the blades supplied with the saw had little tangs on their ends, suggesting that universal blades, even though they fit, don't do the best job in the saw—it bogged down noticeably, and though its cut was straight it just couldn't compete.

Milwaukee tools have a place in my heart, so it is with sorrow that I must report on its mediocre performance in the race. The Milwaukee #6255 (top photo) has a 1-in. stroke, 3.8-amp motor and a sturdy base with a well-designed tilting mechanism. It feels stable and is easy to grip. But to be competitive in the speed test, I guess it needed orbital action. This tool vibrates less than most of the other tools, and has one of the sturdiest and easiest blade attachments of all.

Reactions to the race—After the race there is no doubt Bosch is the favorite jigsaw of the North Idaho carpenter. It lost to the Porter-Cable in our speed test, but only by an inch.

These saws were pushed, I mean really leaned on, and it's amazing that they all didn't break blades. The Bosch, Black & Decker and Porter-Cable saws all took the extreme stress in stride. But the Bosch made the straightest cuts and felt the smoothest. That fact sold the majority of the jigsaw drivers. On the other hand, one carpenter said, "Porter-Cable still has parts for tools that are older than I am. They will have parts for this jigsaw when my kid gets it." □

Craig Savage is a building contractor in Idaho.

Reciprocating Saws

These versatile cutting tools, fitted with the right blade, will take on jobs that other saws can't touch

by Craig Stead

A reciprocating saw is rather like a one-man band—certain melodies sound sweeter played by individual instruments, but it deserves applause just for getting through the score. Few tools are shared by as many trades as the reciprocating saw. It's the right hand of plumbers, electricians and sheet-metal workers as well as carpenters. In a remodeling business like mine, reciprocating saws are invaluable time-savers for salvaging door and window jambs, cutting new openings, removing studs, and sawing out holes for pipes, ducts or new lighting. I seldom have a job where demolition work isn't required, and there isn't any tool that can match the raw power and maneuverability of a reciprocating saw. When our crew of three is going full bore on tear-out, it's not unusual for us to have three of them in constant use.

This tool, which is often referred to as a Sawzall or Cut-Saw (brand names of two popular saws), is just a large linear jigsaw with the blade mounted in the nose. It is powered by what amounts to a ½-in. drill motor, averages 16 in. in length and weighs about 7 or 8 lb. To a large degree it has replaced the hacksaw, keyhole saw and handsaw in modern construction. The reciprocating saw has an amazing range because of its shape and the variety of blades available for it. With the blade out front, it can sneak into seemingly inaccessible places and cut almost any material.

The reciprocating saw does not do all cutting jobs well. Its long unsupported blade makes it difficult to get accurate, straight cuts, so a circular saw is often a better choice. A jigsaw is better for cutting curves because it has a larger shoe for its size, and you have a better view of the blade. But a jigsaw can't make a sink cutout flush with the backsplash. And a circular saw can't rough-cut big beams in a single pass. If you've got a lot of rebar to cut, borrow a cutter-bender or a torch, or use a circular saw with an abrasive wheel. But if you need to, you can get by with a reciprocating saw fitted with a metalcutting blade.

In 1975 I bought my first reciprocating saw, a Sawzall, when I started a full-time renovation business. Before, I was a part-time carpenter building my own house. A few months later I was running a crew of six. The Sawzall got such constant use that we picked up several. Now I have reciprocating saws made by Black and Decker, Milwaukee, Makita and Porter-Cable (formerly Rockwell).

Drawing the saw along a line puts more teeth in contact with the work, increasing the vibration. But it also allows the depth of cut to be easily and quickly changed with good control.

Buying a saw—You want a saw that is lightweight, fast cutting, well balanced, low in vibration, and durable. It should have a good view of the blade through the shoe. The saws I own combine most of these features, and all are basically good machines. There are some minor differences between them, and matching your needs to the strengths and weaknesses of the different saws will help you decide which to buy. As with any tool, it pays to try different brands if you can before buying.

Three companies (Milwaukee, Makita, Black and Decker) offer an adjustable shoe on their saws. By loosening one or more screws, the shoe can be moved up to an inch out from the saw body. This feature is convenient when you have dulled the teeth on one part of a blade and you want to use another part of the blade, where the teeth are still sharp. This need is common because the average blade stroke of a reciprocating saw, the amount the blade moves in and out, is 1 in. However, blades range from 3 in. to 12 in. in length. Depending on the thickness of material being cut, many of the teeth on a blade don't get any use. The Black and Decker saw with a single adjustment screw works most easily, and Makita runs a fair second. I don't use this feature on my Sawzall much because you have to pull the rubber nose boot off the Milwaukee saw to make the adjustment.

All the saws I own have two speeds, controlled by a separate switch on the handle. The higher speed is for cutting wood and the lower speed for cutting metal. You can get the Black and Decker and Milwaukee saws with an optional trigger-controlled, variable-speed drive. This helps if you do a lot of metalcutting because it lets you start your cut slowly before coming to cutting speed. But having variable speed seems to reduce the top cutting speed on the Black and Decker saw, which makes it slower in cutting wood. Variable-speed switches also have a reputation for burning out faster than two-speed switches.

Porter-Cable's Tiger Saw has an action that's orbital as well as reciprocal. Instead of just moving in and out in a linear way, the blade is pushed down on the work on the in-stroke (cutting stroke), and it pulls up slightly on the out-stroke. This elliptical orbit helps clear sawdust from the kerf and digs the teeth of the blade into the wood on the cutting stroke, making the tool more aggressive. This feature, along with a high-end cutting speed of 2,800 strokes per minute, makes it the fastest woodcutting reciprocating saw made. The price you pay for this speed is a heavier tool (8¾ lb.) with more vibration in use. When cutting metal you have to switch off the orbital action on the body of the saw, which leaves you with a straight reciprocating motion.

Although this saw is aggressive, a real advantage in the demolition phases of my renovation business, it vibrates a lot, and has a shoe that limits your view of the blade and makes accurate cutting difficult. The Tiger Saw also has a reputation among people at rental yards and repair shops for wearing out its front-end bearings because of the stresses placed on them by the orbital action.

Milwaukee is justly famous for its durable power tools, and the Sawzall has been the standard in the industry for many years. It is the slowest of all the saws for cutting wood, with a ¾-in. stroke and a top speed of 2,400 strokes per minute, but is a good compromise for many tasks where speed isn't the only requirement. The shoe design provides a very

From *Fine Homebuilding* magazine (August 1983) 16:45-49

Woodcutting blades

Metalcutting blades

Scrollcutting blades

good view of the blade as it cuts, important if you do a lot of precision cutting or scrollwork.

Makita makes a lightweight, low-vibration saw that's reasonably priced. It's particularly nice for overhead work because it weighs just 6.4 lb. The stroke on the Makita is the longest of any of my saws (1³⁄₁₆ in.), but unfortunately the shoe obscures a full view of the blade. I have heard that this design flaw is to be corrected in new models.

My overall favorite is the Black and Decker two-speed Cut-Saw. It's fast cutting because of its 1-in. blade stroke, it doesn't vibrate much in use, and it has an easily adjustable shoe that gives a clear view of the line of cut. This same saw is sold by Sears. It's listed in their industrial line of tools as the Craftsman reciprocating saw.

List price on reciprocating saws runs from $144 to $180, with the Porter-Cable at the upper end, the Black and Decker mid-range, and the Makita the least expensive. All models are commonly available discounted, either through mail-order or lumberyard sales, and they can go for as low as $100 on sale.

I keep each of my saws in a case with the blades, spare allen wrench, and grounded plug adapter. Milwaukee's old case with the saw cradled above the blades was a great design. You could place your boxes of blades in the bottom of the case, and put the dullest blade at the top of the pile. Unfortunately, most of the new cases, including the one offered by Milwaukee, are like suitcases, with no partition between saw and blades. Every time you pick up the case, you end up with a blade stew in the bottom. Instead of buying one of these new cases, pick up an old, used mechanic's toolbox with a top tray to hold your blades. Just make sure the box is long and deep enough for your saw.

Milwaukee makes two accessories for their Sawzall. I haven't found the need for either, but I have friends who do. The first is a cut-off fixture to ensure square cuts through steel and plastic pipe up to 4½ in. o.d. It's a simple blade guide combined with a bicycle-chain grip that will also work on irregular shapes. The second accessory is an offset blade adapter that lets you flush-cut in close quarters without having to put a big bend in the blade.

Blades—A reciprocating saw is only as good as the selection and quality of blades you carry. But deciding which blades to buy can be bewildering. Milwaukee alone lists more than 70 different blades. Most people find a few types that they like, and then try to make these fit every situation.

To make sure you are buying the blades that will be useful to your kind of work, you need to ask yourself a few questions. First,

A versatile assortment of blades. The five blades at the top of the photo are primarily for cutting wood, and range from 3 in. to 12 in. in length, with 3 to 10 teeth per inch. The three metalcutting blades at bottom right have more teeth. The three narrow blades at bottom left are for scrollcutting in wood (7 teeth), composition material (10 teeth) and metal (24 teeth).

what general shape of blade do you need for your cutting task? How long, how wide and how thick does the blade need to be? Cutting a curve calls for a narrow, short blade like a jigsaw blade. If you have thick stock or need to be cutting at a distance, then use a long blade. A straight cut requires a wider blade, which will wander less in the kerf.

Once you have decided on the shape of the blade, then figure out how many teeth you need per inch. This is called tooth pitch. The fewer the teeth per inch, the more rapid and coarse the cut, and the faster the sawdust and chips are cleared from the kerf. The greater the number of teeth, the slower and smoother the cut. Blades are available with as few as 3 and as many as 32 teeth per inch.

What material you are cutting and how smooth the cut needs to be should determine the tooth count of the blade you choose. Soft woods such as pine need a coarse-pitch blade (3 to 7 teeth per inch) because the material is easily penetrated, and will give up a large chip. If you try cutting pine with a fine-pitch blade, the teeth clog and stop cutting. When this happens the blade overheats, and the teeth can lose their temper.

Hard materials, on the other hand, produce smaller chips, so a finer pitch is better. Composition materials like plastic laminate, tempered hardboard and particleboard are best handled with an intermediate number of teeth. I use the coarsest possible blade, so I can cut fast without chipping out the surface material where I want it to look good.

One question frequently asked is whether the blades are interchangeable among different brands of saws. For all of the saws I own, the answer is yes. However, not all blades are the same quality, and this affects the cut and the blade life you can expect. Inexpensive blades are stamped out of coil stock and heat treated. The teeth are formed by the stamping die and the burr left from the stamping process. Better-quality blades have milled or ground teeth—processes that give sharper teeth and more uniform tooth configuration. I prefer milled or ground blades because they cut faster, smoother and hold a line better with less pressure on the blade. You can generally tell these blades by the newly ground metal surfaces of the teeth and gullets.

In my toolbox, I carry ten types of blade, which seem to cover just about all the cutting problems I typically encounter in the remodeling trade. I carry five to ten blades of each type. Most of the blades I buy that aren't bimetal are Milwaukee's because I like their quality and long life.

My basic rough-in blades are 6 in. and 12 in. long with 7 teeth per inch, and work on nail-embedded wood. In nail-free wood, a useful blade is the 6-in. or 12-in. 3-teeth-per-inch blade. These really make sawdust.

Cutting curves in wood calls for scroller blades. I carry 7, 10 and 14-teeth-per-inch blades. With them, I can cut at different speeds and produce finished edges in fiberglass, Formica, and particleboard.

For cutting metal, you need a hacksaw-type

Bimetal blades

Bimetal reciprocating sawblades are relatively new, having been on the market only about five years. Before their introduction, spring steel—the material used to make handsaws—was used exclusively for woodcutting blades. Spring steel cuts wood well, but isn't hard enough to cut any more than the occasional embedded nail.

The other alternative was M2 tool steel, a tungsten-molybdenum alloy commonly called high-speed steel (hss), which is used to make the cutters for metalworking tools. M2 steel can be heat-treated to a high hardness, which makes the teeth last longer when cutting metal. As a result, high-speed steel blades have hard, durable cutting edges. But they are very brittle. They will break when bent, and even shatter when subjected to the shock loading that occurs when a blade is bumped when it's in motion.

A bimetal blade is a marriage of the best qualities of both types. Using space-age technology called electron-beam welding, a thin strip of tool steel is welded to a flexible spring-steel back. The tool-steel strip is ¹⁄₁₆ in. to ⅛ in. wide, and forms the cutting teeth of the blade. After heat treating, the cutting edge is very hard, but the body of the blade is still flexible and tough.

The first bimetal blades I used were Fit-Al, made by Rule Industries (Cape Ann Industrial Park, Gloucester, Mass. 01930). Bimetal blades are now being made by most of the major saw manufacturers as well, and are not hard to find in any of the general types or tooth counts available in conventional blades. They are, however, more expensive. Bimetal blades designed for cutting metal cost about twice as much as regular metalcutting blades. Woodcutting bimetal blades cost about three times their spring-steel equivalents. Depending on the blade and the circumstances, I find that they last anywhere from two to ten times longer than conventional blades.

A couple of my friends—one a builder, the other a tool dealer—had recommended Lenox Hackmaster blades, made by American Saw and Manufacturing Co. (301 Chestnut St., East Longmeadow, Mass. 01028). I found they were manufactured only a few hours from where I live, and visited the plant at the invitation of Marty Kane, Manager of Technical Services, to see first-hand what makes a bimetal reciprocating sawblade different from conventional blades.

American Saw has been making bimetal bandsaw blades since 1960, when the technology became available. While remodeling the company offices, a local contractor broke one metalcutting blade after another on his reciprocating saw while trying to cut away a long run of conduit. Realizing the problem, the machinists in the tool room fabricated a reciprocating sawblade out of bimetal bandsaw-blade stock and gave it to the contractor to try. The blade finished the job, but the contractor had to be told, "No one makes them," when he asked where he could get some more. That changed four months

later, when American Saw introduced the first line of bimetal reciprocating sawblades.

Bill Downing, Technical Services Representative for American Saw, told me that they use an M2 matrix tool steel for their blade edge. This steel is also used for general-purpose lathe tools, milling cutters, taps, dies and reamers. He gave me a bench demonstration of what bimetal blades can do in practice. First, he drove a hardened masonry nail into the end of a 2x4, and then cut off the last inch of the board using a typical spring-steel 6-teeth-per-inch blade. When the blade got to the nail, it stalled and the teeth burned off. Downing then repeated the test using an equivalent bimetal blade. It easily cut through the nail. Some teeth were dulled, but the blade was still usable.

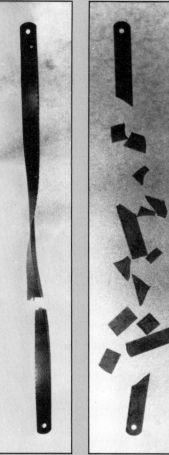

I repeated this test in my shop using a 16d common, a softer nail and one you're more likely to encounter with a reciprocating saw. I was able to cut through the nail with both blades. The teeth on the bimetal blade stayed sharp, while the teeth on the spring-steel blade were rounded over in spots. It required more force on the saw to cut wood as quickly after that.

Next I tried cutting just the exposed shanks of a series of nails driven into a 2x4, still using the two 6-teeth-per-inch woodcutting blades. The teeth on the spring-steel blade were completely worn away after 11 nails. The bimetal blade managed 21 nails. The blade was still cutting, though a number of the teeth had been sheared off by the shock of hitting the nail shanks.

The second of Downing's demonstrations showed the difference in flexibility between blades made from spring steel, high-speed steel and bimetal. Downing took hacksaw blades of all three types and inserted them one at a time into a fixture that would twist the blade until it broke. The spring-steel blade twisted a full revolution and broke in half. The high-speed steel blade made only a one-third revolution before it shattered into 15 pieces. The bimetal blade behaved the same as the spring-steel blade, making a full revolution before snapping.

The third demonstration involved using a reciprocating saw and bumping the end of a metalcutting blade against a steel plate. In this test, the high-speed steel blade broke into three pieces. The bimetal blade was badly bent, but was easily straightened on the flat surface of an anvil with a hammer. —C.S.

Bench tests. Some of the differences between bimetal and conventional reciprocating saw-blades are demonstrated in bench tests that sim-ulate job-site situations. In the first test, spring steel (photo, top) is matched against bimetal on a masonry nail driven into a 2x4. The middle photo shows the results of a test for flexibility with hacksaw blades made of spring steel (left), high-speed steel (center) and bimetal (right) that were twisted in a fixture until they broke. The last test (photo, bottom) demonstrated the effects of bumping the end of reciprocating saw-blades into a steel plate. The high-speed steel blade shattered, but the bimetal blade only bent and was straightened for further use.

Photos this page: Craig Stead

blade. The rule here is always to have three saw teeth in contact with the metal. Thus, thin tubing and sheet metal require a high tooth-count blade, up to 32 teeth-per-inch. Bolts and rebar, which are thicker, are best cut with a coarser blade. I carry 18 and 24-teeth-per-inch blades in the 6-in. length, and a 32-teeth-per-inch scroller blade for cutting circles in panel boxes and ductwork. The conventional metal-cutting blades of hardened high-speed steel are notoriously brittle, and can shatter if they are pinched or bent. You've got to use them carefully.

In the past few years, bimetal blades have become available. They cut metal easily and yet are flexible, giving them a much longer life. I used to break one or two metalcutting blades a day cutting nail-embedded wood until I stumbled onto my first bimetal blade, which lasted me four months until the teeth wore out. Many companies now distribute them under their private label, so you need to check for the word *bimetal* on the blade.

Installing the blade in a reciprocating saw is a straightforward proposition. The blade is attached to the reciprocating shaft using the clamping action provided by a hex-head cap screw. A conventional allen wrench is used for tightening. All the saws except the Black and Decker have a cross pin that goes through a hole in the blade tang. You should be sure that the blade clamp is free of chips when you insert the blade, and be careful to get the cross pin through the tang hole.

The Black and Decker Cut-Saw relies solely on the compression of the blade clamp to hold the blade. This system has several advantages. First, when you are doing precise scroll cutting, you can flip the blade over so the teeth are in full view; you will find that this is a great aid to staying exactly on the pencil line. You will also find it easier to blow the sawdust away from the line as you are cutting. When the blade jams in a cut, it will often pull out of the saw instead of breaking at the tang or bending. If the blade does break, the third advantage is that you can rework a broken blade on a grinding wheel by taking ⅛ in. off the tooth side of the blade butt, creating a new tang.

It pays to carry a spare cap screw for the blade clamp in case one gets lost or worn. You'll also need an allen wrench to turn the screw. For about $4 you can get one that is extra long, and bent to form a T-handle. It's much harder to lose this key, and you get plenty of torque with just a turn of your wrist. The end of your allen wrench will wear with time and the facets will get rounded, allowing it to spin in the socket. Don't throw it away; just grind it down to an unworn portion of the shank, and it will work like new.

Straight rough cutting with a reciprocating saw is an easy skill to develop, but knowing when to use the tool, what blade to use on it, and how to perform delicate tasks with it calls for some experience. In the photo at left, a pocket cut alongside the rafters and through the drywall is made using a short stiff blade with only a few teeth per inch.

Reciprocating saws are ideal for work in tight places, a constant problem in renovation. To reduce vibration when breaking into old plumbing runs (left), keep the shoe held tightly to the work. When cutting through stud walls (right), make a full-depth circular-saw cut first.

Cutting—Reciprocating saws are are made for a two-handed grip—one hand in the D-handle that houses the trigger, and the other either supporting the nose of the saw from below for control, or bearing down on the nose for faster cutting. It's important to stay loose using any tool. Your grip should be firm but light, letting the saw do the work. If you are cutting stock that hasn't yet been installed, make sure that it's clamped down securely to reduce vibration. This is most important in starting a cut, since you will need both hands to establish a kerf without bouncing the blade all over the work. To begin, press the shoe of the saw against the material and lower the blade. You will be using the teeth farthest back on the blade, which will give you the least vibration and the most control.

How much pressure to apply while cutting is a matter of experience. Too much or too little pressure will produce needless vibration, which increases friction and dulls blades. The blades will also break much sooner, usually at the tang. For faster cutting, rock the saw gently. This action keeps the blade's cutting area smaller, making each tooth in contact with the work penetrate deeper and rake a larger chip.

To make blades last longer, it's common practice to back the saw away from the material once a kerf is established so you can also use the teeth nearer the front of the blade. I usually do this when the increased vibration isn't a problem, but I'm careful not to extend too far or the blade will leave the kerf on the retraction stroke and bend or break when it hits the material on its next forward stroke.

One rule for straight cutting is to match your blade to your material, and make sure that the blade isn't bent and that the teeth are uniformly sharp. Teeth designed for cutting wood are set alternately to either side of the cutting line of the blade. Blades that have been used to cut nail-embedded lumber can develop teeth that are dulled on only one side of the blade, which will cause it to drift to the sharp side when it's cutting. If you get into a cut and you find that the blade is wandering, you may be able to compensate by twisting or angling the saw. You will find that soaping the blade will reduce friction and smoking as you try this maneuver. When cutting metal, use a light oil for lubrication.

In many situations, you should use your circular saw to establish a straight kerf, and finish up with your reciprocating saw. Cutting a window opening into an existing stud wall is a good example. I snap a horizontal chalkline across the exposed studs, and square this mark across each stud face on one side or the other. Using the chalkline for a reference, I cut each stud to the maximum depth (about 2½ in.) using a circular saw with a nail-cutting blade. Then I use my reciprocating saw with a thin woodcutting blade to finish the job.

Holes for large waste pipes, heat-duct floor registers and foundation vents are places where you'll need to make a pocket cut, or plunge cut. Begin by resting the saw on the shoe and blade tip, and then let the point of the blade dig a hole through the wood. This method works best in pine and plywood less than 1-in. thick. Make sure that you are using a short, stiff blade with sharp teeth at the free end. I've found that a variable-speed saw makes it easier to plunge-cut, but a two-speed saw will do. Milwaukee, Black and Decker and Porter-Cable all make a plunge-cutting blade that has teeth on both edges.

For pocket cuts in thicker material, such as cutting register openings through several thicknesses of floor, it's easier to drill holes at the corners. Use a circular saw for the straight runs and then finish off with a reciprocating saw to prevent overcutting your marks.

Safety—Safety glasses or goggles should be worn for overhead work or when using conventional metalcutting blades, which could shatter in use. If you're cutting through siding, floors and interior walls, check before you cut to determine whether any electrical wires are in the blade path. Since this is sometimes impossible, get into the habit of holding the saw only by the plastic nose covering and handle, not by the metal shoe or saw body.

When cutting timbers, in-place studs, pipe or tubing, it is common for the blade to bind in the saw kerf and bend. The immediate impulse is to grab the blade with your bare fingers and straighten it out. You really don't want to do this. It's easy when fighting a kerf to turn blades blue from the heat of the increased friction (about 600°F) and that can mean a nasty second-degree burn. Let the blade cool a few seconds, and then slip on a glove to protect your fingers from getting cut on the teeth or from a blade that snaps when you're straightening it. Use a hammer and a convenient hard surface to take the bend out of a bimetal blade.

Maintenance—Once a year, I do preventive maintenance on all my power tools in the interval between Christmas and New Year's, when I'm typically not working. On my reciprocating saws, I check the brushes for wear. If they're at all short, I replace both of them. I also remove the gear head, clean out the old grease, and repack it two-thirds full of lubricant. To guard against dust, I blow out my power tools once a month with compressed air. This makes the tool run cooler and reduces brush and commutator wear. If I'm cutting a lot of plaster with the saw, then I blow it out daily. □

Craig Stead renovates houses in Putney, Vt.

Log floor systems like the one shown below demand smooth, accurate cuts of 40 ft. or more—a job that many portable mills can't handle. The chainsaw mill shown above is a portable, carriage-and-track system designed to provide capacity and accuracy that are comparable to most commercial sawmills.

Chainsaw Mill

A log builder's track-and-carriage design handles big logs

by Harold Sandstrom and Marg Shand

Here in British Columbia, a plentiful supply of tall, straight spruce, fir and cedar has fostered a long tradition of log work. With such fine stands of timber on or near most building sites, it's no surprise that builders often have chosen to use what's at hand rather than pay for lumber milling and transport.

In the old days, logs were hewn with a broad-ax and trimmed or shaped with an adze. When the chainsaw arrived on the scene, it was naturally used by log builders, at first for freehand cutting. In the 1950s, chainsaw mills became commercially available, and they significantly broadened the scope of on-site lumbermaking. Some builders have a favorite commercial mill, while others have built their own, coming up with a number of interesting designs. The one shown here is the creation of Duncan Morris, of Traditional Log Homes in Salmon Arm, B. C. His

design is actually a variation on the mill that log builder Ed Campbell, of Blind Bay, B. C., built just over 10 years ago.

The early chainsaw mills relied on a saw guide that had to be fastened to the log with spikes or lag screws. After each cut, you had to remove the guide and set up again for the next pass. This system, which is still in use today, is fine for small-scale production. But for log and timber frame builders, it's too time-consuming to remove and realign the guide repeatedly. Accuracy can also be compromised if irregularities in the log surface translate into the guide.

Morris' mill operates independently of the log, so the irregularities of individual timbers have no effect on the precision of the cut. The carriage-and-track system (photo above) enables you to adjust the kerf easily and exactly, keeping it level throughout the length of the cut. Safety, speed

From *Fine Homebuilding* magazine (August 1987) 41:49-5

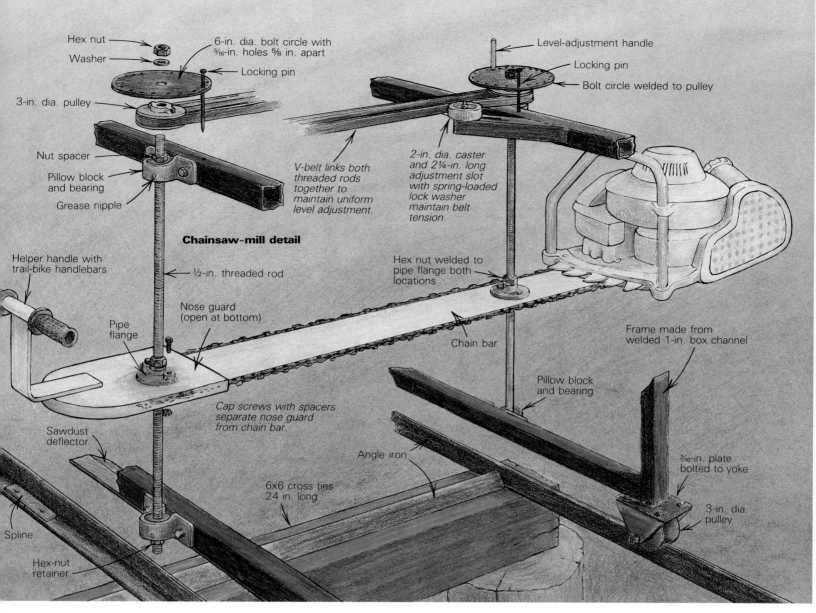

Hex nut

Washer

6-in. dia. bolt circle with ⁵⁄₁₆-in. holes ⅝ in. apart

Locking pin

3-in. dia. pulley

Nut spacer

Pillow block and bearing

Grease nipple

Chainsaw-mill detail

Helper handle with trail-bike handlebars

½-in. threaded rod

Pipe flange

Nose guard (open at bottom)

Sawdust deflector

Spline

Hex-nut retainer

Level-adjustment handle

Locking pin

Bolt circle welded to pulley

2-in. dia. caster and 2¼-in. long adjustment slot with spring-loaded lock washer maintain belt tension.

V-belt links both threaded rods together to maintain uniform level adjustment.

Hex nut welded to pipe flange both locations

Chain bar

Cap screws with spacers separate nose guard from chain bar.

Frame made from welded 1-in. box channel

Pillow block and bearing

Angle iron

6x6 cross ties 24 in. long

³⁄₁₆-in. plate bolted to yoke

3-in. dia. pulley

and unlimited length of cut are added benefits. Log floor systems, like the one shown in the bottom photo on p. 74, often demand straight, true cuts at least 40 ft. long. Morris' mill makes this a routine job.

In addition to conventional milling, Morris can use his rig to make the odd-angled cuts that are frequently required for ridgepoles, log-stair treads and cap logs (photo p. 75, right).

Carriage—The Morris mill has three main parts: carriage, track and saw. The carriage is the moving part, with four wheels that ride on a twin track of angle iron.

The carriage frame (see p. 75, left photo), is a cubic skeleton made of nominal 1-in. square box channel (outside dimensions of the channel are 1¼ in.). At the corners, the channel is welded and reinforced with welded steel gussets. The carriage is 20 in. high and 21½ in. wide. This "throat width" will accommodate a 19-in. dia. log. This is the largest size Morris anticipated having to mill; carriage size can be increased or decreased to suit your needs.

Double-flanged, 3-in. dia. steel pulley wheels are mounted at the bottom corners of the carriage. Aluminum yokes, salvaged from industrial cart casters, carry the axles. The yokes are bolted to square steel feet welded to the carriage corners. Standard steel washers, ganged together along each axle, act like crude thrust bearings on either side of each pulley.

The mounting and adjustment system for the chainsaw bar allows for quick, accurate leveling and a precise kerf (drawing, previous page). Two ½-in. dia. threaded rods run through holes drilled in the chainsaw bar. The rods are mounted vertically, seated in pillow blocks and bearings that are attached to the carriage. Hex nuts welded to pipe flanges bolted to the bar and nose guard allow the threaded rod to rotate and lift or lower the bar.

In order to raise and lower the chainsaw bar evenly, the threaded rods have to rotate synchronously. They are linked to each other by a V-belt-and-pulley assembly that's located on top of the carriage. Belt tension is maintained by an adjustable caster wheel that runs in a short piece of box channel on one side of the carriage.

To lock the bar height, you insert a pin through the steel bolt circle on top of each pulley and into a hole in the carriage frame. Without this locking feature, the vibration of the chainsaw would cause the threaded rod to rotate randomly, drifting the chain off its level cut-line. A steel handle, fastened to the bolt circle closest to the chainsaw motor, allows the opera-

tor to adjust the height of the cut once the locking pins are pulled.

When the mill isn't in use, Morris uses rubber tie-downs to compensate for the extra weight of the engine on one end of the bar. The tie-downs are simply wrapped around the upper part of the frame to relieve the bar of the engine's weight.

Sawdust deflector skirts are a final feature of the carriage. These metal strips are welded to the bottom frame member on the nose-end side of the carriage to prevent sawdust buildup in the pulley wheels. This helps to keep the carriage riding smoothly on its track.

Angle-iron track—Portable track sections give the system the capability of sawing almost any length log. The angle-iron track is supported by cross-ties and footings (see p. 75, left photo). The footings are log ends embedded 3 ft. in the ground, with their tops leveled. The height above ground can vary, but Morris prefers to show 2 ft. of log because this keeps the chainsaw handle at about waist level. This mill allows the operator to stand comfortably, without bending over —an advantage over some other models.

The footings are spaced about 4 ft. apart in pairs along the length of track. On-center spacing of each pair is about 21 in.—the same as the track gauge. Cross ties are 6x6s, 24 in. long, spiked across each pair of footings.

The track itself consists of twin rails made from heavy-gauge angle iron: 1½ by 1½ by ¼ in. thick. The track is kept parallel by gauge bars, welded at 4-ft. intervals to the inside face of each rail. These bars are made from the same angle iron, but it's turned on edge to allow clearance for the carriage wheels.

Morris makes up his track in 20-ft. sections, but the length can be changed depending on how you plan to transport the mill. Sections 8 ft. long are more convenient if you use a pickup rather than the flatbed truck that Morris uses.

The track sections are fastened to the cross ties with 4-in. lag bolts through holes drilled in the bottom web of the angle iron. Where track sections join, the butted rails are held in alignment with a splice of flat bar stock. The splice piece is welded to the top of the bottom web of one rail and overlaps the adjacent rail, where a lag bolt through both splice and rail secures the joint to the cross tie.

The chainsaw—Morris uses a Stihl chainsaw (model 090) with a 36-in. bar for this mill. Chainsaws are designed for crosscutting with the engine operating primarily in a vertical position. Ripping as you do with the mill, with the engine in a sideways position, calls for some important adjustments. You need a ripping chain rather than a crosscutting one. And you need to take into account the extra strain on the motor. Ripping demands more power than crosscutting, so you'll be operating at full throttle through most of the cut. A two-cycle fuel mix with slightly more oil than normal and a rich carburetor setting can prolong engine life. These and other tips can be found in Will Malloff's book, *Chainsaw Lumbermaking* (The Taunton Press, 1982).

Holes in the bar for the support rods should not be drilled until the carriage is fabricated and

the threaded adjustment rods have been fitted in the pillow blocks and bearings. Once the rods are in their fixed positions, it's safe to locate and drill the holes in the bar.

The nose guard mounted on the tip of the bar is a safety feature that also holds a hex nut and threaded rod for level adjustment. The guard is fastened to the bar with cap screws that extend through spacers to hold the guard away from the chain. The guard extends around the chain but not under it, so that sawdust can clear freely. The helper handle welded to the guard was made from flat stock, bent into an L and welded to a pipe crosspiece. The grips came from a trailbike handlebar.

Operation and payback—This chainsaw mill can be operated by one person, but for large-scale milling a team of two people works better. Offloading slabs and maneuvering logs often require two people. Besides giving a balanced push to the carriage, the helper can observe the kerf on his side of the log, warning of knots or disengaging log dogs that are too close to the approaching blade. The helper can also insert wedges into the kerf as the cut progresses, to keep the saw from binding.

The weight and size of the log determine the ways and means of getting it on the track. Morris frequently works with logs that weigh up to 1,800 lb., so he hoists these behemoths into place with a truck-mounted crane.

Once the log is on the track, it frequently needs to be leveled to compensate for slight bows or natural taper. Morris accomplishes this with one or more Volkswagen scissors jacks. Log blocks, positioned beneath the jacks, elevate them to a height where they can act on the log to be milled. When all the adjustments are made, the log is secured with log dogs. These pointed anchors, attached at one end to the track, are driven into the log to prevent movement during milling.

The cutting layout is marked on the end of the log. Then the carriage is rolled up to the face and the elevation of the chainsaw bar is adjusted by turning the level adjustment handle. The bar height is locked by inserting pins through the bolt circles into holes in the frame. When the cut is completed, the bar is lowered to make the next cut, and the carriage is simply pushed back in the opposite direction.

Morris had the carriage and 60 ft. of portable track fabricated at a local machine shop. He estimates that it would cost about $900 (Canadian) to have the mill made today. If you can salvage some of the steel angle iron or box channel and if you're handy with a welder, building the mill would cost considerably less.

One pass through a 40-ft. log takes a two-man crew between 15 and 20 minutes. The smoothness and accuracy of the mill mean that little time is wasted cleaning up the cut. Compared to cutting freehand and cleaning up your work with an adze or drawknife, the mill saves a great deal of time. According to Morris, his rig paid for itself in one season. □

Carriage, track and saw. **The drawing and the photos on page 75 show the mill's three principal parts. While the saw is idle (bottom left), rubber tie-downs, tensioned around the carriage frame, take some of the engine's weight off the chainsaw bar. Pulley wheels at the base of the carriage ride on a twin track of angle-iron rails that sit atop 6x6 cross-ties, spiked into embedded logs. Bar level is adjusted by a pair of vertical threaded rods on either side of the carriage. At bottom right, log stair treads and other odd-angled cuts are made with the aid of a jig to hold the log steady.**

Marg Shand is a freelance writer and photographer. Harold Sandstrom is a forester.

A Mill for the Chainsaw

With this easily made accessory, you can mill your own boards and beams

by Will Malloff

Editor's note: During the last five or six years, with the advent of commercially made chainsaw mills, growing numbers of owner-builders have discovered the advantages of harvesting their own trees and sawing them into boards and timbers. Will Malloff has been milling wood with chainsaws for 20 years. In his new book, Chainsaw Lumbermaking *(The Taunton Press, 63 South Main St., P.O. Box 355, Newtown, Conn. 06470, $23.95), he tells what he has*

learned about cutting-tooth geometry for ripping chain and about the various milling accessories he's developed to make the work easier and more efficient. His book begins with instruction on how to maintain and modify the saw and mill, continues with methods for lumbering in the field and ends with a chapter on specialty milling operations. Malloff uses a Stihl 090 saw engine with either a bearing-roller or bearing-sprocket bar end. But what

makes his system work is what Malloff calls the ultimate chain for lumbermaking, a refined version of the ripping chain he invented and patented in the early 1960s.

The following selection is a description of how to make and use one of his specialty mills. Malloff calls it a 2x4 mill because its working parts are all cut from ordinary 2x4 framing lumber; the mill can be used to produce both boards and beams.

An accurate and inexpensive mill can be built from a dressed 2x4, two feet of ½-in. threaded rod, four ½-in. flat washers, six ½-in. nuts, and a few scraps of 2x2s and plywood for spacers. Use several thicknesses of plywood, such as ¼ in., ⅜ in., ½ in., ⅝ in. and ¾ in., so you can set the cutting height accurately.

Drill two ½-in. holes in the bar of your chainsaw for mounting. Lock together two of the nuts on the bottom ends of the threaded rods. Then drill two ½-in. holes in the 2x4 guide rail, using the bar holes as a template. You can substitute a dressed 2x6 or a wider board for the 2x4 if you wish.

1. To mill a square timber with the 2x4 mill, first set up the end boards and guide plank. The end boards, pieces of 2-in. thick dressed lumber, hold the guide plank parallel to the pith of the log—make sure the top edges of both boards are the same distance from the pith. The guide plank I use is just a 10-ft. long dressed 2x12. Determine mill height by measuring from the top of the guide plank to where you want to make the first cut.

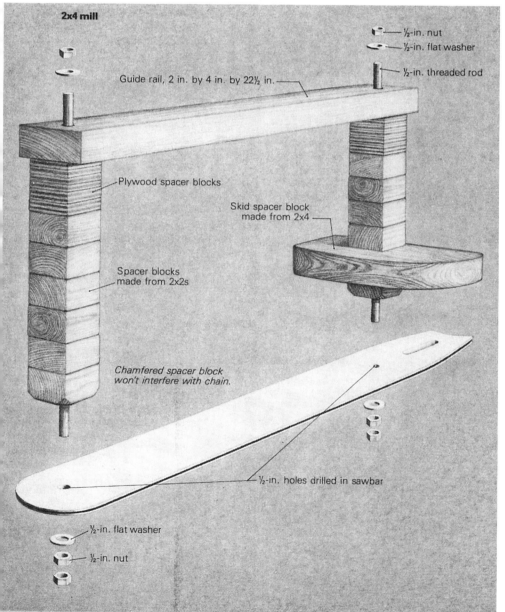

2x4 mill

Guide rail, 2 in. by 4 in. by 22½ in.

½-in. nut
½-in. flat washer
½-in. threaded rod

Plywood spacer blocks

Skid spacer block made from 2x4

Spacer blocks made from 2x2s

Chamfered spacer block won't interfere with chain.

½-in. holes drilled in sawbar

½-in. flat washer
½-in. nut

1

2. Assemble the mill with the necessary number of spacers, positioning the skid block below the bar with a regular block in between to keep the chain from pinching the skid. Stack surplus spacers above the guide rail of the mill and secure the assembly with a flat washer and nut. Double-check cutting height by measuring from the edge of an inside chain tooth to the bottom of the guide rail.

3. Mill through the first cut, pressing down firmly on the guide rail to keep it level on the plank. Drive in end dogs when the guide rail is just past the end board. The dogs tack board and log together so the board can't deform during the cut. Use kerf wedges as necessary to keep the top slab from sagging into the kerf and pinching the chain.

5

4. Reassemble the mill to adjust for the depth of your next cut, positioning the skid block above the bar with a regular spacer block in between so that the skid will ride against the log during milling. The blocks next to the bar should be chamfered on one side so they can't interfere with the chain.

5. For the second cut, lay the guide plank back on top of the slab. Because the 2x4 mill has only one guide rail, you need to use the plank with every cut to control the mill during exit and entry. Torque down the top nuts, double-check mill height and make the cut, using end dogs and kerf wedges. Then set the cant on edge and install the end boards as before.

6. Adjust the mill to the correct height and mill through the third cut, then the final cut.

Below, the completed timber. ☐

Power Tools and the Timber-Frame Revival

Changing from hand work to machine production in American timber-framing means going abroad for tools

by John Lively

Gang-cutting rafters is common practice in German and Swiss carpentry shops. In the photo above, two Swiss carpenters are using a 25-in. circular saw to make the plumb cuts for the ridge on a set of twelve rafters that have been clamped together on a pair of steel horses. To gang-cut the bird's mouths in a single pass (right), they use a circular saw that has been fitted with a special three-knife cutterhead. The saw is tilted at the angle needed to make the seat and heel cuts, and a fence tacked to the rafters guides the tool as it plows through the wood.

In the beginning, the revival of timber-frame carpentry in America was something of a religious movement, and was confined mostly to New England. This neglected and almost forgotten way of building, using large-dimension timbers and wood-to-wood joinery, was resurrected by a handful of craftsmen/scholars who respectfully studied surviving examples of 17th and 18th-century houses and barns. They rediscovered how these structures went together and learned anew how to size sills, posts and girts, and how to cut fat tenons and chop deep mortises in 10-in. square stock. And they learned how to assemble everything from common bents to ecclesiastical-looking hammer-beam trusses.

Along with this veneration of old wooden buildings came a reverence for the long-gone carpenters who put them up, and for their methods of hand craftsmanship. And so it was quite natural for this new generation of timber framers to find a special virtue in cutting joints, chamfering posts and carving lamb's tongues by hand, just like the old guys did. With the exception of electric augers, worm-drive skillsaws and thickness planers for dimensioning stock, there wasn't much place for power tools and standing shop machinery in those early days of the timber-frame revival, or for the kind of secular, production-paced pursuit of quantity and financial reward that machines could offer.

Being a timber framer in 1980 was as much a political statement as it was an occupation. It was standing up and quietly reasserting the practical and spiritual values of workmanship. It was, in a studied (if not romantic) defiance of bottom-line thinking, an effort to dignify labor and deliver to those few who could appreciate it a hand-wrought product.

These days things are a little different. In the first place, timber-frame houses are growing out of the ground all over the country, and there are small to medium-size building firms from Maine to Tennessee, Michigan to California, that specialize in building timber-frame and post-and-beam houses. Secondly, while timber-frame builders still stress their use of high-quality materials and strive for precision in joinery, most of them are careful to avoid coming off as hand-tool junkies who'd rather hone their way to the perfect edge and carry on a rapport with trees than build good houses and make a comfortable living at it.

So what began as a druidic mallet-and-chisel cult in the Northeast is becoming a nationwide business, as more and more home buyers become conscious of good quality in construction and find themselves won over by the traditional look and solid feel of timber-frame houses. As a result, many of yesterday's hand craftsmen are today's businessmen, who spend as much time negotiating prices on materials and land and dealing with their growing number of clients (and quizzical building inspectors) as they do in their shops cutting frames.

Along with all this, of course, has come the machinery that makes it possible for builders to crank out the frames for twenty houses or more a year, instead of the two or three they were laboriously producing only five years ago. Even those framers who choose to keep their output small and who still do a lot of hand tooling have benefited from the fast cleaning up of surfaces and roughing out of joints that machines can do.

Tooling up—In Western Europe, where the timber-framing tradition never died out and so never had to be born again, and where the guild system has remained intact for almost 1,000 years, the shift from hand work to machine production took place gradually over the last several hundred years. In fact, it's a common sight to see a wooden hand plane lying on a carpenter's bench next to an 11-in. wide power plane. When I visited West Germany and Switzerland last spring with a group of American timber framers, we were all pretty surprised to see the huge investments made in work spaces and machinery in the German and Swiss shops we toured. Much of the framing and finish work we saw being done there was accomplished with stationary shop machinery—hulking thickness planers, long straight-line ripsaws, swing-and-pivot crosscut saws, massive jointers and several species of molders, shapers and single-end tenoning machines capable of handling big timber.

But there's a whole range of carpentry operations there (and here) that can't be done with standing shop equipment, and there are other jobs that make more sense economically and logistically to be carried out with portable power tools. As a result, the Germans have pioneered the development of a breed of hand-held power tools that are specifically adapted to working on big timbers. It was these tools and how they were used in the typical German carpentry shop that we had gone all that way to see.

The trip was organized by Winter Panel Corp. (RR #5, Box 168B, Brattleboro, Vt. 05301) and by Mafell-Maschinenfabrik as a non-profit service for American timber framers (other trips are planned in the future). Mafell is a small German company that for over 50 years has produced a line of power carpentry tools that are used all over Western Europe, as well as in the Soviet Union. In the past few years, Mafell tools have been sold in this country by Mafell North America, Inc. (Box 363, Lockport, N. Y. 14049). But because many of their larger tools are powered by three-phase motors, these haven't been offered in the U. S. Though a few other companies (notably Makita and Hitachi) make tools for working timbers, the only ones they market in this country are their oversize circular saws. Mafell is the only company that specializes in portable tools for the timber-frame carpenter.

I was especially interested in what Mafell calls Product Group B (Carpentry Machines). Included in this group are four large circular saws, two portable chainsaw mortisers, a portable bandsaw, three wide portable power planes, a boring machine and a plunge-cutting chainsaw.

Circular saws—In German and Swiss shops, it's standard practice to clamp up all the identical rafters for a house on a big framing table and gang-cut the tails and the plumb cuts at the ridge with a large circular saw (top photo, facing page). The 25-in. three-phase saw shown here is the largest Mafell makes. It cuts to a depth of 9¼ in. and has an extra handle on the front of its formidable cast-iron base so a second worker can help by pulling the saw through the cut. You can buy this saw in the U. S., but its three-phase motor limits it to use in industrial zones.

In typical Swiss and German roofs, each rafter sits atop several purlins as well as on the wall plate, and thus it will have a number of bird's mouths. Instead of cutting these one at a time on individual rafters, they are gang-cut while they are all still clamped together. This is made possible by special cutterheads that fit on the arbors of two of Mafell's circular saws. For each size cutterhead there's a guard that screws onto the saw. Ranging in width from 1$\frac{9}{16}$ in. to 3⅞ in., these three-knife cutterheads will plow out a two-sided notch, forming the heel cut and level cut, when the saw is tilted to the proper angle.

The Swiss carpenters shown in the bottom photo on the facing page have tacked a fence across the group of rafters and are forming the bird's mouths for all of them in a single cut. These cutterheads won't fit on the single-phase saws Mafell sells in America. This is too bad, because the system of gang-cutting rafter stock—especially the bird's mouths—is just the kind of method that could be used effectively in ordinary platform-framing operations in the U. S., as well as in timber framing.

New Hampshire timber framer Tedd Benson owns a Mafell 14-in. circular saw (model MKS 125), which he says performs well cutting the compound angles on hip and valley rafters. Because the shoe of the saw tilts to 30°, it's more versatile for this kind of work than saws that stop at 45°. It cuts 4⅞ in. deep at 90° and 2 in. deep fully cranked over at 30°. Benson used to use a 12-in. Rockwell saw (model #542), which he had to special-order, but he finds the Mafell saw lighter and easier to control.

New Jersey timber framer Mitch Rowland, who was along on the tour, uses a 16-in. Makita, but thinks it's underpowered and too flimsy for regular sawing on the big stuff. He said once he was using the Makita and strayed off his cutline a bit, and when he redirected the pressure on the handle to get back on the mark, the guard distorted, was snagged by the blade and went slamming down, taking a little flesh with it. He's thinking about getting a 14-in. Mafell saw, but isn't comfortable spending the $800 it will cost.

Jeff Arvin at Riverbend Timber Framing, Inc., in Blissfield, Mich., has used a couple of 16-in. Makita saws for several years and says they're real workhorses. At half what the Mafell 14-in. saw costs, they are the tool of choice for some. His crew uses mostly 14-in. Mafell saws now because they have more power, especially for ripping. But the extra power can be a liability. Because the motors on these saws normally draw 18 amps, they're always throwing the 30-amp breakers in Riverbend's shop when they're laboring through tough cuts. Another drawback, says Arvin, is that you can't use long extension cords, and the limited mobility can make things awkward. The factory people say that using a heavy-gauge cord will solve this problem.

Mortising machines—Chainsaw mortisers have been used by cabinetmakers for several decades. Mounted above a compound-action

From *Fine Homebuilding* magazine (October 1986) 35:54-59

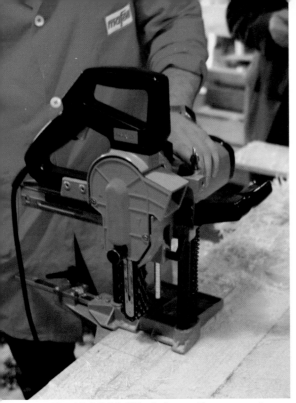

Mafell's 11-in. power plane (model ZH 280) can surface most beams and posts in a single pass, leaving a crisp surface that needs little sanding. Its two-knife cutterhead turns at 9,500 rpm; the disposable knives, sharpened on two sides, can be replaced at a cost of about $10. A light cut and slow feed are essential when cutting oak to avoid strain on the brushes and bearings.

The Mafell LS 101 chain mortiser can cut mortises up to 3⅛ in. wide, depending on the chain set installed, and 5⅞ in. deep. An adjustable fence gauges the tool off the side of the timber, and a stop rod controls the depth of cut. The tool rides on a pair of steel bars, and is plunged by hand into the cut. Designed for working in softwood timber, the machine gives less than accurate results when cutting oak, according to American timber framers. So they use the tool primarily to rough out mortises, and then pare the walls straight and clean with a chisel.

table just like a hollow-chisel mortiser, these cutters perform reliably (as long as you maintain proper tension on the chain) and cut quickly. Portable chainsaw mortisers, on the other hand, are fairly new on the American market, and since Makita no longer sells theirs in the U.S. (they were available during an early test market phase), Mafell's two models are the only ones available in this country. As shown in the photo above left, the tool is equipped with a fence and is plunged into the wood inside the mortise layout lines.

In pine, spruce and other softwoods—the only materials used for timber framing in Germany and Switzerland—the mortisers cut extremely fast, and the resulting rectangular hole in the stock is fairly precise and clean. But in America, timber framers more often than not use oak, which is harder on tools, mortisers in particular. Tedd Benson has used both the Makita and the small Mafell mortiser, and he doesn't like either one of them. He thinks they're adequate as roughing-out tools to be used like a boring machine to waste most of the wood in a mortise, which is then squared up and cleaned out with a sharp chisel. Benson, who used to cut all his mortises by hand, no longer objects to using power tools. He has in fact, along with machinist Rees Acheson, concocted a tool that uses parts from a milling machine to cut finished mortises with a spiral end mill designed for tooling aluminum. Benson's chief objection to mortising machines has been that you have to design

your joints around the size and capacity of the tool, but with his new invention, he can accurately cut mortises of any size, and so has the freedom of hand tools and the speed of machinery.

Mitch Rowland also uses the smaller Mafell mortiser for roughing out. He thinks the tool would be better if an automatic oiler for the bar were incorporated into the design. He points out that maintaining proper chain tension depends on consistent lubrication, so he sprays the bar periodically during use with WD-40. If the chain is too tight, it cuts an undersize mortise; if it's too loose, the hole it cuts is too big.

At Riverbend they use both Makita and Mafell mortisers, and Arvin says as far as performance goes, the two are about the same, though the Mafell mortiser is a little lighter, a small advantage in his opinion. The chief advantage of the Mafell mortiser is that you can buy one.

Power planes—One of the most useful of Mafell's carpentry tools, to American carpenters anyway, is their 11-in. power plane, shown in the photo above right. Its closest competitor is the 6-in. wide Makita, which isn't getting much use in shops that have adopted the wider Mafell tool. Almost all the builders I talked with about the model ZH 280 were skeptical about the tool's $1,800 price tag until they put it to work in their shops.

Using the 6-in. Makita, Benson told me, requires two passes to surface most beams and posts, but the Mafell plane will do the job in a single pass, and leave behind a crisp surface, without the little ridge or ledge that inevitably happens where the two surfaces meet when two passes have to be made. The two-knife cutterhead turns at a fast 9,500 rpm, which means that you get a high number of cuts per inch, unless you race down the beam. Knife marks, where they appear, can be sanded out quickly.

The plane's disposable knives are sharpened on two sides, so when one set of edges gets

dull, you remove the knives, flip them over and reinstall them. When the second side is dull you toss the blades and put in another pair, for about $10—close to what it costs to have a pair of knives reground. Setting the knives is a snap because they're a consistent width and can be registered against adjustable stops in the cutterhead. But the knives are very thin, and touching them up with a stone means removing them from the cutterhead. This annoys Benson, who'd like to be able to hone the edges periodically during use without having to take them out.

Arvin says that their Mafell planes are two of the most productive tools in their shop, and have cut their finishing time by two-thirds because so little sanding is needed. That's the good part. The bad part is that both of their machines have gone through a set of brushes and a set of bearings in less than six months on the job. The Mafell people say this can happen if the machine is forced through the work, or if the depth of the cut is too deep. To avoid excessive strain on the motor and bearings, a light cut and slow feed are in order. Arvin says replacing the brushes involves taking the machine apart, and replacing bearings on any tool isn't fun. But even with these mechanical difficulties, Arvin and his crew are happy with the wide Mafell planes because they're so easy to use and produce such good results.

Boring and slotting machines—German and Swiss timber framers see nothing wrong with using metal fasteners and joining plates. In some cases, local building codes specify metal connectors and prohibit wood-to-wood joints at certain junctures. This is particularly true for roof framing, as their tests have shown that metal plates and rods on the inside of the wood won't fail structurally in a fire as quickly as wood-only joinery or exposed metal connectors, which can weaken rapidly when exposed to intense heat. The wood beams actually pro-

In European timber frames, metal connectors often take the place of wood-to-wood joints. In the photo above, the faces of plumb cuts are being bored to receive steel rods that will hold the rafter pair together at the ridge. To cut the slots for steel connecting plates, Mafell makes a chainsaw rig that clamps onto the stock (right). Turning the handwheel plunges the nose of the bar into the cut. Fire codes in parts of Germany and other countries call for internalized hardware, which can hold up longer than exposed connecting plates and gussets. The wood itself insulates the metal from the intense heat, and keeps the building standing those extra minutes that can make the difference between escaping unscathed and being crushed by a falling roof.

tect the metal from the fire and keep the structure standing longer.

The Swiss carpenters shown in the photo above left are boring into the plumb cuts on rafters with a Mafell model K drilling machine. The base of the tool centers the bit and ensures that the axis of the bore is at 90° to the surface. Instead of being slot-mortised or lap-joined at the ridge, these rafters will be joined by large-diameter steel pins that will fit into these holes.

Mafell also makes a special plunge-cutting chainsaw (KSF 500) for mortising slots in timbers to receive metal connecting plates. This tool (photo above right) is essentially a chainsaw that's attached to tubular ways, which are clamped to the stock. The bar of the saw is held steady where it enters the wood by a little guide that rides in grooves on both sides of the bar. Turning the handwheel advances the nose of the saw into the wood and retracts it when depth of cut is reached. No sane person would attempt to drive the nose of a chainsaw into a piece of wood, but this tool makes the job safe, and very precise. Slots thicker than the chain are made by adding a metal disc to the bottom of the bar. It rides on the floor of the slot and guides the chain into the uncut wood above, and thus widens the existing mortise.

A portable bandsaw—Embellishing rafter tails, purlin ends and truss-web pendants is serious business in the Black Forest and Switzerland. To make the scrolled cuts, Mafell developed a portable bandsaw (photo bottom right), since the

To do the kind of decorative scrollwork on structural members that's characteristic of houses in Switzerland and the Black Forest, carpenters use portable bandsaws. The bandsaw shown at right will cut wood 12 in. thick. Reciprocating saws aren't very good for this kind of work since their depth of cut is limited and because they can wander off the perpendicular when sawing through thick stock.

timbers are much too large to be maneuvered on a bandsaw table. This tool cuts wood 12 in. thick. Since the blade is exposed on both sides, it can negotiate tight curves on either side of the stock. This double exposure could present a safety problem, so Mafell provides a guard that covers the down-tooth side of the blade, although they report that many fail to use it.

Other tools—While Makita and Mafell market portable power tools for the timber framer in the U. S., I saw several stationary tools in German carpentry shops that aren't commonly available here. One is a scaled-up version of the furniture-maker's single-end tenoning machine. This large machine is built for cutting tenons on beams, and consists mainly of a sliding table to hold the timber and a series of sawblades (top photo at left). The first blade trims the timber to length, a second pair, mounted horizontally, cuts the tenon's cheeks and a third pair cuts the shoulders. All the operator has to do is clamp the timber to the table, push it through the blades and unload it at the other end. The one shown here is made by the Schnieder Co. in Corbach, West Germany and is imported by Mafell North America.

In the U. S., it's common practice to cut tenon shoulders and cheeks just shy of the line with a skillsaw. This takes much more time because the cheeks are pared with a slick and the shoulders have to be trimmed with a framing chisel. A few East Coast shops have cobbled up radial-arm saw rigs to cut tenon cheeks in a single pull, and the shoulders in a couple of strokes. The framers in these shops are among the few in America who have ventured to do finish cuts with power machinery. But if tenoning machines were available here at affordable prices, there would be less time wasted cutting to the line with chisels and mallets.

In a couple of German carpentry shops, we saw combination jointer/planers (middle photo at left). Most of the really wide jointers, say 12 in.

This carpenter is using a router fixture to cut tread housings in a stair stringer. Instead of working off the template-and-guide-bushing setup used in the U. S., this fixture lets the router work like a milling machine. The router is clamped to a base that rides on steel rods, and its range of motion is limited by adjustable stops along the ways and side to side. The ways can be rotated to the desired angle once the frame of the tool is clamped to the stock.

or better, in shops around the U. S. are pretty old machines, bought at bargain prices from used-machinery dealers. You'll find antique Olivers, Yates Americans and Northfields in carpentry shops here, though occasionally you'll see a new machine from Taiwan or Japan. The German jointer/planer not only saves space, but it also makes logistical sense. You can joint two adjacent faces of all the stock you're going to run, flip up the jointer table and plane the other two. No need to walk the timbers to another machine. This machine is made by Kupfermuehle (Bad Hersfeld, West Germany), and is also imported by Mafell.

A shop we visited in Switzerland employs about 15 carpenters. They cut the frames for about 75 houses a year, and the owner says he could double that if he had the business. Aside from framing houses, they make all the windows, doors, stairways and trim for the homes they build. The windows are of the triple-glazed, cam-lock-and-gasket variety, every bit as good as what you'd buy from a quality manufacturer in Europe or the States. Two shop carpenters build all of these, using an automatic-feed shaper and pneumatically actuated clamps.

Nosing around his shop, I noticed in one corner a carpenter routing a stair stringer for tread housings. What intrigued me was the router fixture he was using. I've never seen anything like

it in this country. What the thing did was turn an ordinary router into a portable milling machine (photo above). Its main frame clamps to the stock, and it has a base (to which the router was affixed) that slides on a pair of steel rods. The rod assembly can be rotated to any angle, and a series of adjustable stops limits the travel of the router in two directions. The fixture is made by Scheer in Stuttgart, West Germany.

Coming home—As I walked out of this last shop we visited, past the large stacks of lumber stickered neatly in the bole, still slightly ablaze from the dram of schnapps I'd tossed down as a farewell to our host, I asked myself for the third or fourth time that week why these carpentry operations seemed so sensibly and solidly successful. Why were the tidy forests all around cultivated and harvested with such care and intelligence; why were the shops so spacious, light and airy, and fully equipped with new machines? Sitting on the bus, wondering about all these things, I turned to Dieter Pollmann, the man from Mafell who led our tour, and asked him how these guys came up with the money it took to capitalize ventures like this. In America, such a shop would cost millions, and would have to make millions in short order to stay afloat.

Pollman smiled and said such shops were expensive in Europe too, but that these people

were in it for the long haul, that businesses like these passed from father to son and that the builders there weren't driven by the kind of entrepreneurial get-in-and-get-out thinking that gives birth to so many small businesses in America. European shop owners put on their black corduroy overalls with the double zippers at the fly (the sartorial ensign of the carpenter's guild) and work alongside their journeymen and apprentices. They're more concerned with maintaining their way of life and work and with passing on a thriving enterprise to their children than with making big money and selling out.

Playing the game that way is a balancing act—embracing traditional values and long-range plans on the one hand, while competing in a kind of Darwinian economy on the other. Surviving means looking at the craft with a pragmatic eye, and buying those machines that save time and ensure accurate work. And it means making compromises here and there.

Even though American timber framers have tried to accomplish in less than a decade what the Europeans have had a hundred years to work out, they've not done so badly. In the end, as in the beginning, it will be their attitude toward their craft that will keep them in business, an attitude that puts tools at the service of materials and of design, and one that puts good work ahead of fast money. □

Framing Hammers

Longer handles, heavier heads and milled faces can make a surprising difference

by Paul Spring

Generations of beautiful homes have been built with the classic 16-oz. curved-claw hammer, and most carpenters have a beat-up favorite that they use for finish work. But with the advent of production framing in the early 1950s, a new kind of hammer appeared. Heavier than finish hammers and with handles that are 2 in. to 4½ in. longer, framing hammers have straight rip claws and faces that look like deeply etched checkerboards.

These long-handled nail drivers (they can be up to 17½ in. in overall length) are well designed for their task. Most framing these days is done flat on the deck or slab, and unlike the toenailed studs of a stick-nailed wall, almost everything is end-nailed or face-nailed. That calls for longer nails. This means many blows with a light hammer, but just a few whacks with a heavier hammer.

When you are framing a wall flat on the deck, you work bent over at the waist with your legs slightly flexed. Your hammer makes nearly a 180° arc before hitting the nail (photo left, p. 88). As a result, gravity does a lot of the work, so you can handle a hammer with more ounces of metal in the head and a longer handle for balance, leverage and reach.

Head weights and handles—Framing hammers are made with various head weights and handle materials. The usual weights are 20 oz., 22 oz., 24 oz., 28 oz. and 32 oz. The most common is 22 oz., although Vaughan makes a wood-handled 24-oz. model that has become very popular in the last few years. A heavy head has its advantages when it comes to coaxing the bottom plate of a wall onto its chalkline. Extra head weight also helps if you're trying to toenail the edge of a trimmer back into line with its neighboring king stud. But you can overdo it too. If your hammer is too heavy, it's doing you a disservice.

Save your heaviest hammer for framing walls and nailing off subfloors and roofs. Use something a bit lighter for toenailing. I used to use a Plumb 22-oz. hammer with a wood handle for rafters and joists, and then I dropped down to a 20-oz. smooth-face hammer for siding. Exterior trim and siding don't really call for a framing hammer, but I liked the grip on the long wood handle better and it gave me some extra extension when I was nailing out in thin air from a ladder or scaffolding.

What's important is comfort. If you don't drive nails all day long, stay with an all-

Framing hammers are used where a full swing can be taken, letting gravity do some of the work. A mill-face head delivers this force to the nail even when the blow is misdirected.

purpose 20-oz. or 22-oz. hammer. How you swing and how well you keep that form after driving a pound or two of nails is what counts. Few carpenters I know consistently swat in 16d nails with one blow. Two or three strokes is more typical, depending on how wet the wood is and how the nail is coated.

Handles are made of fiberglass, wood, tubular steel or solid steel. Fiberglass was championed by Plumb for years and has now been put to use by all of the other major manufacturers. Its advantages are that the handle and head are permanently joined, and that it is nearly impossible to break the handle. Solid-steel hammers have these same advantages, but opinions about them run strong. I've asked carpenter friends from all parts of the country about them and get one of two responses each time—they either love them or hate them. I hate them. Swinging a framing hammer all day long puts a considerable load on your wrist and elbow. This isn't the muscular fatigue that you feel in your forearm after returning from a few months' layoff from heavy nail driving. It is the shock that runs up your arm and is absorbed by your tendons and joints. A wood handle absorbs some of this shock and vibration, but a solid-steel shank, even with a rubber grip, feels like it sends every bit of that shock right up my arm. My elbow gets tender after just a morning with one. But the slender shank profile of these hammers (Estwing makes the most popular model) gives them wonderful balance. They are also almost indestructible.

I don't have the same vibration problem with tubular-steel handles (True Temper's Rocket and Stanley's Steelmaster are two brands in this category), but I've never found one that feels right. My choice is wood. Wood handles need a steel shim occasionally to cure a loose head, and you have to be careful about putting your body weight behind the handle when you're pulling a nail. But for me, the resilience of wood outweighs its disadvantages. You can feel the nails enter the wood every time you swing because you are holding the hammer itself and not a rubber sheath. Yet the sound and shock of each blow is softened and dispersed.

All of the major tool manufacturers make wooden-handled framing hammers, with Plumb and Vaughan being some of the best known. The first 20-oz. Vaughan hammer I owned vibrated at an audible pitch every time

From *Fine Homebuilding* magazine (October 1984) 23:32-35

it struck a nail. Although it's a little disconcerting to swing a tool that peals like a bell, it was an excellent hammer. I've compared notes with other guys who have had the same experience in the past, but tool-store managers just look blankly at me and mumble about improper tempering of the hammerhead.

Another long-handled hammer worth mentioning is the rigging ax or rig hatchet. This is also a tool that carpenters tend to feel strongly about one way or the other. To a large degree, it's a matter of image and fashion. In the 1960s, the rigging ax was one of a handful of well-balanced heavy hammers on the market. Once they became popular with West Coast piece-workers, they rapidly got an undeserved reputation as quick-and-dirty tools. It got to the point that if you showed up on a custom job with an ax, you were branded as someone whose skills were limited to framing and who wasn't interested in anything but speed. But I was taught to frame with one by a carpenter who appreciated production tools and techniques, and yet was uncompromising on quality. I continued to use a rigging ax throughout my career when I framed walls, and I did only custom work.

A rigging ax combines a typical hammerhead with a hatchet face instead of a claw. This distributes a lot of weight well back of the head for excellent balance. This is really the main advantage of the blade, and for safety's sake, the hatchet edge should be kept less than razor sharp. A notch in the bottom edge of the hatchet is designed for pulling nails, although it's not very good at this job. I've seen tract framers weld claws on their axes to try to get the best of both worlds.

The rigging ax I've seen used most often is a Plumb. It has a slender handle that is slightly contoured a little more than halfway down and is almost oval in section. You don't hold the ax right at the end, but up around the contouring. This sounds clumsy and amateurish, but held this way it has marvelous balance. Of all my framing hammers, my rigging ax delivers the most force for the least effort, although the Vaughan 24-oz. hammer seems to have a similar combination of power and balance.

Be selective about where you use a rigging ax. For instance, because of its broad profile, I found it clumsy for joisting and blocking. But it's perfect for unconfined framing, and for nailing off roofs and subfloors. It's also especially useful for applying 2x6 T&G decking on a cathedral ceiling. Here you use a 16d toenail down into the rafter on the leading (tongue)

A long-handled sampler
The popularity of different styles of framing hammers varies from region to region. Of the three hammers above, the 22-oz. Estwing, shown with a smooth face at the top of the page, seems to be the Eastern favorite. The Plumb rigging ax in the middle is still common among production framers on the West Coast, while the 24-oz. Vaughan, above, has gained wide acceptance throughout the country for its power and balance.

Illustration: Frances Ashforth

Framing walls on a deck (left) lets you use a 24-oz. or even a 28-oz. hammer because much of your swing is assisted by gravity. A rigging ax (above) has a similar weight, although it is distributed differently. If you work overhead a good deal (top), a 22-oz. hammer is often more comfortable to swing for a long period of time. In any case, the long handles (up to 17½ in.) of framing hammers are designed to be gripped higher than a typical finish hammer.

edge of each board to drive it tight. Doing this often mashes about 1 in. of the tongue. A couple of swings on either side of the damaged part of the tongue with the ax edge and it will fly off, with no damage showing below.

Mill face or smooth face—Most manufacturers of long-handled hammers offer a choice of a traditional smooth face or a checkered (or waffle) face. This milled grid forms squares of hardened steel that look like little truncated pyramids. These will dig into the softer steel of the nailhead and grip it, transferring the force of the blow even when the hammer doesn't hit the nail squarely. Even if only a few of these teeth make contact with a nail head, the nail will be driven straight. The mill face will sink the head of the nail slightly below the surface of the framing lumber, which is the way it should be. Don't worry about the hammer dings—you're not building a piano bench. In fact, the rough surface created by the waffle head is a great way to knock down the edge of a stud when you want to start a toenail on the corner of the angle.

A mill face is almost a necessity if you're driving cement-coated nails (sinkers). On a smooth face, the build-up of resin from these nails will lubricate the striking surface and can cause the hammer to glance off the nail heads. You'll feel like a dog with fleas as you try to scrub the black stuff off by dragging the hammer face back and forth across the plywood deck or slab.

Hammerheads are forged from tool-steel blanks; thus they are harder than the milder steel used for nails, prybars and other tools meant to be struck by a hammer. But with this hardness comes a degree of brittleness. The face of a good hammer is slightly convex, and the rim is beveled. These features help to prevent square edges from fracturing off upon impact and whizzing through the air at a dangerous velocity. But still, bits of steel can fly off.

Under no circumstances should you strike two hammerheads together. This isn't an idle safety precaution. A former partner of mine once had to take a fellow worker to the hospital with a piece of steel lodged in his chest. Instead of using a prybar, he had been driving the claw of a hammer between two boards by pounding on its head with a second hammer. I have also chipped hammer faces by using them to enlarge the hole in a concrete slab for a bathtub drain.

Try not to use your mill-face hammer when you strike harder steel tools like cold chisels, nail sets or cat's paws. This flattens the little surfaces and eventually turns the hammer into a smooth face. It also chews up the surface of the tools you strike, making them look like the victims of tiny meteor showers. If you find yourself carrying only a mill-face hammer, use the side of it (the *cheek*) to deliver an occasional blow. You can recover the mill pattern once it becomes worn by running a thin file in the grid or turning it over to a saw sharpener for a facelift. The result doesn't work as well as a new hammer, but it'll save your aging favorite from an early retirement.

Using a rip claw—The claw on a framing hammer has several uses; the most obvious is pulling nails. Although you'll seldom bend more than a few nails in a day if you're an experienced framer, when you do need to pull a nail it will likely be a 16d, and could very well be hot-dipped galvanized or a coated sinker. Both of these are tough to pull even with the leverage a long-handled hammer gives you. With smaller nails you can slip the claw under the nailhead and rock the hammer forward. But with big coated nails, that technique will produce a tug of war that is likely to have you staggering backward with the headless nail shank still firmly embedded in the wood. And if you are using a wooden-handled hammer, you also risk leaving the hammerhead back with the nail shank. I learned this lesson the hard way as an apprentice when I broke my framing hammer, bought with my first paycheck, on the day I got it. I also nearly went flying off the second-story subfloor.

The trick, I learned, is to ignore the head of the nail, and use the sharpness of the claw to grip the shank of the nail tight (you can keep the claw sharp by pulling nothing but nails with it, and even then you should avoid hardened concrete nails). Hold the hammer down as close to the surface of the wood as you can, and slide it along toward the nail in a quick, hard motion—this will literally trap the nail in the claw edges. Then lever the nail by pulling the hammer handle down on its side in a single motion. This will pull less than an inch of the nail, but can be repeated another time or two. Using the side edge of the hammer as a fulcrum, you've got plenty of leverage and you're less likely to break the handle.

In addition to pulling nails, the claw on a framing hammer ends up being used often as a combination peavey and crowbar. Although it sounds a little extreme at first, the safest, most efficient way of moving a heavy header or wall a few feet on a deck or slab is to bury your rip claw in the wood and pull the piece toward you. This will prevent the strained back and crushed fingers that can result if you try to pick the object up and move it.

The swing—Swinging a framing hammer is not much different from swinging a finish hammer, except that the stroke is designed for more power and is therefore exaggerated—a bigger backswing is coupled with a more forceful follow-through. Assuming that you are framing in a bent-over position, you begin by raising your arm with your elbow fully bent so that the hammer hovers around your ear. Then you should bring the hammer almost straight down—first by lowering your arm, and then by extending your elbow—in a slow, smooth motion. Your hammer should make contact with the nail about the same time that you begin to extend your wrist. If you are really swinging hard, you'll end up following through with your wrist and the body English that comes from straightening your knees somewhat.

The grip you use on the hammer handle is also important. First, it should be fairly loose; a white-knuckle grip will only wear your forearm out faster. Your thumb should be wrapped around the handle, not sitting up on top of it pointing to the head. You may have to break yourself of this habit at first, because there is a natural tendency to want to direct the hammer with your thumb. But your control should come from your forearm and wrist, which will also make your swing more fluid. It's also safer, since your thumb is the opposing lock that will make your grip effective, particularly when your hand is sweaty.

Where you grip is also important, and will surprise a lot of people. Most hammers are held near the bottom of the handle to get the best leverage when swinging. Choking up on the handle is one of the classic errors of novice carpenters. But heavy framing hammers are not always held out on the end. Because of their long handles, you can achieve the best compromise between power and balance when you frame bent over by gripping the handle just down from the midway point. Most wooden handles are contoured, and swell at this point. Grip the narrower part lower down if you need to generate a lot of power, and are not too concerned with accuracy—when you're driving a beam, for example, or making sure a king stud is tight to a header.

What your nail hand (the one that isn't clutching the hammer) is doing while all of this is going on is most important. How to feed the nails to the hammer is a matter of practice and your individual style, but coordinating when that hand should be in the line of fire and when it shouldn't is something you can't afford to get wrong. Big hammers with milled faces can literally tear away part of a finger, so be careful to keep your nail hand far away when you are swinging hard. If you find it necessary to get in the habit, put that hand behind your back except when you're actually starting a nail.

Buying a framing hammer—A new framing hammer or ax will cost you between $15 and $25. It pays to buy one of the major brands. Still, check to make sure that the hammerhead is mounted straight—it's surprising how often you will find one that's slightly cocked.

If you're looking for a used one at a flea market or secondhand shop, check that the head is secure, the inside edges of the claw are still sharp, and that the mill face isn't badly worn. In the case of a wood handle, it pays to buy new. Handles eventually break, and even if you spend a lot of time getting the replacement handle just right, it never seems to feel the same. Lightly sand the grip of a new wood handle from the halfway point down to the butt where you hold the hammer most. This will take off the finish and give you a better grip when you're sweaty and swinging hard. Some carpenters carry a paraffin block for rubbing down the handle to increase their grip. Wiping your hand across a pitch pocket on a stud will also give you that George Brett advantage. Even then, lots of framers wrap tape around the butt end of the handle as a stop for the heel of their hand. □

Powder-Actuated Tools

Fastening to concrete or steel without using a drill or a hammer

by Steve Larson

Neglecting to include all the foundation bolts during the insanity of a concrete pour is easy. Adding them later isn't. You can get a roto-hammer and a masonry bit, drill down several inches into the concrete, put in an expansion shield and finally bolt down a sill plate. But if you have to drill more than just a few holes, consider using a stud driver.

Stud gun, stud driver and Ramset (a trade name) are common terms for a type of tool known more formally as a powder-actuated fastening device. They are specialized nail guns, commonly powered by .22-caliber cartridges, that shoot a variety of nail-like fastening pins through wood and steel into concrete. Although it's not a tool that you are likely to carry around every day, if you can beg, borrow, buy or rent one when the need arises, you'll save yourself a lot of time.

Anchoring sill plates to concrete is the most common use for the powder-actuated tool in residential construction. The charge-driven pin is widely substituted for the occasional forgotten foundation bolt, and drive pins have even begun to gain acceptance as primary fasteners for some bearing walls (see the sidebar on p. 92). Stud guns are also commonly used to replace short sections of rotted sill during renovation work, to anchor non-bearing walls to a concrete slab, to attach furring strips to concrete walls, to anchor sleepers, to add plywood subflooring to a slab and to secure braces on concrete formwork.

In addition to nailing wood to concrete, special pins and brackets let you quickly hang a suspended ceiling or anchor electrical conduit. And at the fringe of residential work, steel plates, brackets and anchors can be fastened directly to either concrete or steel.

High and low-velocity tools—Although the operation of powder-actuated tools is simple, there are many brands and models (see the list on p. 94), and each one has special operating and safety procedures, which you must get to know. There are three basic types of powder-actuated tools: high velocity (HV, sometimes called standard velocity), medium velocity and low velocity (LV). But 95% of them are HV or LV.

A high-velocity tool (drawing facing page, left) works like a firearm. As the photos below show, a fastener called a drive pin is inserted into the barrel, then a charge (it looks like a .22-caliber blank) is loaded into the firing chamber. The muzzle of the tool is then placed against the work. By bearing down on the butt of the tool to release the safety, you can fire the charge by pulling the trigger. The resulting explosion in the chamber forces the pin out of the barrel, like a bullet.

A hood called a spall shield fits over the end of the barrel and protects you from flying bits of concrete or a deflected drive pin. The spall shield also holds the tool perpendicular to the work as it's fired. This is very important. A pin fired at an angle can ricochet with dire consequences.

Spall shields are absolutely necessary with HV tools, and manufacturers offer an assortment of specialized shields to allow perpendicular fastenings to irregular materials like corrugated metals and steel channels.

A low-velocity tool (drawing, facing page, right) uses a piston to drive the pin. The charge pushes the piston, which forces the pin out of the barrel at about 330 ft./second—much slower than the almost 500 ft./second of HV tools. The LV tool doesn't scatter bits of concrete at high speeds when it's fired, so it isn't always fitted with a spall shield. As a result, you can poke the barrel right into corners and other tight spots. Even so, I wear goggles when using either kind of stud gun.

Both high and low-velocity tools are commonly available at construction rental yards for a daily fee of about $12 to $20. The cost for pins, washers and charges varies radically—from about $.35 to $.90 for a complete load—so it can pay to shop around. These yards are required by OSHA to show you how to use the tool, and to have you read the operating manual and take a true-false test about the particular tool you are renting. Make sure you get this instruction. The best education would be on the job site, from a certified instructor.

For years, the standard has been the HV tool. Because it takes a stronger charge and will drive a larger pin farther into concrete or steel, it is sometimes the best choice. Concrete hardens with time, and low-velocity tools may not have enough punch to drive a large pin all the way into aged concrete.

Even so, the industry trend is clearly toward the LV tools because they are safer than

Loading sequence for Speed Fastener's high-velocity tool: A drive pin is inserted into the barrel (above) and then pushed into position with a rod made for this purpose (right). The powder load is put in the firing chamber (far right) before the hinged handle is closed.

Photos this page: Steve Larson; Illustrations: Frances Ashforth

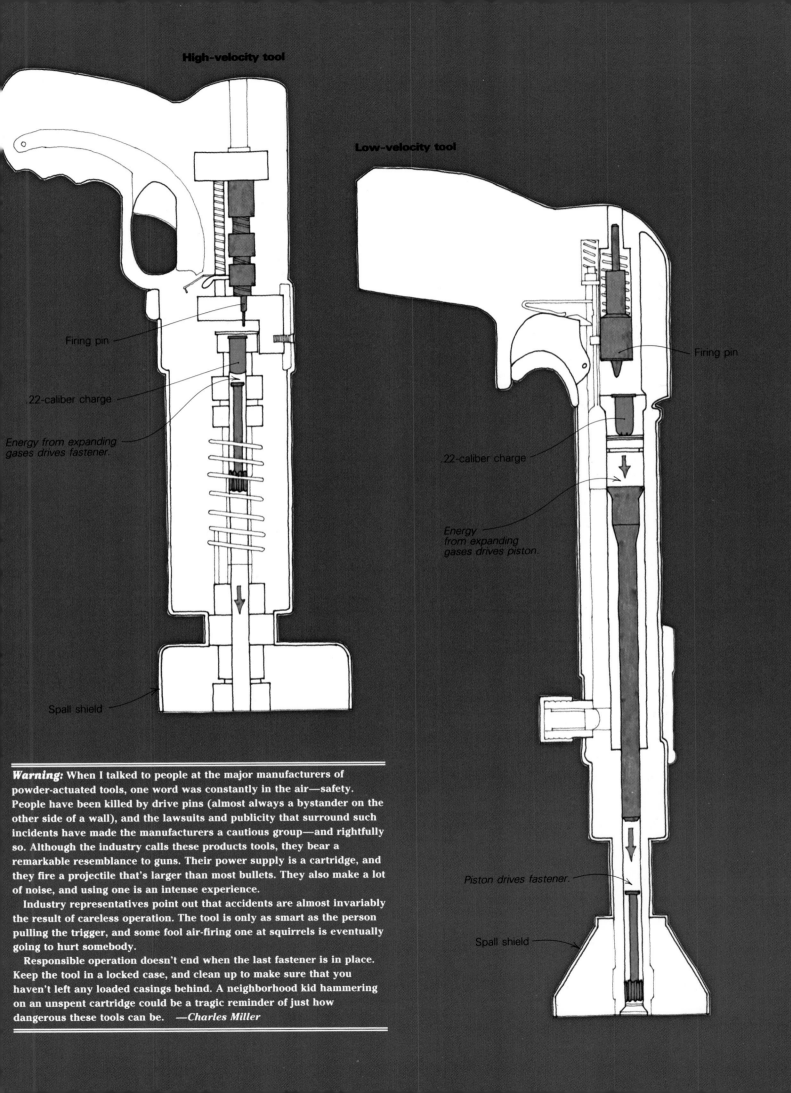

High-velocity tool

Low-velocity tool

Firing pin

Firing pin

.22-caliber charge

.22-caliber charge

Energy from expanding gases drives fastener.

Energy from expanding gases drives piston.

Piston drives fastener.

Spall shield

Spall shield

Warning: When I talked to people at the major manufacturers of powder-actuated tools, one word was constantly in the air—safety. People have been killed by drive pins (almost always a bystander on the other side of a wall), and the lawsuits and publicity that surround such incidents have made the manufacturers a cautious group—and rightfully so. Although the industry calls these products tools, they bear a remarkable resemblance to guns. Their power supply is a cartridge, and they fire a projectile that's larger than most bullets. They also make a lot of noise, and using one is an intense experience.

Industry representatives point out that accidents are almost invariably the result of careless operation. The tool is only as smart as the person pulling the trigger, and some fool air-firing one at squirrels is eventually going to hurt somebody.

Responsible operation doesn't end when the last fastener is in place. Keep the tool in a locked case, and clean up to make sure that you haven't left any loaded casings behind. A neighborhood kid hammering on an unspent cartridge could be a tragic reminder of just how dangerous these tools can be. —*Charles Miller*

Drive pins vs. foundation bolts

The powder-driven pins used for fastening wood sills to concrete look like common framing nails (photo facing page, bottom). The usual range is from 0.143 in. to 0.25 in. in diameter and from 2 in. to 3 in. in length. However, they are made from much harder steel than normal nails, so they can penetrate concrete and resist bending better than the nails in your tool apron. Even so, common sense suggests that a thick, deeply embedded bolt with a hook on its end will hold more tenaciously than a thin, straight, short pin. Research bears this out. For example, a common ³⁄₁₆-in. dia. drive pin embedded 1¼ in. in concrete has a withdrawal (tension) resistance of about one ton. A ½-in. wedge-bolt anchor embedded 2¼ in. has a resistance of over three tons; and a standard concrete-embedded ½-in. foundation bolt, over 10 tons. This tenfold advantage of foundation bolts over drive pins is the reason they have been preferred for anchoring load-bearing sills, and why they continue to be specified in areas with high winds or seismic activity.

Recently, however, the International Conference of Building Officials (5360 S. Workman Mill Rd., Whittier, Calif. 90601) approved the use of powder-driven pins for anchoring interior and exterior load-bearing walls and shear walls in some circumstances (see ICBO Report No. 1147, March 1982; and check with your building inspector for local acceptance). The researchers found that properly embedded pins driven through ¾-in. washers or 2-in. discs at intervals of 2 ft. to 3 ft. (depending on pin diameter and length, and penetration depth) produced lateral resistance equivalent to using ½-in. anchor bolts 6 ft. o. c. You might not want to hold down an entire house with drive pins, but you don't have to be bashful about using them when they are right for the job and you want to save some time. —S. L.

Attaching sill plates to foundations is a common use for the powder-actuated tool. Here a short section is fastened with a high-velocity driver. A C-clamp will keep the wood from splitting when a pin is driven this close to the end of a sill plate.

their high-velocity counterparts. Most of the serious accidents have happened when a drive pin from an HV tool somehow missed or passed through or was deflected by the base material and hit a bystander at high speed. But a pin leaving the muzzle of an LV tool loses velocity so quickly that such an accident is much less likely. Manufacturers estimate that 95% of the fastenings done with HV tools can now be done with the LV devices, and they say in the next few years the LVs will close that gap and take over completely.

Another advantage of the LV tool is the placement of the drive pin within the barrel of the gun before firing. In HV models, the pin is loaded from the firing chamber, and it has to travel all the way down the barrel. In LV tools, the pin sits at the very end of the barrel, and it is loaded from the front, or muzzle, of the tool. Because the pin doesn't travel down the entire barrel of the LV tool, washers or mounting clips can be attached directly to the pin. The HV tool requires that you center the barrel over the washer or clip, and I have missed more than one washer because the spall shield blocked my vision. Although special spall-shield adaptors are available to hold a variety of washers and clips to eliminate this problem, they cost extra and you have to remove them when you aren't using washers or clips. Also, some companies are discontinuing many of their spall-shield adaptors because the LV tools with their pre-assembled clips and washers are clearly more efficient for light to medium-duty uses such as installing conduit outlet boxes and drywall track.

A third advantage of the LV muzzle-loader is apparent during repetitive fastening of furring strips or plywood subflooring to concrete. The pins can first be tacked into the wood by hand and then shot into the concrete by slipping the barrel of the gun over the pin and firing. Low-velocity tools usually cost less than high-velocity tools—$250 to $400 vs. $300 to $500. If you are going to buy one of these tools, shop around. There is a great deal of competition between manufacturers and dealers, and prices vary dramatically.

Some more expensive LV tools feature a semi-automatic magazine that holds up to ten charges at a time, eliminating the time it takes to handle each individual charge. This tool is probably more appropriate for the commercial or large-scale builder who uses a lot of concrete and steel. As a small-time builder and remodeler of wood-frame houses, I wouldn't need one unless I started building a lot more tilt-up or masonry walls. I don't often need ten consecutive identical charges, but I do frequently need a variety of charges of differing strength and pins of different sizes to deal with remodeling situations.

At the low end of the price curve ($30 to $80) are the hammer-detonated tools. Both Remington and Speed Fastener make them. These simple devices use the low-velocity, piston-drive technology. A pin and a charge are inserted into the tool, and the operator fires the charge with a hammer blow. These are handy devices, and I keep one in my tool-

box, but some are limited to a 2½-in. pin. Also, since it takes two hands to fire one, I have found them a bit awkward to use at times, with parts of my body uncomfortably close to the detonation point.

Charges—Although there are a few exceptions, charges for the powder-actuated tools are divided into two categories: high and low power. The most visible distinction between the two is that the low-power loads come in brass cases, and the high-power loads are packed in nickel-colored cases. Also, the loads for HV tools are sealed with a cardboard wad, while LV loads are crimped. This is because the cardboard wadding would eventually plug up the piston chamber in the LV tool. Don't pop any old load into your tool. Make sure that the brand and power of charge you are planning to use are appropriate. This information should be printed both on the inside of the tool's case and in the operation manual. If in doubt, check with the tool's distributor. Don't ever use a blank .22 cartridge or bullet in a powder-actuated tool.

Within each category, there are six color-coded levels of strength. If the powder charge is too low, the pin will not penetrate fully; if it's too high, the pin will go in too far. For example, if you're fastening a sill plate and the charge is too low, the pin will be left above the sill and thus won't hold it down. If the charge is too high, you'll blast the pin through the sill, often splitting it along the grain.

You can reduce these problems by shooting the pin through a solid washer. It is more difficult to drive a pin plus washer all the way through a board, and the increased area of compression provided by the washer also holds the wood more securely. When I'm shooting into especially short or brittle lengths of sill, I'll also put a C-clamp on the sill before I fire to keep it from splitting apart (photo left). When the pin doesn't go in all the way, I've found it nearly impossible to bash it home with a sledge or to pull it out with a prybar. If it's in the way, I usually bend it back and forth until it breaks, or just saw it off with a hacksaw or a reciprocating saw.

Pin selection—The first consideration here is safety. Make sure that the pins are designed for your tool. Drive pins are sometimes not interchangeable, and may be dangerous if used in the wrong tool. Consult your supplier or tool manual. The pin-head diameter must match the bore of the tool. Also, some of the specialized low-velocity tools can't handle the long pins needed for anchoring sill plates.

Aside from compatibility with the tool you're using, selecting the proper pin length depends on what you are fastening, and on what you are shooting into. To anchor a mudsill, the pin would have to be at least 1½ in. long to get through the wood, plus enough shank to penetrate the concrete. In average-strength concrete allowed to cure at least 28 days (3,500 to 4,000 psi), the pin should be long enough to penetrate about eight times the shank diameter—about 1½ in. for a ³⁄₁₆-in.

dia. pin. Thus, you need a 3-in. pin to hold down a 1½-in. sill plate. In soft masonry (2,000 to 2,500 psi), penetration should be nine to ten times the pin diameter. In hard masonry (5,000 to 6,000 psi), penetration of five to six times the pin diameter will ensure a firm anchorage.

Each manufacturer offers a wide variety of pins in various lengths and diameters, and there are charts that give tension and shear values for the various combinations when they are embedded in concrete with different psi ratings. In addition, each company, through the home office or the local distributor, offers technical advice to builders with unusual fastening requirements.

Generally speaking, the holding strength of a powder-actuated pin in concrete increases with the depth of penetration and the compressive strength of the concrete. A pin holds in concrete because the concrete tries to return to its original shape after the pin is driven into it. The resulting compression grips the shank of the pin. Mortar, green concrete and low-strength concrete require even deeper pin penetration for adequate holding power— up to ten times the shank diameter. Don't use a stud gun on concrete that has cured for less than seven days, and even then, the tension resistance will be half as much as for a similar pin in fully cured concrete.

If you're working with brick, never shoot the masonry itself. Instead, aim for a horizontal mortar joint and use a low-power charge.

Testing the base and the fasteners—Although most concrete on construction sites will be suitable, some materials may be too hard or too brittle for firm fastening. Hard materials include hardened steel, welds, cast steel, marble, natural rock and spring steel. Here is a quick test that will help you decide. Take a drive pin and, using it as a center punch, tap it with a hammer against the base material. If the pin is blunted, the base is too hard, and a charge-driven pin will not penetrate. It may even bounce off, inflicting injury.

If the base material cracks or shatters when you hammer the drive pin, it is probably too brittle and may fly to pieces under the pin's impact. Brittle materials include glass block, glazed tile, brick and slate. If you can drive the pin in substantially with a normal hammer blow, the material is too soft and the pin will end up penetrating too far. If the pin makes a clear impression, but isn't blunted, the base material is probably okay and you can try a test fastening with a loaded charge.

If the base material passes this density test, you need to make sure it's thick enough to accept the pin without allowing it to go all the way through or causing bits of masonry to break away on the opposite side. For masonry, the base material should be at least three times as thick as the pin's penetration. This is especially important if someone might be on the other side of a concrete wall or working under a thin-pour concrete floor.

If I don't know how hard the concrete I'm going to fasten to is, I make a test fastening to

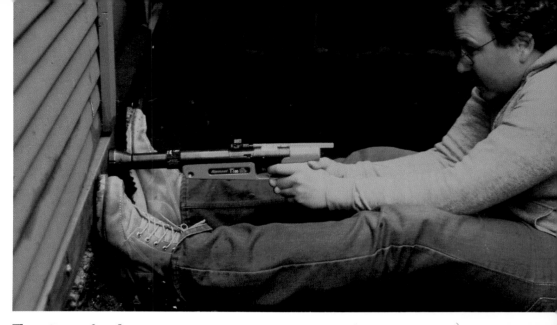

Three types of tools. Powder-actuated tools are especially useful when remodeling and adding on. Above, the author attaches a ledger strip to the side of an old foundation, using 3-in. drive pins fired by a low-velocity tool. At right, low-velocity hammer-detonated tools are inexpensive and handy, and they can be used to fasten preassembled clips. However, some are limited to a 2½-in. pin, and because it takes both hands to use one, they can be awkward in situations where you need a free hand to position and hold the work. In the photo below, a high-velocity tool quickly and effectively secures concrete-form bracing to a slab floor.

Typical drive pins are shown here next to a 16d nail. Unlike the nail, the pins are case-hardened by heat-treating to produce an outer layer that is tough enough to stand up to concrete or steel. The washer is used along with a drive pin to secure sill plates to concrete.

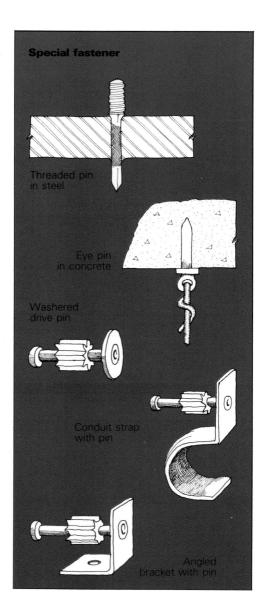

Special fastener

Threaded pin
in steel

Eye pin
in concrete

Washered
drive pin

Conduit strap
with pin

Angled
bracket with pin

Sources of supply

The following companies are the major manufacturers and distributors of powder-actuated tools in the U. S. They all have catalogs on their tools and manuals on how to operate them. For more on stud-gun fundamentals, consult the "Powder-Actuated Fastening Systems Basic Training Manual," a booklet available free from the Powder-Actuated Tool Manufacturers' Institute (435 N. Michigan Ave., Suite 1717, Chicago, Ill. 60611).

Bostitch, East Greenwich, R. I. 02818.

Gunnebo Corp., 293 Lake Ave., Bristol, Conn. 06010.

Hilti Inc., P.O. Box 45400, Tulsa, Okla. 74147.

Impex/Allied Fastening Systems, 5600 W. Roosevelt Rd., Chicago, Ill. 60650.

Ramset Fastening Systems, Div. of Olin Corp., Shamrock Rd., East Alton, Ill. 62024.

Red Head, ITT, Phillips Drill Div., Construction & Fastening Operation, 5209 SE International Way, Milwaukie, Ore. 97222.

Remington Fastening Systems, AMCA International, P.O. Box 719, Bowling Green, Ky. 42101.

Speed Fastener Corp., 11640 Adie Rd., Maryland Heights, Mo. 63043.

Uniset, P.O. Box 26273, 4130 N. Englewood Dr., Indianapolis, Ind. 46226.

select the proper charge. For safety's sake, I start with a small charge and work up until I get the proper penetration. As you gain experience you'll find that you can usually guess pretty closely what the charge should be.

When I'm working on a base of undetermined compressive strength, I like to use HV tools because I can adjust the effective power of the charge by changing the position of the pin during loading. Increasing the distance between the charge and the pin cushions the charge, reducing the pin's velocity. The trick is useful if you're running short of weaker charges. Several HV models come with a calibrated loading rod for just this purpose. Most of the piston-driven, low-velocity tools are less adaptable; to reduce pin speed, you have to use a smaller charge.

Sometimes a pin will bend on impact, an occurrence called fish-hooking. This may be caused by the pin hitting a dense chunk of aggregate or a piece of rebar, and it will reduce the pin's holding strength. If this happens, drive another pin nearby. Also, the pin's impact may cause the concrete to chip out (spall), making a little crater around the pin. Flying bits of concrete can be dangerous, but spalling, unless it's severe, rarely reduces the holding strength of the pin significantly.

To prevent the drive pin from cracking the concrete, keep it away from the edge of a slab or footing—at least 3 in. if you are firing directly into the concrete, or 2 in. if you are shooting through a sill plate. For much the same reason, don't put successive pins closer together than 6 in. Remember that you are driving a hard steel pin into a brittle substance at high speed. Protect yourself with goggles, always use the spall shield and keep other people away from you. I like to wear heavy boots and stand well balanced with my firing arm fully extended and my head directly above the tool. In a confined space, I use ear protection.

Safety—Safety is a big issue in the use of powder-actuated tools. Some states require special training and certification to operate them. Each tool has its own set of procedures, and you should make sure you know the precautions for the tool you are using.

Maintenance is important. Powder-actuated tools should be cleaned and lubricated after each use. As with any firearm, gunpowder residue will build up in the barrel and firing chamber. On LV tools, disassemble the barrel and remove the drive piston to clean it properly. A lightweight rust-preventive lubricant such as WD-40 should be sprayed on these parts and then wiped dry. Don't use heavier oils because they tend to collect dirt. Most manufacturers also recommend a complete disassembly and cleaning of the tool after firing several thousand rounds or after several months of use. Check your tool's manual.

Special uses—In residential building, stud guns are most often used to fasten a sill or furring strip to concrete. But there are many other kinds of fastening pins and applications for

the powder-actuated device, some of which are shown in the drawing at left. These are used more commonly by the big commercial builders, but shouldn't be in their exclusive domain. You can drive pins into steel members like I-beams and metal studs. And you can also fasten soft things like wood or insulation to steel or concrete, steel plates to concrete, steel plates to steel beams and so on.

The pins used for anchoring to steel have knurled shanks and are usually shorter than the pins used for concrete. Since steel is harder than concrete, less penetration is required, but the tip of the pin should penetrate all the way through the steel approximately twice the pin diameter. This is because the pin can be squeezed back out by the steel unless the tip goes all the way through.

Charges need to be selected in relation to the thickness of the steel, and HV tools can shoot through thicker steel than can LV tools: ¾ in. maximum for HV vs. 7/16 in. for LV models, depending on the brand of tool.

Both HV and LV tools are ideal for fastening light-gauge metals to concrete. I use 1-in. pins with washers to fasten such things as outlet boxes and masonry ties to concrete walls. And using a drive pin to anchor a light-duty post base is a good alternative to anchoring the base with a lag bolt and shield.

Two other types of pins are also commonly used. One is the threaded stud, which allows you to screw a nut onto it. It is often used to fasten conduit clips to concrete walls, and can serve as an all-purpose anchor anywhere you need to fasten removable hardware. Another is the eye pin for hanging acoustical ceilings from concrete and steel.

There are also pre-assembled clip and pin combinations, which are used only in LV tools. These include washered drive pins for fastening wood, rigid insulation, corrugated-metal roofing and steel siding to concrete or steel structural members. A combination conduit strap and pin is useful for fastening electrical conduit, and angled bracket pins are handy for hanging suspended ceilings or bolting on ductwork or pipe supports.

More than once I've had wall locations changed by clients between the time I've poured the slab and the time to start framing walls. And more than once I've had to cut off a row of misplaced foundation bolts. Now I anchor interior non-bearing partition walls with a stud driver, and save myself aggravation.

Whether you use a stud driver just to get yourself out of a scrape or as a regular part of your tool arsenal will depend on your imagination and your projects. But in any case, time and money are important factors for all builders, and powder-actuated tools can help you save both if you pick the right one for the job and use it safely. The more familiar I have become with these tools, the more I've gone from using them as an emergency backup to using them as a planned part of my construction activities. □

Steve Larson is a building and remodeling contractor in Santa Cruz, Calif.

Nail Guns

Pneumatic nailers and staplers give even the small builder affordable speed and precision not possible with hand nailing

by Angelo Margolis

Nail guns used to be considered the exclusive domain of tract builders—quick and dirty production tools for huge projects. These days, they are also found in cabinet shops and on building sites where pride in craft is still the dominant influence. Pneumatic fastening tools use compressed air to drive nails, staples, corrugated fasteners and brads. The air is delivered to the tool by a portable compressor through small-diameter flexible hose. The guns, which are usually aluminum-alloy castings, range in weight from 2¼ lb. to 10 lb. and are balanced for one-handed use.

The primary virtue of nail guns and staple guns is the speed you can develop building with them. A subfloor that would take half a day to nail off with a hammer can be completed in an hour with a nail gun or stapler. The time that you save can be spent on more creative work, which requires the judgment and experience a machine can't provide. Even more important, the time saved can mean building a high-quality house for less money. I saved about 15 days of labor on my own house by using pneumatic fasteners.

I do new construction and remodeling on a modest scale, and would no more build a house exclusively with a hammer than I would with a handsaw, though there is a place on every job for the limited use of each.

I first used a nail gun in 1964, when, as an apprentice, I put down a subfloor in an apartment complex. The work was still hard, but it was undeniably faster than nailing off with a hammer. In my mind, however, nail guns were relegated to use by large crews on big projects. It took me ten years to rediscover them.

In the meantime I built a number of spec houses by myself. Because of the hours of tedium that come with siding a house or nailing off the roof, building became a seige, and I often felt I was barely gaining ground. I still work by myself much of the time, but nail guns and staplers have reduced the drudgery.

Guns and staplers—Pneumatic fastening tools were originally developed for the assembly-line production of wood pallets, but residential construction has been the biggest market in recent times. Though nail guns and staplers are most often thought of for nailing off structural work like plywood subfloors, roof sheathing and wall framing, they can also be used on a wide variety of materials including asphalt and wood roofing, drywall, ply-

The biggest advantage of nail guns and staplers is the time you save when nailing off sheathing, siding or subflooring. However, new generations of pneumatic tools can fasten roofing, drywall, and even fine finish work without any sacrifice in quality.

wood and board siding, interior wood paneling, trim and other millwork items. Some guns even shoot a fastener that will penetrate concrete, something that used to require powder-actuated fastening tools.

Most guns operate on an air-pressure setting between 60 psi (pounds per square inch) and 110 psi. The nose of the gun is fitted with a spring-loaded safety, often in the form of a wire bail, that has to be depressed against the work before the trigger will release. The gun fires when a charge of compressed air fills a cylinder and forces a piston forward. The piston strikes a nail or staple in the guide track, and drives it out of the gun and into the work at high speed. Fasteners can be driven in one blow as fast as you can trigger the tool.

Most nail guns can also be used for bounce nailing, or bottom tripping, when you nail off large areas. Keeping your finger on the trigger will fire the gun as fast as you can depress the safety by tapping the surface of the work.

Nail guns and staplers vary slightly according to brand, but all the major manufacturers (listed at the end of this article) produce a variety of guns for different uses. Staples and nails are typically not interchangeable between brands. The trend seems to be toward specialized tools that can handle one type of fastener in a range of sizes appropriate to the task. Paslode, for instance, sells a gun designed for hanging drywall. It weighs just under 6 lb. and drives a ring-shank nail at the same time it dimples the gypboard, something drywall tapers like because the nail is always centered in the dimple.

Guns designed for framing, siding and nailing subfloor and roof underlayment are the most versatile. They generally shoot headed nails from 16d down to 8d or 6d. The magazines of these framing guns are angled away from the surface of the work so that the tool can be used in tight spots for toenailing, fireblocking and the like. Guns that will be used strictly for nailing off large areas have extra-long magazines so that the tool doesn't have to be loaded often.

Nail guns also come in smaller sizes. Some of these shoot finish nails or brads for finish work. These guns are light enough to be held vertically or overhead.

One of the guns I own is a T-nailer for cabinet assembly and finish work. The fastener is shaped like a T, and the gun sets it just below the surface. Lining up the long part of the

Framing guns. Nail guns have a place in small-scale remodeling because they make the work faster and easier. A large framing gun like the one being used below to nail off sheathing is usually the first pneumatic tool bought. It can shoot a range of nails—smooth shank, screw shank, and ring shank—in sizes from 16d down to 8d or less. The angled magazine gives these guns surprising maneuverability. Toenailing studs for a grade-beam pony wall, left, shows off this advantage. Unlike the blows of a hammer, a nail from a gun moves the material very little when it penetrates.

Staple guns and T-nailers. Two-legged staples hold better than nails of the same length, and aren't as likely to split the material. The staple gun being used to join two cabinet partitions, above, can also be used for shingles and shakes, and for nailing off shear walls, subfloor, and roof diaphragms. At left, Margolis uses a T-nailer to fasten roughsawn hemlock near a skylight opening. These guns get their name from the fastener they shoot. It's driven with the grain, just below the surface. Brad-drivers are also used for overhead finish work because they are light, and their fasteners are inconspicuous. Photos: Ron Davis.

T-head with the grain makes the fastener fairly inconspicuous. There are also some good small finish-nail guns. One of these will be the next air tool I buy.

Pneumatic staple guns also come in different sizes based on the range of staples they can handle. The larger guns use staples with legs 2 in. or longer for sheathing and framing. Medium-weight staplers can be used for cabinet assembly. Guns that shoot wide-crown staples are used by roofers for putting down felt and asphalt shingles. These staplers are often equipped with an adjustable shingle gauge. Unlike framing guns, the magazines on staplers are usually at right angles to the head of the gun because the stapler is held flat on the work when it's being used.

Fasteners—All pneumatic fasteners are collated either in coils, clips or strips. Headed nails, which come in lengths from 1½ in. (4d) to 3½ in. (16d), are often manufactured with a crescent-shaped piece missing from their heads so that they can be nested with their shanks touching. This economy of space yields between 60 and 80 nails per strip, depending on the size of the nail.

Pneumatic nails have smaller-diameter shanks than hand-driven nails. For example, a standard 16d box nail is .160 in. in diameter. The nail-gun equivalent, which meets all of the required code standards, is just .131 in. in diameter, because it doesn't need to stand up to repeated hammer blows.

Headed nails also come with smooth shanks, ring shanks and screw shanks (drawing, above right). Some companies manufacture a hardened nail for fastening wood to concrete. It penetrates up to ¾ in. into the concrete. This seems like a good way to attach furring strips and mud sills for nonbearing partitions, but I haven't tried it yet. Most nails are available with a galvanized coating for weather, or a resinous coating that heats up when the nail is driven, acting as a lubricant and improving adhesion when it sets—something like hot-melt glue. Senco has a moisture-resistant coating called Weatherex, which the company claims is as good as a hot-dipped galvanized coating used on nails driven by hand. I've had good luck with them, and they don't seem to leave black marks on siding the way galvanized nails do. Stainless-steel nails are also manufactured for some guns, but they're very expensive, and you can't always get them at a moment's notice.

The wide distribution of pneumatic fastening tools has brought with it a real increase in the use of staples. They are classified by their crown width (the distance across the top of the staple), leg length and gauge (metal thickness). Crown widths range from ³⁄₁₆ in. to 1 in., the wider ones for asphalt roofing and tacking up building paper. Staple leg lengths vary from ⁵⁄₃₂ in. to 3½ in., and gauges vary depending on the shear value needed.

Staples are said to have greater holding power in straight withdrawal tests than nails of equal length. I have tried to remove plywood sheathing after it was stapled down and

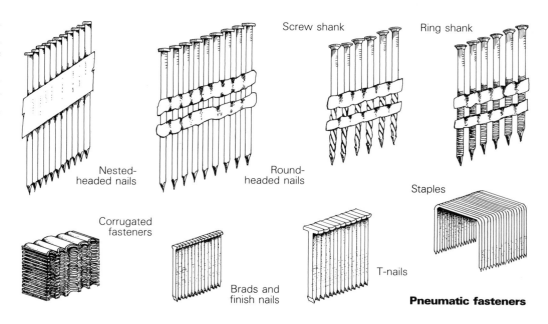

Screw shank Ring shank

Nested-headed nails Round-headed nails

Staples

Corrugated fasteners

Brads and finish nails T-nails

Pneumatic fasteners

destroyed the wood in the attempt because the staples held and the wood tore. Nails have more strength than staples in resisting horizontal movement, but you can use more staples in a sheathed wall to increase its shear strength. Sometimes I feel as if I'm actually stitching a building together. If you tried to use the same quantity of nails, you would just split the studs.

Staples are even being used for 2x wall framing. A 14-ga. staple 3½ in. long can now be used as a 1:1 equivalent for a 16d nail with code approval in many areas—a significant fact considering that staples cost a lot less than nails. Staples are also much less liable to split the wood than a nail is, particularly when driven near the end of a board or when several fasteners are needed in a small area. If you have questions about whether staples can be substituted for nails in a certain application, check with your building department, or write to the Industrial Stapling and Nailing Technical Association (ISANTA) or one of the manufacturers listed on p. 99.

Most manufacturers offer a tool that drives corrugated fasteners. As the fastener is driven, it pulls the two pieces together for a tight fit. A friend of mine built some machines for joining mitered picture frames using one of these guns. The frame is held against a fixture, and the gun is lowered and fired with a pedal. The machine works beautifully.

Buying a gun—The first decision to make when you're buying a pneumatic tool is not which brand, but which type of gun. Consider your needs carefully, and buy the tool that best covers the range of work you do the most. If you are buying a gun to nail off plywood for roofs, floors, sheathing and shear wall—a good place to start with nail guns—consider buying one of the larger pneumatic staplers instead of a nail gun.

The best way to get started is to buy a package. Pneumatic-gun manufacturers and their dealers make their profit primarily from the sale of the ammunition, so they can be very competitive with the price of compressors,

hoses, and guns. It is in their interest to have their equipment in the field. In areas where there is a lot of new construction going on, some companies offer a nail gun free if you buy ten cases of nails at the list price. It pays to shop around, but when you compare price, consider the cost of the entire package you want, and not just one component.

I have used three makes of guns—Bostitch, Paslode and Senco—and they have all performed well; so differences in quality will probably not be the deciding factor in which brand to buy. Instead, consider the price, and the quality and speed of service you can get on the tool you buy. These things will vary according to where you live. Some of the manufacturers will repair a nail gun or stapler right on the job site within a day for a minimal charge. Check with other builders to see if they have gotten the attention they needed once they bought the tool. The service that will be most important to you is being able to get fasteners when you need them. An empty nail gun is useless.

For my first gun, I made a choice based principally on price and bought a package from a Senco dealer. It consisted of a SN IV gun, which shoots nails from 16d to 6d, a Rolair compressor, a hose, a regulator and some nails. My most recent catalog (winter 1983) lists the following prices on these tools: nail gun, $518; 50 ft. of ⅜-in. hose with connectors, $49.94; filter and regulator mounted in a frame, $82; and compressor, $689. You'll probably be able to do better than list.

Compressors—The compressor I bought is quite different from the small, top-heavy, single-tank compressors that you see in shops. It is designed to be moved from one location to another on a job site, or to ride easily in the back of a van or pickup truck at the end of the day. With one wheel mounted between two low tanks that support the pump and motor, it maneuvers like a wheelbarrow. This keeps the center of gravity low, so it doesn't tip over easily. Emglow (Johnstown Industrial Park, Johnstown, Pa. 15904) and

This compressor has twin tanks, a front wheel and a low center of gravity; it won't tip when moved around a site or transported. The small steel frame on the left contains a filter to trap moisture, and a regulator that adjusts the air pressure delivered to the tool. Photo: Ron Davis.

Finish nailers that shoot brads or finish nails can be used both in the shop and at the site. Adjusting the pressure of the air delivered to the gun determines whether the nails are driven flush, or countersunk. Some of these guns are fitted with a removable rubber nose to protect the work from being marked. Where trim or paneling is to be stained or left natural, the heads of the nails can be painted to match the material.

Using a nail gun can give a carpenter working by himself the extra hand needed for stubborn material. Only one hand is necessary to drive a 16d nail into this decking, leaving the other one free to lever the board into line with a framing chisel. Photo: Angelo Margolis.

Dayton Speed Air (W.W. Grainger, 5959 West Howard, Niles, Ill. 60648) sell similarly designed compressors.

The motor on my compressor has a rating of 1½ hp. It was sized to produce enough compressed air to operate the large framing gun I bought with the package. This motor also allows me some versatility in where I can get power. When a compressor switches on under load it will draw over twice the current than when cycling without a load. Many compressors use 220 volts, but this can be a problem when remodeling or adding on. My 1½-hp motor allows me to plug in to any 110-volt, 20-amp circuit.

The output of a compressor is measured in cubic feet of air per minute (cfm). There are several methods of rating this flow, and you should check with the manufacturer of your gun about the size compressor you'll need for the guns you'll be using. I bought a compressor that gives me the reserve power to bounce-nail 16d nails or run more than one gun at a time. Roofers and cabinetmakers can use smaller compressors because their finish

nailers and staplers require much less air than a framing setup.

The difference between home-owner and industrial equipment is usually obvious, and this is as true with compressors as with other tools. Lower-quality compressors can be bought cheaply on sale, and I would encourage you to buy one of these, rather than miss out on using a nail gun because you can't afford a better unit. The compressors that Sears sells seem to fall into this category.

Hose, regulator and filter—You will need at least 50 ft. of hose to get started. Although auto-parts stores sell 150 psi, ⅜-in. hose, it is sometimes not as well reinforced or as flexible as the hose you can buy from the dealer who sells you the nail gun or stapler. Make sure the hose has the correct end fittings, or couplers, to fit your compressor, regulator and gun. Unlike electricity, whose drop in voltage on long runs can damage tools, compressed air can be delivered over distances by turning up the regulator, so you can leave the compressor at the power source and use more air

hose. You can also run more than one tool off a single compressor by making up a simple T-shaped adapter.

Down line from the compressor is a filter and regulator. The filter reduces the amount of moisture in the air coming from the compressor. A small cock at the bottom of the filter lets you drain the water that's collected.

From the filter, the air goes to a regulator—essentially a valve with a gauge on it. This is where you can adjust the amount of air pressure the gun receives. Many companies sell a filter and gauge that are combined into a single frame that is separated from the compressor by just a few feet of hose. This is a helpful combination because it's compact and protects the regulator and filter from the usual beating that tools take on a job site.

The operating pressures of pneumatic tools are usually stamped right on them, with final adjustments left up to the operator. Keep in mind that the pressure gauge on the compressor will always give higher readings than the regulator, because the compressor will be cycling on and off to keep pressure up in the tank. My compressor cycles between 125 psi and 140 psi. The regulator settings most often used on a building site range from 80 psi to 110 psi. Hardened concrete nails, large framing nails and screw shanks require settings at the upper end of the scale. Small brads take less pressure. You can adjust the regulator to countersink them or not.

Maintenance and safety—Maintenance is simple, and should be a part of setting up and shutting down each day. Most failures in guns and compressors result from dirt or moisture in the system, and from insufficient lubrication. Clean the compressor's air filter regularly and watch the oil level. I set up my compressor away from where I am working to minimize how much sawdust it inhales.

The setup procedure is simple, too. Make sure the drain cocks are closed on the compressor; then connect the filter, regulator and hoses, and start it up. I usually leave the drain cock on the filter open just briefly to blow out any residual moisture in the system. Once you close it, the gauge on the compressor should begin to register increasing pressure. Set the regulator for the psi you'll need at the gun. While you're waiting for the system to come up to pressure, put a few drops of oil—I use mineral oil kept in a small squeeze-bottle—in the air inlet of the gun. If it blows an oil mist after you've used it for a while, give it a little less the next day. Only highly refined oils should be used, and check with the field representative for your tool if you have a question. Some manufacturers recommend an automatic oiling device that attaches to the air inlet of the gun, but I've had no trouble with any of my pneumatic tools when following a strict regimen of adding oil every time I hook up the gun. This lubrication is for the inner workings of the gun—the piston and cylinder walls. Be sure to lubricate the nail track of the magazine on the outside of the gun as well, with a non-sticky product like WD-40.

When you connect the gun to the hose, which is now under pressure, make sure it's pointing at the ground. Do the same when you are loading. If the gun jams while you are using it, disconnect it from the air before you work on it. Some guns have a quick-clearing device that doesn't require you to take the nose of the gun apart to get at a crumpled staple or nail. If you want to test-fire the gun after clearing it, check to see if there are some fasteners in it. Dry-firing the gun will make it wear out more quickly.

Safety—Most safety rules for pneumatic tools are common sense. Don't use bottled gases to power the tool—oxygen will cause an explosion, and carbon dioxide will freeze the regulator. Keep an eye on the compressor gauge to make sure that it's cycling on and off properly. Lastly, don't ever pull the safety mechanism on the nose of the gun back manually, or fire the gun at something to see if it will penetrate. Consider the forces involved, and you won't be tempted to fool around.

The compressor should be emptied at the end of the day. This makes it safer to transport, and lets the moisture that has collected during the day evaporate. Open the cocks at the bottom of the compressor tank or tanks, and the filter. Keep them open until the system is drained of air. Treat the hoses with care. Coil or chain them like utility cords and keep the couplers out of the mud. Keep the magazine and the nose of the gun out of the dirt as well, or some of these particles may end up on the cylinder walls of your gun.

More advantages—If you are bidding a job, the labor savings possible with pneumatic tools can mean the difference between making a profit or not. They reduce the time you'll have to spend nailing off to the point that it's not much of a factor in the bid. Pneumatic fasteners can cost as much as three times more than hand-driven nails. But nails are a negligible expense when compared to labor costs for driving them with a hammer.

On time-and-materials jobs, my wage usually includes all my overhead and tools, but my nail guns are an exception. I charge half the local rental-yard price for using them, in addition to my hourly labor figure. Using the guns saves money for my employers.

I do no more than four asphalt-shingle roofs a year, and my roofing stapler has made the difference between my being able to do the roof competitively on a small job, and having to sub it out. An experienced roofer will hold his hammer in one hand, the nail in another hand, and position the shingle with his third hand as he drives the nail home. I have never done enough roofing to develop a third hand. With a roofing stapler I can hold the shingle and staple it down in one easy motion. With the pneumatic tool, I shingle more than twice as fast. I don't think a roofer who worked at it every day would double his time, but the savings would still be significant.

Nailing off exterior plywood sheathing with pneumatic tools is not only faster but safer than leaning way out from scaffolding or ladders and hand-nailing. Instead of having to use two hands, one to hold the nail and the other for the hammer, you can hold on with one hand at all times.

Nail guns can improve the quality of your work. The heads of finish nails and brads can be painted to match the color of thin, solid-wood paneling or trim that has to be face-nailed. This eliminates countersinking and filling, which often looks more conspicuous on a naturally finished wall than the flush-driven heads of these tiny nails. Splitting is seldom a problem, even with narrow trim.

A subfloor will go a lot longer without squeaking or lifting if you drive screw nails or ring shanks. But they require many more blows with a hammer than smooth-shank nails, and this translates to a lot of extra time. They're often not used for this reason. With a nail gun, all you need is a little extra pressure at the regulator.

One of the seldom recognized advantages of pneumatic tools is that they can drive a nail or staple without moving hand-held work significantly. This makes jobs like toenailing and installing forgotten drywall backing blocks much easier. In some cases, this lack of percussion is what makes a job possible. I was involved in building a 12-ft. high single-wall form for a concrete retaining wall up against an excavated hill. Face-nailing the form boards to the 2x4 uprights was impossible because of all the rebar inside the form. The only thing we could do was toenail through the uprights into the back of the form boards. But this just wasn't practical with a hammer because there was no effective way to hold, or buck, the boards while the nails were driven. With the nail gun, there was no problem.

One of the drawbacks of pneumatic nailers is that they won't draw a joint together as repeated blows with a hammer will. This can be a disadvantage in rough-wall framing where headers and sills should be drawn in tightly against the studs and trimmers to prevent problems later on. Another situation where a hammer is a better tool is installing bowed 2x6 decking on a roof. Gaps between boards can be eliminated by toenailing the leading edge and hitting that nail until the board moves into line. A nail gun won't do that. However, all of these boards also have to be face-nailed, and for that part of the job, a nail gun is a better tool than a hammer.

I don't use pneumatic tools everywhere, but I think every serious builder should have at least one. As my collection of nail guns grows, I feel like a golfer with his bag of clubs, using one and then choosing another as the game progresses, reaching for them in the same instinctive way I do my Skilsaw or Sawzall. □

Angelo Margolis lives in Sebastopol, Calif.

Sources of supply
The following companies are the major manufacturers of pneumatic tools and fasteners used in the U.S. They are all members of the Industrial Stapling and Nailing Technical Association (435 North Michigan Ave., Suite 1717, Chicago, Ill. 60611), which acts as the educational and technical arm of this industry.

BeA America Corp., 280 Corporate Center, The Briscoe Building, Roseland, N.J. 07068.
Bostitch, Division of Textron, Inc., 806 Briggs Drive, East Greenwich, R.I. 02818.
Duo-Fast Corp., 3702 North River Rd., Franklin Park, Ill. 60131.
Hilti Fastening Systems, 4115 South 100th East Ave., Tulsa, Okla. 74145.
International Staple & Machine Co., Box 629, Butler, Pa. 16001.
Paslode Co., 8080 N. McCormick Blvd., Skokie, Ill. 60076.
Senco Products, Inc., 8485 Broadwell Rd., Cincinnati, Ohio 45244.
Spotnails, 1100 Hicks Rd., Rolling Meadows, Ill. 60008.

Among Japanese tool manufacturers, Hitachi (Air Nail, 1407 S. Powell, Springdale, Ark. 72764) has entered the pneumatic-fasteners market in the United States.

Power Nailing without Hoses

A look at a new non-pneumatic automatic nailer

by John Lively

How often have you been nailing off a roof deck and almost taken a fall from stepping on an air hose? Or been on a remodeling job and found it impractical to set up your compressor for the small amount of framing to be done? In short, how often have you wished your nail gun wasn't tied to a noisy compressor with a clumsy air hose?

Paslode Corp.'s chief engineer Mike Nikolich pondered these questions and decided that there had to be a way to make a non-pneumatic automatic nailer, one that would carry its power source along with it, and eliminate the ubiquitous umbilical cord.

This summer, after spending six years and a lot of money developing a new technology and testing prototypes and pre-production models, Paslode (a major manufacturer of pneumatic nailing equipment) will introduce its Impulse nail gun. Powered by a liquid-propane cylinder and a rechargeable battery, the Impulse will shoot clips of nails suitable for most framing and sheathing operations. The largest nails it fires are 3 in. long and the shortest are 2 in. long. It can fire as fast as you can depress the nose piece and pull the trigger, but unlike most pneumatic nailers, you can't hold the trigger down and bounce-fire the tool.

The mechanics of the Impulse are clean and simple. When you squeeze off a shot, a measured dose of propane gas is injected into the combustion chamber. There a fan (which also serves to cool the cylinder) mixes the propane and air. Next, a spark ignites the volatile gas and forces the piston downward. The piston, as you would expect, is linked to the rod that drives the nail. After the nail is driven, cooling gases in the combustion chamber suck the piston back to starting position, and the gun is ready to fire another round. All this happens in about $^3/_{10}$ sec. or less.

But while the principle of operation is pretty direct, the engineering problems faced by Paslode were manifold and complex. It seems that nobody knew much about low-pressure combustion engines, and Nikolich and his colleagues had to re-invent the technology for internal-combustion engines—at least for the kind of engine that would drive a 3-in. nail with a head pressure of less than 70 psi and an incredibly low engine efficiency of 5%.

The engine parts are cast and machined from a magnesium-aluminum alloy, and the handle and housing are molded from Du Pont's Zytel, the same stuff football helmets are made from. The tool weighs 8 lb., compared to the usual 8½ to 10 lb. for most pneumatic nailers. The Impulse works well in all climates except

Paslode's new Impulse nail gun is designed around the mechanics of internal combustion. A battery in the handle ignites a spark, causing a metered charge of propane to explode. This drives a piston, which in turn drives a nail.

for cold ones. When the temperature drops below 20°F, the gas doesn't mix well with the cold air; as a result, the gun fires erratically.

Replacement propane fuel cells cost $4.19 apiece. Each cell is good for about 1,400 shots, and the battery will fire about 4,000 times before it needs recharging. All this means that it costs about $3 more to fire 1,000 nails with the Impulse than with a typical pneumatic rig. But this figure doesn't take into account operating costs and setup time for the compressor. Nor does it allow for the fact that the Impulse will run about $900 vs. the $1,400 to $1,600 it costs to buy a good pneumatic gun and reliable regulator and compressor. Plus the hoses.

Job-site trials—We had several carpenters test a pre-distribution model of the Impulse. First we shipped the gun to Berkeley, Calif., and asked builder Jim Servais and his crew, who were framing up a house at the time, to try it out. They were generally pleased with the tool's performance, and found the gun to work effectively and fast. But they were most impressed by the freedom of movement it offered, and by the fact that their favorite rock-and-roll station wasn't periodically drowned out by the compressor.

Servais found that the angled dogs on the nosepiece of the tool really bite into the wood. This feature makes toenailing a snap, although if the angle to the work is too steep the nail won't be driven flush, and you'll have to reach for your hammer. To sum up its advantages, Servais said quite directly: "No compressor, no hoses, no setup time. This thing's ready when you are."

One of the guys on Servais' crew coveted the tool chiefly because it's sleek and black and looks like something Darth Vader would use to subdue squadrons of rebel pilots. But what they didn't like was the fulsome, perfumey smell of spent propane. This definitely isn't a tool you want to use in closed, unventilated spaces.

Back on the East Coast, we lent the nailer to Connecticut carpenter Jim Picton. The second day on the job, the gun broke down. It refused to fire. Picton got on the phone with Paslode's Steve Wilson (Vice President, Engineering). After taking apart the gun and checking potential trouble spots, it still didn't work upon reassembly. Wilson's diagnosis: a faulty micro-switch, a problem that had occurred several times before once the guns got out of the lab and into the dirty world of job sites. According to Bob Bellock, Director of Product Development, they've gone to a hermetically sealed switch that won't get fouled up with dust. When the tools are marketed this summer, Bellock says that they will have reliable electrical parts.

Aside from the malfunction, Picton reported that the gun has good balance and is generally easy to operate once you've mastered the unconventional firing sequence. First you have to squeeze the safety grip on the back of the handle. This actuates the fan. Next you depress the nose against the work, and then you pull the trigger. Do things out of sequence and the gun won't fire. Picton didn't find the fumes obnoxious or the noise of the fan distracting. He was particularly keen on the design of the nosepiece. Clearing the gun of a jammed nail or snagged driving rod is much easier than on a typical pneumatic tool. With the Impulse, you just loosen a locking knob, slide out the nosepiece and shake out the kinked nail.

The people at Paslode (2 Marriott Dr., Lincolnshire, Ill. 60015) say they expect that most builders will use the Impulse not to replace pneumatic nailers completely, but rather to complement them by affording a versatility you can't get with tools attached to hoses. But they do think that the Impulse will make an attractive alternative to pneumatic guns for small contractors and remodelers who need the speed and ease of an automatic nailer but not the inconvenience and expense of a pneumatic setup. It also could be the remedy for many carpenters (not all of whom are past their prime) who spend too much time in the orthopedist's waiting room rubbing their aching elbows and dreading the inevitable long-needled cortisone shot. □

From *Fine Homebuilding* magazine (June 1986) 33:82
Photo: Paslode Corp.

Levels and Transits

Shooting lines and grades involves nothing more than what meets the eye

by Stephen Suddarth

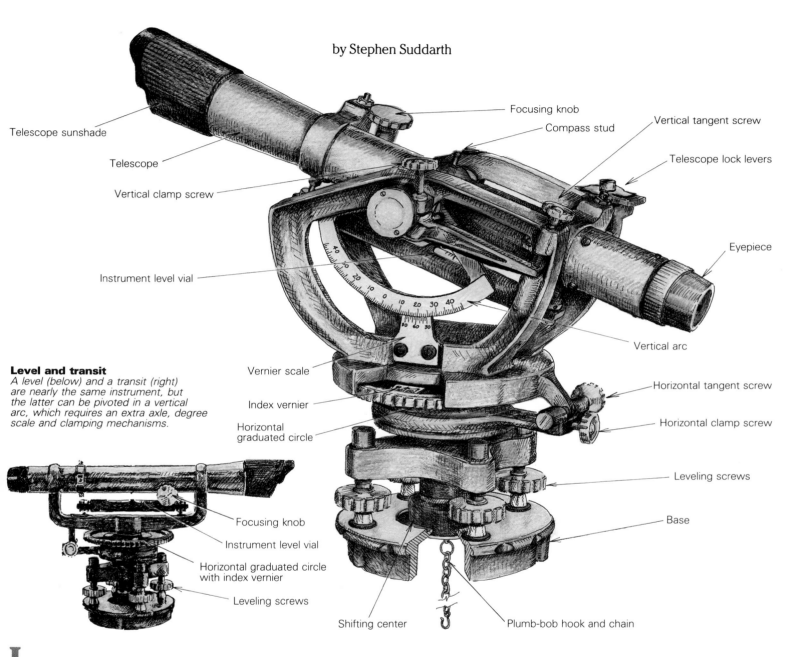

Focusing knob

Compass stud

Vertical tangent screw

Telescope lock levers

Telescope sunshade

Telescope

Vertical clamp screw

Eyepiece

Instrument level vial

Vertical arc

Level and transit
A level (below) and a transit (right) are nearly the same instrument, but the latter can be pivoted in a vertical arc, which requires an extra axle, degree scale and clamping mechanisms.

Vernier scale

Index vernier

Horizontal graduated circle

Horizontal tangent screw

Horizontal clamp screw

Leveling screws

Base

Focusing knob

Instrument level vial

Horizontal graduated circle with index vernier

Leveling screws

Shifting center

Plumb-bob hook and chain

In all my discussions with skilled tradespeople on building sites, the most common complaint is, "it's not square" or "it's not level." From tile-setters, masons and carpenters to plumbers and welders, it seems that the better the job they're trying to do, the more they like to see accurate work preceding their efforts. That means pinpoint layouts in the beginning and follow-up checks as work progresses.

Uncomplicated buildings on level sites can be laid out with simple, inexpensive measuring tools. Water levels, line levels, even spirit levels held against a long straightedge will work to check for plumb and level. And you can put the Pythagorean theorem to work with stringlines and tapes to check for square.

For me though, the right tool for leveling, lay-ing out and double-checking is the builder's transit. Now that I'm used to setting up the instrument, it has become an easy matter to lay out a house, especially if it has more than a simple four-wall shape. Checking the work in progress on walls, floors or columns is also a lot easier if a transit or level is used.

Two instruments—Optical leveling and layout instruments fall into two categories: the level (drawing, above left), and the transit, sometimes called a level-transit or a builder's transit (drawing, above right). Both types are simply telescopes in partnership with an accurate spirit level and a pivoting base mounted on a tripod. They operate on the principle that a line of sight is straight, without sag or curve. When a level is set up correctly, any point along its line of site is at the same level as the instrument's horizontal crosshair. Because it is a telescope, it becomes an extension of your eyesight, giving you the ability to focus on a tape rule or leveling rod from a distance. The vertical crosshair is a reference point that allows you to rotate the scope and lay out any angle in a horizontal plane.

Angle readings are expressed in degrees. They are read off the graduated circle, which is divided into four quadrants of 90° each (top left drawing, next page). The pointer that registers the degree setting is at the center of the vernier, which is an auxiliary scale that slides against a primary scale. It divides the units on the primary scale (degrees) into smaller constituents called minutes (there are 60 minutes in a degree), al-

Reading the vernier

Example 1

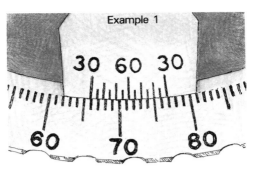

Both levels and transits have degree scales that are divided into 90° quadrants. The scale can remain stationary as the instrument rotates, or it can be moved independently. The vernier moves along with the instrument. To read a degree setting, note the position of the center mark on the vernier. Vernier scales vary—on this one the center mark doubles as the 60' (minute) mark and the 0' mark. Readings begin at zero, move to the right to 30', then continue from the 30'

Example 2

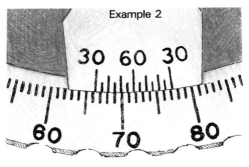

mark at the far left to end on 60'. In example 1, the center mark reads slightly more than 71° on the graduated circle. To determine the minute reading, look for the vernier mark that aligns with a degree mark. In this case the 75° mark lines up with the 20' mark, so the setting is 71° 20'. In example 2, the center mark reads a little less than 72°, while the minute mark aligns at 69°. Reading from the left of the vernier, the minutes equal 45, so our setting is 71° 45'.

lowing very precise readings to be made. On my Realist builder's transit, the vernier is divided into five-minute segments.

A transit is essentially a level with an added axle that allows the telescope to pivot up and down in a vertical plane. This makes it possible to "see" in a plumb line by sighting the vertical crosshair while pivoting the scope up or down. This feature is especially helpful when you are aligning tall walls or laying out stakes on a hilly site. The vertical pivot has its own degree scale and vernier. Surveyors use this feature to calculate angles in a vertical plane, which can then be plugged into simple calculations to find the heights and distances of objects. While surveyors use instruments that are similar to a builder's transit, the surveyor's equipment has to work to closer tolerances—about ± 1/10 in. in a mile compared to ± 3/16 in. in 150 ft. for a good builder's transit.

Because of their greater accuracy, surveyors' instruments are a lot more expensive than those made for builders. But some of their fancier features—specifically those that make it easier to set up the instrument—are now being offered by several manufacturers (see the sidebar on laser levels, p. 107). This article is about the traditional instruments, so let's take a look at how to set them up. In some ways, this is the toughest part of using a transit or a level. It takes calm hands, a careful eye and a lot of patience just to get one of these instruments ready to use. But without an impeccable setup, your results will be worthless.

Setup for leveling—To begin, find a fairly flat piece of ground that is centrally located on the site and position the tripod with its legs about the same distance apart (photo facing page). I like to use an adjustable-leg tripod because it makes it easier to get the instrument to a comfortable sighting height. Adjustable legs also make it easier to set up if you're working on a slope. To guard against bumping the tripod out of its position, stabilize its legs by pressing their metal tips firmly into the ground with your foot.

The bracket where the three legs are joined is called the head, and it is topped by a flat plate with a threaded stud or ring through its center

Attached to the base of the level or transit is a hook that aligns with the instrument's vertical crosshair. When you set up the instrument over a fixed point, a plumb bob hung from this hook is used to position the instrument directly above the point. The slip knot (drawing, right) makes it easy to adjust the bob up and down.

that anchors the instrument. When you begin a setup, try to make the head as level as possible by eye as you adjust the legs of the tripod.

Next lift the level by its base plate and hand-tighten it firmly onto the tripod head. On some instruments the four leveling screws have to be backed up to allow space for the mounting stud to be fully tightened. Hand-tighten all the leveling screws until they make firm, equal contact with the tripod head. The instrument shouldn't shift around.

Start leveling the instrument by releasing the horizontal clamp screw (drawing previous page) so the instrument can spin easily on its axis. For instruments with four leveling screws, turn the telescope and line it up directly over two of them. By turning the screws uniformly with your thumbs moving toward each other or away from each other you'll actually be tightening one and loosening the other, which maintains the even pressure of the leveling screws and levels the instrument as you watch the bubble below the telescope. If you remember that the bubble will travel in the direction that your left thumb moves it will probably make this part of the operation easier.

When the bubble is centered over the first pair of screws turn the telescope 90°, directly over the other pair, and repeat the leveling operation. Go back and recheck the first pair of screws—it's not uncommon to have the bubble go out a little on this first check. Adjust if necessary and recheck both again. The test is to turn the telescope in a complete 360° circle and watch the bubble for movement. It should take no longer than about 10 to 15 minutes (automatic levels can be leveled in two to three minutes) to have the bubble in the spirit level centered and not move while the telescope is rotated in a complete 360° circle.

Fixed-point setup—Levels and transits are made to be centered directly over a fixed spot—usually a nail embedded in the top of a stake (photo left), but it may be a mark on the floor or the intersection of two stringlines. In rocky soil I often use rebar for my stakes.

Begin setting up by placing the tripod and the instrument as a unit over the fixed point. Make sure the plumb-bob chain and hook are hanging freely through the tripod head (they are in a plumb line with the exact center, or vertical crosshair, of the instrument). Using a slip knot (bottom drawing, facing page), hang a plumb bob from the hook. Eventually, you'll want the point of the plumb bob between ¼ in. and ½ in. above the fixed point.

What comes next requires practice and patience. The instrument has to be carefully and exactly placed directly over the fixed point with the tripod head eyeballed as level as possible. Back off the leveling screws until the instrument can slide across the tripod head horizontally in any direction. Start with the plumb bob a few inches above the stake because you'll be pressing the tripod legs farther into the ground. You can now move the tripod in small increments by lifting individual legs, moving them in and out or side to side, and then pressing them back into the ground. This operation is easier if you've got someone to steady the plumb bob. While you move the legs about, be sure to keep the tripod head as level as possible.

Once you've got the bob within about ½ in. of the nail, you can slide the instrument across the tripod head until it's centered over the nail and turn the leveling screws until they lightly but firmly support the instrument. If it has a tribrach mounting (three screws), turn the telescope parallel with two of the three leveling screws. As you watch the circular (target) bubble, rotate the screws simultaneously with the thumb and forefinger. As the target bubble approaches center, turn the telescope 90° so it's directly over the third leveling screw. Raise or lower that screw until the bubble is centered. Now rotate the telescope and watch the bubble for movement, and adjust the screws until it remains dead center. Many of the new self-leveling instruments have tribrach mounting, and for most of them you need only get the bubble within the outer circle of the target. Once your setup is complete, do your best to avoid bumping the instrument, and try not even to touch the tripod.

If repeated attempts fail to level the instrument, chances are the spirit-level vial is out of adjustment. If the bubble is off-center the same amount in all positions, it's possible that the line-of-sight adjustment is off. In that case you'll always be sighting higher or lower than actual level. These two conditions are the most common instrument problems. Although some owner's manuals give instructions for adjusting vials, I don't attempt to adjust my own instruments. I send them back to a factory-authorized dealer.

Orientation—It helps to be familiar with the control knobs (drawings, p. 101) on the level or the transit so you can operate without fumbling for the dials while you're trying to sight a target. First unlock the horizontal clamp so that you can easily rotate the instrument on its base with the touch of a finger. Standing comfortably behind it, sight across the top of the telescope to line up your target. Look into the eyepiece (all sighting should be done with both eyes open), find the target and adjust the focusing knob until the target is sharply defined. Lock the instrument with the horizontal clamp so that the cross-

Setting up the tripod. Begin setting up a level or a transit over a fixed reference point, such as a stake, by spreading the tripod legs equally and pressing their tips into the ground. As you position the tripod legs, watch the instrument—you want it eventually to end up above the stake.

hairs are near the target. Now bring the crosshairs into focus by turning the eyepiece. You can fine-tune the crosshair up or down with the horizontal tangent screw. If it's a transit, the vertical tangent screw works exactly the same way to adjust the vertical crosshair to the left or right. The power of the telescope varies with different brands, but all the instruments I've seen have either 20x or 26x telescopes.

Using the level—Using a level is a job for two people. The operator sights through the instrument, while the rod-holder positions a leveling rod. A typical leveling rod is a sturdy, two-piece sliding rule made of maple or fiberglass that extends to 8 ft., 10 ft. or 15 ft. An architect's rod is graduated in feet, inches and eighths, while the engineer's version is in feet, tenths and hundredths. Commercial rods have sliding targets that can be moved up and down the rod for easier sighting. Builders will frequently use folding rules or retractable tapes instead of a rod, or make their own rod from an old tape.

A tape rule from close range (20 ft. to 30 ft.)

can appear to have such large graduations that you can get distracted. I suggest that you avoid driving your rod-holder (and yourself) crazy by calling out "up a sixteenth" or "down a thirty-second." For a smooth layout, pick a tolerance that you want to work to and stay with it.

Much of a builder's work requires accurate knowledge about the relative heights of objects, or of the elevations of the ground (called grades) around the building site. Suppose, for instance, that you're working on a hill that needs a pad leveled for a parking space, and you need to know the difference in height between the downhill (point A) and the uphill (point B) edges of the pad.

To find the difference, set up the level in a spot roughly between points A and B. Drive a stake flush with the level of the ground at both points to ensure stable reference points that can be relocated. Have your helper hold the rod perfectly plumb on the stake at point A. To get an accurate reading, it helps to have the rod-holder rock the rod slightly toward and away from the instrument. As you sight the rod, the

To find the differences in elevation between two points, set the level between them. Have the rod-holder steady the rod atop fixed points, sight the rod with the instrument and note the rod readings. The difference between the two is your answer. To determine height differentials between distant locations, set up at intermediate points and record the readings. The difference between the totals is your answer.

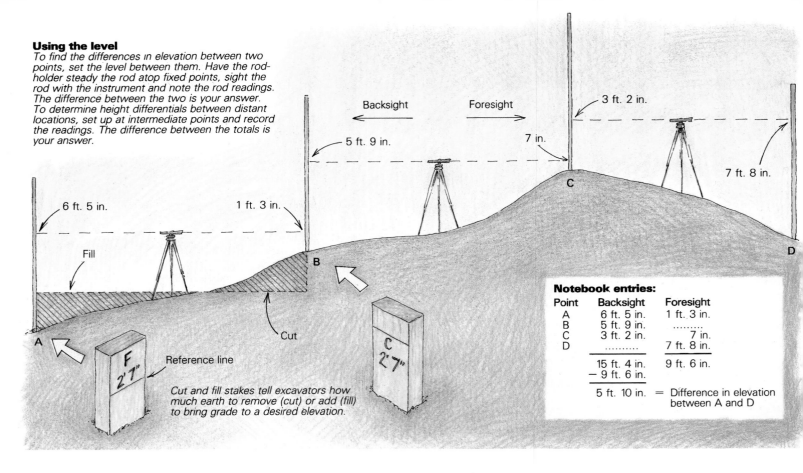

Backsight

Foresight

5 ft. 9 in.

7 in.

3 ft. 2 in.

7 ft. 8 in.

6 ft. 5 in.

1 ft. 3 in.

Fill

B

C

D

A

F
2' 7"

Reference line

C
2' 7"

Cut

Cut and fill stakes tell excavators how much earth to remove (cut) or add (fill) to bring grade to a desired elevation.

Notebook entries:

Point	Backsight	Foresight
A	6 ft. 5 in.	1 ft. 3 in.
B	5 ft. 9 in.	....
C	3 ft. 2 in.	7 in.
D	....	7 ft. 8 in.
	15 ft. 4 in.	9 ft. 6 in.
	− 9 ft. 6 in.	
	5 ft. 10 in.	= Difference in elevation between A and D

horizontal crosshair reads 6 ft. 5 in. Make a note of this figure, turn the level and sight on the rod held on point B. It reads 1 ft. 3 in. The difference between the two is 5 ft. 2 in., so point B is that much higher than point A (drawing, above).

To level the pad, your equipment operator will need to remove earth from the uphill side and place it on the downhill half to build it up. His reference points are lines drawn on stakes that call for cuts or fills, as shown above. The letter C on the cut stakes and an F on the fill stakes tell him which is which, and the depth of the cut or fill is also written on the stake. In our example, about 2½ ft. of earth (half the difference between the points) has to be cut from the uphill side and compacted on the low side.

You may need to find the difference in elevation between two points that can't be seen from one setup. For instance, finding the heights of point A and point D in the drawing above. In this case, set up the level between intermediate stations and keep notebook entries listing your readings. The backsight column contains measurements taken toward your point of origin, while the foresight measurements are taken toward the destination point. When you are done, add all the numbers in both columns. The difference between the two is your answer.

Grade stakes—The great thing about leveling with either the builder's level or the transit is that you can usually set up in a central location and determine the elevation of anything on the site from one place. For instance, here in Florida we usually pour slabs for houses, and sometimes they get pretty big. Without reference points in the middle of the slab, it's possible to get rises and depressions in the slab as much as two or three inches off finished elevation. To

Aligning

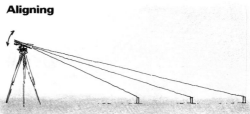

By loosening the lever lock and the vertical clamp screw, you can pivot the builder's transit up and down to align layout stakes.

Plumbing

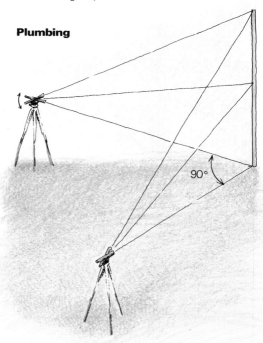

90°

To check for plumb, set the transit's vertical crosshair along one edge of the subject. The two should be aligned at top and bottom. Adjust subject accordingly, move transit 90° and repeat.

eliminate this problem, we place rebar grade stakes on 8-ft. to 10-ft. centers across the entire floor area to guide our pour. We set up the level in the center of the floor and take a reading with the rod held on the perimeter of the leveled formwork. Say this reading is 4 ft. 8¼ in. The rod-holder slides the target to this reading. Then we drive all the rebar stakes, leaving them each a little bit high. Now the rod-holder holds the rod on one of the stakes, and we note how much more it needs to be driven to have the target line up with the level's horizontal crosshair when the rod is on the stake. This is a check-and-tap procedure. When I read 4 ft. 8¼ in. on the rod, I know the top of the stake and the forms are level with one another.

I like to spray-paint the tops of each stake as they are set to grade. That way we know when we're finished with all the stakes, they don't get kicked around as much, and the concrete guys can see them more easily during the pour. Once the stakes have done their job as reference points, they get driven below the surface of the slab before finish troweling.

Straight lines and plumb lines—Unlocking the vertical clamp on a transit allows you to take advantage of its ability to move up and down in a vertical plane. For instance, to align a row of trees, stakes, fence posts or columns with a transit, set up the instrument somewhere along that line. Sighting to another point known to be along the line will give you the required orientation. Now tighten the horizontal clamp screw to preserve the setting, and loosen the lever lock and the vertical clamp screw to allow the telescope to swing up and down in a vertical arc. Now you can align a stake, measure to the next one and align it (middle drawing, left). To extend the line in the opposite direction, turn the telescope 180°.

In this setting it's also possible to see along a plumb line, locating any number of points, whether on the ground or several floors up (bottom drawing, facing page). I think this ability to plumb by line-of-sight is one of the most useful functions of the transit. On several occasions I've used a transit to plumb formwork for concrete columns. They were too tall to be guessing with a 4-ft. level and there were too many angled braces projecting from the formwork to use a plumb bob. But because I could sight the top and bottom of the forms, I could adjust them into perfect alignment.

The transit is also useful when setting tall wood posts that may, and usually do, have a camber in them. This is especially true when it is inconvenient to drop a plumb bob off their tops, and a level won't help because the camber will throw you off. In this circumstance, begin by setting up the transit at least as far away as the object is tall. If the object is square, set up along one projected edge—on the building line for example—if the posts or columns fall on it. Any twist in the object from bottom to top can be detected at the same time you check plumb. Set the intersection of the crosshairs directly on the bottom edge, and raise the telescope. If the edge moves away from the vertical crosshair, you then know which way to move the object to bring it into plumb.

Next, move the instrument to a spot 90° from the first setup and repeat the operation from the new position. To avoid errors, make sure to lock the horizontal movement on the transit while checking for plumb.

Layout with a level or transit—Laying out a building means locating the outside corners of its foundation, and marking them with stakes. Nails driven into the tops of the stakes register the precise intersection of the walls.

The starting point for any layout is the orientation of one side of the building's foundation (a building line) and one corner on that line. Site plans or plot plans usually have enough information about the dimensions of the lot to get you positioned on the site. Assuming that one boundary of the lot is parallel to a building line, I set up the transit over survey stake A at one corner of the lot, and focus the transit on the adjacent corner B (drawing, above right). Sometimes the view to the building is obscured along line AB by trees, bushes or even other structures so I have to find a point (C) on this line that gives me a clear shot of its position. I drive a stake at C, set up the transit, and I have my rod-holder place the rod atop corner stake B. I sight the vertical crosshair on one edge of the rod, and set the horizontal circle of the instrument on 0° (photo right). Rotating the instrument toward the building site, I lock it on 90°.

The rod-holder now moves to a point a few feet inside the building footprint, and adjusts the rod to the left or right until one edge lines up with the vertical crosshair. If the rod-holder is beyond the sound of my voice, I motion with my right or left arm, depending on the direction the rod needs to move. When it's on target, I

Building layout
Layouts typically begin by establishing a point along a property line (C) where the transit can be set up and a measurement taken to the building line. Once the building line and one corner are located, the major corners of the building are pinpointed with stakes and diagonals measured.

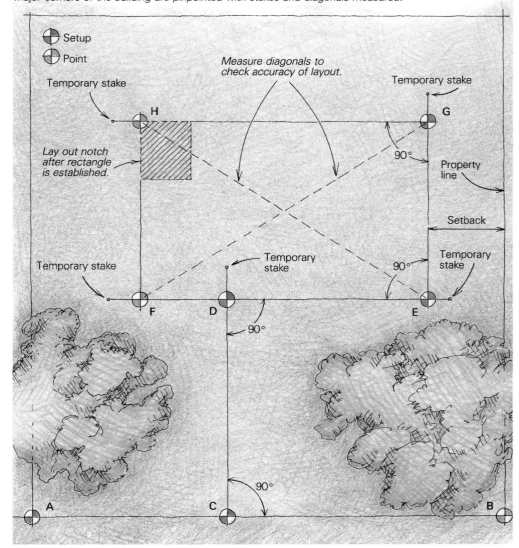

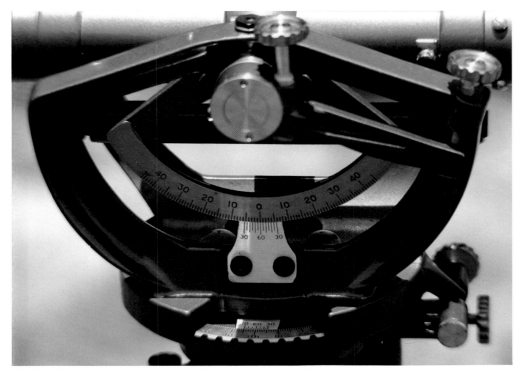

The two degree scales on a transit allow you to read angles in a horizontal or vertical arc. Here both are set at 0°. The instrument is now ready to be used as a level or to turn angles for layout.

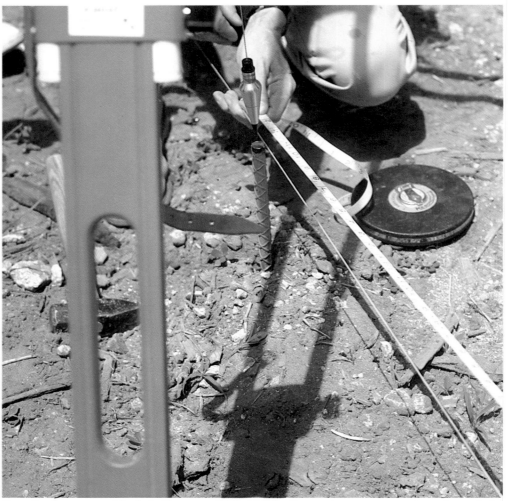

Once the temporary stake is in the ground to establish alignment, a measurement can be made by pulling a steel tape between the new stake and a known corner such as this one.

Setting batterboards

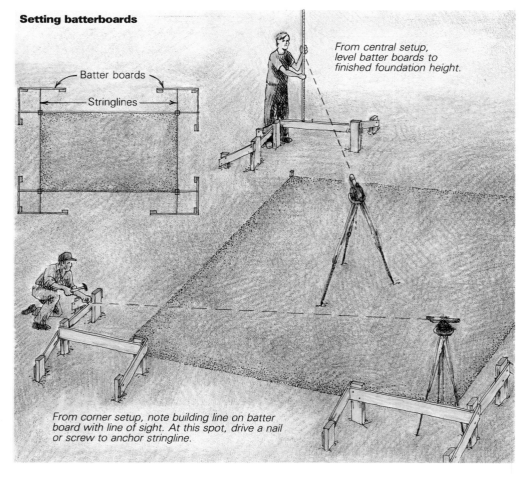

Batter boards

Stringlines

From central setup, level batter boards to finished foundation height.

From corner setup, note building line on batter board with line of sight. At this spot, drive a nail or screw to anchor stringline.

raise both arms to signal "hold it." I then sight the bottom of the rod, where he drives a temporary stake and marks the vertical crosshair with a nail. If I'm using a level instead of a transit I can still do this operation, but my rod-holder has to use a string-line and a plumb bob to locate the placement of the nail. While it's possible to position a stake on the building line without the temporary stake, it usually ends up being easier to put in the temporary reference point—especially if you're using a level.

Now we measure the required distance along this perpendicular line, and with the tape pulled tight, drive stake D on the building line (drawing, previous page). With the transit set up over point D, I sight back to point C, set the horizontal circle at 0° and rotate the instrument 90° to the left. Now I'm sighting along the building line toward point E, which will be the first established corner. We place another temporary stake on the building line beyond point E, and measure the necessary setback from the property line to find point E. If the property line is difficult to locate, we can subtract the setback from line CB. If the lot is rectangular, the result will equal DE. Since I'm set up on the building line, I turn the transit 180° to set a temporary stake beyond corner F. Then I stretch a stringline between corner E and the temporary stake, and measure the distance to F (photo above left).

Now that the first corner and first building line are established, I can set the rest of the corner stakes. The procedure is the same for the corners turned on the way to establishing corner E—setting up over a known point, sighting the building line, setting the degree scale on zero and turning the scope 90°. If the building footprint has a notch taken out of what is essentially a rectangular form (such as at corner H), lay out the rectangle first and check the diagonals to make sure they are the same length. Then you can place the stakes that delineate the notch.

The best rod-holder is one who understands how the level or transit works, so make sure he or she has a chance to look through the telescope, set a few grade stakes and turn a few angles. The rod-holder will also notice that the telescope can make the string appear to be the size of a rope, allowing you to sight either side of a stringline. Consequently the rod-holder's plumb bob must really be still.

With the layout done, the batter boards (see drawing, left) can be set up at the corners, at least 4 ft. outside the building lines. To get the batter boards level with the finished foundation, I set up the transit in the center of the building footprint and have the rod-holder adjust them to the required height (drawing, left). Then I set up the level or transit over each building line. I locate the lines by stretching strings between the corners. I can then extend the building line in either direction by line-of-sight onto the batter boards, where it is marked with a nail. With this arrangement you can stretch the stringlines again and have your location on the site, a level grade reference and the major building lines with corners where the stringlines cross. □

Stephen Suddarth is certified as a building contractor in the state of Florida.

Review of some level-transits

The instruments I've used include my own *David-White 8300 Universal Level-Transit*, shown in the drawing on p. 101. While it's a topnotch level-transit, it has been discontinued by Realist. A few are still available for $448 from Duder Stadt Supply, 2422 E. Southcross, San Antonio, Tex. 78223.

David White 8830 Meridian Level-Transit. This is one of the least expensive models of the instruments reviewed. It's a perfectly adequate beginner's instrument. $315.

David White LT8-300 Level-Transit. This is a new product with conventional features, but an optical plummet is available on the LT8-300P. It has a sleek modern appearance, with the same tolerances as the 8300. Solid and heavy, it turns very smoothly. Its adjustment knobs are simple and easy to find. The horizontal circle does move just a bit too easily however, which could cause errors in a layout. $539.

David White AL8-22 (8860) Automatic Level. This level spoiled me. It sets up quickly, it's accurate and stays accurate if the tripod is nudged. Looks sleek, has air-dampened gravity compensator to keep optics level. It does all its tasks well. $469.

Lietz Model 20 Transit-Level. This basic instrument has conventional features and is the least expensive of Lietz Transit-Levels. It

While the latest levels and transits (such as this model LT8-300 from David White) have become more streamlined, their functions remain the same as their ancestors.

seems well built with a handy magnetic locking device to secure the telescope in the horizontal position. $315.

Sears Craftsman 9 46201 Contractors Transit-Level. This basic instrument has solid brass adjustment knobs and leveling screws, and tolerances similar to competitors. The vial is hung below the telescope, and I found it easier to read while leveling. I had no problems with this instrument in use. $289. —*S. S.*

Manufacturers

Listed below are the names and addresses of the principal American manufacturers and distributors of optical levels and transits, and laser levels.

A.G.L., 2615 W. Main St., Jacksonville, Ark. 72076 (laser levels).

Berger Instruments, 4 River St., Boston, Mass. 02126 (levels, transits).

Carl Heinrich Co., 711 Concord Ave., Cambridge, Mass. 02138 (distributors of Kern and Topcon levels and transits).

Laser Alignment, 2850 Thornhills SE, Grand Rapids, Mich. 49506 (laser levels).

Lietz/Sokkisha Co., 9111 Barton St., Box 2934, Overland Park, Kan. 66201 (levels, transits).

Realist Co., N 93 W 16288 Megal Drive, Menomonee Falls, Wis. 53051 (David White levels, transits and laser levels).

Sears, Roebuck and Co., Merchandise Group, Dept. 824FC, Sears Tower, Chicago, Ill. 60684 (levels, transits).

Spectra Physics, 5475 Kellenburger Rd., Dayton, Ohio 45424 (laser levels, electronic levels).

L. S. Starrett Co., 121 Crescent St., Athol, Mass. 01331 (levels, transits).

Wild Heerbrugg Instruments Inc., 465 Smith St., Farmingdale, N. Y. 11735 (levels, laser levels).

Carl Zeiss Inc., One Zeiss Dr., Thornwood, N. Y. 10594 (levels).

Laser levels

There are two types of laser levels: visible-beam and invisible-beam. Both use a rotating head for transmitting the beam in a level or plumb orientation.

Visible-laser levels emit a low-power, red beam of light that is about ⅜ in. in diameter, 300 ft. from the source. Realist's Blount Electronics Div. makes five models of visible-laser levels, all of which are self-leveling. The Milli-Beam (list price, $3,995) emits one milli-watt of power and covers more than a 600-ft. radius. The other four models emit two milli-watts of helium neon light. These very low levels of energy produce no detectable heat, but you are cautioned not to stare into the beam.

Realist's visible-laser levels operate on 12-volt DC, so they will work off a battery pack, a car battery or a 110 AC converter. Mounted on a tripod, the Milli-Beam rotates at variable speed (0 to 360 rpm), or mounts on its side for plumbing or 90° layouts.

Spectra-Physics offers two visible-light laser levels. Both mount on a tripod, hang on a wall or perch on trivet feet. Once adjusted to near-level, they level themselves automatically. Most contractors I've seen using the 910 (list, $5,995) or 942 (list, $5,195) Laser Level from Spectra-Physics simply hang them on a wall or column exactly at the desired height to do leveling operations. When lying on its side, the

910 Laser Level can lay out 90° angles by emitting a beam of red light straight out of the end of the rotating head, which is also emitting a beam simultaneously in a "plumb" vertical plane.

An invisible-laser level emits an infrared beam that can be detected by a small, hand-held sensor. When aligned with the beam, the sensor beeps and gives an LCD (liquid crystal display) readout. They are best used outside in bright light, when visible-laser beams are very hard to see.

Realist's invisible-laser level is the Electrobeam. It has essentially the same features as the Milli-Beam, including an automatic leveling system that is always in operation. This feature is typical of the higher-order optical transits used by engineers and surveyors, and is very handy when the building you are in is swaying or vibrating from construction operations.

Spectra-Physics' invisible-beam level is called the EL-1 Electronic Level ($2,995). Its range is 300 ft. The detector, called the Level-Eye, has an LCD as well as a fast beep for high, a slow beep for low, and a solid tone for on grade. The LCD flashes an arrow pointing down for high readings, and a line across its center for level. They also offer the model 1044-L Long Range EL-1. Range is 1,000 ft.

Has the laser technology in leveling

instruments made the optical instruments obsolete? I don't think so. Optical instruments are here to stay. It appears that laser levels are quite valuable in specialized areas. They are fast and accurate, and on production-type commercial jobs the expense of a laser instrument is justified. Laser levels aren't designed to lay out buildings, so they lack the versatility of the optical instruments, and there aren't any laser transits.

Recent improvements to optical instruments, such as automatic-leveling, optical plummet (which replaces the plumb-bob operation) and tribrach mounting, all make optical instruments easier to set up. And easy setup has been a strong part of the sales pitch for laser levels. A person who has trouble leveling a conventional instrument should investigate those with automatic leveling.

In my discussions with Realist, a company that manufactures both optical and laser instruments, I was assured that optical levels will be far less expensive than laser levels for many years to come. Look out though. Wild/Magnavox now makes surveying transits that use data from 18 satellites. The readings appear on a terminal linked with a computer. The surveyor sets up in the field and never looks through a scope. —*S. S.*

Portable Power Planes

How these versatile tools can true framing lumber and clean up trim

by Geoff Alexander

Portable power planes can solve many of the problems that come up on the construction site during framing and finish carpentry. By removing a thin layer from a piece of wood, power planes can improve the appearance of the surface by taking out saw marks, dings and other blemishes. And they're good for fitting and scribing trim. With repeated passes, power planes can straighten or taper studs, joists, rafters and beams, as shown in the photo at right. A lot of this work would be unnecessary if all framing lumber were dimensionally stable and free of twists and bows, if houses were built perfectly square, plumb and level, and if all carpenters, sheetrockers and other tradesmen did flawless work. But they don't. So my power planes get steady use.

In size, shape and function, power planes resemble hand planes, but they work like machine jointers, turned upside down and held by hand. On a hand plane, the sole is a single flat surface with a slot, or throat, through which the blade protrudes. You adjust the depth of cut by moving the blade up or down in relation to the sole of the plane. But the sole of a power plane, like the bed of a jointer, has two separate surfaces, one in front of the knives, one behind. The cutting edge of the knives is always aligned exactly with the plane of the rear shoe, and you change the depth of cut by raising or lowering the front shoe. When the front and rear shoes are in exactly the same plane, the knives will just skim the work surface and make no cut at all.

What's on the market—In my view, there are four types of power planes, with slight design variations among manufacturers. The planes all have the same basic working parts (drawing, facing page)—a motor, a rotary cutterhead that holds either fixed or adjustable knives, a two-piece shoe, one or two handles

Geoff Alexander is a carpenter and woodworker in Berkeley, Calif.

Power planes are the best tools for truing up and trimming framing members that have been nailed in place. Here a carpenter levels a crowned gluelam beam to align it with the second-story floor joists.

and a mechanism for adjusting the depth of cut and for aligning the rear shoe with the cutting arc of the knives (or knives with the shoe). Most planes have a detachable fence to help guide the tool past the work, an especially useful feature for trimming or beveling the edge of a door, window or board.

The four types differ by size and by the kind of cutterhead-drive system they have. In my business, we do everything from the rough framing of additions and new construction to finish work and architectural detailing. So I own one of each kind of power plane.

The first type is the direct-drive, or sidewinder (top photo, p. 111). The motor hangs down below the level of the surface being planed because the cutterhead is mounted directly to its rotor shaft. The direct-drive model is designed for edge planing, and its sole is only 2 in. wide. The low-slung motor helps stabilize the tool during long passes down the

edge of a door or a joist or rafter. The sidewinder I own is a Rockwell (now Porter-Cable) 126 Porta-Plane. Of all the power planes I have, this is the one that I use most.

All of the other three types of power planes have their motor mounted above the cutterhead, with a drive belt connecting the motor shaft to the cutterhead arbor. This arrangement gets the motor away from the sole, and makes the tool suitable for surface planing, even in the middle of a wide board or panel.

I group the belt-driven power planes by size because I use each type in a very different way. The smallest and lightest is the Porter-Cable 167 Power Block Plane. It's designed for one-handed use. The on/off switch is right at your fingertip, just where it ought to be. Its light weight and maneuverability let you work in situations where using a larger plane would be awkward or impossible.

The second type of belt-driven power plane is available from many manufacturers. I call it the standard size. It has a 3-in. cutting width, and a shoe length of from 11 in. to 18 in. I use the Makita 1900B, which is on the short end of this range, but others have nice features, too. Porter-Cable's 653 Versa Plane is also standard size. The great virtue of these planes is that they can perform a very wide range of tasks. They are small enough to be highly mobile, yet substantial enough to do fairly precise work; light enough to hold overhead for a short time, yet powerful enough to shave down protruding framing members. If I had to get by with only one power plane, I'd probably choose a standard size.

The fourth type of power plane simply makes possible tasks that otherwise could not be done, or that would be so prohibitively difficult or expensive to accomplish that I would not attempt them. I'm talking about the Makita 1805B. It can remove a swath of wood 6⅛ in. wide and ⅛ in. deep in a single pass. The 1805B was the first power plane of its size to be made available in the United States. Hita-

From *Fine Homebuilding* magazine (April 1983) 14:42-45

chi's six-inch er is now being sold by many tool suppliers.

The Makita 1805B and other planes like it are made for heavy-duty surfacing work on large beams and timbers. If you work often with gluelams or heavy framing, you will want one of these big planes for sure. It also makes a dandy job-site jointer for one who does a lot of finish carpentry.

Another uniquely Japanese aspect of all the Makita planes is that the knives themselves are made of laminated steel. The cutting edge is a relatively small piece of hard, brittle high-carbon steel, while the body of the knife is a softer low-carbon steel. In theory, the harder edge can take and hold a razor sharpness, but the tough body will still be able to withstand shock and abuse.

Cutterheads—There are two basic kinds of cutterheads: those with straight knives and those with spiral (helical) knives. Most power planes have straight knives, but those on Porter-Cable planes are helical. Planes having straight knives have fixed rear shoes, so the knives themselves are adjusted up and down for proper alignment of the cut. Helical knives are permanently fixed to the cutterhead, which means the rear shoe of the plane must be adjustable.

There are advantages to each type of knife. Helical knives have a lower cutting angle than straight knives, and will cut more smoothly, more quietly, with less power consumption and less wear and tear on the machine. Helical knives stay buried in the cut for a longer part of each revolution than straight knives do, and properly sharpened, will leave behind a cleaner, less scalloped surface. Helical knives have a shear-cutting action, which means less chance of tear-out and pecking in woods with irregular grain.

While either style of knives is easy to sharpen with a grinder, razor sharpness requires honing after grinding, and honing is much easier to accomplish on the removable straight knives.

Porter-Cable's 653 Versa Plane has carbide-tipped knives. You have to send the cutter-head out for sharpening.

Principles of use—Like all other cutting tools, power planes work remarkably better when they are sharp. Power planes are designed to work properly when the cutting edges align perfectly with the rear shoe. Set the cutters so that they just touch a straight-edge held against the rear shoe. You will always have to make this adjustment after you've sharpened the cutters. Locking the adjustment in place is easy on all the planes, but Makita has wisely made it more difficult to re-install the knives incorrectly than to install them the right way, though you must be sure to get the mounting screws very tight.

In most situations, you want to use a power plane to create a smooth, unbroken surface from one end of a board to the other. To do so, make each cut in one continuous pass along the full length of the board. Begin by entering the cut with firm downward pressure on the front shoe. Then as the entire sole comes to bear on the stock, shift your downward pressure to the rear shoe. Maintain the pressure on the rear shoe until the cutter has cleared the end of the work.

There is a knack to making smooth cuts, and I usually warm up on scrap stock to check the adjustments and to recapture the rhythm of a smooth stroke before starting a new job. It almost always improves the quality of the cut if you keep two hands on the plane, one in front and one in back. If you have to move your feet during the cut, make sure that your path is clear, and that the cord can't catch on anything (including your feet) during the cut. You don't want to have to stop the cut halfway through and then start up again. Many of the planers have a device for directing the cord away from the path of the cut, and these can be useful, but when I'm making a long cut, I almost always carry the cord over my right shoulder and across my back.

Tapering—In some cases you can't get the desired result by planing from one end to the other in a continuous pass. To cut a slight taper, snap a chalkline down both sides of each piece of lumber,

secure it on edge, and make the first pass 6 in. to 12 in. away from the end from which most of the stock will be removed. Back up another 12 in. or so for the second pass. Increase the length of subsequent passes until your planed surface is parallel to the line, at which point you keep removing wood until you've cut halfway through the chalkline. Snapping a line on both sides of the lumber helps guard against planing an out-of-square edge. For greater tapers, rough-cut close to the line with a circular saw and clean up with the power plane.

Truing framing members—To straighten joists, rafters or beams, it's sometimes necessary to flatten the crown of the bow, which means that the dimensions will remain true at both ends of the member. Snap a chalkline on both sides of the lumber to guide the cuts. Make the first pass about 8 in. in front of the center of the crown to produce a straight surface on the top edge parallel to the line. Increase the length of subsequent passes by 6 in. to 8 in. until you split the chalkline with an unbroken pass from one end to the other.

Concave cuts—If you are trimming to a scribed line that is straight, or nearly so, any of the planes except the big one will do a good job. For irregular or concave cuts, however, I prefer the Porta Plane. I misadjust it so that the cutters protrude slightly below the rear shoe. With this setup, you can remove a lot of wood in a hurry, so start with the depth of cut adjustment fairly shallow and experiment to find the best setting for making concave cuts. Be sure to return the rear shoe to its proper adjustment when you are through. Another method that works more slowly, but with less risk of error, is to leave the rear shoe adjusted correctly. Then, with your left hand on the depth-of-cut adjustment knob, lower the cutters as you pass over low spots in the line, and raise them to skim over the high spots. With both systems, I usually give the cut a final touch with a hand block plane held slightly askew as it runs down the wood.

Surfacing large timbers—The plans for a house I built last year called for a 6x14 exposed ridge beam, but I wanted something

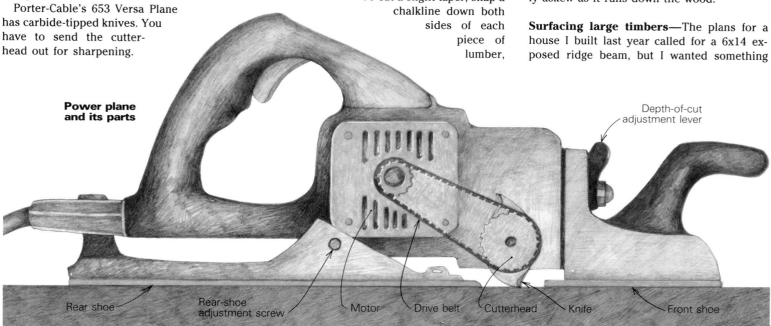

Power plane and its parts

Depth-of-cut adjustment lever

Rear shoe   Rear-shoe adjustment screw   Motor   Drive belt   Cutterhead   Knife   Front shoe

Illustration: Frances Ashforth

much more massive, and I found it at a used building-supply yard—23-ft. redwood 10x16s whose surfaces were so battered that the dealer sold a pair of these to me for $40. I used the Makita 1805B (photo, bottom) to take ½ in. off the bottom edge and ¼ in. off of each side to reveal unmarred wood. The result was spectacular. The beams were almost totally clear, virgin-growth redwood, so straight that I could have milled door stock from them. This one job alone justified the substantial cost of the 6⅛-in. power plane. It took only eight passes to remove ½ in. of wood 10 in. wide—about 15 minutes of work. Without the big power plane, I wouldn't have even considered the job. Not that there aren't other ways to surface a 10x16 beam. I have a friend with a huge 16-in. wide jointer who would have been happy to give it a try. But who would be crazy enough to try pushing a 600-lb. beam down a jointer?

For the rafter beams in the same house, we used 4x12s. Because the drywall was going to

Cleaning up sawn edges with Porter-Cable's Power Block Plane, left, is easy. Because it's light and compact, this plane is well suited to working overhead, and in tight spaces.

For surfacing large timbers, the Makita 1805B, shown below, can cut a path 6⅛ in. wide in a single pass, and makes recycling used materials an attractive alternative to buying new stock.

come up around the rafter beams, I didn't want to use green lumber, as it would inevitably shrink away from the drywall and leave gaps. New, dry 4x12s are expensive, but used ones aren't, and the Makita 1805B made quick work of surfacing the ones I found.

When you're working with used lumber, search carefully for broken nails or other debris lurking at or beneath the surface. Pore over the wood from one end to the other. And do it again. An unseen nail or staple can nick or, in extreme cases, ruin a set of knives.

Fitting doors—Here the power plane shines. Except for prehung doors, almost every door I hang has to be trimmed to fit, beveled a few degrees on the hinge side, and beveled 4° on the latch side. For trimming and beveling the edges of a door, I like to lay it flat over two sawhorses, with its best face down, then make all the trim cuts with my Porter-Cable 126 Porta-Plane (photo facing page, top). With the door flat, I can trim all four edges without having to move anything but the tool.

The Porta-Plane adjusts for bevels quickly and accurately, and when I'm edge-planing on a horizontal surface, the weight of the Porta-Plane's direct-drive motor is almost centered over the edge of the cut. In this position, the plane handles well. I keep my left hand on the fence, at the front end of the plane. And I use both hands to ensure that the shoe and the fence make snug contact with the work.

When I'm planing the top and bottom edge of a door, the cut begins and ends on end grain. Cutting the end grain is no problem, but it can chip out at the end of the cut; so I either stop the cut shy of the end and come back from the other direction, or score the far side of the cut deeply with a utility knife, and plane right through.

Correcting framing errors—Let's say you are getting ready to hang drywall, and you discover that one end of a 4x8 window header stands proud of the wall by ¼ in. The window is in place and the exterior siding is on, so you can't bash the offending member into place. The sheetrocker would keep right on hanging rock, but if you're the guy who did the framing and you're also going to hang the drywall and trim out the window, it's time to reach for the power plane. The smallest standard size you've got is best here. You need some power, but you'll be working on a vertical, overhead surface, so light weight is a big plus. Be sure to set all the nails at least ⅜ in. below the surface before you begin to make repeated passes on the face of the header, using a shallow (1⁄32-in.) setting, and entering the header from the protruding end.

Standard-size power planes are also useful for trimming studs standing proud of a wall, for evening up stair stringers, and for correcting other framing irregularities.

Exterior siding—In sidewall shingling, if you are weaving inside or outside corners, the power block plane is a natural for trimming to fit. If you're siding with plywood or any type of rabbeted horizontal siding, you may well have to custom-rabbet some of the joints. The block plane and several of the standard-size planes can cut crude rabbets easily, if you work carefully and have a steady hand. I use a table saw or router for visible joints.

Removing saw marks—In custom finish work, stock often has to be ripped to width. If the ripped edge shows, the saw marks must be removed. With a power plane, you can clean up skillsaw rips effortlessly. All of the planes are good at this job. For freehand work the power block plane is easiest to handle (photo left), but the Porta Plane makes a smoother cut.

Fitting trim—Let's say that the sheetrockers beat you to that protruding header I mentioned earlier. If you are mitering the joint between side casings and head casing, and the shoulders of the door frame are not flat in the plane of the wall, then you may well have difficulty getting the miters to fit. Patience and a sharp power plane can solve the problem. You need to shape the back face of the stock—it's an ordinary scribing problem turned 90°, and your scribing line will be on the edge of the board. Mark the edge to fit the wall and then plane the back to your line. If you have to remove a little extra material in the center of the board, drop the cutter slightly below the rear shoe. But be careful.

It may also help to back-bevel the miter a few degrees using the Power Block Plane. Work down from the mitered corners, keeping the meeting parts the same thickness. Remember that the goal of finish carpentry is to create the illusion of perfection, not perfection itself. Therefore, if you get the miters to fit tight and flat, quit fiddling. Squirt in some glue, and start nailing. Be sure to get at least one good nail through the miter itself. If the wood is going to be oiled or stained, sand the glued miters immediately after nailing. I use 100-grit garnet paper and sand until there is no glue residue on the surface. Sanding before the glue dries not only provides a final flattening of the joint, but also removes any excess glue and help fill any remaining gaps in the joint with a mixture of sawdust and glue.

Most of the planes have an optional adjustable fence that allows beveling and chamfering. The Makita 1900B has a groove down the center of the front shoe which makes it easy to cut a chamfer without a fence. It's fairly easy to plane skillsawn plywood edges clean enough to glue on nosing. I prefer the Porta-Plane for plywood, because it's the easiest for me to maintain a square edge, and because its high rpm and its helical knives handle the mixed grain directions with little tear-out.

Keep in mind that there's no substitute for a sharp block plane—the hand-powered type—for the final cuts on pieces of trim. You get greater control, and produce a smoother, more polished surface. Power planes are fine for most work and gross stock removal, but a hand block plane will refine your results.

A job-site jointer—Makita makes a planer-stand accessory for each of its power planes. The planer stand is designed to hold the plane securely upside-down for use as a jointer. These have some merit even for the standard-size planes, and when the big Makita is mounted on its stand, it becomes a very reasonable 6-in. jointer (photo below right) that can be carried to almost any job site comfortably by one person in one trip. This has proved so useful as an on-site jointer that I have built a support table on which the planer stand is permanently mounted, and which doubles as a carrying case for the planer stand and other accessories. To improve the plane's capability as a jointer, I have added an auxiliary wooden fence to the stock fence. The new fence contacts the shoe of the plane to prevent the cutterguard from jamming under the fence. I have also painted markings with fingernail polish on the underside of the adjustment knob to make it easier to set the depth of cut while the plane is on its stand.

Sharpening—Porter-Cable and Makita, as well as some of the other manufacturers, sell sharpening kits for their power planes. The sharpening kits that I know about use the plane motor as a power source for a small grinding wheel, and use the plane's body for mounting a jig that holds the knives. Having the sharpening kits on the job is best if you use your power plane on a regular basis.

The Porter-Cable sharpening device is

made to hold the entire cutterhead on a mandrel that is moved laterally and rotated at the same time. This compound action is necessary because the knives are helical. The Makita sharpening attachment works in a more conventional way. It's a hooded grindstone/tool-rest assembly that mounts on the rear of the plane. The knives are clamped in a bar, which slides along a track on the tool rest.

All of the sharpening systems work well, and all are fairly straightforward to set up and operate. I can disassemble, sharpen and reassemble my Power Block Plane in around 15 minutes. The big Makita takes half an hour. I try to keep two sets of cutters on hand for each power plane, and try to sharpen them both with one setup.

The Makita planes also come with a "sharpening holder"—a simple but effective jig for honing the knives on a Japanese waterstone (not included, but an inexpensive accessory). The jig, of course, would also work if you were using an oilstone, but Japanese waterstones

cut fast, stay cool, don't require oil, and are cheaper than oilstones. The jig holds the two knives in such a position that if both knives are kept in contact with the stone, they will be honed at the correct angle. If you avoid planing rough materials and lots of used lumber, and keep your knives free of nicks, you can keep them sharp by honing, something you can do several times before you have to regrind the bevels. In most of my work, I use edges right from the grinder. But if I'm doing pretty work (as opposed to surfacing used timbers), I hone my knives on the stone after grinding all of the nicks out of them.

Safety—Jointers are notorious for eating fingers, and power planes are portable jointers that can be set down on things. A rotary cutterhead can chew away flesh quickly, even when it's coasting to a stop. So be careful. Unplug it when you're fooling with its knives or adjusting the rear shoe. Watch where you put it down, and keep it out of the dirt. □

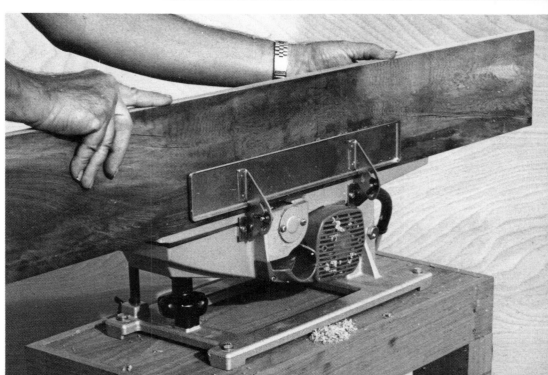

The Porter-Cable model 126 Porta-Plane, above right, is designed for trimming the edges of doors, sash and framing lumber.

The Makita 1805B, shown at right, can be inverted and mounted on a stand to become a job-site jointer that is good for truing and fitting trim. Photo: Geoff Alexander.

On Screw Guns and Screws

How screw guns are different from variable-speed drills,
and a look at power-driven screws

by M. F. Marti

Twenty years ago, the contractor I worked for gave me the task of putting down a plywood subfloor with screws. To make things go faster, he gave me a ¼-in. electric drill with a gear-reduction device in its chuck. A screwdriver blade protruded from its tip. With this tool, I was supposed to drive #12 slotted screws through the plywood and into the joists. It was torture. The blade refused to grip the screws with any consistency, so it twisted out of the slots and then chewed ragged holes in the plywood before I was able to release the trigger.

My next major experience with screwdriver innovations came when a cabinet installer introduced me to Phillips-head screws. I had always cursed Phillips-head screws because the weird screwdriver that they require was never at hand. But this time they made a lot of sense. The cabinet installer got out his Yankee screwdriver, and quickly drove all the screws needed to anchor the cabinets. The

A screw gun's power is transmitted from the motor to the drive tip by means of a positive clutch. In the cutaway exhibit of a Makita drywall gun (above and top), you can see the clutches just to the right of the nosepiece (one of the clutch faces has gear teeth cut into its edge). The clutch consists of a pair of metal discs with interlocking teeth called dogs. The dogs are held apart by a spring until you push on the screwdriver bit. This compresses the spring, engaging the clutch.

flanges on the tip of the Phillips bit captured the head of the screw and kept it centered as the screw was driven home.

I bought a Yankee screwdriver, and found that I could chuck its bit into my variable-speed drill and use it to drive screws faster than ever, and learned to use a pinch of wax from a toilet seal to lubricate the screws. This was progress.

I once used my drill to set quite a few screws, using my wrist as a slip clutch. The next day I complained to another contractor about my sore wrist. He wondered why I didn't have a screw gun—essentially a drill with a clutch—among my tools. I finally realized there was a difference between variable-speed drills and screw guns.

Screw guns have been around since the 1930s, when the Stanley Tool Works produced one to drive slotted screws. But it wasn't until the 1950s, when builders started securing drywall to steel studs with Phillips-head screws, that screw guns

Cutaway display courtesy of Makita

came into their own. Today, most major tool manufacturers make screw guns, and their features and list prices ($100 to $150 for drywall guns, $150 to $200 for Teks or adjustable-clutch screw guns) are roughly comparable. The screw guns discussed in this article are representative of what's available on the market today.

Positive clutches and the screw gun—A screw gun is designed to protect the operator, the tool motor and the head of the screw. It has a clutch (photos facing page) that disengages once the screw has been driven. This prevents the motor from stalling, keeps the bit from tearing up the screw head, and keeps the screw from being driven too far into the material. If you stall your variable-speed drill under load, you risk burning up the windings. Sometimes this is relatively immediate; sometimes repeated stallings are required for the damage to be obvious. Using the slow speed needed to control your drill as you drive screws also means the cooling fan is turning at slow speed, which results in an overheated motor.

Screw-gun clutches vary in design from manufacturer to manufacturer, but all screw guns have what is called a positive clutch. The positive clutch is composed of two interlocking clutch ratchet faces called dogs. Their mating angle and depth of engagement determine the deliverable torque. The dogs are held apart by a spring, permitting you to place a fastener on the driver tip whether the motor is running or not. When you press the point of a fastener against the work you compress the spring and engage the clutch dogs, thus delivering the motor's power to the driving tip. This type of screw gun delivers constant torque to the fastener, and it will keep on driving the screw until you let up on it. When you relax the pressure the clutch faces are pushed apart by the spring, and the shaft stops turning.

The basic screw gun has a nosepiece with a hexagonal socket that retains either a bit or a bit holder. Bits and bit holders both have hexagonal shanks that fit into the socket. The bit is dedicated to one drive tip, while the bit holder has a socket that accepts bits of various drive styles. Most bit holders have a snap ring inside the socket to secure the bits. Some are magnetized, which keeps the screw from falling off the tip and makes it easy to pick up dropped screws. Insert bits are easy to change and relatively inexpensive to replace when they wear out.

Sometimes a screw will go in cockeyed, and you'll have to back it out. For this reason, screw guns have reversing capabilities.

You need plenty of torque to drive some of the screws available for these tools, so manufacturers gear their screw guns to various rpm outputs. The lower the rpm, the higher the torque. A typical screw gun turns (without a load) at about 2,000 rpm, and variable-speed tools are by far the most popular. A representative of Porter-Cable says they sell most of their single-speed screw guns to people who use generator power, because many variable-speed switches won't work off direct current.

I've found the biggest weakness with any electric tool—fixed-speed or variable-speed—to

Nosepieces for different jobs. There are four distinct types of nosepieces found on screw guns. The ones shown here are made by Porter-Cable, but the configurations of others are basically the same. From left to right, the first screw-gun nosepiece accepts either a bit or a bit holder, and it is used to drive any screw designed for power driving. Next is a Teks-screw nosepiece, followed by an adjustable-clutch nosepiece and a drywall-screw nosepiece. The screws from left to right are a particleboard screw, a Teks screw, a sheet-metal screw and a drywall screw.

be the switch. If I'm going on a distant or weekend job I carry spare switches.

Teks screw guns—Teks is the registered trademark of the Shakeproof Company, and it denotes a type of screw used in metal work (more on these later in the article). The depth-sensitive nosepiece of the Teks gun (photo above) is adjustable, which allows you to control the finished depth of the fastener. This feature accommodates screws that need countersinking, or those with washers that don't need to go below the surface of the material. The nosepiece functions by braking the forward motion of the gun but not the driving-tip assembly. When the screw is driven to the depth allowed by the setting, the positive clutch disengages with a nasty ratcheting sound. When you hear that sound don't panic, the tool isn't broken. It's just doing what it was designed to do—protect itself and you. In time clutches will wear down and need replacement, but it will cost you less than replacing an abused drill.

Adjustable-clutch screw guns—Some screw guns have a secondary clutch called an adjustable clutch (photo above). It usually consists of another pair of clutch dogs in the nosepiece that are held *against* one another by means of an

externally adjusted spring. Their mating angles are more obtuse than those on the positive clutch. The more you compress the spring that holds them together, the more torque you can deliver to the tip. To operate a screw gun with an adjustable clutch, you first have to run some test screws into the material to find the right torque setting to sink the screw to the proper depth. When you reach the amount of torque allowed by the setting, the dogs in the adjustable clutch disengage. If the screw isn't all the way in, just tighten the spring a bit more and have at it again.

Alternatives to the adjustable clutch are made by Fein (3019 W. Carson St., Pittsburgh, Pa. 15204) and Black & Decker. The Fein screw gun allows the operator to adjust the positive clutch, though it takes a bit of disassembly. Black & Decker makes a screw gun with a feature called a Versa Clutch that allows you to adjust the angle of the plates on the positive clutch without disassembly, thereby controlling the amount of torque delivered to the fastener.

The finely tuned torque settings allowed by an adjustable clutch can be a blessing or a curse, depending on the nature of the material you are driving the screws into. Manmade materials like particleboard, plastic or metal are ideal for the torque-sensitive clutches because they present a

Builders use drywall screw guns (left) to fasten gypboard to wood framing as well as to metal studs. The high-speed guns available today and the superior holding power of screws over nails make a drywall job that has been screwed down both competitive and less likely to develop surface blemishes as the wood dries. Fein's screw guns (below) feature a handle configuration that requires you to grip the barrel of the tool.

Four drives. Bottom photo, from left to right: a Phillips-head bit, a blade-type bit for slotted screws, a square-drive bit and a hexagonal socket. The Phillips has been the most popular configuration for power drivers, but the square-drive design is gaining on it. The blade type is marginal at best, even with the cylindrical shield that is supposed to keep the bit centered on the screw. Some Teks screws and screws with washers use a hex-head drive socket.

consistent resistance to the screw. You can run tiny screws into delicate plastics or thin sheet metal without stripping either one. Plumbers often use adjustable-clutch screwdrivers to tighten no-hub couplings, and metal-roof installers use them to make sure they don't smash the neoprene washers on their fasteners.

On the other hand, if you're using a screw gun with an adjustable clutch to drive screws into a material with varying density, such as solid wood, the torque setting may require constant adjustment to sink the screws. This is true particularly in remodeling work, where you may have to run screws alternately into new studs and then into old, well-seasoned studs. Most woodworkers prefer screw guns without adjustable clutches.

Drywall screw guns—Like the Teks gun, a drywall gun (photo top left) has a positive clutch and a depth-sensitive nosepiece. The big difference between the two is rpm. At 2,500 or 4,000 rpm, drywall guns spin faster than Teks guns. They are available in either fixed or variable-speed models, and those with variable speed are by far the most popular. Many production drywallers leave the motor on full at all times (some even tape the switch so it's always on) and use the low-speed settings only to back out a cockeyed screw. The 4,000-rpm drywall guns are used primarily to affix gypboard to metal studs, where torque isn't a major issue. If you're driving drywall screws into wood studs, the higher-torque, 2,500-rpm tool is for you. Some people buy the variable-speed 2,500-rpm drywall gun (such as AEG's SCRIE 2500) and with Teks accessories are able to convert the gun into a dual-purpose tool.

On a drywall gun, the driving tip protrudes about ¼ in. beyond the nosepiece. The exact distance has to be determined by trial and error. Once the trial screw is countersunk properly, the adjustment is correct.

In my experience, the greatest hassle with a drywall gun is in extracting a badly driven screw. Once you've cammed out in forward (the bit twists out of the screw's recess) the same usually occurs in reverse, so to extract the screw requires alteration of the nosepiece-to-tip setting. This adjustment is so tedious that you'll quickly learn to do the job right the first time. I'd like to see a quick "correction adjustment" nosepiece on the market.

The nosepiece on a drywall gun has ports cut into it to allow the gypsum dust turned up by the screw to escape. In addition, drywall guns have seals to help keep the abrasive dust out of the clutch and gear assemblies. But as anyone who ever worked drywall knows, there is no escaping the dust. It eventually works its way into the gears and clutches, wearing them down and turning the grease into a goo that resembles toothpaste. Many drywall crews toss the tools after a few big jobs because the hassle and cost of repair outweighs the expense of simply replacing them.

Some personal preferences—When I began researching this article, I came across a German company that was new to me. They make tools

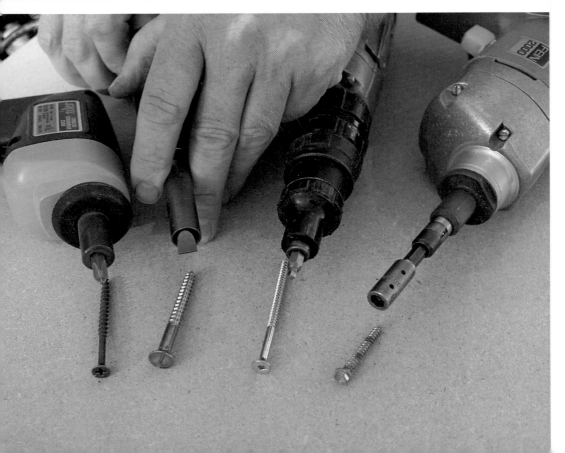

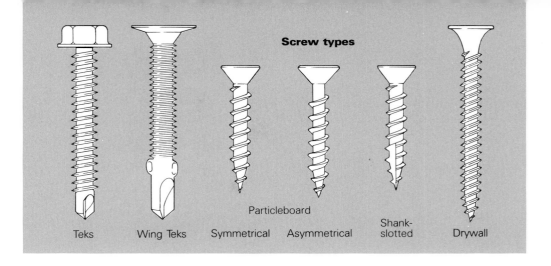

Screw types

Teks · Wing Teks · Symmetrical · Asymmetrical · Particleboard · Shank-slotted · Drywall

under the Fein (pronounced "fine") imprint, and I liked two of their screw guns well enough to buy them. One is their positive-clutch model #ASSE 636 series 2000 (middle photo, facing page), and the other is the #ASSDE 630 adjustable-clutch model. Both tools are beautifully made, and they have smooth-sounding motors and switches that allow precise control over the bit speed. The adjustable-clutch model has 16 readily indexed torque settings, and it's a very light 2.4 lb. I find it especially good at sinking little screws, like the ones I use to secure cabinet hinges, without tearing up the drive sockets. The grip on the Fein tools takes some time to get used to. The hand is forced to sit directly behind the barrel of the tool.

Of all the screw guns that I have used, I like Porter-Cable's tip retainer in their model #7533 (photo p. 113). All other guns, in my experience, have a spring or ball retainer in the hex recess to grip the tip. Frequently a screw head will grip the driving tip tightly enough to pull the tip loose. Porter-Cable's retaining tip holder is a positive mechanical holder that keeps the tip in place. Another desirable feature with Porter-Cable screw guns is the ability to change clutch assemblies so that one can take advantage of their functions without buying another complete tool. A third good feature of this tool is that you can change the positive-clutch dogs yourself when they wear out. Most other screw guns have to be sent back to the factory.

Some screw types—As screw guns become more sophisticated, so do the screws. A sampling is shown in the drawing, above right. The *Teks screw* (Shakeproof Co., St. Charles Road, Elgin, Ill. 60120) is designed for fastening to heavy-gauge steel without the tedious step of drilling a pilot hole. A Teks screw has a short length of drill bit built right into its tip, followed by a length of unthreaded shank, the thread-cutting threads and finally the head. Teks will drill and fasten in one operation, as long as the drill tip reaches through all layers being fastened.

I've found that a magnetic bit holder is a nuisance when I'm installing hex-head Teks. It attracts bits of metal cut by the screws, and these bits interfere with the fit of the nut driver to the screwhead. Non-magnetic holders won't fill with bits of metal.

A Wing Teks screw is designed for fastening wood or similar soft material to steel. There are two little tabs just behind the drill tip that ream a clearance for the threads. When the tabs encounter the steel, they shear off and permit the threads to engage. These screws are quick, clean and solid.

Particleboard screws have thin shanks and aggressive threads for good holding power. They are considered thread-forming screws because they force their way into soft materials such as wood and plastic. Southern Screw (P.O. Box 1360, Statesville, N. C. 28677) makes two versions of the particleboard screw. One has symmetrical threads for use in standard-density particleboard, and the other has asymmetrical threads to give it better holding power in high-density particleboard. Both have a 30° point for easy penetration and quick starting. There's little

material distortion with this type of screw but if you're going into the edge of particleboard or wood it's best to drill a pilot hole. Bore pilot holes large enough to accommodate the screw shank in the first piece of material, then bore a hole into the second piece that is slightly smaller than the thread diameters and half as long as the threaded portion entering the material. A tapered bit, such as those made by Fuller (PO Box 8767, Warwick, R. I. 02888-8767) can usually achieve the clear bore and pilot bore in one shot, but be careful near the end of boards, where you may split the grain.

In my opinion, particleboard screws have far better holding power than drywall screws. Drywall screws are adequate for securing drywall, but their narrow shanks aren't strong enough to drive into high-density materials. They usually break where the shank meets the screw head.

Shank-slotting (self-tapping) screws are offered by many manufacturers. This kind of screw has a wedge taken out of its tip, creating both a void and a cutting edge that cuts the female threads. These are used in materials that are hard and brittle. Cutting threads in these materials decreases internal stresses, which lessens the chance of splitting the material. In some brittle materials, a thread-forming screw would create cracking and chipping. My own experience dictates using a thread-cutting screw and a pilot hole whenever you can't afford any splitting or breakage—at the ends of boards or into very thin material.

Drywall screws were invented for fastening drywall to metal studs, but lots of builders use them in wood studs because they eliminate the nail pops that can occur when wet framing lumber dries out. When used along with a panel adhesive, you can space the screws quite far apart. The UBC permits spacing of screws that penetrate wood to a distance of ⅝ in. at 12 in. o. c. (nails are required at 7 in. for ceilings and at 8 in. on walls). The screw spacing increases to 24 in. o. c. when you use adhesive.

A drywall screw has a noticeable bugle-type flare from the shank into the head. The head is eased or rounded at its edges. These configurations are designed to limit tearing of the face paper. If the paper is torn, another fastener should be installed correctly nearby.

Drywall screws typically have a #6 shank, and a #2 Phillips head. They receive a phosphate

coating to prevent rust, but considering the rust I've seen on them, this is minimal protection.

A sturdy all-purpose screw is the zinc-plated tapping screw (sometimes called sheet-metal screws at hardware stores). They are case and core hardened, and threaded their entire length. I keep a supply of #6 and #8 tapping screws on hand from ½ in. to 2½ in. long. I use them to hang cabinets, and in 15 years I've never broken a screw. They are zinc-plated, so I can use them outdoors with relative impunity, and I can get them in pan, flat or oval head styles.

New styles—With the advent of power drivers, manufacturers have developed new styles of fastener recesses for better transmission of the torque from the tool to the fastener. The square drive is the best of them, but the Quadrex looks very good too.

Square drive is exactly what it says. Just as your socket wrench has a square drive, so does the bit used to drive these screws (bottom photo, facing page). The driver's edges are slightly eased, but there's a definite grip between driver and screw. Apparently, this screw is gaining rapidly on the Phillips, the old favorite for power drivers. My own experience with square-drive screws has been positive. Compared to the Phillips the square drive has almost no tendency to twist out of the socket, even with a worn driver.

Quadrex is a registered trademark of Isotech Consultants, Inc. It is a new design that combines the features of a Phillips head and a square drive. Its claimed advantage is that you can use a square drive to install a screw with a Quadrex recess, and use a Phillips screwdriver to work on it in the field.

Sources of supply—Very few hardware stores or lumberyards have a wide range of the many screws available these days. City folks can usually find a big supplier that sells over the counter to professionals, but if you live in the country chances are you'll be shopping for fasteners through the mail. Two outfits that I have dealt with are A and I Bolt and Nut (209 Kalamath St., Denver, Colo. 80223) and Thunander Corp. (P.O. Box 1166, Elkhart, Ind. 46515). Both have given me good service, and both carry an extensive stock. Catalogs are available on request. □

M. F. Marti is a contractor who divides his time between jobs in Oregon and Colorado.

Routers

Knowing the basic bits and how to guide the router will help you get the most from this versatile tool on site and in the shop

by Craig Savage

I build custom homes for a living. This requires that I set up, at least for a short period of time, a millwork shop on the construction site. Bringing my two routers along lets me leave several heavy machines at my permanent shop. At various times I've used the router to perform the work of a shaper and a slot mortiser, and with my 3-in. trim bit I can put an edge on a board that looks as though it has been passed across a jointer.

Rabbeting, grooving, dadoing and edge shaping are the simple operations that most people associate with routers. But routers are versatile enough to do dozens of other useful operations, including pattern cutting, laminate trimming, mortising, dovetailing and finger jointing. Routers can cut all of the wood structural joints, including tongue-and-groove, half-laps and splines. Other more esoteric operations include straightening and flattening boards, plunging holes, making dowels, inlaying, freehand carving and even sharpening tools.

Choosing a router—A router, in its basic form, consists of a direct-drive motor/arbor assembly, a base assembly and a chuck for holding the router bits, as shown in the drawing on the facing page. The motor-assembly housing nests inside the base assembly (like concentric cylinders). A threaded-collar device for raising and lowering the motor assembly relative to the base unit changes the depth of cut.

There are many routers on the market. Their rated outputs range from ¼ hp to 3¼ hp, while their rated speeds range from 18,000 to 30,000 rpm. Because of this they can produce smooth, crisp cuts and leave the wood fairly free of tell-tale mill marks. There are specialty routers that only trim plastic laminates, overhead pin routers that do pattern cutting and edge trimming, and stationary routers, set upside down, that function as small shapers.

I think a good general-purpose router should be moderately large—at least 2 hp. A router this size can do everything that a small one can do except get into tight corners. This much power will keep you from overloading the motor by running it at lower than rated speeds. Small routers can manage deep cuts that remove a lot of wood, but you have to make several shallow cuts instead of a single pass. If you are thinking of using the router for more than edge-shaping, then buy a 2-hp or better router.

Rating systems for router motors vary among manufacturers, much as they do for skillsaws and other power tools. This makes comparing performance a difficult if not impossible job. And don't think that just because your Brand A electric drill is a good tool that Brand A's router will also be good. It doesn't always work that way. Your best bet is to consult someone who uses routers on a regular basis, or a tool dealer you trust.

Routers come with several different handle configurations. At first all of them seem awkward to hold. Two handles low and at the sides work best for me; others prefer the D handle in front, with trigger switch. Some routers have no handles at all. These are usually small routers that lend themselves to one-handed work like laminate trimming and freehand carving.

Some routers just have a toggle switch, which means that if the switch is on and the cord plugged in, the tool will come to life. This is a very dangerous design. I recommend a spring-loaded switch in a handy position so the power is turned off if the switch isn't depressed. Another thing to look for is wrench access. Most collet systems require two wrenches and some allow ample room for them, but others are built as if you were never going to change the bit.

You'll have to pay for performance. Good ball bearings, horsepower and close-tolerance castings cost money, and usually the more you pay the more you get. Look for value not only in initial price, but in dealer support. Ask about spare-part replacement time. Even quality tools break down, and it's frustrating to have to wait four to six weeks because your top-of-the-line router needs a switch unit that's on a siding in Topeka or Tokyo.

Routers commonly accept three sizes of bit shaft—¼ in., ⅜ in. and ½ in. Naturally, a ½-in. shaft is stronger than a ¼-in. shaft, and if you're trying to put a 1-in. wide groove ¾ in. deep in miles of maple, then you're going to want a powerful router and a bit with a ½-in. shaft.

Routers that accept ½-in. shafts can usually be converted to smaller sizes by inserting smaller-diameter collets into the arbor. This is another reason for starting out with a larger router, since it will accept any bit. Also, some bits just can't be made with small shanks because of cutter size or the bearing-guide design.

Plunge routers are becoming popular in the United States, and with good reason. They have a motor that rides up and down inside the base assembly (photo facing page) or on a pair of posts anchored to the base. This allows the bit to be turned on above the work, then lowered vertically into it. Plunging turns the router into a slot mortiser. Slot mortising is a convenient and fast way to get strong mortise-and-tenon joints. With the use of a few jigs, slip-joining has replaced doweling as my main method of joining cabinet face frames and door frames (more on this later).

The plunge router can also do blind dadoes and grooves, and it can be locked to function as a normal router. This makes the plunge router the most versatile of the routers, and I strongly suggest you consider purchasing one—especially if it is going to be your only router.

I think that plunge routers also have the edge in safety. I'm in the habit of raising the bit into the body of the router after each cut, even if I'm not plunging. This gets the cutting edges out of the way of fingers, and lets me set the router on its flat, stable baseplate rather than on its side.

Baseplates—The surface that rides on the work and frequently guides the router is the baseplate. It is usually made of black phenolic-resin plastic. You can custom-make your own out of Plexiglas, aluminum, plywood, medium-density fiberboard or hardboard. Bases can be round or square.

I thank Makita for introducing me to the square baseplate. The square baseplate gives a constant distance between bit and base edge. The round base, even when accurately made, isn't always perfectly concentric to the bit. This error, although slight, can double in certain operations and become a nuisance. Even if your baseplate starts out round with a centered bit, the screw holes in the base eventually get worked out of round, and the result is the same. Of course, you'll need round baseplates to follow curved templates. The trick then is to mark a spot on the baseplate and always keep the mark pressed against the guide surface.

I find that the round bases that came with my routers are most useful as screw-location templates for the baseplates that I custom-make to perform specific tasks. I usually make these of ¼-in. hardboard, tempered on both sides. They range from 8 in. by 8 in. to over 24 in. by 24 in. The small one rides on a template, and I use the large one to increase my baseplate bearing when I'm doing edge-forming work (photo facing page). The big one can also ride on two guides, allowing the router to float over the workpiece as it flattens an uneven surface (drawing, above right).

Bits—The bit is the business end of the router. Bits have hundreds of profiles, but they all fall into two basic categories: piloted and unpiloted. A piloted bit has a cylindrical surface on the

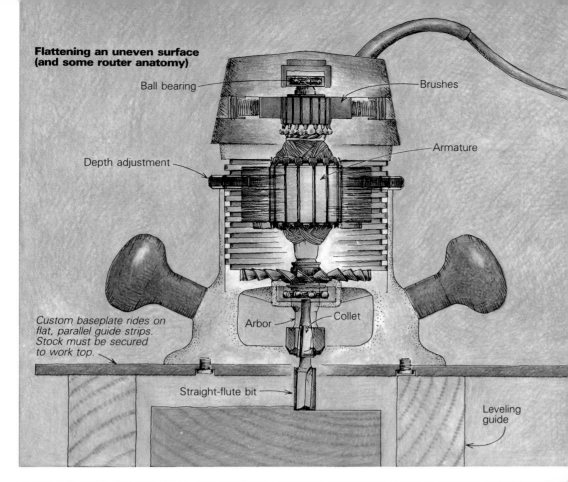

Flattening an uneven surface (and some router anatomy)

Ball bearing · Brushes · Depth adjustment · Armature · Custom baseplate rides on flat, parallel guide strips. Stock must be secured to work top. · Arbor · Collet · Straight-flute bit · Leveling guide

Savage uses a ¾-in. radius roundover bit with a bearing pilot to soften the edge of a redwood handrail (facing page). A 2-ft. square router baseplate allows more contact between the work and the router, which makes it easier to keep the bit perpendicular to the work during the cut. The motor assembly in a plunge router (right) moves up and down inside the cylindrical base casting. The vertical bar is an adjustable depth stop. Here a 3½-hp Stanley (now Bosch) plunge router cuts louver mortises in a door stile. The dowel in the 2x4 is a registration mark for the particleboard template. The 8-in. square hardboard baseplate makes it easy to align the template fences, and keeps the bit a consistent distance from the fences.

Drawings: Christopher Clapp

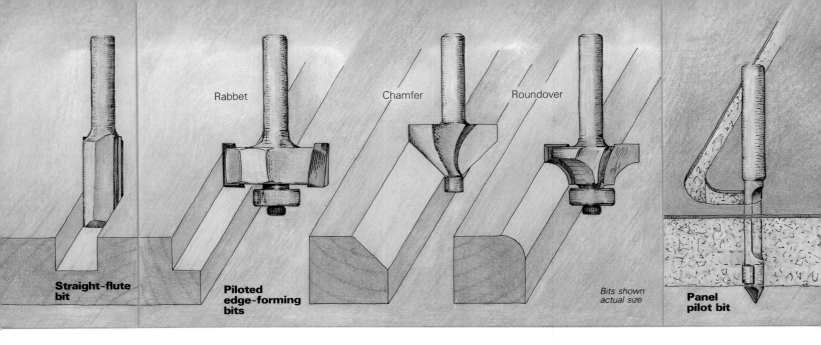

Rabbet Chamfer Roundover

Straight-flute bit

Piloted edge-forming bits

Bits shown actual size

Panel pilot bit

shaft of the bit that bears against the edge of the work during the cut. This surface guides the router, and it can be either above or below the flutes, or cutters. At least 1/16 in. of the original edge must remain for the pilot to follow. Some pilots are solid and some are ball-bearing. Solid pilots use a polished portion of the shaft as the bearing surface, but these can burnish and sometimes burn the work. Ball-bearing pilots are the best because they won't mar the work. Unpiloted bits lack this built-in guide.

A bit's cutting edge can either be high-speed steel (HSS) or carbide. There are production bits that use exotic coatings such as diamond and zirconium, but only HSS and carbide are affordable. Carbide bits (some are solid carbide, most are carbide tipped) cost three or four times more than HSS, but they last seven to fifteen times longer, depending on the material they are used to cut. Most of my bits are carbide tipped. If you do one-of-a-kind pieces and need only a few feet of some unique profile, then go ahead and buy the HSS bit. It won't hurt to have it around. With a grinder you can even change its shape, to reproduce old moldings or make new ones of your own design.

Within the broad categories of piloted and unpiloted, there are distinct families of bits, shown in the drawings on these pages.

Straight-flute bits. These unpiloted bits cut grooves, rabbets, and dadoes (grooves across the grain), and they can have one, two or three cutting edges (flutes). The more flutes, the smoother (and slower) the cut. They can also be used to template-cut, flatten or remove lots of wood. They are among my busiest bits.

Edge-forming bits. These bits do decorative cuts, such as chamfers, ogees, roundovers and coves. For routers with 1/2-in. collets, you can get a matched pair of piloted bits that will cut a bevel-and-tongue profile that's 15/8 in. wide. Rabbeting bits also fall into this category. Many edge-forming bits don't have pilots. You use a fence to guide them.

Piloted edge-forming bits cut a profile that can be varied only in the vertical plane, by raising or lowering the bit. Unpiloted bits, because they have to be used with the router's fence,

can be adjusted vertically and horizontally, and so are more versatile.

Panel pilot bits. These bits are used for drilling through the workpiece, and then cutting laterally. They are used for scrollwork and latticework. The pilot underneath can follow a template and do things like sink cutouts and curved designs.

Groove-forming bits. Like the straight-flute bits, these unpiloted bits make grooves, dadoes and rabbets. They include core-box bits, which can make the half-round flutes in a column or pilaster, and V-groove bits, which can simulate chamfered plank construction. They also include hinge mortise bits and dovetail bits.

Plunge bits. These unpiloted bits have cutting edges on their ends as well as on their sides. They can be straight or spiral fluted, carbide or HSS. They have two tasks: to cut material and to remove it from the hole—not an easy job. This probably explains why there's so much variety and confusion concerning plunge-bit configuration. I've had good luck using the Ekstrom Carlson spiral-flute HSS plunge bits (Ekstrom Carlson & Co., 1400 Railroad Ave., Rockford, Ill. 61110). They come in 1/4-in. to 3/4-in. sizes with 1/2-in. shafts. They last a long time and remove chips better than straight-flute bits. They can also be used to cut grooves and trim edges.

Slotting cutters. If you've got to cut a groove in the edge of a board, slotting cutters are what you need. They have two, three or four "wings," and each has a carbide cutting edge brazed to it. A slotting cutter's pilot bearing allows the wings to penetrate to a preset depth. Both dimensions, the depth of cut and the distance off the face of the workpiece, are very consistent. With one of these, you can cut a slot to accept the panel in your frame-and-panel door, or the tongue on your T&G flooring.

The slot width is determined by the cutter face. It can be from 1/16 in. to 1/4 in. It is possible to get arbors, wing cutters and bearings, and interchange them to get the size slot that you want. These are very useful bits.

Laminate trimmers. Laminate trimmers are usually straight-flute carbide bits with a ball-bearing pilot that's exactly the same diameter as

the bit's cutting arc. The bearing travels along the vertical surface of the workpiece, and trims the overhanging horizontal sheet flush with it. There are laminate-trim bits with 71/2°, 10° and 22° bevels to ease the sharp edges on countertops where laminates meet at 90°.

Trim bits. This kind of bit resembles a laminate trimmer, but it is larger. And because the pilot bearing is positioned above the cutter, it can be used to follow a pattern or template that's mounted on top of the workpiece. These bits come in all sizes, from 1/2 in. to 3 in. long, and from 1/2 in. to 1 in. in diameter. They usually have straight flutes, but I have a 3-in. long, 1-in. diameter version made by Oakland Carbide Engineering Co.(1232 51st Ave., Oakland, Calif. 94601) that has spiral cutters. With this bit I

Trim bit
A trim bit is used with a pattern to produce a finished surface. In the photo below, a 3-in. bit with a bearing above the cutters follows a straightedge clamped to a door.

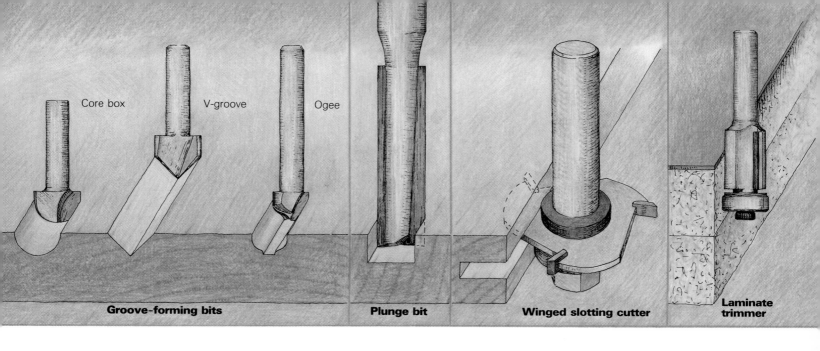

Core box   V-groove   Ogee

Groove-forming bits   **Plunge bit**   **Winged slotting cutter**   **Laminate trimmer**

can trim the bottom of a 2-in. thick door by using a straightedge clamped to the door as a guide (drawing and photo on facing page), or I can make a pattern out of ¼-in. hardboard for curved surfaces. Curved or straight, the bit cuts a faithful copy of the pattern. Panels that are too large for the table saw can be cut with a skillsaw and then trimmed precisely with this type of bit.

Router-bit care—I keep my bits stored upright in a block of wood. Their shanks rest in holes drilled ¹⁄₆₄ in. oversize. Stored this way, they never touch anything that could damage them, especially neighboring bits.

A stubborn sludge of resin and wood dust can build up on the faces of router bits and actually make them duller by compacting right on the cutting edge. This can cause bits to overheat and sustain permanent damage. I keep my bits clean with a strong detergent like 409. I've tried various ammonia and commercial blade cleaners, but none seems significantly superior. I just give the bit a squirt and then wipe it clean in a few minutes. Every so often I'll mist all my bits with a light oil like WD40. Pilot bearings should get an occasional drop of oil. If you get contact cement on the pilot bearing while you are doing plastic-laminate work, take the time to soak the cement off in a solvent like lacquer thinner. Otherwise the bearing may seize, putting a decorative burn in your work.

After I've cleaned a bit, I drag it across my fingernail to see if it's sharp. A sharp one will drag and dig into the nail—dull ones simply slide across. You can hone and sharpen steel bits yourself, and I'm told that carbide bits can be successfully touched up with a diamond hone. But to tell the truth, I don't mess with sharpening bits. It doesn't cost much, and the pros are set up to do it right.

I clean the collet and bit shafts with fine steel wool. This helps to keep the bit from freezing in the collet. When I run up against a frozen bit, I take out a small brass mallet and gently tap someplace on the bit that is not a cutting edge. I try to tap at an angle that slightly tweaks the bit in the collet. I turn the shaft frequently between the slight taps. Eventually the bit comes free.

Putting router to wood—Before you install a bit in the collet, unplug the router. This is one rule I never break. Insert the bit shaft, and make sure it extends at least ½ in. into the collet. Better yet, put the shaft to the bottom of the collet, lift it ⅛ in. and then tighten the nut.

Now adjust the depth of cut—the distance between the baseplate and the cutter tip. Some routers have a threaded motor case that screws up and down into a threaded base. Others have rack-and-pinion gears that move the motor relative to the base. I measure the bit extension off the baseplate with a steel ruler scaled in 64ths, and I add a known amount to compensate for the slight movement that happens when you tighten the depth-lock wing nut. This slop is built into most routers, and you must take it into account if you want accurate results. Precise settings are critical in such operations as dovetailing drawers and mortising for hinges. Then I make a test cut and repeat; loosening, adjusting, tightening, until it's correct.

Before I turn on the router, I go over a mental

Directing the router
Because of the high-speed clockwise rotation of the bit, there's a right and a wrong direction to enter the work. The router should be moved around the work so that the cutters are exiting the material as the router advances. In wood, the end-grain edges should be cut first.

Bit spins clockwise.

list of safety checks. Is the work snugly clamped? Are the fences secure? Is the bit tightened? Is the cord out of the way and free to travel the distance of the cut?

If you've never used a router before, try a test cut in softwood with an edge-forming bit. The bit should enter the wood at full speed, so make sure the two aren't touching when you turn on the router. With the baseplate flat on the workpiece, slowly let the bit into the wood until the pilot touches the edge. Now lead the router around the edge so that the cutters are exiting the wood as the router advances from left to right, if the edge is facing you (drawing, left). If you go the opposite direction (back cutting), the bit will want to dig into the wood—self-feeding, it's called—like a little high-speed, steel-studded tire, taking the router with it. In some cases, however, back cutting can be useful. When routing across the grain, making a little back cut at the extreme right-hand edge of the work will eliminate the chance of the wood splintering out when the bit exits the cut.

Listen to the router. When you turn it on it will sound like it's running too fast. When it enters the wood it will have a lower pitch. As you feed more forcefully into the wood it will be lower still. But these changes in pitch are nothing compared to the lowering of the pitch when you begin to force the feed and overload the motor. Feed rates are affected by the obvious things—the power of the router, the sharpness and number of the cutters, the depth of cut and the type of material you're working.

If your feed rate is too slow, the router will spin too fast, burnishing, often burning, the edges of the cut and tossing out chips that resemble baby powder. When it is cutting correctly, the router glides smoothly across the work, making mounds of large, smooth, clean chips. A router doesn't have to be gripped too tightly, and it doesn't have to be guided with too much force. If you relax and try to feel what the cutter is doing, you'll get consistently good results.

Fences—Most routers come with a fence attachment (called a guide assembly by manufacturers). It is typically made of two steel rods that attach to the baseplate, and a metal fence that slides over the rods. These fences work but they are inevitably too short or slightly skewed to the base, or the cutter is too large and the fence interrupts its arc. I hardly ever use factory-made fence attachments.

A fence can be clamped to the work (photo below) or to the router baseplate. It's usually a straight piece of scrap, but it can have an inside or outside curve in order to follow a matching curve on the workpiece. When you use a straightedge to guide a cut—for instance, a groove with a straight-flute bit—you should lead the router in a direction opposite the one that it's inclined to take (drawing below right). This way the router will snug itself against the fence, rather than try to push away from it.

The router mounted upside-down can act like a shaper. I had a machinist mill away some of the webbing under my table-saw wing, and drill a hole for the bit and some smaller holes for flathead screws that hold the router to the wing. This lets me mount my small router to the saw table (photo facing page, top left). The cutters protrude perpendicularly through the hole in the wing. A notched wooden fence clamps around the cutter (photo facing page, center left). I use fingerboard hold-ins and hold-downs made of Baltic birch plywood to steady the work. I can move the saw fence right up to the cutter, letting me make linear passes for moldings and casings. The saw's miter gauge can be used to make crosscut passes, easing the construction of finger joints, slip joints, half-laps and tenons.

Bushings—Guide bushings are collars that are screwed to the router base and surround the bit. The guide bushing (drawing, bottom left) is de-signed to bear against a template, allowing you to make accurate pattern cuts. These guides work especially well for small jobs where repetitive, accurate setups are required, such as hinge mortises (photo facing page, bottom left), dove-tails and box joints. I find setting up bushing-and-template systems tedious, and they're frustrating to use. Often it's difficult to install the guide bushing so it's concentric with the cutting diameter of the bit. And when making templates, it can be a pain to figure the small offsets that have to be taken into account when using guide bushings. I prefer fences and templates, though some jigs and fixtures have to be used with guide bushings. This is certainly the case with stair-routing jigs and dovetail fixtures, where precise depth-of-cut adjustments are important.

Templates—I made a simple template to mortise the butt hinges into the stiles and jambs of some custom doors. It works in conjunction with a custom-made square baseplate, and consists of a 7-ft. 1x4 with three identical mortise templates (photo facing page, right) made of ¼-in. particleboard. I can clamp this entire unit to a door, ensuring equal hinge spacing every time. I used hot-melt glue to position the fences, and then I tested each one for accuracy with a cut. The hot-melt glue lets me fabricate a template quickly, though the bond isn't very strong. When I'm satisfied with the fit, I anchor the fences with screws.

To cut a hinge mortise, I use a straight-flute bit set to a depth that equals the hinge thickness plus the template thickness. The bit enters the stile from the side, in a space cut into the template for this purpose. As I pass the router baseplate around the confines of the template fences, the bit cuts a mortise. If the mortise is a little wide, I stick a few strips of tape to the inside of the fences for shims.

Louver-door jig—My co-worker Peter Feirabend came up with a jig to cut louver mortises in a door stile. It takes advantage of the plunge router's capabilities and the square baseplate. A pair of 2x4 rails are clamped to the stile, and a template fits atop the 2x4s (photo p. 117). Holes drilled in one of the 2x4s are spaced one louver apart. They accept a dowel registration pin. Peter made the template by placing the square baseplate on a piece of ¼-in. particleboard, and gluing fences to the template on opposite sides of the baseplate. These fences lightly touch the baseplate, guiding the router in a straight line. Then he added stops to the template to limit the router's travel. These determine the width of the louver. In use, the template is oriented at 30° to the stile. Using a ¼-in. plunge bit, Peter lowers the bit into the work and makes a few passes back and forth. Then he retracts the bit, slides the template down the stile and moves the registration dowel to the next stop.

To make the louvers, I rip stock to the right dimension, and then I run it by a roundover bit mounted in the router/table-saw setup.

Cabinet doors—I use slip tenons (sometimes called loose tenons or inserted tenons) instead of dowels to reinforce doors and face frames at

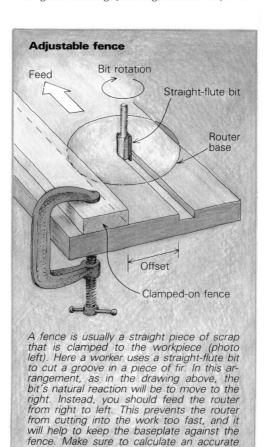

Adjustable fence

Feed

Bit rotation

Straight-flute bit

Router base

Offset

Clamped-on fence

A fence is usually a straight piece of scrap that is clamped to the workpiece (photo left). Here a worker uses a straight-flute bit to cut a groove in a piece of fir. In this arrangement, as in the drawing above, the bit's natural reaction will be to move to the right. Instead, you should feed the router from right to left. This prevents the router from cutting into the work too fast, and it will help to keep the baseplate against the fence. Make sure to calculate an accurate offset distance from the cut to the fence.

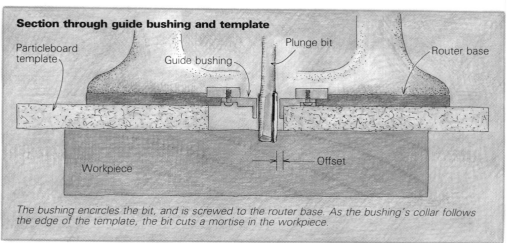

Section through guide bushing and template

Particleboard template

Guide bushing

Plunge bit

Router base

Workpiece

Offset

The bushing encircles the bit, and is screwed to the router base. As the bushing's collar follows the edge of the template, the bit cuts a mortise in the workpiece.

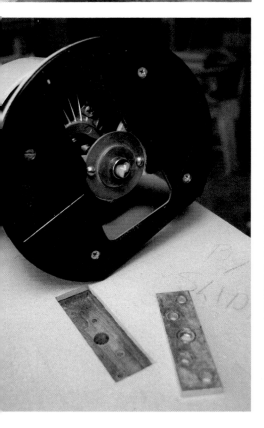

A router mounted under the wing of a table saw turns the saw table into a shaper (top left). The bit protrudes through the table, where a clamped-on wooden fence is aligned with it. At center, the author uses an ovolo bit with a fillet to carve a decorative edge on a door rail. A slot for the door panel was cut with a winged slotting cutter. The template at left is used along with a guide bushing (drawing facing page, bottom) to cut a hinge-plate mortise. As with all routed mortises, the corners are rounded and have to be squared with a chisel. Above, this template uses fences to guide the router base as the bit cuts mortises for butt hinges. The rectangular hole in the center of each template shows the area where the bit cuts. The slot in front of the stile is an entry hole for the bit.

Plunge-router door frames. Savage's frame-and-panel doors are reinforced at the corners with slip tenons (above). The tenons are inserted into mortises cut with a ⅜-in. plunge bit. Where the rail and stile meet, the ovolo pattern must be mitered at 45°. To cut the miter, Savage uses a V-groove bit mounted under the wing of his table saw to act as a shaper (above right). The saw's miter gauge guides the work during the cut.

The fixture in the photo below secures door-frame members while they are mortised with a plunge bit. The penciled centerline on the rail aligns with a centerline on the face of the fixture. During the cut (right), the router base rests on the fixture and travels between the two clamped-on stops. A fence clamped to the router base guides the cut. The first cut is ¼ in. deep. Subsequent cuts are ½ in. deep, until the final depth is reached.

the joints (top photo, far left). These joints aren't limited to light duty—I've used them with great success on entry doors up to 3 ft. wide.

I start by cutting grooves for the door panels in the rails and stiles with a ¼-in. winged slotting cutter, mounted shaper style under the table saw. At this point I could slot the end of the rails and butt-join the stile to the rail with a spline and have an acceptable frame for a cabinet door. But these doors have a pattern running on the inside of the frame, and they meet at 90°, so they must be mitered where the patterns join, as shown in the photo.

Next I run the pattern, in this case an ovolo with fillet, on the inside edge of the rail and stile stock (photo previous page, center left). Then I lay out the frame as if it were to be butt-joined, and I draw centerlines for the mortises across the rail and stile faces. Next I miter the decorative edge with, you guessed it, a V-groove bit (top photo, left).

Now I can plunge the mortises for the slip tenons. For this operation I use a fixture that clamps to the edge of my workbench. It has slots cut into it for various clamps to hold the frame parts and the stop blocks. The fixture's front panel has a penciled registration mark that aligns with the mortise centerline drawn on the rails and stiles (photo bottom left). The fixture's front and back panels are at the same height, creating a surface for the router baseplate to ride atop that is perpendicular to the workpiece (photo center left). A fence clamped to the baseplate regulates the horizontal relationship between the cutter and the workpiece. To cut the mortises, I use a HSS ⅜-in. spiral-fluted plunge bit.

Finally, I make tenon stock the same way I shaped the louvers, and I cut them to length. The various parts are easy to assemble, and a strong custom door is the result.

Maintenance and safety—Most of the bearings in today's routers are sealed and don't need any maintenance other than wiping or blowing away the dust and dirt. The same goes for the motor and brushes. If you don't force the tool and overload it, it will do lots of work.

Routers are noisy, they make a lot of dust and they sometimes send bits of wood and metal flying about at high speed. Ear protection, dust masks and goggles are standard precautionary garb. To be honest, I don't always wear these things when I'm doing plunge cuts because the bit is contained by the work. But if I've got my snout down there at ground zero watching the bit make a cut, I've got every piece of safety equipment in the shop on my head.

When you are back-cutting around a corner where the change in grain direction causes tear-out of the fibers, use great care. Hold the router firmly and be ready to counter a good amount of pull.

A safer way to get the same result is to clamp a scrap piece to the edge of the workpiece for the bit to exit through. This protects your finished edge from tear-out. □

Craig Savage builds custom homes near his home in Kootenai, Idaho.

Photo top right: Dick Oniell

Cordless Drills
Assault with battery

by Bill Phelps

Power drills without power cords. It's an appealing proposition to anyone who has unraveled a tangled drill cord to drill one hole, or dragged 75 ft. of extension cord to the roof, or looked in vain for a nearby outlet. With the help of modern battery technology, cordless drills are now available from most manufacturers of small power tools.

Although they can't produce the high speeds or the torque that a cord-powered drill does, cordless drills are powerful enough to handle countless drilling jobs with ease. They can also substitute for their cord-connected cousins in tight spots, where a power cord is more a nuisance than an impossibility. In wet or damp areas, cordless drills are safer because they nearly eliminate the hazard of electric shock.

These versatile tools often double as cordless screwdrivers, and several manufacturers have designed their drills to work as well driving screws as they do drilling. There are, however, specialized tools called screw guns that excel at this sort of work, and you should investigate these if driving screws is what you'll be doing most (see pp. 112-115).

The best way to learn about cordless drills is to take them to the job site, and that's exactly what I did. I used tools by Bosch, Skil, Black & Decker, Porter-Cable, AEG and Makita to drill steel, aluminum, plastic, hardwoods and softwoods. I drilled ⅝-in. bolt holes through 6-in. beams, drilled pilot holes for lag bolts, and drove 2-in. grabber screws through subflooring into Douglas fir joists. I used them to hang cabinets and doors, and even fitted them with a nut-driver bit to install metal roofing. After all that, I'm very impressed with how well these drills work—whenever it can handle the job, a cordless drill is the one I reach for first.

What follows is a detailed look at what makes cordless drills work. After that, I'll tell you what I found out about the particular drills I tested, which are shown in the photos on this page. To give you some basic information on what other cordless drills are available, I've included some of them in the chart on p. 126.

Batteries—The really tough jobs, like drilling ⅝-in. holes clear through a Douglas fir beam, are the ones that define the limits of what cordless drills can accomplish. This limitation is largely due to the battery.

The battery, or *battery pack*, is a cordless drill's most important component. The pack is actually a package of several small batteries

Among many cordless drills on the market are (top to bottom) the Skil #2725, Bosch #1920-VSRK and Porter-Cable #800.

Top to bottom: AEG EZ-506, Makita 6012-HDW and Black & Decker #1940. The drills in these photos were tested by Phelps for this article.

connected in series, contained in a plastic housing. All cordless drills use rechargeable nickel-cadmium (ni-cad) batteries, which can maintain a relatively constant voltage during use. The drill will continue to operate near full power until the battery charge is depleted, and then it will stop quickly. Ni-cad batteries can be stored for months, either charged or discharged, without damage or loss of capacity, so you don't have to worry about them if your drill has been gathering dust on a shelf for a while.

One of the two specifications that appear on the nameplate of a cordless drill is its DC voltage (VDC) rating. This is the combined voltage of the ni-cad batteries in the battery pack. Each individual battery has a rating of 1.2 VDC. When the batteries are connected in series, the total voltage is the sum of their individual voltages—six batteries will produce a total of 7.2 VDC, and eight will produce 9.6 VDC. These are the most common voltages for cordless drills. The two extra batteries in the 9.6-volt drills provide more energy-storage capacity and more power potential. They also add somewhat to the weight of the drill.

The professional models have battery packs that can be removed from the drill for recharging. This has a couple of advantages over plugging the whole drill into the charger, as is done with most lighter-duty drills. If you have a second battery pack to use while the first is being recharged, you can operate the drill continuously by simply alternating packs all day; they can usually be completely recharged in one hour. The battery packs for different makes aren't interchangeable, however.

Another advantage of this system is that it allows the battery pack to be replaced when it wears out. The packs have a lifespan of between 300 and 800 charges, depending mostly on how the drill is used. Even if the battery pack is used very little, it will wear out in about three to four years as the separators between the positive and negative electrodes of the batteries oxidize. The rate of oxidation of the separators increases geometrically as their temperature rises. Since hard use and frequent recharging generate heat, they will decrease the lifespan of the batteries. As batteries age, their storage capacity will gradually decrease.

Another important factor to consider when using a cordless drill—or any ni-cad tool, for that matter—is the ambient temperature. Even when they're new, battery packs will last longer and work best at temperatures between 50°F and 104°F, and they won't even take a charge below 32°F. Since the batteries depend on chemical reaction to store and release energy, they don't function efficiently when it's very cold and the chemical reactions are slowed down. If the tem-

Cordless drills are particularly useful when electrical outlets aren't easily reached. In this photo, a worker is using one to drive hex-head screws in the metal roof of an agricultural building.

perature of the battery pack rises above 122°F, serious damage to its storage capacity will result. At high temperatures, water vapor and other gases produced by the batteries are released through safety vents designed to prevent the packs from exploding under pressure. The battery pack still works after venting, but loses some of its storage capacity. So keep batteries out of the trunk of your car on hot days, and put the drill in a shady spot when you break for lunch. In cold weather, you can put spare batteries in an inside pocket of your coat to keep them warm.

The storage capacity of the batteries can also be reduced by what is called the *memory effect.* If you top off a partial charge frequently, the total storage capacity of the batteries will be reduced to the amount of the partial charge. The memory effect shows up when the drills are used in a consistent—and incorrect—pattern. One manufacturer told me about a complaint he received from a drywall contractor whose workers drove drywall screws with cordless drills. The workers had a habit of changing battery packs during coffee breaks and at lunch, before the batteries had fully discharged. The repetitive partial recharges eventually reduced the storage capacity of the batteries. To restore the full charge capacity of ni-cad batteries after their storage capacity has been reduced, they must be completely drained and fully recharged several times. A small percentage of the capacity will be lost forever, though.

Battery chargers—The battery charger is separate from the drill and plugs into 120-volt household current. Each drill manufacturer makes a charger designed to accept only its own battery packs, but they are all very similar in function. The alternating current voltage (AC) of household current is reduced with a transformer and converted to direct current (DC), which charges the batteries.

As the batteries become fully charged and their temperature rises, a temperature-sensitive switch turns off the power supply. Some chargers use an electronic switch that senses when the batteries are fully charged to turn off the power supply. With either method, though, you can leave the battery pack in its charger for long periods of time without damage. In addition, all of the chargers I've seen have one or two indicator lights that let you know when the charger is working and when the batteries are fully charged. Some manufacturers offer a charger that plugs into the cigarette lighter of your truck, so you can power up on those jobs in the middle of nowhere, too.

Speed controls—The speed and torque produced by a drill bear an inverse relationship to each other. As speed increases, torque decreases (torque is the force that turns the chuck). This means that manufacturers can control the torque of a drill by employing a speed control of some sort—generally a trigger switch—thereby making the drill more versatile.

The second specification that appears on the drill's nameplate is the no-load drill speed in revolutions per minute (rpm). This is the rotational speed of the drill chuck when it is turning freely, and indicates what jobs the drill will do best. When I drilled ⅛-in. holes in both 26-ga. steel roofing and ¹⁄₁₆-in. aluminum sheets, I found that a faster drill speed noticeably reduced the time required to drill the holes, and the job didn't require much torque. Faster speeds are also best for drilling plastic, glass or any hard, brittle material that is likely to fracture if the drill bit snags. On the other hand, drilling through wood with an auger bit requires slower drill speed and much more torque. The slow-speed, high-torque combination also works best when the drill is used to drive screws.

Faced with these different drilling requirements, manufacturers use different approaches for controlling the speed of their drills. The simplest and most economical method is a simple on-off trigger switch. These drills have one speed that's somewhere between 600 rpm and 1,850 rpm. They are less expensive to manufacture and tend to be more durable because the speed-control mechanism is quite simple. If your drill will be used for a similar drilling task over

		CORDLESS DRILLS TESTED						
Company	Model*	Battery voltage	Speed	RPM	Clutch settings	Weight, lb. (incl. batt.)	Price (incl. batt.)
AEG	EZ-506	7.2	Variable	100-600	6	3.0	**
Black & Decker	1940	9.6	One	800	0	3.1	$174.00
Bosch	1920-VSRK	7.2	2-speed variable	0-300 0-650	0	2.9	$169.00
Makita	6012-HDW	9.6	Two	400/1100	5	3.5	$188.00
Porter-Cable	800 Hammer drill	9.6	Two	350/1000	0	4.5	$195.00
Skil	2725	7.2	Variable	0-250 0-750	0	3.25	$139.00

*All drills include ⅜-in. chuck and reversing switch.   **Information unavailable.

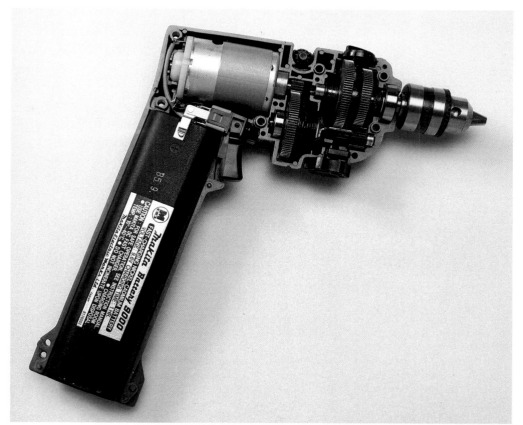

Anatomy of a cordless drill. The motor of the Makita #6012 (above the trigger) transfers power through an adjustable clutch to the two large spur gears on the chuck spindle. The clutch shaft and the chuck spindle are each supported by a brass bushing at one end and ball bearings at the other.

and over again, a single-speed model is all you need. The two-speed models are more versatile, with one high speed between 600 and 1,100 rpm, and a low speed around 300 to 400 rpm. A dial or lever on the drill mechanically shifts gears so that you can easily adjust to different drilling situations.

Variable-speed control is the most versatile approach for drilling or for driving screws. It gives you the ability to begin drilling at a very slow speed to prevent the bit from wandering, and then increase the speed while you are drilling. It also allows greater control when driving short screws or when working with finish materials. I grew accustomed to variable-speed con-

trol on my cord-carrying drill, so I was pleased to find this feature on cordless drills.

For a manufacturer, variable-speed control on a cordless drill presents some engineering problems. To make it work, sophisticated electronic control circuits are required. One type converts the direct current coming from the batteries into alternating current so that the power can be varied, and then converts it back into direct current to power the drill's DC motor. As the pressure applied to the trigger changes, the control circuit constantly adjusts the power to the motor, which varies the motor speed.

The AEG drill goes one step further. It has a tachometer that monitors the motor speed and

sends a signal pulse at each rotation back to the control circuit. When the drill starts to slow down, the power input to the drill motor is increased even though the pressure on the trigger is the same. This is called feedback and is very much like cruise control on a car. Another type of circuit, used on the Bosch #1920, has a silicon control rectifier that electronically adjusts the electrical resistance and hence the power flow to the drill motor.

The electronic circuits used with the variable-speed control are vulnerable to power surges when the drill is overloaded, and can be burned out as a result. It's important not to run a cordless drill when a bit jams or when it's under load at a very slow speed. Various techniques are used to protect control circuits. The safest is an additional circuit that shuts off the drill when it senses a power surge. Another method uses an electronic device that diverts the power surge into a heat sink built into the drill. A plate of aluminum is used as the heat sink to absorb the excess energy created by the power surge.

To find out if a variable-speed cordless drill has a cut-off circuit, run the drill at a very low speed and then increase the load by squeezing the drill chuck with your hand. If the drill has a protection circuit, the drill motor will quit when the drill chuck stops turning, and will start up again after you release the trigger and start over. If the drill does not have a cut-off circuit, the motor will continue to moan after the drill chuck stops turning. Electronic circuits tend to drive up the price of a drill, but I think they're worth the extra cost.

Motor and gear train—Most cordless drills use a standard DC motor like those used to operate windshield wipers in automobiles. Motors in most of the drills have power outputs of about 75 watts. It's the gear train between the motor and the drill chuck that determines what the speed and torque of the drill will be.

For drilling wood, torque is more important than high rpm. Most drill bits designed specifically for drilling wood take a larger bite than twist drills do at each revolution. The drill has to produce enough torque to cut through the wood or the bit will jam. Most often, the high-speed setting of a cordless drill cannot produce enough torque to drill large holes in wood. I discovered that when I used a ⅝-in. auger bit to drill holes in the same 2x Douglas fir stud with all the drills. I was careful to ensure that each drill was fully charged and then counted the number of holes that each could drill before the charge was depleted. At the high-speed settings, most of the drills couldn't turn the ⅝-in. auger bit. At low-speed they got through, but it was tough going, and all of them got pretty hot from the strain.

In a car, shifting to a lower gear will increase the torque at the driving wheels, and will decrease the rotational speed of the wheels. The same is true for drills. A greater gear reduction will produce more torque at the chuck. Extra voltage—more batteries—makes more power available, but that doesn't necessarily mean that the drill will produce more torque.

Parallel-shaft gear trains similar to those in most 120-volt AC drills are used in almost all of the cordless drills as well. Different-size gears rotate on shafts positioned parallel with each other, and the gear reduction depends on the number and size of the gears.

A second type of gear train is called a *planetary* gear train. The primary gear on the main shaft coming from the motor meshes with three smaller gear wheels evenly spaced around it. The three planet gears in turn, mesh with the inside of a larger gear that rotates around all of them. This makes the gear train compact, and allows greater gear reduction in a given space.

The gears themselves are made from machined steel, sintered metal or nylon. Since the strain on cordless drills isn't as great as it is on cord-powered drills, some manufacturers feel that the more expensive, higher-quality machined steel gears aren't necessary.

More important than the type of gear train, however, is whether ball bearings or bushings are used to keep the gears precisely aligned. The output shaft behind the chuck and the primary gear shaft at the motor are the two highest stress points in any drill. A cordless drill that uses ball bearings or needle bearings at these locations will stand up to the rigors of job-site use better than a drill that relies on bushings. This is particularly true at the main output shaft, since it receives side pressure frequently during normal drilling and must stay aligned to keep the drill bit from wobbling.

Clutch—Several cordless drills have a clutch that automatically disengages the drill chuck at a preset maximum torque. This feature makes the drills more useful for driving screws because it guards against stripped screw slots and over-driven screws. The clutch is typically adjusted by a dial on the body of the drill, with four or five settings to choose from. I often find, however, that the torque I need to set a screw perfectly falls in between two settings. Variations in the density of the material receiving the screws adds to the problem. But the clutch is still a very handy feature and one that I use frequently. If the work calls for a precise depth for the screw, I choose a torque setting on the light side to drill them most of the way. Then I increase the torque and carefully finish off the screws. Another method would be to finish the screws off by hand. If the screw depth is not critical, I set the torque on the heavy side; the clutch will prevent me from stripping or grossly over-driving them.

Other features and accessories—Broken chucks and switches are two common causes for breakdowns with cordless drills. The chuck should be a good one (industrial grade) if it's going to hold up on the job site. Most cordless drills come with a ⅜-in. capacity chuck.

With a cordless drill you can't tie the key to the cord, so drill manufacturers provide a holder on the drill itself. Take a look at the chuck-key locations on the drills I tested (photos, p. 123). Remember that you'll want to get at the key quickly and conveniently, and that the key should be held securely out of the way so it won't get pulled loose while you work.

All of the professional models of cordless drills can reverse to remove a jammed drill bit

Company	Model*	Battery voltage	Speed	RPM	Clutch settings	Weight, lb. (incl. batt.)	Price (incl. batt.)
AEG	EZ-505	7.2	Two	300/600	4	2.7	$162.00
	EZ-560	7.2	Two	300/800	6	3.25	**
Black & Decker	1910	7.2	One	600	0	2.5	$141.00
	1920	9.6	One	1850	0	3.1	$174.00
	1942	9.6	Variable	0-800	0	3.1	$184.00
	1970	9.6	One	750	Var.	3.5	$188.00
	1980	9.6	One	800	5	3.5	$184.00
	1982	9.6	Variable	0-800	5	3.5	$192.00
Bosch	1921-VSRK	7.2	2-speed variable	0-300 0-650	5	3.5	$189.00
Fein	110-03	7.2	Two	300/650	5	3.5	$155.00
Hitachi	DTC-10	7.2	Two	280/700	0	2.6	$143.00
	DRC-10	7.2	Two	300/650	5	3.3	$159.00
	D-10DB	7.2	2-speed variable	0-300 0-650	0	2.6	$155.00
	D-10DC	7.2	2-speed variable	0-300 0-650	5	3.3	$170.00
Makita	6010-D	7.2	One	600	0	2.4	$124.00
Metabo	D 80/2	7.2	Two	250/700	6	4.0	$219.00
	D 80/2 VSR	7.2	2-speed variable	0-250 0-700	6	4.0	$249.00
Milwaukee	0210-1	9.6	Two	350/750	4	3.5	$189.00
	0212-1	9.6	2-speed variable	60-280 200-1000	6	3.8	$209.00
	0214-1	7.2	Variable	100-600	6	2.25	189.00
Sears	27131	9.6	One	800	0	3.5	$130.00
	27133	9.6	One	800	5	3.5	$140.00
Skil	2520	7.2	One	600	0	3.25	$99.00

*All drills include ⅜-in. chuck and reversing switch.   **Information unavailable.

or back out a screw. The most common reversing mechanism is a lever located above the trigger that swings left or right, though some drills have the switch on the drill body. A trigger lock can be important when you're carrying the drill around in the pocket of your nail belt—having it start up accidentally while you are straddling a beam isn't good.

Many accessories are also available from drill manufacturers. They include metal or plastic carrying cases (sometimes a case is included with the basic drill), holsters, Phillips-head and slot-head screw-driving bits, and hex-head screw-driving bits. Magnetic hex-head drivers are a handy accessory since the screw is held securely by the driver head and your other hand is left free.

Choosing drills: what to look for—A drill's voltage and speed specifications do not by themselves give enough information for evaluating capacity or output torque. In promotional literature, most manufacturers rate drill capacity by counting the number of holes drilled in a given material cn a full charge. But you can use these figures to compare drills from various manufacturers when the same size hole is drilled

in a material with consistent characteristics, like metal—the variability of wood doesn't provide an accurate comparison. What is sometimes more important than the number of holes that can be drilled on a full charge, however, is the maximum-size hole that can be drilled in different materials. In general, professional-grade cordless drills are rated at ¼-in. holes in mild steel, ⅜-in. holes in aluminum, and ⅝-in. holes in wood.

The first step in choosing a cordless drill is to match the drill speed and the type of speed control to the type of work you will be doing most often. Single-speed, 9.6-VDC drills offer more power for tough drilling, while 7.2-VDC variable-speed drills are lighter and allow more control for drilling or driving screws.

Each cordless drill also has a unique feel or balance that is a product of its weight, how the weight is distributed, and the length and thickness of the handle grip. Some manufacturers locate the battery pack in the handle of the drill, and there it usually adds a characteristic bulge below the grip. Locating the batteries here makes sense because they counterbalance the weight of the drill body when you're using it. But because so much weight is concentrated at the end of the handle, this style of drill is difficult to carry in the pocket of your tool pouch—the weighted handle hangs out and tends to pull the drill out as well. A special holster sold as an accessory by most manufacturers is the only secure and convenient way to carry this style of cordless drill.

When you've evaluated price, special features, and the little things like the chuck-key holder and placement of the reversing switch, you'll soon realize that it's impossible to pick a best drill. But it's an easy job to pick a drill that will suit your particular needs.

AEG (1 Winnenden Rd., Norwich, Conn. 06360) offers a variable-speed drill and two two-speed drills. The EZ-506 variable-speed drill is the model I tested. In addition to variable-speed control (100 to 600 rpm), it has a six-position clutch and produces impressive torque with quiet nylon gears and a planetary gear train. The clutch is adjusted by rotating a cylinder located behind the drill chuck; it's quick and easy to do. The 7.2-VDC battery pack is located in the drill body above and behind the handle, so that the weight of the drill is balanced above your hand. This also allows the handle to be small and comfortable to grip. A clip that stores inside the handle holds the chuck key and two extra driver bits—a handy and very secure place for them. The forward/reverse switch, located on the side of the drill, operates easily with your thumb (if you're right-handed). The trigger lock is separate from the reversing switch and is positioned under the trigger.

The variable-speed control is very smooth, thanks to a feedback control circuit that automatically adjusts the power input to the drill motor when it comes under load. It also has an overload-protection circuit that cuts off the drill if there is a power surge or overload. Unfortunately, however, this circuit prevents the drill from boring large holes in wood. When I used the EZ-506 to bore ⅝-in. holes in a Douglas fir 2x, the overload-protection circuit cut off the drill each time the bit started to snag. Consequently, the drill quit several times while drilling each hole, and I gave up after boring only five holes. The protection circuit was never a problem when driving screws, since screw-driving produces a steadily increasing load rather than an abrupt one. This drill makes an excellent screwdriver because of the feedback variable-speed control, the clutch, and the most conveniently located reversing switch of any of the cordless drills that I tested.

Makita (12950 E. Alondra Blvd., Cerritos, Calif. 90701-2194). I tested model 6012-HDW. It has a 9.6-VDC motor, two speeds (400 and 1,100 rpm) and a five-position clutch, effectively doubling the number of torque settings. The clutch is adjusted with a dial located on the underside of the drill body, an awkward position that forces you to turn the drill upside-down so you can see what setting you're changing to. A smaller dial located on top of the drill body changes the speed. The reversing switch is recessed into the drill body above the trigger and also doubles as the trigger lock. It's a short lever and can be difficult to operate, particularly if you have gloves on. The chuck key snaps into a clip that's re-

cessed into the top of the drill. The plastic clip is secure, though the key sometimes gets snagged.

Makita uses a long, narrow battery pack that fits completely inside the drill handle. It eliminates the bulge below the grip but adds girth to the handle itself. The extra width in the handle makes the drill seem heavier and a little clumsy when it is held with one hand, even though the drill weight is evenly balanced at the trigger. The tool feels solid and is one of the heaviest drills (3.5 lb.). It has machined steel gears and ball bearings at both the output shaft and the primary gear shaft of the motor, and is the only drill I tested that included vent holes in the drill housing to help cool the motor. It was also the most powerful drill that I tested and bored thirty-four ⅝-in. holes through a 2x Douglas fir stud—other drills bored between five and twenty-one holes in the same material.

Black & Decker (U. S. Power Tools Group, 10 North Park Dr., Hunt Valley, Md. 21030) was the first company to offer cordless drills, and they have many models. I tested the #1940. For a single-speed drill, 800 rpm is a good compromise. It's fast enough to run twist drill bits quickly through metal sheeting or wood. But boring ⅝-in. holes in Douglas fir with an auger bit proved to be tough going—the drill completed only nine holes before the charge was used up. All of the other drills that I tested had plastic housings, but Black & Decker uses a cast-magnesium gear housing so that the ball bearings at the chuck and the motor output shaft are mounted in metal. The rest of the body is plastic. The tool has a Black & Decker-built motor with serviceable brushes.

The 9.6-VDC battery pack of model #1940 forms a sizable bulge under the handle of the drill, and limits the length for a comfortable grip. I think I have an average-size hand—the bottom of my palm and my little finger wrap around the top of the battery bulge. The chuck key is stored just below the grip in a very secure and easy-to-use recess that keeps it safely out of the way. The reversing switch is a small but convenient lever on the left side of the handle, and it also locks the trigger. The #1940 is noticeably light for a 9.6-VDC drill. The low battery pack acts as a counterweight to the drill body and gives the drill a light, well-balanced feel.

Porter-Cable (Youngs Crossing at Highway 45, P.O. Box 2468, Jackson, Tenn. 38302-2468) sells one cordless drill. It's the #800, a 9.6-VDC, two-speed (350/1,000 rpm) model, and Porter-Cable calls it a "hammer drill/screwdriver." Hammer drills are generally heavier than other drills—this one weighs in at 4.5 lb. It's a sturdy drill that feels solid and uses ball bearings and needle bearings at the high stress points. It bored twenty-one consecutive ⅝-in. holes in the Douglas fir 2x stud and drilled masonry block with ease. The battery pack forms a large squarish bulge below the grip. But it is outweighed by the drill body, so the drill feels a little top-heavy. I found it easiest to use two hands even though the grip area of the handle is comfortable.

One feature of the #800 that sets it apart from the other drills is its automatic brake. When the trigger is released, the chuck stops. That allows better control when the drill is used to drive

screws. And when the drill bit begins to wander when you're starting a hole on metal, you can stop it quickly and continue with short startup spurts until the bit is started. Porter-Cable also offers a 12-volt charger in addition to the standard 120-volt AC charger.

Skil (4801 W. Peterson, Chicago, Ill. 60646) makes two professional models. I tested the #2725, a two-range variable-speed drill. It has an industrial-quality chuck and ball bearings at the chuck.

Having two gear ranges with the variable-speed control is a nice feature. It enables the drill to produce greater torque in the low range for tough jobs. The Boar Gun, as Skil calls it, completed eighteen ⅝-in. holes in the 2x Douglas fir stud, considerably better than the other variable-speed models I tested. The drill is mechanically shifted between ranges with a sliding lever located on the side of the drill. There is no overload-protection circuit, so the motor will continue to hum if the drill chuck jams.

The added weight and the leverage of the long drill body make the drill feel a little top-heavy, especially if you're using a large drill bit. The grip, however, is slim and comfortable. The battery pack locks into place with a plastic clip. It holds securely, but I'm not sure how well it will survive. The drill trigger is protected by a trigger guard, but it can be awkward. With gloves on, I invariably shifted the reversing lever, above the trigger. The trigger lock is a separate lever that works from either side of the drill handle, and the chuck key fits into a hole in the bottom of the battery pack. Skil provides a chuck key with each battery pack, so you don't have to switch the key each time you change packs. You can turn your pickup into a mobile power station with Skil's optional 12-volt charger.

Bosch (Box 2217, New Bern, N. C. 28560) makes two cordless drills. Both are 7.2-VDC models that have a two-range variable-speed control. The #1920-VSRK that I tested is a little lighter than the clutch-equipped #1921-VSRK, but the drills are very similar in other respects.

The #1920 uses machined steel gears and has ball bearings at the output shaft and the primary gear shaft at the motor. The drill is shifted between high and low range with a mechanical slide located on top of the drill, making it easy to tell which range the drill is in. The variable-speed control uses a silicon control rectifier (SCR) and an additional SCR provides overload protection by directing power surges to a heat sink built into the drill.

The drill is very well balanced and has a comfortable grip. The trigger guard on the Bosch presents the same problems as the guard on the Skil. The trigger lock is located below the trigger. A secure clip holds the chuck key in a recess on the drill body that covers the entire key—it's snag-proof. A recessed holder in the top of the drill holds a Phillips-head bit. The #1920 is very handy for driving screws and for most drilling jobs, but it didn't do well boring into the Douglas fir 2x—the battery held a charge for only eight holes.   □

Bill Phelps is a building contractor in Jackson Hole, Wyo.

Hinge Butt Mortising Templates

The perfect tool for a quick and accurate hinge job: a product comparison

by Stephen Suddarth

The sweet smell of ponderosa pine filled the room as Howard, my boss and teacher, deftly routed the mortises for door hinges. He was using an old router and an ancient-looking device tacked to the door jamb, a contraption of metal rods and plates with lots of thumbscrews. I was watching, for the first time, a hinge butt template in use.

As we moved from doorway to doorway through the custom home we were building and I carried a door to each opening, Howard set the template nails, quickly routed the jamb and door, and offered advice to me every so often in his own quiet way. Soon the mortises were cut for doors throughout the house, and Howard left as I began screwing in hinge leaves. I remember being surprised at the speed with which he worked, particularly since it had taken me what seemed like days to set all the jambs.

That happened years ago. Now, as a building contractor, I have to hang all sorts of doors, and usually within strict time constraints. Once I hung 8-ft. tall oak church doors in the morning and spent that afternoon hanging a number of interior residential doors. On a day like that, a hinge butt template can make the difference between getting home in time for supper or snarling at the dog when you finally arrive home around midnight.

A good template will give you a dependable and versatile way to do the trickiest part of hanging a door: cutting the mortises. Templates will work for most interior and exterior doors, and I've found mine to be an invaluable aid for saving time and ensuring accuracy. Just as important, it gives me the confidence to tackle a demanding job without balking. In fact, I don't hesitate to use the template even if I have only one door to hang.

Basic template anatomy—A hinge butt template (some manufacturers use the term "butt hinge template") is a tool for spacing, sizing and guiding the cutting of hinge mortises in doors and door jambs. Since the templates are basically router accessories, it's no surprise that the major manufacturers of hinge butt templates also make routers. These companies each make one version of the tool except for Bosch, which offers two.

All the templates I've seen are similar. They consist of three metal template bodies arranged along adjustable extension rails. A separate one or two-piece collar (usually called a template guide or guide bushing) attaches to the base of

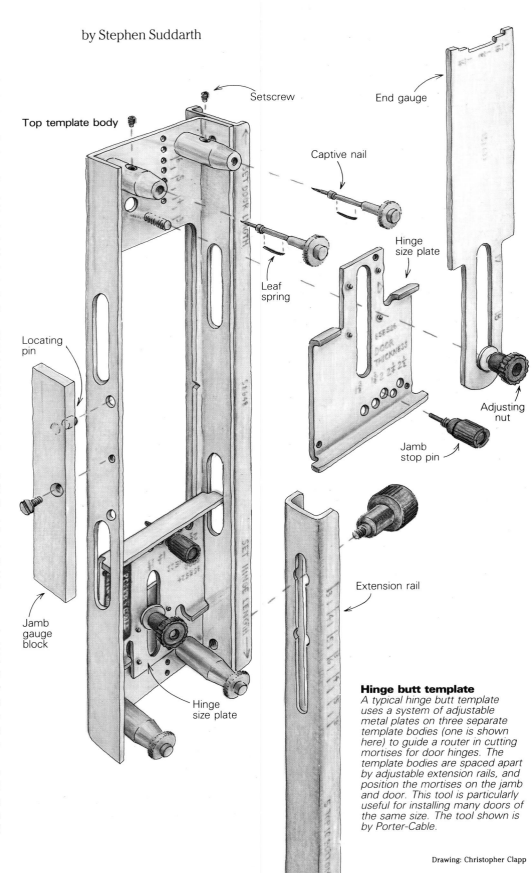

Hinge butt template
A typical hinge butt template uses a system of adjustable metal plates on three separate template bodies (one is shown here) to guide a router in cutting mortises for door hinges. The template bodies are spaced apart by adjustable extension rails, and position the mortises on the jamb and door. This tool is particularly useful for installing many doors of the same size. The tool shown is by Porter-Cable.

Drawing: Christopher Clapp

the router and guides the router bit within a space in the template body.

The action happens at the template bodies—the extension rails space them along the jamb or door. Each template body incorporates metal hinge size plates, usually tightened with thumbscrews. They slide toward or away from each other, and are easily set to match the length of hinge you need. On the template bodies are adjustable stop pins that rest against the edge of the jamb or the face of the door. They ensure that the template is properly positioned and will produce a mortise of the correct width.

Once the template is set for the mortises you wish to cut, it's temporarily fastened to the door or the jamb with captive nails, pins or clamps, depending on the manufacturer. These hold the template sections securely to the surface; the small holes they leave in the woodwork can be concealed with a bit of wood filler.

When you purchase a template, you also get the guide bushing to fit the base of your router. The bushing is a metal sleeve through which the router bit extends. When the router base is held in cutting position against the hinge butt template, the outer surface of this sleeve rides against the inner edges of the hinge size plates, and guides the router bit. Since each template is designed for a guide bushing of a particular outside diameter, you have to make sure that the bushing and the template match. Some routers won't accept certain guide bushings without modification. To see if your router will work with one or all of these templates, check the chart below.

When you purchase a hinge butt template, you'll have to put it together. This will take you anywhere from five minutes (Bosch) to ninety minutes (Skil). Instruction booklets range from cryptic to complete, but it's not a big deal to assemble most templates. Some carpenters even partially dismantle the tool between jobs and store it in the box it came in. I prefer to keep mine fully assembled and set up for the size of doors I usually work with. The whole assembly is only about 6 ft. long, and since it's pretty slender I never have any trouble tucking it away in my van. Because I don't take it apart, I don't have to spend time putting it together when I get to the job site, and the parts don't get lost.

Routers and router bits—Hinge butt templates require the use of a special two-flute hinge-mortising router bit. These bits are avail-

able in high-speed steel or carbide-tipped versions. With two cutting surfaces, the bit's special configuration leaves the floor of the mortise with a smooth finish. Another characteristic of these bits is their longer-than-normal shank, which gives them extra reach to extend through the hinge butt template.

A ½-in. bit is generally used, though bits are available from ½ in. to 1¼ in. The size you choose depends in part on the type of hinges you're using. With square-cornered hinges, the smaller bits leave less material in the corners of the cut, so you'll have less to clean out with a chisel. If you're installing hinges with rounded corners, choose a bit that best fits those corners. Bits are available to match the radius of most round-cornered hinges (a ½-in. bit for hinges with ¼-in. radius corners, for example).

The template sets I've seen all come standard with a high-speed steel hinge mortising bit, but if you want a carbide-tipped bit, you'll have to shop around—many suppliers don't carry them as part of their regular stock. When I used high-speed steel bits, the first ⅛ in. or so of cutting edge was quickly dulled, probably because of heat buildup. So now I use only carbide-tipped mortising bits. Both types of bits are available from router manufacturers.

I have found several good routers for hinge mortising. The Bosch #1601, the Black & Decker #3310 and the Porter-Cable #690 are comparatively light in weight and have good service backup. They're not the only routers you can use, but they are heavy-duty machines that are well suited to the purpose. Hitachi and Makita have guide bushings that fit the templates I tested, but I haven't tried them yet.

Setting up—In new construction, once the jambs are installed, doors can be cut to length, edges can be eased, and the doors can be taken to the proper openings. At this point, I always check the plans and door schedules again, especially if I have a question about hardware, hinge specs or whether the door is to be right-handed or left-handed.

Door hinges are traditionally installed at certain heights. The top edge of the highest hinge is usually 5 in. to 7 in. below the top of the door, and the bottom edge of the lowest hinge is usually 11 in. from the floor. If a third hinge is used, it's placed halfway between the others.

In laying out the hinges, I've found that mistakes are minimized when I mark the location of

a hinge on both the door and the jamb. Then I can step back and double-check my work before any cutting is done. I put an X in a hinge-sized rectangle about where the top hinge will go. Once I've marked the door, I turn it over and bevel its lock edge at a 5° angle with a power planer. Returning the door so its hinge edge is up, I mark the depth (thickness) of the hinge leaf on it with a sharp pencil or a knife, and then do the same on the jamb. When the template is in place, I will use this line to set the depth of the router bit. The bit depth has to be set only once for all the hinges of a given thickness that you plan to use.

Mortising the jambs—I set up the template assembly on the jamb first. I know that many carpenters cut their door mortises first, but I've found that if anything goes wrong, it usually happens on the first cut, and I'd rather make that mistake on the jamb than on a door; it's often cheaper and easier to replace a jamb. Also, a small test cut on the jamb can be easily and unobtrusively filled, while the patch is more likely to show on a door.

The only measurements you'll need are the thickness of the door, its height and the hinge size. Once you have these, you can put your tape measure away, because each template incorporates a system that allows you to set the hinge sections without measuring. You just slide each hinge section to a scribed mark on the extension rail and tighten it down. These settings correspond to standard hinge sizes. Most of the templates are easy to set up, usually taking me about five minutes to adjust to a new setting.

Setting up the template on the jamb is fairly straightforward. If the door stops are already on the jambs, there's no need to remove them—the templates can be adjusted to work around them. Stand in the doorway facing the hinge jamb, and place the template assembly against the jamb. Slide the template up until the top gauge touches the head jamb, then move it in toward the centerline of the jamb until the edge guides touch the jamb edge. With your hammer, drive in both pins on the top template body, and do the same with the center and lower template bodies (if you have a template that uses clamps, tighten those instead of nailing).

Now is a good time to check the templates—they must be tight and flat against the jamb. If you're hanging interior doors with only two hinges per door, you might want to stick a piece

Capacities of some hinge butt mortising templates

Brand	List price	Hinge sizes*	Door heights	Door thickness	Collet fits these routers
Black & Decker 58129 2-pc. guide ⅝ in. o.d.	$175	2½ in. to 5½ in. 2, 3 or 4 hinges	5 ft. 10 in. to 7 ft. 7 ft. to 8 ft. with conversion kit	Up to 2¼ in.	Black & Decker Porter-Cable Milwaukee
Bosch 83037 Bosch 83002 Milwaukee 49-54-0100 1-pc. guide ⅝ in. o.d.	$168 $131.60 $155	2½ in. to 5½ in. 2, 3 or 4 hinges	6½ ft. to 7 ft. 7 ft. to 9 ft. with conversion kit	1⅜ in. 1¾ in. 2 in. 2¼ in.	Bosch Milwaukee
Porter-Cable 59380 2-pc. guide ¹³⁄₁₆ in. o.d.	$165	3 in. to 6 in. 2, 3 or 4 hinges	6 ft. to 7 ft. 7 ft. to 9 ft. with conversion kit	1⅜ in., 1¾ in. 2 in., 2¼ in. 2½ in.	Black & Decker Porter-Cable Milwaukee
Skil 71022 1-pc. guide ⅝ in. o.d.	$120	1¾ in. to 5 in. 3 hinges	6½ ft. to 7 ft.	Up to 2¼ in.	Skil

*These ranges include all standard sizes in between.

Cutting hinge mortises. Once the hinge butt template has been set for the hinge size and spacing, lift it into the doorway and slide it against the edge of the hinge-side jamb (top left). At the same time, make sure the top of the template is against the inside of the head jamb. Once it's in position, nail it to the jamb. Attach the guide bushing to the base of your router (center left), and set the depth of cut by holding the router in the template and adjusting the elevation of the bit. Make a test cut to check the cutting depth, and then cut all jamb mortises. The same setup can be used to cut hinge mortises on the door. Kneel on one knee to maintain balance and control while cutting the mortises (below left).

of masking tape across the center hinge section as a reminder not to cut there. The template body can't be easily removed because there's no provision for joining the extension rails directly to each other.

The router you use should feel comfortable in your hands as you work. I wouldn't dream of using my 3-hp production router for hinge mortising. Instead I use a lightweight, no-frills, heavy-duty 1-hp or 1½-hp machine. Attach the correct guide bushing to the router base, chuck a sharp hinge-mortising bit in the router and set the cutting depth. Hold the router in the template and lower the bit to the mark you made previously on the jamb. When you have the right depth and the setting has been tightened, hold the router in the template, turn it on and guide the bit into the edge of the door. I like to make a quick test cut before routing all the mortises, and use the brass sliding section at the end of a folding rule as a depth gauge. Reset the bit depth if necessary, because the appearance of your work will be enhanced by hinges that are flat and flush with the surface of the jamb and door edge.

Once the router is set for the correct depth of cut, position it so that the bit is in the open area of the template body. Switch on the router and slowly move it toward the jamb, making light cuts as you excavate the hinge mortise. I cut the edge of the jamb first to avoid splintering, then finish off the rest of the cut.

Repeat the process at the remaining templates. When you finish a jamb, turn off the router and remove the template assembly by pulling out on the pins with the claw of your hammer.

Mortising the door—A door buck will steady the door as you use the hinge butt templates. You can make one from scrap wood with a plywood base, or buy readymade. Porter-Cable and Bosch both make adjustable door bucks.

With the door secure in the buck, place the template assembly on the hinge edge of the door. A small spacing device at the top of most templates allows you to offset the entire template assembly, which compensates for the clearance between door and head jamb, while ensuring that the hinge leaves will match when the door is hung. The spacer will allow you 1/16-in. clearance (the thickness of a dime) or 1/8-in. clearance (the thickness of a nickel). Here in humid south Florida, I find that 1/8-in. clearance is the safest bet.

If there were ever a time for concentration, this would be it. It's real easy to cut the mortises

into the wrong face of the door (and real embarrassing when you do). Make sure the edge stop on the template is tight up against the door. Once you're satisfied that the template is in position, carefully drive the pins home one template body at a time, as you did on the jamb. It doesn't hurt to check that router-bit depth once more, either. Then rout the mortises.

Hanging the door—When all the mortises are cut and the template assembly has been removed from the door, it's time to install the hinges in the jamb and the door. Then stand the door upright and set it in the opening with the hinge knuckles facing you. Slip the top hinge leaves together first, holding the door with the toe of your boot at the bottom and one hand near the top. Reach in your pocket or nailbag for the pin and drop it in the hinge barrel. Follow with the bottom hinge, then the center hinge. Placing the top hinge pin first will hold the door in position until you can put the lower pins in place. This may save you from crushing your fingers or from damaging the work you've just done. Tap the hinge pins partway down, leaving them extended about ½ in. Take a quick look at the door's fit, and if it looks good, tap the pins home and go on to the next door.

Templates available—I tested hinge butt templates by Black & Decker, Bosch, Milwaukee, Porter-Cable, and Skil (photo facing page), and they're not exactly cheap. But if you install doors on a regular basis, then it's costing you money not to use one. I've cut hinge mortises **by hand with a good butt chisel and a hammer, with jigs that were built on-site, and free-**hand with a router, and in terms of productivity, my hinge butt template has made far more money than it ever cost. You can do more work in less time with the tool, and that alone makes it worth the price.

As far as I know, Makita, Ryobi and Hitachi don't make hinge butt templates. They do, however, offer guide bushings that fit some of the templates noted below. Here's what I've found about the templates I tested:

Black & Decker model 58129. The Black & Decker, with cast-aluminum template bodies and formed plated-steel guide rails, is fairly light in weight at about 4½ lb. I found it easy to put together. To set up for routing, you have to finger-turn six knurled nuts in order to adjust for the thickness of the door. Once set up, though, the clever design of the template lets you flip it front to back for routing doors and jambs without changing the setup. It's fastened to the jamb with flat-tipped nails that make smaller holes in the workpiece. The tops of the template body castings were a bit rough to ride over with the router, so I had to file them slightly to get a smooth surface.

The Black & Decker is the only model I tried that includes metal gauge blocks that allow you to match the template to existing jamb mortises, like the ones you find on metal jambs or in remodeling work. It also comes with a metal case and a corner chisel.

Bosch 83037. This is my favorite. It's a refined and sturdier version of the old Stanley template,

From bottom to top in the photo above, the hinge butt templates are: Skil, Porter-Cable, Bosch 83002 (identical to the Milwaukee), Black & Decker and an old Rockwell. Not pictured is the Bosch 83037, which is identical to the Bosch 83002 except that it is a heavier-duty tool. Sears offers the Skil template under its Craftsman label.

which is no longer produced. Carpenters who have used the Stanley told me that it was a bit on the fragile side, and didn't take well to knocks and bumps. But with its strengthened extension rails, the Bosch should hold up. At 5¾ lb., it's the heavy-duty model of the two Bosch templates. It was the easiest of all the templates to assemble, and the only one with spring-loaded nails that retract when they're not holding the template to the jamb. That's a nice feature, since the nails on other templates can scratch woodwork if you don't retract them entirely before carrying the tool from one jamb to another.

The 83037 has excellent balance and adjusts easily to different door thicknesses. The hinge size is easier to set than on other templates, but this adjustment requires using a locating pin that can get lost if you happen to drop it in a pile of sawdust. One thing I really like about the 83037

is that it allows you to make fine adjustments of the hinge gauge. I've found lots of hinges that are slightly off-size, especially solid brass hinges, and this adjustment lets the template change slightly to match that difference. Unfortunately, however, there are no graduations on the hinge guide that allow you to find a previous setting, so I scribed a mark on the cast-aluminum guide before adjusting it. Other than that, the 83037 is nearly foolproof in use. Metal gauge blocks are available as an accessory.

Bosch 83002. This is a lighter-duty version of the 83037. There is no provision for attaching metal gauge blocks to the edge. The 83002 weighs about 4¾ lb. I'd definitely go to the 83037 for production work.

Milwaukee 49-54-0100. The Milwaukee has exactly the same features as the Bosch 83002. It even looks exactly like the Bosch 83002, except

that it comes in a red metal case instead of a blue one. That's because Bosch makes them for Milwaukee. I was a bit surprised to find that Milwaukee offers only the lighter-duty model of the Bosch line, though.

Porter-Cable 59380. With its plated all-steel construction, this is the heaviest template at over 7 lb., and is probably the most durable. I think it runs a close second to the Bosch 83037 in overall utility. Part for part, it's exactly the same tool as my Rockwell 59380, which has been in use for almost ten trouble-free years now. It's the only template that can accommodate, without modification, the largest bits generally available for hinge mortising. Placed on the inside of the template sections, the optional metal gauge blocks become spacers to allow for weatherstripping on exterior doors. One minor problem with the tool is that the extension rails, even when well tightened, don't seem to hold the template completely straight. I found that I always had to lightly spring the unit straight on the door or jamb before driving the nails.

Skil 71022. This template functions in a completely different way from the others, but its innovations aren't necessarily improvements. Assembling it was difficult, and trying to use it was awkward. Because it has to be adjusted for each hinge, changing a setup takes about fifteen minutes, compared to five minutes for the other templates. But a couple of good ideas are evident in its design. Since the hinge gauge adjusts to the actual hinge itself, irregularities in the size of each hinge are automatically accounted for. The cast-aluminum template bodies clamp to the door and jamb, instead of having to be nailed. If I owned a Skil template, I'd leave it set up for the most common type of door I encountered and use it only for that. This would get around the difficulty of changing the settings.

Template accessories—If you're buying a hinge butt template, do yourself a favor and get the jamb gauge-block set as an accessory. You'll find it very useful on door replacement jobs, when you have to match door mortises to preexisting jamb mortises. The gauge blocks allow you to index the template setting to the existing mortises. On commercial construction, you'll often have to hang wood fire doors in metal jambs, and the gauge blocks are helpful here, too. You'll need a set of blocks for each size of hinge you use. The Bosch 83002 can't use gauge blocks, nor can the Milwaukee or the Skil.

Hinges with rounded corners appeared after carpenters and millwork shops began using routers for cutting hinge mortises, and now you see them everywhere. Some people still like square-cornered hinges. I find the small corner chisels offered as an accessory with some templates (with Porter-Cable and Bosch) really handy to pop those corners out of router-cut mortises.

Black & Decker, Porter-Cable, Bosch and Milwaukee offer accessory packages that allow you to use the hinge butt templates on unusually long doors. These packages include an additional extension rail and a fourth hinge section.

Stephen Suddarth is a building contractor and cabinetmaker in Miami, Fla.

On Pulling Nails
Use good tools and the right technique

by Gene Schnaser

Unless you specialize in salvage work, chances are you'll hear five times more about hammering nails than you will about pulling them. Carpenter Duane Clarke, of Burnsville, Minn., has a theory on why this might be. His hunch is that there's a stigma attached to the subject of pulling nails, which probably stems from when we were all beginners and were taught that pulling a lot of nails on the job was a sign of incompetence.

Another reason, Clarke speculates, is that pulling nails is more or less a personal thing. There are no hard-and-fast rules. How you do it depends not only on the tools you use, but also on techniques you pick up by watching others and trying different ways yourself.

According to Clarke, there are two basic kinds of nail pulling. First there is pulling nails that are bent while hammering or mistakenly driven into the wrong place. Anytime you watch a crew frame up a house, you'll see a fair share of this. Knots, slippery hammer faces, defective or weak-shanked nails and awkward nailing positions can all lead to bent nails. So can poor hammering technique.

Then there's pulling nails in order to dismantle or recycle lumber. Here nail pulling may be a secondary objective; the first order of business is to get that lumber apart, and then take care of the nails later.

The difficulty of removing a nail depends on the nail itself, how it was driven, and what it was nailed into. Hot-dipped galvanized nails, spiral or ring-shanked nails and cement-coated nails are harder to pull because the shank surface creates a lot of friction. The resin-type adhesive on a cement-coated nail actually "sets" when the nail is driven, creating a bond between wood and metal. Duplex nails, on the other hand, are made to be pulled. They're used for temporary fastening of such things as scaffolding, wall bracing or concrete forms.

Leverage—Over the years hand-tool manufacturers have come up with quite a variety of nail pullers. The photo at right shows a sampling. These tools have either claws or slots to capture the nail head, a prybar to loosen nails by forcing lumber apart or a blade to sever nails. Many nail-pulling tools combine these features. Unlike other areas of carpentry, nail pulling hasn't been motorized. There are no pneumatic or electric nail pullers.

All nail-pulling tools use what physics teachers call first-class and second-class leverage. With

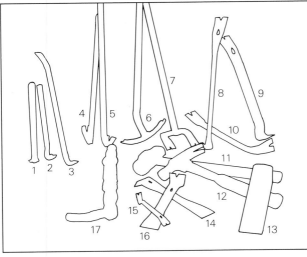

A nail-pulling arsenal. Size, shape and chief purpose are diverse in nail-pulling tools. #1, #2 and #3 on the silhouette are cat's-paws. #4 and #5 are wrecking bars (often mistakenly called crowbars). #6 and #7 are double-headed wrecking bars. #8 and #9 are prybars. #10 is a ripping bar. The hand drilling hammer (#11) is the tool to use if you have to pound on a nail puller. The framing hammer (#12) can pull most nails 16d or smaller. The wedge (#13), commonly used for splitting firewood, is also useful when two pieces of lumber have to be pried apart. #14, #15 and #16 are small prybars sometimes referred to as handy bars. They're good for removing trim that will be reused. #17 is a sliding-handle nail puller.

From *Fine Homebuilding* magazine (April 1986) 32:53-55

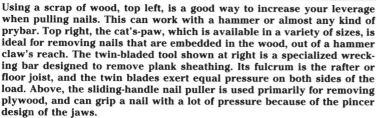

Using a scrap of wood, top left, is a good way to increase your leverage when pulling nails. This can work with a hammer or almost any kind of prybar. Top right, the cat's-paw, which is available in a variety of sizes, is ideal for removing nails that are embedded in the wood, out of a hammer claw's reach. The twin-bladed tool shown at right is a specialized wrecking bar designed to remove plank sheathing. Its fulcrum is the rafter or floor joist, and the twin blades exert equal pressure on both sides of the load. Above, the sliding-handle nail puller is used primarily for removing plywood, and can grip a nail with a lot of pressure because of the pincer design of the jaws.

first-class levers, the fulcrum (or pivot point) is between you and the load, or the nail you are pulling. This is the leverage you get with hammers and other tools with claws at 90° to the handle. The second-class lever has the load between you and the fulcrum. This is the kind of leverage you get when you pull up on tools with nail slots in the handle.

The hammer—The basic hammer is also the most widely used nail puller, though some carpenters hate to use it for that task for fear of breaking the handle. Clarke, for example, uses 22-oz. and 16-oz. framing hammers, and prefers straight claws to curved claws for a couple of reasons. Straight claws can easily be forced between two pieces of lumber to pry them apart. And the straight claws don't require bending over as far to get the claws under the head of a nail. Other carpenters like curved claws because they provide better leverage for nail pulling.

Hammer handles can be wood, fiberglass or steel. Wood and fiberglass have good shock-absorbing qualities, while a one-piece, steel forged hammer is generally thought to be the most durable. Any good-quality hammer should last through many nail-pulling sessions if the proper technique is used—a steady, smooth pulling motion that avoids sudden jerks.

When you buy a hammer, it's good to evaluate it as a nail-pulling tool as well as as a driving tool. Make sure the claw is heat-treated and well tempered. The V of the claw should be clean and sharp so that you can get a good bite on a nail as big as 16d. Good claw hammers have ground and polished heads of drop-forged steel, not brittle cast iron.

The weakest part of any hammer is where the handle enters the head. To reduce strain on this part of the handle when pulling nails, many carpenters use a scrap block of wood as an added fulcrum under the tool. It can be a piece of 1x, or any scrap of wood (top left photo, p. 133). Gaining this extra mechanical advantage is especially helpful for deeply embedded nails or nails driven into hardwood. To make extra nail-pulling leverage a permanent feature, some carpenters weld a short stub of steel rod across the top of the hammer head. Improving leverage this way results in straighter pulled nails. Even though used nails haven't much status today, there are times you run out of spikes and need just a few more to finish. That's when a bucket of used nails comes in handy.

Wherever the point of the nail protrudes, you can drive it back to make the head accessible. If the end of the nail just barely penetrates through the lumber, you can use a nailset to back the head out enough to get your hammer claw under it. The cupped end of a ¹⁄₁₆-in. or ³⁄₃₂-in. nailset will fit nicely over the nail's point to keep it from slipping off. Clinched or bent-over nails can be restraightened for backing out by using the claw of the hammer. Alternatively, you can pry the two boards partially apart, then hammer them back together. This usually exposes the nail head.

Once in a while the head of the nail will break off when you're pulling it. If this happens, one way to gain purchase on the nail is to push it as far into the V-notch of the hammer claw as possible and twist the hammer a quarter turn to each side. The sharp inside edges of the V-notch will groove the nail to provide grip as you pull it. Another way is to use pliers or nippers, along with a scrap wood fulcrum if necessary, to inch the nail up and out.

Some beginners are tempted to use a second hammer to get a tight grip on tightly embedded nails, striking the face of the hammer that has the nail engaged in its claw. This can be extremely dangerous. Two hardened metal surfaces striking with force are likely to cause a brittle metal chip to fly off at high speed. In one eyelid, Clarke still carries a small metal fragment from a cross-hatched framing hammer as proof of hammering hazards. Today most hammers are sold with warnings that advise users to wear safety goggles. This is sound advice. If you do need to snug up a hammer claw on a nail, it's best to use a mallet or a drilling hammer, or a short length of 2x.

Other nail pullers—There are plenty of nail-pulling situations where a hammer isn't the tool of choice. If you need to pull nails that have their heads set below the surface of the wood, it's possible to expose the head by chiseling carefully around it to give the hammer's claw some purchase. But it's much easier (especially on your chisels) to use a cat's-paw. The claws on these tools—which are usually curved 90° from the handle but may also include a straight claw—are made to be driven into the wood and under a nailhead (top right photo, p. 133). Cat's-paws are made of bar-steel stock and can be struck with a drilling hammer or sledge. Nevertheless, you should still wear eye protection.

Nails bigger than 16d usually demand more leverage than a hammer or cat's-paw can provide. This is where wrecking bars come in. The terms "wrecking bar" and "crowbar" are often used interchangeably. But technically, crowbars are 5 ft. to 6 ft. long, while wrecking bars are generally smaller, with one end that's slightly angled and another that's curved 90°, gooseneck fashion (photo, p. 132).

On the racks of a well-stocked hardware store today, you'll see some newer variations on the wrecking bar. Prybars and ripping bars are similar to wrecking bars but flatter in section. A specialized type of wrecking bar has a double head, and looks something like a claw-tipped horseshoe attached to a steel handle at about 45°. This tool can work well for prying up flooring, siding, sheathing and roof boards. Set on the joist or rafter with its two-pronged head under the boards, the tool lets you use a fast rolling action to loosen the wood (bottom right photo, previous page). Homemade versions of this tool exist, but you have to be a fair welder to make one up.

The sliding-handle nail puller is the most expensive nail-pulling tool you can buy. It usually costs between $30 and $40, and it's worth every penny. During general construction you won't get that much use out of it. But if you're removing plywood sheathing or if you're doing a lot of remodeling, it's a worthwhile investment. The tool has a sliding handle that acts like a pile driver to push one of its jaws under the nail head. Then you simply push or pull the tool and the second jaw grabs under the nail head. As you continue the motion, the tool pulls the nail out (bottom left photo, p. 133).

While not exactly for nail pulling, iron wood-splitting wedges can come in handy for unfastening nails. Wedges are especially helpful when you need to separate large nailed-together beams or headers. Instead of trying to pull nails out individually, put the lumber on edge and, with prybars or wrecking bars, use the "buddy system" to separate the pieces. When you get them separated enough at one end, insert a wedge. Then keep moving down toward the other end of the lumber. Keep adding wedges as the split opens up while you work from one end to the other.

Removing trim—Salvaging lumber can sometimes call for a more delicate touch, particularly if you are pulling nails from trim or molding that you want to re-use. I carry two small, flat prybars, the Wonderbar (Stanley Tools, Slater Rd., New Britain, Conn. 06050) and the Superbar, (Vaughan & Bushnell Mfg. Co., 11414 Maple Ave., Hebron, Ill. 60034) for this kind of work. The Superbar is the cheaper of the two (about $3), and I grind an end of one bar down quite thin. This gives me a very fine edge that won't leave an indentation when I slip it behind a piece of molding. After the molding has been raised slightly, I insert the second bar; then I use both bars alternately to pry the trim off.

Another way of taking off trim is to use a nailset to punch the nail completely through the wood. Large trim that won't pry off easily is a good candidate for this treatment, but it can only work if the trim is fastened with finish nails. The disadvantage is that you end up with larger holes in the wood. Smaller holes will result if you pry the trim off and then pull the nails through the back of the trim with a hammer or pliers. For this job I use some nippers, or a pair of channel-lock pliers. Nippers, because of their sharp bite, can really take hold of a nail, but to exert strong pulling pressure you need a long-handled pair.

If trim is attached with flat-headed nails, you can first pry the molding out and then push it back in the hope that some nail heads will be exposed so that you can pull them. The only problem here is that flathead nails—especially when they've been set and covered with wood putty—will probably tear out some of the surrounding wood as they're pushed (or hammered) out head first.

When removing doors and windows installed with casing nails, what works well for me is to use either a Sawzall or a hacksaw blade to cut the nails off between the jamb and rough opening. Then, after pulling the unit out, you can either back out the nails, or leave them in place and nip off what's left on the back side.

What about hardened nails in concrete? If you are removing walls and prying up a bottom plate, cut nails will usually pull right through the 2x stock. So you end up with nails sticking up out of the slab. If they don't pull out easily, one solution is simply to break them off. Cut nails are brittle, and a whack with a sledge does the job. Be sure to wear protective goggles when you do this. If the plate was glued down, as well as nailed, your only answer may be a sledge and ripping bar, though this approach will generally leave you with a bunch of kindling wood.

Choosing the best tools—The best nail pullers are made from heat-treated high-carbon (1078 or 1080) steel. The 10 stands for a straight carbon series steel; the last two digits indicate the percent of carbon. Many flat prybars are made of 1095 spring-tempered forged steel. The claws or "working" ends of the tool should be forged, ground and painted.

Because of the competition in today's tool market, a higher price means higher quality most of the time. Another thing to go by is how long the manufacturer has been in business. Many name-brand nail-pulling tools are made by companies that go back to horse-and-buggy days. Even these companies get tools returned to them occasionally, but returns amount to less than 1%. Of these, most have been misused. Many have been overly muscled with extensions. Others have been overheated during grinding, with a resulting loss of temper.

Nail-pulling tools forged in one piece will generally be stronger than those with welded parts. This is not to say you should avoid welded tools. But if you are buying a tool that's been welded, take time to examine the bead closely. Pass up any tool that looks like it might have a defective bead. It's bad business to break such a tool, especially if it's being used under heavy pressure and you're perched on a roof or a top plate, or standing on a ladder.   □

Freelance writer Gene Schnaser lives in St. Paul, Minn. Photos by the author.

The Carpenter's Toolbox
A close look at some old and new designs

by Tom Law

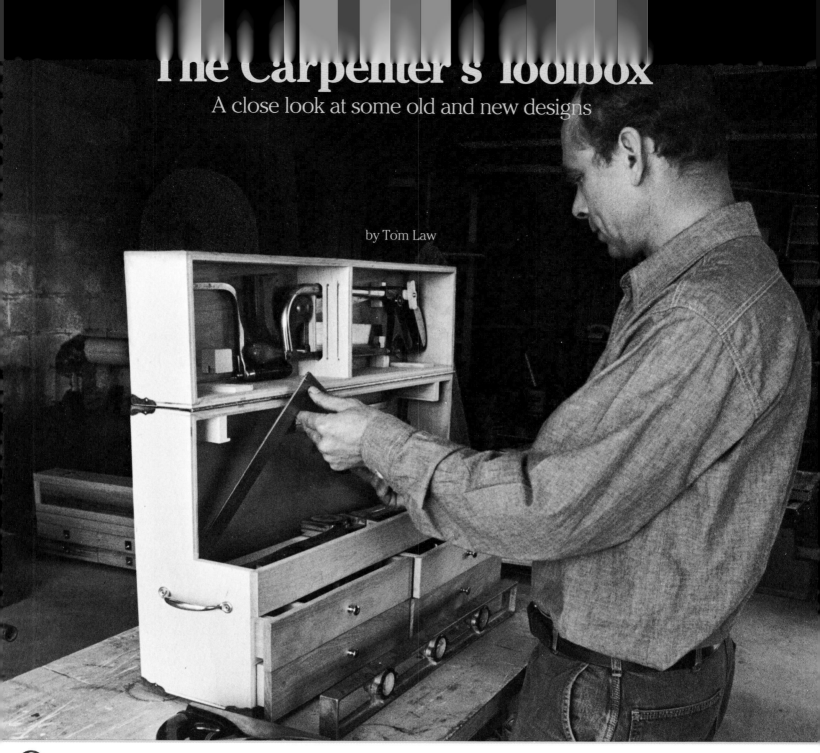

Over the years I've seen plenty of tool-boxes. Most of them are variations on several basic designs that have stood the test of time. Now and again I build a new toolbox, either to replace one that's worn out or because I think I've got a better design.

Before looking at particular toolbox designs, it's important to acknowledge some general design guidelines. The most important requirement of a good toolbox is capacity. It's got to be able to hold all, or at least most, of the tools for a specialized or general job. It has to be spacious and durable without being so unwieldy that you can't move it comfortably from place to place. A toolbox doesn't merely store tools; it protects them when they're not in use. This means that

Consulting Editor Tom Law is currently building a house in Schuylkill Haven, Pa.

edge tools like chisels and planes shouldn't be allowed to knock around in the box. Levels, saws and files need similar protection.

Tools should be readily seen, easily accessible when they're needed and conspicuously absent when you're packing up at the end of the day. And last, a good toolbox makes a good impression. If you're on a job with new clients or among unfamiliar carpenters, your toolbox is a resumé of sorts. Sure, you can carry your tools in a 5-gal. joint-compound bucket, but chances are your clients or your fellow carpenters will spend a lot of time looking over your shoulder.

The open shoulder box—With today's widespread use of portable power tools, the framing carpenter might get by without an open shoulder box. In the old days, though, these simple toolboxes were standard equipment. Typically

narrow and 2 ft. to 3 ft. long, the open shoulder toolbox has a closet-pole handle that extends the full length of the box. The ends of the box are higher than the sides to keep the handle up out of the way so that tools can be picked up and replaced quickly. These boxes are meant to be moved around a lot, so they've got to be ruggedly built and symmetrically proportioned in case you need to put the thing on your shoulder and climb a ladder. Handsaws, pencils, hammers, a prybar, a level, try and framing squares, a few chisels, a chalkline and a tape measure or folding rule are some of the tools the average shoulder box is meant to hold.

To keep tools from banging into each other, most carpenters build a few compartments into these boxes. Kerfs for handsaw blades can be cut into one end of the box and the saw handles can protrude outside the box, or you can simply

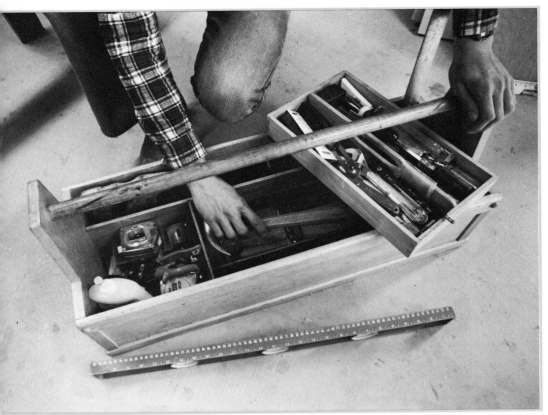

Long and narrow, the open shoulder box has traditionally been the workhorse toolbox of the framing carpenter. Elaborate versions, like the one shown above, are divided into compartments to keep edge tools or delicate tools like handsaws and levels separate from the jumble of tools below. Portable and rugged, this type of toolbox has two main disadvantages: It offers no protection from sawdust or bad weather, and tools often have to be hunted for.

The cabinet-type toolbox shown above was developed in the 1960s by the Douglas Fir Plywood Association. Its display-case design makes tools easy to find and also makes it obvious what tools are missing at the end of the day. Webbing, metal hooks or brackets and simple wood latches are used to secure different tools. Two disadvantages with this type of toolbox are its tendency to blow over easily and its lack of storage for small items. Photo courtesy American Plywood Association.

make the box long enough to accommodate the full length of the saw. In the better shoulder boxes that I've seen, there is a long compartment for saws on one side. And there are several lower compartments and one or more small, shallow boxes that rest inside the box on top of the lower partitions (photo top left).

Tool cases—The utility of the open shoulder box is compromised by the fact that it offers very little protection from the weather or from sawdust, dirt and other construction debris. Tool cases do. At just about any hardware store or building-materials supplier, you can buy metal tool cases in a variety of sizes. I don't really consider these as carpentry items, though. Most of them are poorly made, and their metal compartments can't be modified easily to fit the tools you want to carry. Wood is a far better material for a carpenter's toolbox.

Wooden tool cases have been made in a number of sizes. The simple ones are about the same size as a shoulder box, but have a hinged top with a handle on it. Handsaws are usually kept in the top. The base is divided into several compartments, and there's usually a shallow lift-out box as well.

To enclose the framing square, you need a box the size of a suitcase. Small cases are usually designed so that the short blade of the square protrudes through a slot in the top of the case.

The APA case—Trade-offs between weight and capacity have always caused problems in toolbox design. In 1960, the National Association of Home Builders conducted a time-and-motion study of carpenters at work. It was discovered that carpenters sometimes spent more time looking for a tool than they did using it. Soon after this fact came to light, the Douglas Fir Plywood Association—now the American Plywood Association—designed a tool cabinet that, when open, resembled a display case of common hand tools (photo bottom left).

The APA tool case actually came in two versions: one that opened as two compartments and one that opened as three. Of course, it was made mostly of plywood. The most impressive thing about these cases was the way that every tool was secured. Chisels were held in brackets or webbing adjusted to individual blade widths; saws were secured with their blades in slots and their handles latched; screwdrivers and pliers were held by brackets or broom clips. With this type of setup, it's virtually impossible to put a tool back in the wrong place. It's also easy to spot a missing tool. Unfortunately, the APA no longer sells plans for either of these toolboxes.

What the APA case demonstrates is the concept of custom-building the toolbox around the tools it's supposed to hold. This isn't a new idea, and in fact many versions of the APA's toolbox design were developed by the Stanley Tool Corporation during the early part of this century. For years, Stanley published a nifty catalog of tool cabinets and cases. Each one contained an array of hand tools that were clamped or latched in place. Yes, the tools came with the box, and at prices that would make a modern carpenter cry.

The author's toolbox, shown open and closed at right and above, combines display-case design for large tools with drawer space for smaller items. The top section swings open on a piano hinge, revealing saws, squares, hammers and planes. The legs of the framing square slide behind the small platform above the drawers. In a good toolbox, the storage space is tailored to the tools. Remaining photos: Top, chisels occupy their own drawer and fit into individual slots to protect honed edges. Center, carrying slots for the level, try square and sliding T-bevel are made from solid wood glued to the back of the box. Bottom, the hacksaw, backsaw, keyhole saw and coping saw are secured in slots cut in a piece of ½-in. plywood. The two outer slots are for full-size handsaws.

My design—A few years ago I made a cabinet-style toolbox similar to the APA toolbox. It was slightly larger and heavier, so I mounted it on caster wheels. I could roll it around the workspace, and it was nice to be able to see my tools out in front of me. The trouble with this and other cabinet-type boxes is that they blow over easily in a wind, or are just as easily knocked over accidentally. My cabinet's numerous topplings finally did it in. Rather than glue it together once more, I disassembled it and used the wood and the wheels for other things.

In my next toolbox I tried to combine the best features of the cabinet toolbox with the best features of the case-type toolbox. This hybrid, shown in the photos on this page, seems to work best for me. Its overall dimensions are as follows: 16 in. high; 8 in. wide, 30 in. long. Its top half hinges up, revealing an upper section reserved for saws—two full-size handsaws, a backsaw, a hacksaw, a keyhole saw and a coping saw. The back of the case revealed by the fold-up top is used to hold the level, try square, sliding T-bevel and framing square. The framing square slips behind the small platform above the drawers, where I keep a smooth plane, a block plane, a tape measure, a Yankee screwdriver and a couple of hammers.

The four shallow drawers in the bottom part of this toolbox are important features. One holds nothing else but my set of chisels (photo right, third from bottom). Notches cut into wood spacer strips hold each sharpened edge away from its neighbors.

The other three drawers hold a variety of small items: nail sets, a full drill-bit index, coping and hacksaw blades, pliers, snips, pencils, a utility knife, a compass, an adjustable wrench and several files. What's in the drawers weighs quite a bit more than the tools stored above

them, so the box is bottom heavy, as it should be for stability.

Toolbox construction—Plywood is the best material to use for the body of the case and for drawer sides and bottoms. I built a fancy version of my latest toolbox design using solid hickory and sassafras boards that came from trees on my property. Rather than rabbeted joints and flat sides, this one has dovetails and raised panels. It's more beautiful to look at than my plywood version, but it's also a lot heavier and—I suspect—less durable.

Half-inch birch-faced plywood is what I used for the toolbox shown here. I constructed the top part of the case—down to the tray above the drawers—as a whole and then ripped out the hinged section on my table saw. I had to finish this cutout using a handsaw where the circular-saw blade wouldn't reach.

I used a piano hinge to make the top open. It's easy to mount and distributes the weight in the hinged portion evenly. The handles, corner shields and drawer pulls are either thin-gauge brass or brass-plated steel.

The fixtures in the upper part of the box that hold the larger tools were made from pine scraps and simply glued in place (photo middle right). I cut the handsaw slots in the hinged portion (photo bottom right) on my table saw. The only latch inside the box is the one that holds the hacksaw handle.

Drawer fronts shouldn't be made of plywood because they'll get dinged up too easily. I used maple for my drawer fronts, but almost any hardwood will do. Each front is dadoed to receive its sides and grooved to accept the bottom panel of ¼-in. plywood. I left my plywood box unfinished, but for extra protection you can apply a couple of coats of polyurethane. □

The Renovator's Tool Kit

A versatile collection
that fits in a carpenter's toolbox

by Craig F. Stead

If your business is renovating houses, you are typically faced with a sequence of tasks requiring several skills, many unknowns and a number of different tools. Replacing a water heater, framing a wall and installing new outlet boxes could easily fall into a day's work schedule. The workspace is usually cramped, the work itself unpredictable, and it's easy to spend half the day driving back and forth just picking up tools you forgot to bring. Wasting time on gofer runs can put a renovator out of business.

To work efficiently and to minimize hunting trips, I've organized my tools into a basic core group that goes to every remodeling job. The power tools—a 7¼-in. circular saw, a ⅜-in. variable-speed reversing drill and a reciprocating saw—have their own carrying cases. All the hand tools in the kit can fit into a standard carpenter's toolbox. Mine is 9 in. wide, 9 in. deep and 32 in. long, and has the usual tray on top. Packed with the renovating gear you see above, it weighs just under 50 lb.

One indispensable item that doesn't go in the box is a folding, clamping bench (mine is a

The author with his tool kit. All the tools shown at the top of the page fit into Stead's 9-in. by 9-in. by 32-in. toolbox.

Black & Decker Workmate). There's not much room to set up a work surface on most remodeling jobs. I've seen people use chairs, cardboard boxes or even their knees to support stock for scribing and cutting. This isn't very safe or accurate. The clamping feature of the bench means you don't need a heavy bench vise or C-clamps, and I can set up just about anywhere. I organize the rest of my tools by use.

Layout equipment—You don't need anything longer than a 25-ft. steel tape for renovation work. I use a Stanley Powerlock II. I carry a framing square and a combination square. A sliding bevel is indispensable for fitting angled framing and trim on old houses. My aluminum level is 30 in. long, and just fits into the toolbox. You'll also need a chalk box and refill for snapping layout lines, as well as nylon string, and a plumb bob and sheath. The sheath keeps the bob's point sharp, and gives you a place to wind the string. I find a 6-in. machinist's rule comes in handy for measuring drawings and doing precision layout work. For fitting trim to

From *Fine Homebuilding* magazine (December 1982) 12:50-51

uneven surfaces, I carry a small compass, or scriber, and I use a 6-in. compass for laying out curves and circles. My tool kit also includes a compass/divider. For layout on concrete or brick, I use red and blue marking crayons. I also carry flat carpenter's pencils, which last longer than round pencils and are easier to sharpen with a utility knife.

Pliers, snips and strippers—I carry a pair of channel-lock pliers with a capacity of 1½ in. for opening sink traps and loosening large bolts. Side cutters come in handy for service entrance and heavy cable work. Vise-grips can often lend you a third hand, and I carry a 5-in. and a 10-in. pair. I also find frequent use for needle-nose and slip-joint pliers, aircraft-type tinsnips and diagonal cutters. My wire stripper and cutter is adjustable for #24 to #12 wire.

Wrenches and sockets—Renovators need two 1⅛-in. capacity adjustable wrenches for sink plumbing. I also carry a 1½-in. pipe wrench. Rigid makes a good aluminum pipe wrench, which keeps the toolbox lighter. Nut drivers (³⁄₁₆ in. to ½ in.) are for electrical service work and appliances. Deep sockets (³⁄₁₆ in. to ½ in.) will drive lag screws. A square-to-hex adapter allows you to use your ⅜-in. electric drill to drive nuts and lag screws. I carry nine Allen wrenches (⅝ in. to ¼ in.). Eklind makes a set with an integral holder that keeps all the keys together, an important feature.

Screwdrivers and awls—I carry one square-shank screwdriver with a ¼-in. blade, and drivers with ³⁄₁₆-in. and ⁷⁄₃₂-in. tips. A small, instrument-type screwdriver is good to have, as well as #1 and #2 Phillips heads. I prefer Klein rubber-handled screwdrivers, but Stanley Jobmaster and Sears Craftsman are also good. You can save money by buying sets. Include a couple of awls for removing knockouts on electrical boxes, starting screws and scribing.

Files—My standard selection includes a 10-in. flat bastard, an 8-in. mill bastard, a 6-in. slim taper, a 6-in. round bastard, a 7-in. auger-bit file and a four-in-hand. Buy handles for the first four, and you'll work a lot easier. The four-in-hand is the one to carry around in your pocket. You'll also need a good file brush with metal bristles on one side and fiber ones on the other. Buying files as a set is a good idea because they're less expensive that way, and you can use the pack as a carrying case.

Edge tools—I keep my good paring chisels in the workshop. For the rougher, less precise work that renovation requires, a plastic-handled set of ¼-in., ½-in., ¾-in., 1-in. and 1¼-in. butt chisels is adequate. I keep mine in a leather roll to protect their edges. I use a Stanley pocket Surform for fitting drywall and other rough shaping; I also pack a block plane. I prefer a non-adjustable utility knife, because they are more durable than adjustable knives. You can store your spare blades in the handle of either type. I use a cold chisel for breaking rusted bolts free and for cutting cast-iron pipe.

Bars and putty knives—For pulling nails, you'll need a Stanley wonder bar, or a similar cat's paw. Check the claw before you buy; the quality of this forged part can vary. I like a ship's scraper for heavy scraping and removing molding. Red Devil makes a good one that can be sharpened easily with a file. For puttying, I carry a 1¼-in. flexible putty knife, and I carry a stiff knife the same size for scraping and rough patching that will need a lot of sanding over. For cleaning plaster cracks before patching, a machinist's scribe works well.

Saws—For rough work, I use an inexpensive straight-back crosscut, with 8 points per inch. Stanley has a cheap one with hardened teeth that looks to me like just the ticket for renovators. I like hacksaws with tubular backs that hold extra blades. Both Rigid and Milwaukee make good ones. Try to keep hacksaw blades with different teeth counts on hand. In tight spots, I use a Stanley wallboard saw.

Punches—I carry a center punch for starting drill bits in metal, and a Stanley #1113 self-centering screw punch for mounting hinges and lockplates. If you're hanging even a few doors, a self-centering punch will save plenty of time. I use #1, #2 and #3 nailsets whenever I'm installing casing or interior trim.

Electrical—A Romex ripper allows me to strip plastic-sheathed electrical cable without cutting into the insulation, and also avoid cutting myself with a jackknife. It's also good to have a couple of 3-wire to 2-wire adapters for tool hookup. A low-cost pocket electrical tester could save your life. I also make sure I have electrician's tape and a flashlight (the rubber-handled models hold up well under renovation's rigors). One 50-ft. extension cord should reach anywhere inside the house; two will get you to the yard for siding or trim work. Buy only cords with #12 wire. Lighter wire will actually starve a power-tool motor, causing overheating and insulation failure.

The screw box—The Plano Mini Magnum #3213 plastic organizer (available at fishing-tackle stores or from J.C. Penney) holds a versatile variety of screws: drywall screws (3 in., 2¼ in., 1¼ in.) for hanging gypboard and cabinets; self-tapping, hexhead sheet-metal screws, also good for general woodwork (#6 by ⅜ in., #10 by ¾ in., #8 by 1 in., #8 by 1½ in.); joist-hanger nails; flathead wood screws (#8 by 1¼ in., #12 by 1¼ in.). The #12 screw is perfect for mounting a toilet flange.

Hammers—Choosing a hammer is a subjective decision, so look around until you find one that feels right in your hand. I've found that wooden handles break too easily, while steel handles transmit a lot of shock, so for me fiberglass is a good compromise. My tool kit has one rip-claw framing hammer with waffle head, and one curved-claw finish hammer. □

Craig Stead specializes in house renovation, and lives in Putney, Vt.

Shopping for tools

In general, I buy the best tools I can. Renovation work often pushes a tool to its design limit, and failure can be dangerous and costly. If you're buying new tools, it may pay to wait for the annual January and July sales. You'll probably get discounts of 15% to 30%. If you are an established contractor, get a contractor's account with W.W. Grainger (look in the Yellow Pages under Electric Motor Distributors), which will allow you discounts on many items, particularly Milwaukee power tools.

The used-tool market can offer substantial savings for the knowledgeable buyer. A power or hand tool in good condition is worth 50% to 60% of its new list price. If you are buying a tool privately, 30% to 50% of current list is a fair price. Examine any second-hand tool carefully. Look for clean, high-quality tools with little evidence of wear. Don't buy any worn, off-brand or very old power tools because replacement parts are often unavailable or very expensive. January and February are good times to buy used tools because this is when contractors sell equipment they don't need to raise cash for taxes. Keep a list in your wallet of tools you want to buy, along with approximate retail prices. This allows you to evaluate whether you're getting a fair price.

Auctions can be a good source for tools if you are well prepared. Before the auction, list all the items you'd like to bid on and the price you are willing to pay. Use catalogs such as Sears, Silvo and W.W. Grainger as price references. Test power tools before the bidding, and examine them for wear. Don't bid over your intended price unless you have a very good reason. A single dollar increase bounced back and forth between two eager buyers can quickly add up to much more than you wanted to pay.

Patience and a little homework can occasionally be highly rewarding. I once attended an auction for a large tract-house builder who had filed for bankruptcy. The notice read like a builder's letter to Santa Claus. Saws, drills, sanders and other shop equipment were featured. I was interested in many items, so the morning before the auction I inspected equipment and prepared my wish list. Then I called local distributors to determine market prices.

The day of the auction broke cold and rainy, but a crowd of over 400 people was milling around the tools and equipment. Bidding was hot, and most of the tools were selling for close to list price, far in excess of any maximum price on my want sheet. I had my eye on a 14-in., 5-hp radial arm saw for my cabinet shop. It looked to be in excellent condition, but I couldn't test it, so I wasn't sure. Fortunately, I found a man at the auction who had worked with the saw. He informed me that the saw had hardly been used. He also said it was wired to run on single-phase current. The list price for the saw and accessories was over $1,600. My limit was $400. It was getting dark when the auctioneer finally got to the saw. Only one other person bid against me, and he dropped out at $375, I got the saw for my planned price of $400. Today that saw is still one of my main shop power tools, every bit as good as a new one. —C.S.

On the Edge

An overview of grinding and honing for the carpenter, wherein the author argues for more skill and fewer gadgets

by John Lively

I revered my Arkansas stones, until I met Apolinar. He worked as a carpenter in a Texas shop that made custom doors, windows, interior trim and furniture for rich clients. He came across the river from Mexico, where the guild system that followed the conquistadores into the New World still spawns craftsmen who serve out formal apprenticeships. Apolinar at the age of 50 was a master of his trade, with a measure of self-esteem to match his skills. He could not be coddled or coerced into sweeping the floor, he thought it entirely beneath his station to maintain or adjust any of the machines in the shop and he steadfastly refused to use sandpaper. He got paid by the piece, worked his own hours, and made about six times the money he would have earned in his native Mexico City. Not bad for an illegal alien.

Apolinar didn't have any whetstones. Yet his chisels and plane irons were always impeccably sharp. Nobody ever saw him sharpen a single tool, yet every morning there they were, freshly honed and ready for another day's service at the bench. One night when I was working late, I noticed Apolinar fussing around his bench in an unaccustomed way. He was getting ready to go home, and kept acting like he'd forgotten something. Finally he gave a demure grin and a resigned shrug, and said he'd touch up the edges of his tools before he left. So at last I got to witness the Apolinarian mysteries of sharpening.

He disassembled his three planes and lined up his six or seven chisels. From under his bench he produced a dirty 8/4 board, about 16 in. long and 6 in. wide, with a cleat nailed along the bottom, like a keel. He reached under his bench again and came up with a small cardboard box, which was fairly filled with neatly cut strips of, God forbid, sandpaper—240-grit, 400-grit and 600-grit aluminum-carbide wet/dry paper, to be precise. He clamped the board up in his vise, squirted some viscous fluid (which I later found out was a mixture of motor oil and kerosene) on the surface and spread it around with his fingers. Then he took a strip of 240-grit paper, patted it flat onto the oozing surface of the board and secured it there with two thumbtacks, using the same timeworn holes. He squirted some more fluid on the paper and began to hone one of his plane irons.

He was fast, taking no more than 15 seconds or so to have done with the bevel. He

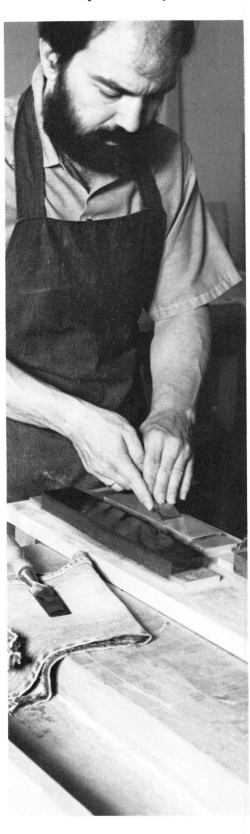

followed with his other plane irons. Next came his chisels. When the paper stopped cutting, he'd put on a fresh piece. Stage two—400-grit paper. He went through the same routine as before, making sure the paper was kept wet with the oil/kerosene mixture. Then came a final round with 600-grit paper, which went the same as the first two stages. This time, though, he finished each tool by flipping it over and backing it off—holding the back of the tool flat against the abrasive surface and rubbing back and forth for several strokes to remove the wire edge that results from honing the bevel.

Ten minutes from the time he started, he was rubbing the oil off his fingers with a handful of jointer shavings. I stood there aghast. It seemed almost immoral that with all the honing jigs and grinding rigs on the market and with all the hush-toned lore surrounding this sacred subject, Apolinar should get such serviceable edges from strips of sandpaper and a grungy board.

The lesson is clear and direct. You don't need expensive sharpening equipment to get sharp edges. What you do need is to know what you're doing, to understand what happens when steel is rubbed against an abrasive surface and the effect this has on the edge. Once you have this understanding and have practiced the mechanics of grinding and honing, sharpening tools stops being an onerous, contraption-cluttered task that's consigned to weekends and rainy Monday afternoons.

The fundamentals of sharpening are learned early in a society that still values apprenticeships, but in our own country many builders and craftsmen are self-taught, and so seek instruction from tool catalogs and other self-taught tradesmen. There's no shortcut to acquiring these skills, but once you've got them you won't have to put up with dull chisels and planes that jump and chatter down a board. If your kind of carpentry involves considerable joinery, finish woodwork and cabinetmaking, you need efficient sharpening skills because your work requires using chisels, gouges and planes, and because these tools just don't work unless they are sharp. And even if most of your work is confined to rough framing, nothing takes the place of a chisel or plane when you need one.

To maintain edge tools you have to know how to grind and how to hone. Grinding shapes the bevel on the tool, and honing fin-

From *Fine Homebuilding* magazine (December 1983) 18:56-61

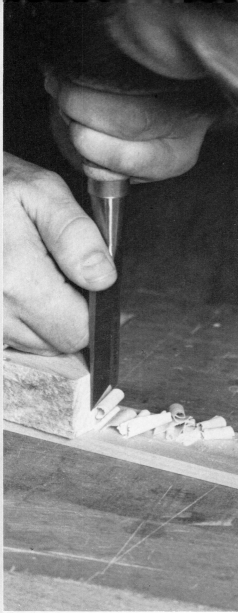

How sharp is sharp?

Look at the forearms of some timber framers and cabinetmakers, and you might see patches of scabby-looking bare skin where they've pared the hair away, testing their chisels and plane irons for razor sharpness. As a dramatic gesture (and testament to one's sharpening acumen), nothing beats showing the amazed onlooker that a fat hunk of tool steel can shave one's arm. While testing your edges on your arm can give you an indication of relative sharpness, it's not a method a dermatologist would recommend. A better way to assess the sharpness of an edge is to see how easily the blade will slice tiny slivers of wood from the edge of a board. The smaller the slivers, the sharper the edge. Another way is to pare away wispy curls of end grain, as shown above. If the wood powders and flakes, your edge is dull, but if you can slice off translucent, tissue-thin pieces that stay in one piece, you've got a sharp, serviceable edge. A third way to test for sharpness is to rest the edge, bevel up, on your thumbnail and slowly raise the back end of the tool. The lower the angle at which the edge will bite into your nail, the sharper it is. —*J. L.*

ishes the edge by removing the small ridges and ruts left by grinding. The edge can be further refind by buffing or stropping.

Grinding—Shaping the bevel of a tool by grinding (backs of blades are never ground) is something that should happen infrequently. There are only three reasons to take your tool to a grinder. The first and most common is that the edge has been nicked or dinged, and you need to regrind the bevel back into undamaged steel. You can minimize dinging up your good chisels by keeping them sheathed and using a junk chisel for nasty work that doesn't call for a sharp edge. A second reason to regrind is that the width of the micro-bevel (more about this later) has become too wide, and you have to restore the original 25° bevel. Lastly, you might want to regrind a new tool to alter the angle the factory put on it.

Most grinders can be taken onto a building site if necessary, but it's usually more convenient to do your grinding at home, where the machine and its accessories can be permanently set up. To avoid investing in a commercial grinding machine (and to make do in emergency situations), you can improvise. I know a cabinetmaker who uses a plywood disc faced with 100-grit sandpaper and fitted with a mandrel so it can be chucked in a drill press. I've seen others use a belt sander turned upside down and clamped to a table.

The two most common types of grinders have abrasive wheels (bench grinders) or abrasive belts. There are rules of use that apply to them both. The abrasive surface—whether an emery or vitrified aluminum-oxide wheel or an aluminum-oxide belt—has to be kept clean. Clogged wheels and glazed belts don't cut effectively, and they cause you to apply excessive pressure to the tool. This overheats the steel and ruins its ability to hold an edge. To get around this, dress the wheel often or replace worn belts. They're a lot cheaper than new chisels and plane irons.

While grinding, quench the tool often in a can of cold water. Watch the little beads of water at the edge of the tool as you grind. When they begin to fizzle or evaporate quickly, dunk the tool again. All the grinding and honing you do will be wasted if you overheat the tool and ruin its temper, and the edge—no matter how sharp you get it—won't last. A brittle, distempered edge will fray, splinter off in tiny pieces, and soon become too dull for anything but spooning yogurt.

If the steel turns blue, the edge has been heated beyond its original tempering temperature. The only way you can salvage the tool is to grind past the blue area into good steel. So take your time when you grind, holding the tool against the wheel or belt with a firm but

> *All your grinding and honing will be wasted if you overheat the tool and ruin its temper, and the edge—no matter how sharp you get it—won't last.*

light touch. Keep the steel cool, and inspect the bevel often to make sure you're removing metal in the right place, in the right amount.

Bench grinders—Most motorized bench grinders accept 7-in. or 8-in. dia. wheels, one coarse-grit, the other fine. Many people think that you shouldn't grind a good tool on a coarse wheel, and so make the mistake of using the coarse wheel only for the rough shaping of metal parts. The truth is that a coarse wheel (say, 36-grit), freshly dressed, will cut faster, cleaner and cooler than a fine wheel. After all, the point of grinding is to shape the bevel, not to finish it. A fine wheel will glaze over quickly, and even if it's clean, you'll have to apply more pressure to remove the same amount of steel that requires less pressure on the coarse wheel. This means you have to spend a lot more time grinding, and that you

risk burning the tool. A coarse wheel will yield an edge that's quite fit for honing.

Because of the relatively small diameter of grinding wheels, the radius of the hollow grind they produce is correspondingly small. This deeply hollowed bevel, as opposed to a bevel with a shallower concavity or a flat bevel, is fragile at the edge, and requires considerable honing to get a flat surface wide enough to give support to the cutting edge.

The purpose of grinding is to produce a uniformly flat or hollow-ground bevel on the tool. But holding a chisel or plane iron at the proper angle, using nothing more than the little tool rest that comes with most bench grinders, and being able to return the tool to the same position repeatedly after numerous quenchings isn't easy. And those unpracticed at grinding often end up with multifaceted bevels and cutting edges that aren't square to the sides of the blade. That's why there are several sliding tool rests on the market that will attach to a grinder, hold the tool at the angle you choose and guide it past the wheel. But these devices have drawbacks. Using a sliding tool-rest attachment can double your time at the grinding wheel. To set one up, you have to adjust the angle of the tool rest, clamp the tool on the slide and then unclamp it when you're done. The ones that have a rack-and-pinion feed mechanism keep you from feeling what's going on between the wheel and the edge of the blade because you're turning a knob instead of holding the tool.

Freehand grinding—For grinding on a wheel, the best method I know uses nothing more than the stock tool rest on your grinder, yet gives you a high degree of control over the grinding angle and lets you regulate the pressure against the wheel with considerable sensitivity. Quite simply, it involves using the tool rest as a fence rather than as a surface to rest the tool on. Set the angle of the tool rest so that it's slightly lower than the bevel angle on the tool. With the motor turned off, place the edge of the tool against the wheel so that grinding will happen across the full width of its bevel and so the blade contacts the outer edge of the tool rest.

Now grip the tool firmly, thumb on top and forefinger underneath, perpendicular to the blade, and push your forefinger smartly against the edge of the tool rest (photo left). This grip turns your hand into a jig and lets you use your forefinger to gauge the distance from tool rest to wheel. You just slide your entire hand back and forth, keeping your forefin-

Freehand grinding uses the standard tool rest as a fence rather than as a flat surface for supporting the tool. The blade is gripped so that the right forefinger passes underneath and perpendicular to the side of the tool. With the forefinger pressed firmly against the edge of the tool rest, you can move the blade from side to side to grind the full width of the bevel. The distance from the tip of the tool to the forefinger determines the grinding angle. Fingers on the left hand deliver pressure to the cut, and sense when the steel heats up.

ger pressed against the tool rest and using your thumb to deliver pressure to the cut. If your grip remains firm, you can remove the blade from the grinder as often as you wish to inspect the edge or quench it.

Dressing the wheel—The point of dressing a wheel is to remove a very small layer of clogged and dulled abrasive particles from its edge, and thus expose a new surface of clean, sharp particles. Some diamond-tipped wheel dressers lock onto a jig that slides on the grinder's tool rest. The jig ensures that you dress the edge of the wheel at 90° to the sides. But you can use a diamond dresser freehand by making several deft, deliberate passes across the edge of the wheel with the tip. Excessive pressure can cause you to remove too much material, gouge the wheel and end up with an uneven grinding surface.

Other kinds of dressers—star dressers and carbide dressers—are also available, but a diamond-tipped dresser lasts longer and cuts cleaner. Dressers are sold by industrial-supply houses and mail-order tool companies.

Belt grinders—There are quite a few belt grinders on the market. Rockwell makes two different types—one is a 7-in. grinder/finisher equipped with a grinding wheel on the right of the motor unit and a platen-backed, 2-in. wide belt on the other side. It's more expensive (about $600) than their sander/grinder ($120 to $235, depending on the model), which comes with a single 1-in. wide belt, a tilting table and a platen to back up the belt.

The Mark II Sharpening System sells for about $500 at Woodcraft Supply Corp. (41 Atlantic Ave., Box 4000, Woburn, Mass. 01888). Like the expensive Rockwell belt grinder, the Mark II would be a good investment for professional shop carpenters and timber framers. But unless you do a lot of grinding, a cheaper machine would be a wiser choice. The Mark II (photo above) has an 11½-in. dia. cast-urethane contact wheel that drives a 2½-in. wide, 60-in. long belt around an idler that contains the belt-tracking device. Because of the wheel's large diameter, the hollow grind it produces is minimal, and the edge is therefore more substantial than one ground by a small-diameter wheel. The grinding side of the machine is fitted with a sliding outrigger arm that has a block at the end for holding the butt of a chisel or plane iron. By sliding the arm in or out, you adjust the grinding angle the tool makes with the contact wheel. On the left side of the arbor there's a muslin buffing wheel, something I'll comment on a little later in the article.

Rockwell's belt grinders, because the belts are backed up by a platen, produce a flat bev-

el on the tool. And both come with standard tool rests, rather than with the arm-and-block rest that's part of Woodcraft's machine. The craftsmen and tradespeople I've talked to who own belt grinders prefer them to bench grinders. They say that the belts cut faster and cooler, and that they have more control over the tool. The wider the belt, the better, as you can grind butt chisels, framing chisels and plane irons without having to slide them back and forth across the cutting surface.

As with wheels, coarse-grit abrasive belts will cut faster and clog less quickly than fine-grit belts. Don't use anything finer than 80-grit or 100-grit belts, or you risk overheating the steel. You can clean grinding belts with the crepe sole of an old sneaker, or you can go buy a bar of the stuff (sold as a "dressing stick") for about $9. But after several cleanings the abrasive particles will have been dulled, and many of them worn away; so it's best to replace the belt.

One last thing about grinding. Wear goggles.

Honing—With a magnifying glass, you can see that grinding gouges the steel. Even to the naked eye, a freshly ground edge looks a little ragged out on the tip. Such a sawtooth edge might even be sharp, but after a couple of cuts into wood the fragile slivers on the end will bend and fracture, and you'll have a dull edge. The purpose of honing is to polish the bevel, to smooth out all the ridges and trenches left by grinding and to produce an edge that ideal-

ly is straight across. A polished edge is sharper and sturdier because there are no unsupported slivers of steel to break off.

Honing is done on stones that are usually about 2 in. wide and 8 in. to 12 in. long. Arkansas stones are natural; other stones—Carborundum, Crystolon, India, and Japanese waterstones—are manmade. You begin with a fairly coarse stone, progress to a medium-grit stone, and end on a fine-grit stone.

The more finely honed an edge is, the sharper it will be and the longer it will last. And, paradoxically, the more frequently you hone a tool, the less time you spend at the stones. Because honing is tedious, messy and repetitive, and because it requires discipline and practice to hold a tool at a constant angle while rubbing it on a stone in a back-and-forth or figure-eight motion, many carpenters never develop an effective, reliable technique. This is why the tool catalogs peddle honing guides. These roller devices hold the tool at the proper honing angle while you move the edge over the stone. As with grinding jigs, these things just get in the way, slow you down and discourage you from developing a valuable skill.

Posture and grip—Stance and grip are critical to proper honing. The grip I'll describe enables you to hold the tool at a constant angle while honing, and it lets you work without getting tired. Grab the blade in your right hand with your forefinger extended down the right side of the tool so that your fingertip is about

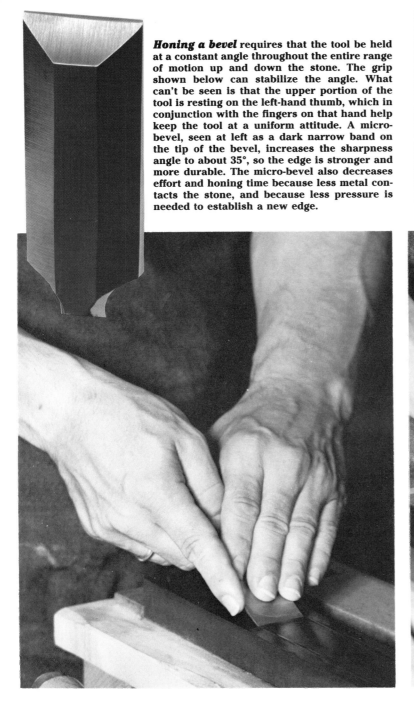

Honing a bevel requires that the tool be held at a constant angle throughout the entire range of motion up and down the stone. The grip shown below can stabilize the angle. What can't be seen is that the upper portion of the tool is resting on the left-hand thumb, which in conjunction with the fingers on that hand help keep the tool at a uniform attitude. A micro-bevel, seen at left as a dark narrow band on the tip of the bevel, increases the sharpness angle to about 35°, so the edge is stronger and more durable. The micro-bevel also decreases effort and honing time because less metal contacts the stone, and because less pressure is needed to establish a new edge.

Backing off removes the wire edge that results from honing and keeps the unbeveled face of the tool polished. It's done by holding the back flat against a fine stone and moving the tool up and down the stone's length, as shown below. The back of a new tool, like the chisel at left, has to be flattened on a coarse stone and then polished on a fine stone. The light areas have been honed, and the dark areas retain the original surface left by the factory's grinding machine. It's not necessary to flatten the entire back, but the area just behind the bevel must be flattened and honed or the edge will never get truly sharp and durable, regardless of how well the bevel has been honed.

an inch from the edge (photo above left). Your right thumb sits on the blade. Place your left thumb under your right thumb and across the underside of the blade; then put your left-hand fingers on the face of the blade about ½ in. up from the edge. Wide tools like plane irons can accommodate all four fingers. Narrow blades take fewer fingers. The thumb on your left hand acts as a fulcrum, while the fingers on that hand serve to deliver even downward pressure across the width of the blade. Your right hand stabilizes things laterally and delivers energy to the stroke of the cut.

Position your feet a comfortable 18 in. or so apart, bend at the waist and touch the bevel to the front end of the stone, which should be about 10 in. in front of your belly. Work the tool up and down the length of the stone. Let your arms (not your body) do the work. Flex only at your elbows, keeping your back and shoulders still. If you shift your upper body, you'll alter the angle of tool on stone, and end

up with a convex bevel. To hold the tool at the proper angle while you're learning this technique, cut a scrap block at a 35° angle and set it by your stone as a visual reference. With practice, you'll be able to find the correct angle automatically.

Try to distribute your strokes over most of the stone's length and width. If you don't, you'll gouge a rut down the center of the stone. Keep the stone amply lubricated. If you're using oil, wipe the stone clean when the oil gets thick and black from metal filings and apply fresh oil.

Micro-bevels—Most edge tools are ground to a sharpness angle of about 25°, just fine for a nice easy cut, but not so good for a durable edge. A second angle of about 35° honed at the tip of the bevel, called a micro-bevel, can lengthen the life of an edge without adversely affecting its cutting efficiency.

Whether the bevel is flat ground or hollow

ground, working with a micro-bevel increases the speed of honing because substantially less steel contacts the stone. And honing is less tiresome because it takes less pressure than honing the entire face of the bevel. With each honing the micro-bevel widens, and once it gets so wide that you can't get a new edge in a minute or so at the stone, you have to regrind a fresh 25° bevel on the tool.

You can tell when your honing should stop by running your finger along the back side of the edge and feeling for the wire edge—that ever-so-small flap of steel that's produced when the surface of the bevel collapses or wears through to the back side of the tool. If the wire edge is so small (or your fingertip so calloused) that you can't feel it, eye the face of the bevel in raking rays of light. If it's time to stop honing, the micro-bevel will be flat and even from its heel out to the edge (in set, above left). But if you see a line of light reflected off the edge, you're not done yet.

Backing off—The back side of a new tool must be honed absolutely flat and kept that way. This is necessary because the backs of new tools are ground more or less flat (inset, facing page, right), and the trenches left by grinding will form little sawteeth at the edge. It doesn't matter how finely polished the bevel is; if the back of the blade isn't flat, and if the grinding lines haven't been leveled, you'll never get the edge really sharp or durable.

For a new tool, begin backing off by holding the blade flat on your coarsest stone (photo facing page, right). Keep working until you've honed a flat surface at least ⅛ in. wide behind the edge. Don't worry if you can't get the entire back flat; it's only the area immediately behind the edge that counts. Next, proceed to your medium-grit stone, and finally polish the back on your fine-grit stone. Now that the tool has been properly flattened and polished on its back side, never back it off on anything but the fine stone. The deeper the scratches, the duller and less durable the edge will be.

You should back off a tool every time you hone its bevel; eight or ten strokes up and down the length of the stone should remove the wire edge. It's not unusual, though, to go from backing off to stroking the bevel a couple of times, back to backing off again, possibly four or five times, to remove a stubborn wire edge. The lighter your touch when honing the bevel, the thinner the wire edge, and the easier it will be to remove.

Oilstones vs. waterstones—Oilstones (Arkansas stones) are novaculite. Mined from pits and caves near Little Rock, they come in four grades (grits). The coarsest is a reddish-looking Washita stone (about 800 to 1,000 grit). Next comes the mottled slate-colored soft Arkansas (about 2,000 grit), followed by the hard Arkansas (about 3,000 grit), which looks like white marble. The finest stone is a black hard Arkansas. Because these are natural stones, the grit in each grade can vary from stone to stone; indeed, from spot to spot on the same stone.

Arkansas stones are fast cutting and durable, but have to be kept clean, or their pores clog with a paste of oil and metal filings. These stones should be cleaned after each use by flushing the surface with fresh oil, rubbing it into the stone and wiping it clean with a lint-free cotton rag. Badly clogged stones can be cleaned by soaking them in mineral spirits or some other solvent that will soften and remove the gunk.

It's pretty easy to gouge a Washita stone

(especially with the roller on a honing guide), and all the natural stones will get uneven after years of use. You can flatten them anew with a diamond whetstone (from Diamond Machining Technology, Inc., 34 Tower St., Hudson, Mass. 01749).

Japanese waterstones are made from abrasive particles that are bonded into bricks. The binder, which softens with water, lets worn particles on the surface float away so that the steel always contacts new sharp particles. For most honing you need only two waterstones—a coarse (say 1,000 grit) and a fine (about 4,000 grit). Before honing can begin, you have to immerse the stones for several minutes in water to let the pores fill up. Otherwise, the water you try to pour on the surface to lubricate the cut will get soaked up, and you'll have a dry stone. But it's not good to keep the stone submerged for a long time because the binder will soften to considerable depth and the stone will wear out too quickly.

Waterstones cut fast, don't clog and make less of a goupy mess than oilstones, especially if you do things right and fix the stones in a rack over a trough of water. This way you can scoop handfuls of water over the stones as you hone without getting spills all over the table and floor. But waterstones will wear faster than oilstones, and these days they are not much cheaper (a black hard Arkansas sells for about $48, and a fine-grit waterstone for about $47). Because waterstones are manmade and therefore consistent all the way through, you get a more uniform cut with them than you do with natural oilstones, which vary in density, porosity and cutting ability. People who use waterstones like them and say that they wouldn't go back to oilstones.

Buffing—To go that extra step toward the perfect edge, you might want to polish the bevel of a tool by buffing, a refinement that almosts gets rid of honing scratches altogether. A buffed edge is sharper and stronger than a honed one, and you can keep it sharp by fre-

quent buffings, though eventually you'll have to re-establish the bevel by grinding and honing. Buffing is done by loading a cloth or felt wheel with a polishing compound (usually grey buff that comes in ingot-size bars) and applying the edge to the wheel just as if you're grinding it, though it's a good idea to adjust the angle to 35° to produce a micro-bevel.

A muslin buffing wheel (a stock item with the Woodcraft Mark II sharpening system) consists of 80 plies of cloth sewn together. The edge of the wheel yields quite a bit under pressure, and so can round over the edge of the tool at an angle much steeper than 35°. I think that a hard felt buffing wheel (photo below) is a better choice because its edge is firm and it won't round over the bevel appreciably as it polishes. Also the hard-felt wheel smooths out honing scratches better than a muslin wheel.

I've made the mistake of trying to buff bevels straight from the grinder, something you can do if you're in a hurry, but not if you want a good edge. You should hone the edge first, then buff it, and buff it thereafter as often as you need to. A buffing wheel shouldn't be used for backing off the blade. Several strokes on your finest stone will remove any wire edge that comes from buffing the bevel.

Compared to grinding, buffing produces very little heat, but you can lean on a tool hard enough to burn it, so take it easy, and load the wheel often with fresh compound. Because buffing is so fast and gives such good results, it's something that site carpenters, as well as shop woodworkers, ought to try. A good setup, one that could easily be made portable, is to take a common bench grinder and equip one arbor with a coarse grinding wheel and the other arbor with a hard felt wheel. Used in conjunction with bench stones, buffing can be part of a format for quick, effective sharpening.

But if you're traveling light, far from home, you can always use sandpaper, kerosene and motor oil. □

Tool Pouches

Pick the right rig for your task, and develop a routine to avoid wasted moves

by Douglass Ferrell

When a builder gets to the job site and puts on a tool belt, everything changes. As the buckle snaps together, the time for designing and negotiating is over, and hands-on work begins. This is one of the reasons those of us who get to wear one all or part of the time feel so strongly about our tool belts.

A properly organized nail and tool pouch contributes to the smooth flow of work. Pulling the right tool from your pouch and finding it in your hand at the moment you need it can become a reflexive act. It can be easily achieved through a combination of well thought-out equipment and patterns of use.

Two kinds of carpenter's belts—There are two distinct styles of waist-mounted storage systems for carpenters: the apron (top photo) and side bags (photo at right). Both are designed to carry commonly used tools, as well as a selection of fasteners. The apron is the traditional style, and it usually hangs in one piece across the user's front from a waist-high belt. Side bags are also held in place by a belt around the waist, but they're positioned on the hips. The question of which is better can be endlessly debated.

The apron's slim profile makes it easier for the wearer to negotiate narrow passages, like the openings between studs. And if you've got to sprint after the coffee truck at break time, you are less likely to leave a trail of hardware. That's because an apron has deep, flat pockets, which

Tool belts fall into two distinct categories: aprons and side bags. The leather apron at top has four pockets and a pair of loops. It's a good choice when you don't need to carry a wide selection of tools. Side bags, on the other hand, are designed to carry a lot of fasteners and tools. Wearing his old standby belt in the photo above, the author demonstrates his two-handed approach to tool-belt organization. Having already measured the board for length, he has marked a cutline with the combination square. Now the skilled hand returns the pencil to its pocket, while the unskilled hand tucks the square into its sheath. These pouches have loops at the top and ride on a woven belt that is fastened with a twist buckle.

also means that its contents are more apt to st. put when you take your belt off at the end your workday.

Most builders who started out as house fram ers prefer side bags to aprons because whe you are bent over you can still get at your na and tools. Most side bags have greater capaci than the front-apron style, and you can car more nails and bulky tools like flat bars, pop ri eters and cordless drills. Many side bags have loop at the top, allowing them to be threade onto the belt of your choice. This lets left-hande workers shuffle bags and components around position tools and fasteners where they wa them. This is another advantage over mo apron-style pouches, which come assembled one piece and are mostly available in only rigl hand models.

Whichever style you choose, consider wearir overalls, or suspenders to hold up your pants. tool belt riding on top of the belt in your jea will just make you uncomfortable, especially you're carrying a lot of weight. Heavy suspende designed to clip directly onto the tool belt c; get some of the load off your hips and onto you shoulders, and keep the flesh on your belly fro being pinched between two belts. McGuir Nicholas and Action Leathercraft both mal suspenders for use with tool belts (see the sid bar on the facing page for addresses).

For general carpentry, a tool belt should b outfitted with a hammer, tape measure, penc

Side-bag rigs: sources of supply

Recent developments in tool-belt manufacturing have created three types of side bags, representing different solutions to the problem of carrying tools and fasteners.

The old standby—Most tool belts in use in this country fall into a category I call the old standby. These weigh from 2 lb. to 3 lb. and come in many styles but generally include a web-type belt with twist buckle and leather side bags (bottom photo, facing page). Many styles and accessories are available for this type of rig. While some bags are sewn onto their belts, others have a loop so you can thread them onto your own belt to create a custom storage system.

One of the nation's largest manufacturers of tool pouches and aprons, the McGuire-Nicholas Co. (2331 Tubeway Ave., Commerce, Calif. 90040), publishes a catalog that is a real eye-opener. It illustrates and describes hundreds of aprons, bags and pouches in all price ranges (from $50 to $80 in premium grades). Their premium-quality bags are considered to be state of the art by many workers. Besides a vast selection of products for general carpentry, McGuire-Nicholas makes specialized tool pouches for surveyors, masons, drywall hangers and blacksmiths. The catalog also includes leather and canvas chisel and bit rolls, shop aprons, and eight styles of knee pads. If you know what tools you want to carry and where you want to carry them, you can probably find a product to suit your needs in this catalog. If not, you might get some inspiration.

Action Leathercraft (5340 Harbor St., Commerce, Calif. 90040) has a similar catalog, although not as extensive. All common styles are well represented, including unusual items like a bag that hangs from the shoulder and rides on the hip and a staple-gun pouch.

The leather saddle—Both Occidental Leather (P.O. Box 364, Valley Ford, Calif. 94972) and McRose Leather (P.O. Box 9325, Truckee, Calif. 95737) make tool belts and bags that I call leather saddles (top photo at right). They are made from the best thick and supple top-grain leathers, and they feature wide leather belts with roller buckles. Although fairly heavy, (nearly 5 lb. without tools and nails) the rigs are surprisingly comfortable. They are also beautiful.

The side-bag-only styles made by these companies are available in a couple of configurations. Tool placement is mostly logical but not very flexible, and they have room for all commonly carried tools. Most are snugly cradled in form-fitting leather sheaths inside the main pockets and against the body. There they don't rattle around or fall out, but they certainly encumber the side pockets somewhat; if you don't like their location, you don't have many other options. The leather tape-measure cage on Occidental's belt feels in the way to me.

These rigs are beautiful, durable and well made with plenty of smooth, sturdy rivets and top-quality stitching. They are handmade and expensive ($90 to $125) versions of regular side bags. If you like the wide belt and buckle and the arrangements for tool storage, you might like one of these rigs.

The nylon alternative—Two manufacturers have recently introduced belts and bags made of Cordura nylon. The complete assemblies weigh less than 2 lb., about half as much as the old standby, and offer some interesting advantages. The belts have a quick-release plastic clasp buckle like those found on backpacks, and the assemblies are washable and require no break-in.

The bags made by Nailers (10845 Wheatlands Ave., Suite C, Santee, Calif. 92071-2856) come in a variety of colors and feature two layers of Cordura surrounding durable foam padding, even on the belt (bottom photo at right). Developed by Du Pont, Cordura is often used to make luggage and backpacks. It staunchly resists puncturing, scuffing and tearing, and does not unravel around a cut.

The Nailers' rigs were designed by a carpenter and include two models in three sizes. They make both right-hand and left-hand versions. Besides conventionally designed side bags, a third bag hangs in the back with one large roomy pocket for excess gear. Removable pockets that attach by way of a touch-fastener flap can be added to the top of each side bag. They are suitable for things like a calculator, glasses and paperwork. Nailers bags cost about $125.

The bag itself is light, so you can carry more seldom-used tools without fatigue. The Nailers' line also has chisel and screwdriver-size tool pockets mounted inside the pouches. This doesn't make it any easier for me to get my nails

Occidental's side bags hang from a wide leather belt secured with a hefty roller buckle (top). A nylon tool belt from Nailers (above) has room for a third pouch in back. The small pouch affixed to the top of the right-side bag is held in place by a touch-fastener flap, and can be easily removed or added as the need arises for more mobility or more tools.

out, but there is sufficient storage for all common tools.

A company called Bear Wear (8733 S. 300 West, Sandy, Utah 84070) also makes nylon belts and bags in five standard designs, all of which are made of a single layer of Cordura. Complete assemblies weigh 1 lb. or less and retail for around $50. The trouble is, no combination of these bags allows a carpenter to carry two or three sizes of nails and a minimum of necessary tools in anything like logical locations. Sheetrockers or other specialists who don't carry many different tools and fasteners might give Bear Wear a try.

Obviously the major question

regarding nylon bags is whether they will hold up. Since they are so new, this is hard to judge. My initial fears of sharp nails and tools poking through the bags have proved unfounded. The material is hard to tear and very tough. The Nailers' bags are well riveted and all double-stitched, but on a Bear Wear bag I tested, an improperly clinched rivet failed right away. Nylon hammer loops on the Nailers' bags don't look very durable. And I don't think the plastic belt buckles will take five years of constant use either, especially if a 2x4 falls on them. But the person who wants to carry less weight on the job should appreciate them.   —D. F.

Photos this page: Doug Windle

An electrician needs screwdrivers, a wire stripper, pliers and knives on the side of the skilled hand. Consequently, an electrician's pouch (top) is a series of pockets made of stiff leather. A plumber's hand tools come in a range of shapes, so a pouch divided into several compartments (above) is a good way to carry them. Along with other tools, this plumber has in his rig a nut driver, a tubing cutter, a torpedo level and a torch striker hanging on a chain.

combination square, razor knife, framing chisel, big and little nail sets, and maybe a four-in-one screwdriver. When I'm doing finish carpentry I add a four-in-hand rasp, a block plane, some sandpaper, a scribe and a butt chisel. If I'm working on framing, I take along a chalkline, a lumber crayon, a saw wrench and the rarely used cat's paw. Early in a project, I might also carry a 100-ft. tape, a mason's line and a plumb bob. Besides this equipment, I usually want nails in three sizes, and I don't want them covered by loose tools.

My work habits are by no means universal, and it's always been interesting to observe how two workers will carry different tools in different ways to tackle the same job. When this is the case, the same pouch setup won't be well suited for both. Fortunately, there is a big selection of different pouches in various sizes and styles, and with a variety of different features.

Tool-belt organization—When you load each tool into its loop, pouch, pocket or niche, put it where it takes only one hand to retrieve it—the one that will use the tool. This is important because it saves motion and lets you use your other hand for something else.

If you consider the routine procedure of preparing a board to be cut, you will see how the correct-hand/correct-tool arrangement works: At the same time the skilled hand gets the pencil, the unskilled hand reaches for the tape. After measuring and marking the board for length, the unskilled hand replaces the tape and brings out the square in one motion. The board is marked square at the tick, and both hands return their tools to their spots.

The same principle applies to your other tools. Hang your hammer on the side of your skilled hand, and keep the things you hit with it, like nails, chisels and nail sets, on the unskilled side. Block planes, utility knives and screwdrivers stay on the skilled side—the chalkbox and the cat's paw live in the unskilled pouch.

Once you get used to carrying your tools in a consistent, rational manner, you'll misplace them less and get more work done. I think this kind of organization at routine operations is one of the great joys of manual labor.

Specialty pouches—For other trades the considerations of using the pouch are similar, although the specifics differ. Wiring, for example, normally requires only one tool at a time in the skilled hand, while the other one holds the work. It is no coincidence that electricians usually carry just one big pouch on their skilled side (photo top left). It may look unbalanced, but it gives them the tool they need in the hand that uses it.

Electrician's pouches are usually stiff leather, while a carpenter's are soft and flexible. This is because carpenters need to reach into the pouch to get nails, and may carry a variety of different-shaped tools like hand planes, chalklines, plumb bobs or tin snips. Electricians want to grasp the handles and pull out their screwdrivers or wire strippers. The stiff bag and many individual pockets keep the various tools separated and easy to withdraw and return. Most

electrician's pouches also feature a convenient way to carry a cable stripper and tape, and they have a steel hook for a wrench or knife.

Like an electrician, a plumber wears a single pouch on the skilled-hand side (photo bottom left). Once you get used to where things are, you can plumb or wire faster with these dedicated tool rigs than you can with a jumble of tools in a general-purpose pouch.

Specialized pouches for drywallers (bottom photo, facing page) can save time for someone hanging a lot of rock. They usually hang on the skilled side, where the tools are used; a large single-pocket pouch holds fasteners on the unskilled side. Accessories like screw-gun holsters can be added to this rig. Because hanging drywall requires few tools and a lot of fasteners, these bags are relatively simple and inexpensive.

Since maneuverability is critical in the trades, it's important to carry no more tools and fasteners than are absolutely necessary. Nowhere is this more important than on the roof.

While I think canvas work aprons are virtually useless to the serious carpenter (they don't have enough room for tools, and it's too hard to get them out of the limp pockets), they do make sense on a roof. A roofer nailing down asphalt shingles generally needs only a hammer, a utility knife and a sack of roofing nails (top photo, facing page). A roofer needs a rig that's flexible enough to allow sitting or kneeling, and canvas is the perfect material for the job.

The most elaborate roofer's aprons (such as those made by McGuire-Nicholas) have pockets mounted high along the waist, where they won't drag on the roof. They are set up for carrying nails, a hammer, a tape and a razor knife, with room for things like a chalkline, tin snips and felt stapler. I have also seen rigs adapted to carry the bulky fasteners for air-driven shingle staplers, along with a hook where you can hang the stapler. Although it might not be practical to carry the heavy stapler around on your waist this way, such a hook frees both hands on a steep roof that has no place to rest the tool. Off the roof, I think canvas work aprons are best used by ticket takers at high-school football games.

What to look for—Once you know what tools you want to carry and what hand will use them, you can select pouches and accessories, or modify your present setup. Professional-grade carpentry pouches in top-grain leather cost from $40 to $120, depending on the quality of the workmanship and the materials.

Serviceable full-sized pouches made of synthetic materials cost about half as much as their leather counterparts. Although most of these won't do for steady use, they can greatly increase a part-time worker's efficiency over the old canvas apron. A big lumberyard or home center is probably the most convenient source for a new pouch, but catalog sales generally offer a bigger selection.

Accessories like tape holders, hammer loops, pliers pockets and sheaths for combination squares can customize a stock bag to improve its efficiency, and help lefties position individual tools where they want them. Special fiber-lined pockets are available for carrying sharp tools

ke chisels and exposed-blade knives. If you like
o carry a Speed Square, look for a bag with a
pecial pouch for this tool.

A good hammer loop will pay for itself in a
ay by letting you get your hammer out rapidly
ith one hand. A metal ring is infinitely better
or this purpose than leather, which tends to
ling to your handle both coming and going.
he "free-swing" metal loop, which pivots to al-
ow your hammer to remain vertical even when
ou aren't, is easier to use when roofing, kneel-
ng or bending. Some belts have a loop in back
o your hammer hangs down at the base of your
pine. This has always seemed awkward to me. I
arry my hammer near the front of my skilled-
ide bag on a factory-installed steel loop. Here it
s near the fingertips of my hand at rest.

One problem tool for tool pouches is the steel
ape measure. Like the hammer, this common
ool should rate a setup that's quick and easy to
se. But most arrangements I've seen for carrying
a tape are not very satisfactory. The special
eather cage-type pouches for tapes often re-
uire some fumbling on removal, and their loca-
ons don't seem convenient to me. Carrying a
ape loose in a nail pouch interferes with getting
he nails. Some bags made by Action Leather-
raft feature a conveniently located metal clip
nto which a steel tape snaps securely. I clip my
5-ft. tape on a stiff leather loop low and near
he front of the side bag on my unskilled side.

Experiment with your setup. It took me a
ouple of years of experimentation to arrive at
my present tool arrangement, so don't be dis-
ouraged if everything doesn't fall together right
way. One interesting way to experiment is to
rade pouches with co-workers and see how
heir setups work for you. It's easy to move tools
bout on a given setup until they feel right, but it
akes a while to get used to any change. If you
move your pencil to a new location, you will
ind yourself continuing to reach for it in the old
pot for some time.

When you figure out what you'll need and
where it's handiest, don't be afraid to modify a
ag. I bought the side bags I have worn for years
off the shelf at a lumberyard. They didn't have a
sheath for a combination square so I just cut out
he bottom of a pliers-type pocket behind the
nail pouches on my unskilled side. This works
well for me, and I think it's a little easier to find
on the return than the inflexible slit on the spe-
cially designed metal sheath.

Materials, buckles and maintenance—Nail
bags can be made from leather, synthetic imita-
tions or nylon. Leather's intricately interwoven,
twisted fibers account for its great strength and
flexibility, and give it excellent resistance to
abrasion, puncturing and tearing.

The best-quality leathers are called top grain
and will be identified as such on well-made
products. Top-grain leather is taken from the
outside layer of cowhide, which is too thick for
most leather products. Consequently, the leather
is split into layers. The inner layers are referred
to as split leather and are not as resistant to tearing and abrasion. Split leather has a rough suede
finish on both sides and is more likely to absorb
water. Sometimes split leathers are rolled and

painted to make them look like smooth top
grain. Any leather product not advertised as top
grain is probably a lower grade. A vegetable tanning process is used for most stiff pouches,
while mineral tanning yields a softer product—
mainly for nail bags.

Even if you are not familiar with the fine points
of leather quality and the various synthetic imita-
tions, you can tell a lot simply by feeling and
inspecting the product. Better-quality materials
will feel more supple and substantial, and the
finish will have more depth than on cheaper materials. Double-stitched pockets with lots of rivets are an indication of good-quality construction, as is sturdy, nickel-plated hardware. The
rivets should be smooth on both sides. Nail
pouches should easily accept your hand, and
they should have their seams on the sides, not
on the bottom, where they can trap nails.

I think that 100% cotton web belts are more
durable and comfortable than the cheaper polypropylene alternatives, especially in hot weather.
But I know several carpenters who prefer wide
leather belts. They like the better weight distribution and back support that they get from a
wide belt.

Most tool belts require only a twist of the
wrist to fasten or unfasten, whether they fasten
in front or in back. I like front buckles—it's just
a lot more convenient to take the thing off when
the buckle is readily accessible.

Some all-leather belts use a conventional roller buckle. The twist buckles are both faster to
operate and longer lasting, since the main wear
point is metal on metal, as opposed to metal on
leather or fabric. But nothing lasts forever under
heavy use. I wore out a twist buckle in about five
years of more or less steady use. The prong
eventually wore down enough to slip through
the slot in the keeper whenever I bent over,
dumping the whole works on the floor in a
shower of nails and loose tools.

A well-made pouch doesn't require much care.
I try to keep mine out of the rain—at least when
I am not in it. I have not treated mine with leather dressing, and after ten years of mostly heavy
use, the leather is bleached out but still supple
and comfortable to the touch.

Most manufacturers assume no particular
maintenance will be given to their products and
don't specifically recommend any. But if a pouch
gets dry, a leather dressing like saddle soap or
mink oil will revive it. Just work it thoroughly into
the leather so no residue remains to attract dirt.

I've sewn my bags twice. Once I sewed up the
stitching around a pocket cut from years of carrying a framing chisel. Another time a shoe re-
pairman sewed a patch where a bag was wearing
thin, on top along the belt. Waxed nylon thread
should be used for any stitching of this kind.
You can also use braided fishing line or dental
floss. Use a hand-held awl stitcher to sew on a
patch, and make sure you pull the stitches tight
and tie the ends securely. A temporary repair
can be made in the field with a pop rivet. But a
leatherworker can install a permanent rivet so
inexpensively that I rarely do it myself. ☐

_General contractor Douglass Ferrell lives in
Trout Creek, Mont._

While canvas work aprons have limited applications, they are just right for working on a
roof (top). They have a hammer loop and room
for a knife and a bunch of nails. The flexibility
of a canvas apron lets you get comfortable in a
spot where comfort is at a premium. Drywallers
need two bags—one to carry tools for the
skilled hand (above) and one for fasteners. On
the skilled side, this rig carries a drywall circle
cutter, a Surform plane, a utility knife, a
drywall hammer, a keyhole saw and tin snips.

Pickup-Truck Tool Storage

Long sliding drawers let a builder get to his tools, even when they're under a stack of plywood

by Ray Lincoln

I'm a builder who works on a variety of jobs at different locations during a typical week. As a consequence, my pickup truck is a rolling hardware store, and I often need to haul around a stack of building materials to boot. Anyone who's had to carry both tools and materials in the same pickup knows what kind of problems can result—the tools inevitably end up under a pile of lumber or drywall, inaccessible when they are needed.

Because I carry so many tools, I want them to be safely locked up inside a shell that covers the bed of the truck. The shell eliminates the easy addition of a lumber rack, so I needed some other way to carry tools and materials that allowed ready access to both.

My solution is a simple one. I keep my tools in a pair of 8-ft. long drawers made of 1x14 knotty pine boards and plywood. The drawers are subdivided into compartments for various kinds of tools and supplies. Over the years I have noted which tools I use with the greatest frequency, and I keep these—my carpentry tools and tool belt, extension cords and general-

purpose hand tools—in the compartments closest to the tailgate. In the middle bays I keep three toolboxes devoted to door-jig equipment socket sets and wrenches and miscellaneous hardware. In the back bay of one drawer I keep my power tools, and in the other I stash painting equipment, shim stock, nails and other fasteners. To speed up loading and unloading, I keep related tools in lift-out trays or toolboxes that nest into the compartments.

The drawers fit into a steel and plywood carcase that is covered with four plywood lids. If

Lincoln's pickup-truck storage system consists of two 8-ft. drawers that ride in a steel and plywood carcase. Here the drawers are fully extended, with their inboard ends bearing on the second steel crossbar. The drawers are divided into compartments for related tools, hardware and supplies. Four plywood lids atop the unit make a flat surface for carrying cargo. The carcase stays put between the wheel wells without mechanical connections.

don't have a load of cargo resting on the plywood, I can get at the drawer compartments through the doors in the side of the shell. Notches cut into the plywood sides of the carcase allow me to sneak a hand under the plywood lids so that I can lift them away to gain access to the tools.

If, on the other hand, I've got a load of materials resting on the cargo platform, I can pull the drawers out so that about 6 ft. of their substantial length is readily accessible (photo facing page). When the drawers are extended this far, their inboard ends bear on one of the steel crossbars, which resist the considerable upward thrust of the fully loaded drawers.

A steel framework—A local welding shop fabricated the steel skeleton of my storage system. As shown in the drawing below, the outside dimensions of the frame are 49 in. by 97 in., which gives me a little wiggle room on the top of the platform for loading 4x8 sheets of plywood or other material.

The top and bottom frames and the corner posts are made of ¾-in. angle iron, while the uprights on the side and the three-sided border around the top frame are made of flat iron. To

beef up the frame at the tailgate end, I had the welder add a piece of ¾-in. by 3-in. rectangular steel tube as a header. On the inboard side of the header, a piece of angle iron picks up the edge of the plywood lid. It takes four lids of equal dimension to cover the carcase. Their edges bear on angle-iron flanges.

I paid about $300 to have the steelwork portion of this storage system built. That price included grinding down the rough spots and a coat of primer. For a finish, I bought some cans of black lacquer spray paint and applied a few coats myself.

Since the steel parts are ⅛ in. thick, I used ¾-in. solid-core birch plywood for the lids and the bottom of the carcase. That way the wood ends up a little above the edges of the angle iron. The sides are ½-in. thick plywood, held in place by ¼-in machine bolts through the flat iron uprights. I used self-locking nuts for the sides because I was concerned about road vibration eventually working the nuts loose. I've driven a lot of miles since I installed the storage unit, and to date the nuts have hung on tight.

Because I sometimes rest lumber on top of the platform that is longer than the bed of the truck, I installed three tie-downs on each side of

the carcase. They are secured by machine-thread screws driven into T-nuts embedded in the plywood sides.

The carcase fits just inside the wheel wells, and gravity and friction have proved to be strong enough forces to keep it in place. I didn't use any mechanical fasteners between the plywood bottom and the frame either. It just rests there, held in place by the plywood sides and the angle-iron flanges. Three runners divide the bottom into two bays for the drawers. The space between the runners is about ¼ in. larger than the width of the drawers to keep things from binding up. I think the only time the runners are really necessary is when I'm working in the hills. Then they help to keep the drawers from shifting around in their slots.

I have been using this storage system for a couple of years now, and I've noticed that it has a hidden benefit. Not only do I keep my trips to the hardware store to a minimum, but I often have an obscure tool or part that one of my subs needs. And that can keep a job from stopping dead in its tracks. □

Ray Lincoln is a licensed general contractor based in Castro Valley, Calif.

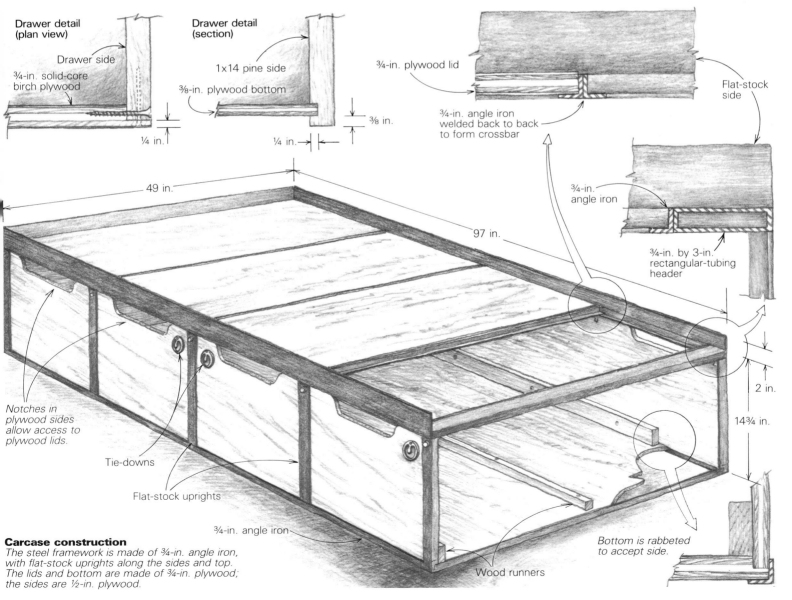

Drawer detail (plan view)

Drawer side

¾-in. solid-core birch plywood

¼ in.

Drawer detail (section)

1x14 pine side

⅜-in. plywood bottom

⅜ in.

¼ in.

¾-in. plywood lid

¾-in. angle iron welded back to back to form crossbar

Flat-stock side

¾-in. angle iron

¾-in. by 3-in. rectangular-tubing header

49 in.

97 in.

2 in.

14¾ in.

Notches in plywood sides allow access to plywood lids.

Tie-downs

Flat-stock uprights

¾-in. angle iron

Wood runners

Bottom is rabbeted to accept side.

Carcase construction
The steel framework is made of ¾-in. angle iron, with flat-stock uprights along the sides and top. The lids and bottom are made of ¾-in. plywood; the sides are ½-in. plywood.

Drawing: Christopher Clapp

On-Site Shop

A portable table saw and jointer and several useful jigs

by Sam Clark

Given enough big-shop tools, it's fairly easy to do accurate work quickly; given more time and skills, accurate work can be done by hand. But often there is a need to do accurate work quickly when shop tools are not available. In my work, remodeling, many jobs require accurate cutting but are too small to justify bringing in the 10-in. table saw. For such jobs I have developed a traveling shop consisting of light, portable jigs and setups that extend the uses of portable circular saws and routers. All these gadgets are cheap; convenient to make, move and set up, and precise.

Plywood-cutting jig—I learned about this gadget from John Borden, a designer from Cambridge, Mass. Carpenters commonly make long

cuts in plywood, counter stock and other large panels by clamping a straightedge to the work and running a circular saw against it. Setting up is tedious, particularly if many such cuts must be made, and usually the cuts are off a bit. My plywood-cutting jig has a fence, but it also has a base that aligns exactly on the cutting line so you don't have to measure.

You can make this jig in five or ten minutes. First cut a strip about 5 in. wide off the long edge of a piece of ½-in. or ¾-in. fir plywood. I use A/B, A/C or A/D grade. Flip the strip over so the factory-cut edge ends up as the working side of the fence, and screw it down firmly to the remainder of the sheet with eight or ten screws. Leave enough of the sheet sticking out to the left of the fence so that you can clamp it to your

work surface without obstructing the saw. Run the saw down the track once to cut the jig free from the plywood. To use the jig, line up this edge with the line you want to cut, clamp the jig down, then saw.

Homemade table saw—The heart of the traveling shop is the homemade table saw. George Carson of Bloomfield, Conn., rigged up a table saw in his basement by suspending a circular saw upside down underneath a table. My gadget is based on his idea. The table is simply a piece of ¾-in. plywood with a hole for the saw and a routed slot for the crosscut fence to slide in. It rests on a pair of folding sawhorses, braced to prevent sagging. I used A/B, A/C or A/D grade Douglas fir, which will stay flat for years if it is

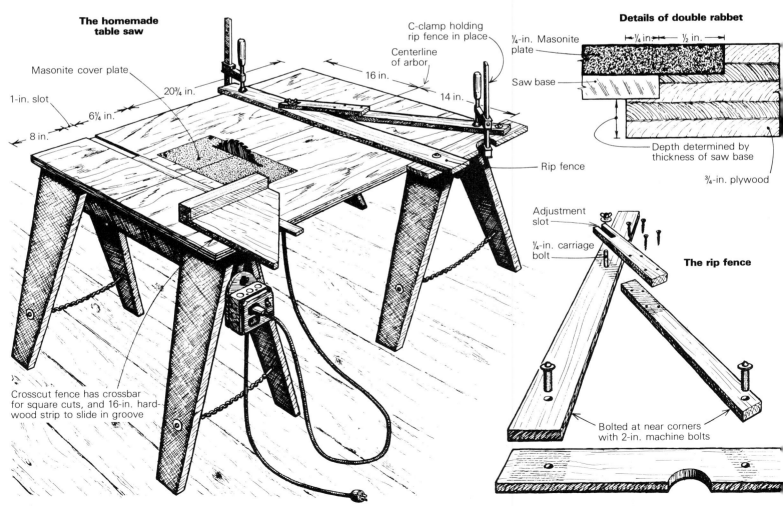

The homemade table saw

Masonite cover plate

1-in. slot

6¼ in.

8 in.

20¾ in.

C-clamp holding rip fence in place

Centerline of arbor

16 in.

14 in.

Rip fence

Crosscut fence has crossbar for square cuts, and 16-in. hardwood strip to slide in groove

Details of double rabbet

¼ in.   ½ in.

¼-in. Masonite plate

Saw base

Depth determined by thickness of saw base

¾-in. plywood

Adjustment slot

¼-in. carriage bolt

The rip fence

Bolted at near corners with 2-in. machine bolts

stored in a dry place. Cut the plywood table using the plywood cutting jig; the drawing gives table dimensions.

The accuracy of this homemade table saw depends on aligning the rip fence precisely parallel to the rabbets around the saw hole and the groove in which the miter gauge slides. The simplest way to accomplish this is to use the rip fence itself when you rout the saw hole and the miter gauge slot. Therefore, it's best to make the rip fence first.

The rip fence is simply an L-square with a two-piece diagonal brace for rigidity. It is bolted at the two near corners with 1-in. machine bolts. At the apex, a $\frac{1}{4}$-in. carriage bolt and wing nut ride in a slot cut in the diagonal brace to allow for adjustment. In operation, the fence slides side to side against the near edge of the table, much like a drafting T-square. Once set up for a cut, the fence is simply C-clamped in place. Use a rafter square to square up the rip fence, then tighten the wing nut. A wood screw installed at the apex, next to the wing nut, will serve as a set-screw to make the adjustment permanent.

Use the rip fence to draw the location of the saw hole on the table. This hole is double-rabbeted. The lower shelf supports the saw base and the upper one holds a slotted $\frac{1}{4}$-in. Masonite cover plate, which should be fitted flush with the table top. This cover deflects sawdust and keeps small scraps from falling through. The saw is

sandwiched between the lower rabbet and the cover plate, which is screwed down to the table. No other fastening is necessary. Rout the top rabbet first, fencing your router with your new rip fence. After completing both rabbets, cut the hole out with a saber saw. The precise dimensions of these cuts will be determined by the size of your portable circular saw. Now make the crosscut fence, a 45° triangle of plywood with a crossbar screwed to its top for square cuts, and a $\frac{5}{16}$-in. by 1-in. by 16-in. hardwood strip screwed to its bottom. Rout a groove, using the rip fence. Make the fit snug, and lubricate with wax or silicone spray.

If you fasten the hardwood strip perfectly square to the plywood triangle, the guide will stay accurate. I've been using mine for five years now and it's still true. It would not be hard to make an adjustable miter gauge, but when I need precise angled cuts, I sometimes make a jig similar to the plywood cutting jig, but only 16 in. long for convenience. This jig is particularly useful when less experienced people are on the job, because anyone can make precise cuts easily with it.

Now you're ready to insert the saw. Use a good saw with a rigid base. I prefer the Milwaukee. Hold the saw trigger down with a clip or tape, and plug the saw into an extension cord fitted with a switch, so you can turn it on and off like a regular table saw.

The most annoying aspect of the homemade table saw is that blade height and angle adjustments are awkward. I'm not sure this problem can be solved.

Router table—The homemade table saw cannot cut dadoes, but you can solve this problem by hanging a router underneath the table. Replace the saw cover plate with one of $\frac{1}{4}$-in. Masonite drilled to receive the router bit. Remove the plastic disc from the router, and bolt its metal base to the plate. For greater rigidity, use $\frac{1}{2}$-in. plywood, which will necessitate rabbeting the edges of the bottom side of the plate. The router table can be used for dadoing, sliding dovetail joints, rounding over and similar operations using the crosscut and rip fences devised for the circular saw.

With a special fence, you can also use this setup to join the edges of boards with reasonable accuracy and speed. On a power jointer, the outfeed table lines up exactly with the jointer knives. The infeed table is slightly lower but parallel, so the work travels over the cutters in a straight line even while part of the wood is being cut away. To make a jointing fence for your router, take a straight board at least 4-in. wide and rip between $\frac{1}{32}$ in. and $\frac{1}{16}$ in. off half of its length. You can use the homemade table saw for this cut if the blade is sharp. The full-width part of the board will be the outfeed fence and the narrower part will be the infeed fence. Cut a hole for the bit. Clamp the fence to the plywood table so that the outfeed fence lines up perfectly with the router bit. Use a sharp $\frac{1}{4}$-in. straight bit. Because the jig's capacity is determined by the length of the bit, make sure the one you use is at least $\frac{3}{4}$-in. long.

Dadoing jig—I have found this jig indispensable. It consists of two 1x2s screwed with drywall screws to a base of $\frac{1}{4}$-in. Masonite. The 1x2s are spaced a distance equal to the diameter of the router base. They form a track for the router. The jig in the drawing is for $\frac{3}{4}$-in. dadoes. When the strips were in place, I put a $\frac{3}{4}$-in. carbide bit in the router, lowered the router into the track, and made the slot in the base. To make a dado, clamp the slot directly over where the cut is to be made. Because there is no measuring, this jig is precise. For angled cuts or cuts in slightly warped pieces, it is often more convenient than a table saw.

On deep cuts, make several passes with the router. Set it for the maximum cut, but make the first pass with two thicknesses of $\frac{1}{4}$-in. Masonite between the router base and the base of the jig. Make the second cut with one thickness, and the final pass with none.

Plywood cutting jig

Fence is screwed to sheet, then jig is cut free

Flip 5-in. piece so factory-cut edge becomes work side of fence

Overhang for clamping

← 3 in. → ← 5 in. →

Detail of jointing fence

Outfeed

Router bit

Infeed portion of jointing fence is $\frac{1}{32}$ to $\frac{1}{16}$ in. narrower than outfeed

Dadoing jig

Use different sized slots for different sized dadoes

$\frac{1}{4}$-in. Masonite

1x2

Sam Clark, 36, of Cambridge, Mass., is the author of Designing and Building Your Own House Your Own Way *(Houghton Mifflin Co., Boston, 1978).*

Job-Site Shack

A modular tool shed that's roomy, well lit and secure

by Bill Young

I sometimes envy my subs because they can practice their trades neatly out of their trucks, and drive blithely on to the next job after a week or two. As a general contractor, I'm married to the site. I build large custom houses, and my small crew does everything from complex hillside foundations through cabinet-grade finish work. We use a variety of hardware and tools, and often end up working at the same location for a year.

My situation calls for a job shack—a lockable outbuilding where tools and hardware can be stored. This means you don't have to haul your equipment back and forth on a day-to-day basis. It also safely houses the job telephone, and provides a place to tack up the building permit and the clean set of plans. Lastly, the job shack is a place to sip coffee and plan strategy when it's pouring rain.

The shack shown here grew out of my dissatisfaction with dark, low sheds that rarely survive more than one or two jobs. I wanted a durable job shack that was a manageable load for a standard pickup, and easy to assemble. Even more important, I wanted enough natural light inside so things wouldn't get lost on the backs of the shelves. The building also needed to be secure enough to discourage all but the most determined burglar.

The modular design that I came up with bolts together. It consists of ten 4x8 plywood panels edged with 4x4s, four roof trusses, two 5-ft. by 8-ft. pieces of expanded metal, and five 2-ft. by 10-ft. corrugated-fiberglass roof panels (see the materials takeoff on the facing page for the complete list).

My shack cost me about $700 to build, but there's little reason to think that I'll ever need to replace it. Considering how long we spend on the site over the course of a year, the two hours it takes to assemble the completed modules is well worth the result. The shack is secure enough that I can store things like my transit there, with little worry of theft. And it's big enough (over 60 sq. ft. of floor space, and 48 sq. ft. of shelf space) to store tools and materials that I don't use everyday—the same things that would normally send me scurrying back to my garage if the need arose. I've even stocked my shack with a cast-off refrigerator that makes pail lunches a little less boring, and keeps the Friday afternoon staple colder.

Bill Young is a general contractor in the San Francisco Bay area.

This modular job shack knocks down quickly and fits in the back of a pickup truck. Yet with over 60 sq. ft. of floor space and 48 sq. ft. of shelving, it holds the normal complement of tools and hardware, a wheelbarrow, a compressor and even a refrigerator. The translucent fiberglass roof panels keep the shack well lit, and the expanded metal screwed to the purlins and trusses helps keep burglars out.

Floor and walls—The floor is made of two 4x8 sheets of ¾-in. AC exterior plywood. I fastened fir 4x4s with glue and pneumatic staples flush with the four edges of each plywood sheet. After carefully aligning the two panels side by side, I joined them with three ⅝-in. by 8½-in. machine bolts that extend through the butted 4x4s.

I used 4x8 sheets of plywood for the walls also, but ½-in. AC exterior seemed sufficient. I fastened 4x4 ledgers back 4 in. from the top and bottom edges of all eight of these panels to form a lip. The top lip provides a positive seat for the ends of the roof trusses. The bottom lip overlaps the floor panel. The floor and wall panels aren't joined through this plywood lap, however. Instead I used two ⅝-in. by 8½-in. bolts through the bottom 4x4 on each wall panel and into the plywood and 4x4 of the floor panel.

The four wall panels that I used under the eaves on the two sides of the shack were identical, with 4x4s set flush with their long edges. I laid these panels out flat in pairs, drilling and bolting the two butting 4x4s in the same way I joined the floor panels. On the remaining two pairs of panels that form the gable-

end walls, I inset the 4x4 on one edge of each by 3½ in. to allow for overlap with the side panels at the corners.

To make the door, I laid down one of the end panels with its plywood side facing up, drew the dimensions of the door, set my saw depth for ½ in. to avoid ripping into the 4x4s and cut free the rectangle. This door panel overlaps the inside edge of the 4x4 perimeter by ½ in. on all sides, forming a kind of stop. I reinforced the plywood door face with an inner frame of 2x4s, holding the frame shy of the edge of the plywood by ¾ in. all around to accommodate the overlap. Then I braced the door with horizontal 2x6s laid flat to add strength and to provide solid backing for the carriage bolts that secure the hinges and hasps. I nailed ⅜-in. shear panel on the inside of the frame for rigidity. The heads of the ⅝-in. by 7½-in. machine bolts that secure the panels on either side of the doorway were set in counterbores so the extra-thick door would clear the bolt heads in the 4x4 jambs.

Roof—The roof trusses are pitched for a 6-in-12 gable. I used 2x6 rafters with nearly full ⅜-in. CDX plywood gussets on each side. By setting the end rafters out to the edge of the frame, the plywood on the trusses serves as gable-end sheathing.

The tops of the trusses were notched to receive flat 2x4 purlins, three on each side of the slope. I used bugle-headed screws to secure them. I held the trusses down on the walls with sheet-metal angles called seismic-hurricane ties. The ties I used for the end trusses were Simpson H2.5s (Simpson Co. 1450 Doolittle Drive, San Leandro, Calif. 94577), with a Simpson H1 on each of the middle trusses.

Although I wanted a roof that gave me good natural light, security was just as important, and the 9-ga. expanded metal I used fits the bill. I was able to get 5-ft. by 8-ft. pieces, one for each side of the roof. I attached them to the purlins with screws and fender washers. An even more secure method would be to weld short pieces of angle iron to the underside of the steel fabric that could be screwed to the rafters from below.

The corrugated-fiberglass roofing keeps the rain out and allows good natural lighting. I overlapped the panels a few corrugations and attached them to the purlins with screws and neoprene washers to prevent leaks. □

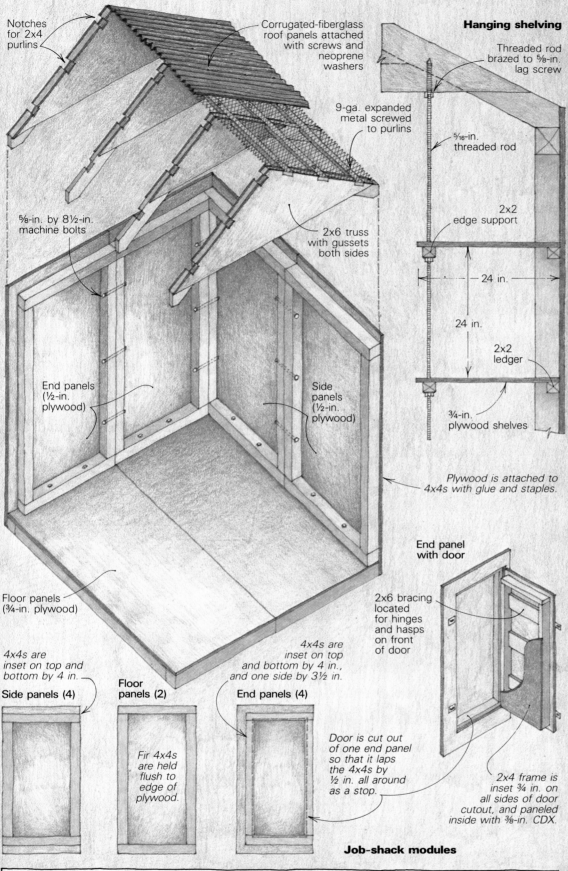

Notches for 2x4 purlins

Corrugated-fiberglass roof panels attached with screws and neoprene washers

9-ga. expanded metal screwed to purlins

⅝-in. by 8½-in. machine bolts

2x6 truss with gussets both sides

End panels (½-in. plywood)

Side panels (½-in. plywood)

Floor panels (¾-in. plywood)

Plywood is attached to 4x4s with glue and staples.

4x4s are inset on top and bottom by 4 in.

4x4s are inset on top and bottom by 4 in., and one side by 3½ in.

Side panels (4)

Floor panels (2)

Fir 4x4s are held flush to edge of plywood.

End panels (4)

Door is cut out of one end panel so that it laps the 4x4s by ½ in. all around as a stop.

End panel with door

2x6 bracing located for hinges and hasps on front of door

2x4 frame is inset ¾ in. on all sides of door cutout, and paneled inside with ⅜-in. CDX.

Job-shack modules

Hanging shelving

Threaded rod brazed to ⅝-in. lag screw

⅝6-in. threaded rod

2x2 edge support

24 in.

24 in.

2x2 ledger

¾-in. plywood shelves

Materials takeoff

2	¾-in. 4x8 AC ext. plywood	35	⅝-in. by 8½-in. machine bolts
9	½-in. 4x8 AC ext. plywood (incl. gussets)	8	⅝-in. by 7½-in. machine bolts (door jambs)
4	⅜-in. 4x8 CDX plywood (incl. back of door)	86	⅝-in. washers
30	4x4 by 8-ft. fir	43	⅝-in. hex nuts
3	2x4 by 16-ft. fir (purlins)	4	Simpson H1 (center-rafter hurricane ties)
1	2x4 by 20-ft. fir (door frame)	4	Simpson H2.5 (end-rafter hurricane ties)
7	2x6 by 10-ft. (trusses and door bracing)	1	Box 1½-in. bugle-headed screws
2	5-ft. by 8-ft. pieces of 9-ga. expanded metal	3	Heavy strap hinges
5	2x10 corrugated-fiberglass roof panels	2	Heavy hasps and locks

Illustration: Frances Ashforth

Supporting utility shelves

Utility shelves that will take a keg of nails dropped off a laborer's shoulder are usually so cluttered with 2x4 supports that the nails end up being stored out in the rain. The shelving system I use takes lots of weight, allows for any number of shelves at adjustable heights, can be easily disassembled, and leaves the floor space under the bottom shelf completely open.

My system doesn't depend on a frame resting on the ground. Instead, the shelves rest on ledgers along the back, and are suspended at the front from the ceiling by ⁵⁄₁₆-in. threaded rod. The front edge of the shelf is stiffened with a 2x2 and supported by a washer and nut.

What makes this top-hung system work is the connection between the all-thread and the ⅝-in. by 5-in. lag screw that is driven into an overhead framing member designed to take the load. I drill out the head of the lag screw about ½-in. deep, and then nickel-silver braze the all-thread to it. If long pieces of threaded rod become cumbersome, you can always buy shorter lengths and use unions.

On the job-shack shelving shown in the photo below, I ran two vertical threaded rods 32 in. apart that were lag-screwed to the bottom chord of the trusses. The rods support the front edges of ¾-in. plywood shelves that are 2 ft. deep and 8 ft. across, and drilled out for the rods. The back edges are supported by 2x2 ledgers screwed into the shack walls. In this case, I left a little less than 2 ft. of clearance between shelves. Leveling the shelves is easy—you just give the nut another turn. —*B. Y.*

A Mobile Workshop

How to get your standing power tools to the job and back again

by Cy Westlake

If you do custom woodwork in homes, commercial buildings or on board boats, you are better off with a complete mobile workshop than with a built-in tool setup in your garage or shed. The mobile shop carries your essential equipment right to the job site where you need it. It can also instantly transform a barn or large garage into a functioning woodshop.

Taking the time to make your mobile shop handsome as well as functional has a side benefit that may not be immediately apparent. The mobile shop is a testimonial to its owner's ability as a craftsman. I'm surprised how often a passerby will stop, make several slow circles around my trailer, watch me work for a while and then ask, "Could you bring that rig over and build me a teak bar in my rec room?"

Equipping the shop—The first task in designing your mobile shop is deciding what tools you want to carry and where to locate them on the trailer. To help in making this decision, lay out the deck of the mobile shop full scale on the floor. I used a rectangle 88 in. by 120 in. Make accurate cardboard plans of your equipment and position them on the deck. It took me quite some time to make sure that one piece of

equipment wouldn't interfere with wood being worked on another, and that the shop would remain in balance on the road. Undoubtedly your shop will be equipped differently from mine to fit your tools and your style of work, and so you'll need to experiment.

My jointer and radial arm saw are both secured to the deck with dovetail slides, the saw because it must be pulled out to adjust depth-of-cut with the elevating handle under the table. Traveling, the saw is pushed back, and a butt hinge on each stationary dovetail flips over onto a locking pin on the sliding dovetail. The jointer has to be on slides because it's impossible to clear shavings from under the machine in travel position. In use, it pulls out, and chips fall directly into a cardboard box below.

I gave a lot of thought to including a lathe. If you stick close to home, you're probably better off with it on your garage workbench so that you can use that extra workspace in the mobile shop. But I bum around the country and have to carry everything I might need to use, so I made space for my lathe.

My sanding machine (12-in. disc, 6-in. wide belt) is indispensable. It sits on a ¾-in. plywood plate that swivels to bring the belt or disc into

working position. The bandsaw is important to me in marine work. It is bolted in place, but is cocked at an angle to allow work to clear the drill-press column.

I decided to include my drill press because it's equipped with a hollow-chisel mortiser and because I often need to cut plugs for screws. Sometimes I use it to drill holes. Supplies such as sanding belts, glue, screws, and even extension cords and portable electric tools can be stored easily in the locking side compartments.

My air compressor was a luxury at first, but I soon found it essential for cleaning up the shop, filling tires and cleaning my pipe. With a good compressor you may also find yourself doing more pneumatic stapling, nailing, spray painting and varnishing on site.

I didn't include a generator in my shop. In my experience the craftsman arrives on the job after the power is in; so I always carry two 50-ft. #10 wire extension cords.

The chassis—A good alternative to making your own chassis is buying a trailer or converting one to your own purpose. Make sure that it is rated to carry your load. I like fabricating my own chassis so that I can equip it exactly as I want. If you're going to do it yourself, the first consideration in choosing wheels, springs, axles and brakes is weight. My gross vehicle weight—trailer and average load—is about 1,850 lb., but I can also stow nearly 1,000 lb. of plywood in the rear compartment if necessary. Typically I carry 300 lb. to 400 lb. of materials in addition to my tools.

Balancing this load is important at highway speeds. I placed the axle center on my shop 9 in. behind the center of the body, so that roughly 12% of the weight is being carried by the hitch of the towing vehicle (I usually use my full-size pickup). Distributing the weight of materials and hand tools can make a big difference. You'll quickly develop the habit of stowing your gear where it makes the trailer track best.

Springs that are too stiff cause the trailer to vibrate badly because the wheels don't have constant contact with the ground. When springs are too soft, the trailer will sway and wander which can affect the tow vehicle also.

For my mobile-shop trailer I chose springs rated at 3,000 lb. This also eliminated the need for shock absorbers with the amount of weight I carry. To stop the load I use surge brakes, which makes braking effort even, and always proportional to the load. These brakes don't

Plan of tool layout Overall dimensions 88 in. by 120 in.

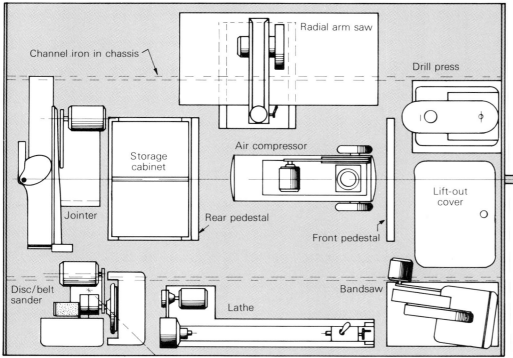

Channel iron in chassis

Radial arm saw

Drill press

Storage cabinet

Air compressor

Jointer

Rear pedestal

Front pedestal

Lift-out cover

Disc/belt sander

Bandsaw

Lathe

require adjustment like electric brakes. And since this load-activated hydraulic system is on the trailer tongue, it doesn't matter what vehicle you happen to use for towing.

Don't skimp on axles. They should be seamless tubing and rated to carry more than your load requirements. Few experiences in life are as maddening as having a broken axle on a loaded trailer far from home.

Putting the chassis together requires some precision if your mobile shop is going to travel the highways without wandering or whipping. Lay out the correct lengths of structural steel (channel and angle iron) on the floor. As if you were reconstructing a fossil skeleton, make sure of each piece in relation to the others. Take the wheels off and lay the hubs and springs in place; the two axle spindles should form the points of an isosceles triangle with the ball hitch. This, along with a toe-in of between ⅛ in. and ¼ in., will give you good straight tracking without excessive tire wear.

Once you have thoroughly checked the layout of the running gear and steel frame, you can weld the chassis together. Don't be dismayed to see how light and flimsy the rig looks. The iron has very little to do with the rigidity of the structure; it merely ties everything together. The strength lies in the body structure, which forms a very strong box girder.

Building the body—I used five 10-ft. sheets of ⅝-in. exterior AC fir plywood for the body of the trailer. The compartment bottoms are made of ½-in. ply, and the front and rear pedestal, the plywood sandwiches that support the roof and gull-wing doors, are ⅜-in. ply, as are the cabinet sides. Everything gets glued. You want to end up with a competely unitized structure in which every component contributes to the strength of the whole.

I made the wheel cutouts after the body was complete, making sure there would be clearance to remove the wheel without jacking up the body as well as the axle.

The top and doors—So I could work with long boards, my trailer design called for four sides, or doors, that would hang from a fixed top with continuous hinges, and give me free, unobstructed access to all of the machines. The configuration of the top and sides had to allow one door to pass another in opening and closing, yet still give a completely weathertight coverage of the trailer sides when they were in the down position.

The end doors are fastened by heavy-duty toggle-type catches. A prop set into a lip on the inside of the door and at the top of each pedestal holds them up. The sides are held open together by means of a bar across the top of the whole rig. This bar hooks the lip of each side door in the open position.

This system offers a shaded working space free from corner posts, with head clearance of 6½ ft. Closed for travel, the entire unit is just over 5 ft. high, and offers very little wind resistance on the highway. It is secure, weatherproof and pleasing to the eye.

I made the gull-wing door frames from spruce for lightness, and used 5/32-in. lauan interior paneling as the skin, which I installed with aluminum screws—400 in all. I used aluminum screws because they could be sanded down if any of them stuck up beyond the surface of the skin. A few of them did.

The top and doors were undercoated with three coats of penetrating epoxy resin, and finished with white gloss marine enamel. The overhanging lips of the doors were formed in place with fiberglass tape and epoxy resin over soft foam weatherstripping. This form fit leaves no room for water penetration, even under highway conditions. By the time I finished, the doors were no longer plywood, but wood-core epoxy panels. After nearly five years, the finish remains smooth and unbroken.   □

Cy Westlake, a retired patternmaker and engineer, is a cabinetmaker and architectural woodworker based in Goodrich, Mich.

This mobile workshop lets you use stationary power tools with a minimal setup time. It includes a jointer, disc/belt sander, air compressor, radial arm saw, drill press, lathe and bandsaw. The working space is shaded and free from corner posts, with 6½ ft. of headroom and plenty of clearance for each tool. The gull-wing doors close for a low wind-resistance profile, with a positive weather seal that doesn't leak even at highway speeds.

Organizing the Project

How one builder creates order at the job site

by David Gerstel

Workers are often blamed for poorly constructed buildings. But I think the builders in charge have to shoulder at least half of the blame because of their bad management practices. Construction sites sometimes tell the story at a glance. I've seen some that resemble public dumps, and others where crews stand idle for lack of materials.

I must admit that once my crew and I have a project underway, we are sometimes tempted to neglect the supportive tasks not directly connected to building. We might want to postpone daily cleanups, stacking materials in rational piles, storing tools and taking measures to protect the client's property. These chores seem to be a distraction from the making of floors, walls

and roofs. But though they may appear costly and irksome at the moment performed, in the long run they are well worth doing.

It is hard to pin down the amount of time workers lose stumbling over debris or digging through sloppily stored materials on a messy site. But I suspect the loss exceeds the cost of keeping the site in order, considering that good site maintenance is necessary for good workmanship, that good workmanship prevents callbacks, and that callbacks can take a substantial bite out of a small company's profits.

Project warehouse—To control the array of equipment and supplies used in residential construction, builders need a coherent storage sys-

tem. When my crew and I first set up a new site we organize a mini-warehouse (photo above) On a remodel, the "warehouse" will likely be the client's garage. Along one wall we place our tools, using heavy wooden crates as modular shelving. Each carpenter gets room for his tools and company tools are stored in another space

Along the opposite wall, we organize our supplies. Fifteen buckets each hold a different type of nail. Fifteen plastic bins (Turnkey Material Handling, Inc.; P.O. Box 2000, 36 Letchworth St., Buffalo, N. Y. 14213), some sectioned with half-gallon milk cartons, hold various categories of hardware. One bin is for joist hangers, straps and similar framing hardware. A sectioned bin holds different types of screws, tacks and sta

From *Fine Homebuilding* magazine (February 1988) 44:46-49

Protecting the clients' house

If we are working on a remodel, we begin the job with a series of protective measures. We cover heating registers exposed to debris with window screening. It keeps the big stuff from falling into an inaccessible run of ductwork, yet allows the heating system to operate. Over the floors, we tape down a double layer of kraft building paper. If one layer tears, the other still provides protection. In areas of heavy demolition we top the kraft paper with sheets of plywood.

To seal off the areas of the house that are occupied by the clients, we stretch polyethylene curtains across passageways. To protect the walls, we cover them with polyethylene sheets attached with duct tape or stapled to wood strips held in place by small finish nails. The holes left by the nails are almost invisible, and easily patched.

At the outset of a job we establish a dump area for waste and debris, which we keep covered with an opaque tarp. When the dump pile grows to a pickup truckload, we have it hauled away. Recently we invested $400 in a Milwaukee industrial vacuum that keeps the site free of the fine dust stirred up by brooms.

Before any demolition begins, we remove doors, windows, trim, hardware and accessories. Since we may reuse the trim, we bundle related pieces (all the casing from one window, for example) into packages and label them. Hardware and accessories we store in a bucket. All the salvaged items are assigned a corner in the warehouse, where they remain until the job is done. That way, we never find ourselves grieving for a piece of molding or a latch that was dear to the client's heart and has now disappeared into the whirlwind of demolition and framing.

Builders who reduce their clients' pain of cohabiting with construction work will find the effort worthwhile. Instead of disgruntled clients calling to complain, the friends of pleased clients will be calling for the builder's services. Many owners have had their properties trashed by careless builders, and will appreciate considerate builders. The tidiness of our sites is the feature of our work that clients and visitors most frequently comment on. It seems that they cannot judge the quality of the carpentry, especially the rough work, but take assurance from the neatness of the site that the construction is also done with care.

When we do new construction, we extend to neighbors the same consideration we give to remodeling clients. Realizing that a messy construction site is a neighborhood blight, we keep ours neater than concern for efficiency might call for. The neighbor of every construction project is a potential client. And honestly, we can't stand working in a mess. —D. G.

Gerstel protects floors with a double layer of kraft paper, and walls with polyethylene sheeting stapled to wood strips. If walls and ceilings are to be removed, he puts down a layer of plywood on top of the kraft paper, and duct-tapes the seams.

---

bles; another holds various tapes: duct tape, plumber's tape and drywall tape. At each site a few bins are set aside to store hardware ordered specifically for that project.

When we shift our supplies around a site or to the next project, the buckets and bins move and stack readily. Most important, they sharply reduce our "go-fer" runs. On many building sites, go-fer runs are a daily occurrence. We go weeks between runs. Our buckets and bins act as an inventory system, giving us advance notice when we are about to run short of a stock item.

As buckets and sections of bins near empty, we note the items on a "needs" list and phone them in to our supplier, for delivery with our regular loads of lumber, drywall, doors and hardware. Occasionally we do have to schedule a separate delivery for depleted hardware and miscellaneous items. Our suppliers will have their drivers drop off a small load for $10 or $15—less than the cost of a trip to their yards. Rarely does one of our crew have to break stride to leave the site for supplies.

Care of the clients—When remodeling, we take steps to protect the clients' home from our work (sidebar, above). At the outset of a job I introduce the clients to the crew and, as they appear, the subcontractors. I frequently discuss details of the project with the clients. But I've found that because of the complexity of construction, clients often lose track of their respon-

sibilities. So early on I also establish a "communication corner," say the fireplace mantelpiece. There I keep a manila folder in which I can place notes and lists of tasks for the clients (choose plastic-laminate color, select tile, get towel bars), and where they can leave me their questions and instructions.

When the job is about one-third complete—the frame is up, rough plumbing is in and work seems to be flying along—I offer the first caution against what a builder friend calls the "90% blues." At this point I warn the clients that the job will seem to come to a standstill. So while they enjoy the swift changes of the rough-in, they should also brace themselves for the long haul of the finish work. I'm never sure the advice does my clients much good, but it helps me to keep the faith during those last phases of the job when it seems that for every detail scratched from the final punch list, three more are added.

Keeping a project on track—Well-organized builders spend much of their day putting items on, and scratching them off, lists. Good lists map a project, so that a builder can complete it with a minimum of missteps. In designing a set of lists, the important considerations are these: Which lists should be kept? Which are redundant? How do master and subordinate lists feed each other? Who should make the various lists—job foreman or contractor? Where are they kept?

Keeping lists is an acquired taste. Often it does not come easily to contractors and carpenters, a freedom loving and hell-for-leather bunch on the whole. One carpenter I worked with hated my list making so much that he not only refused to keep the lists I requested, but nagged other carpenters to refuse, also.

We, however, like our lists. Now that we have cultivated the habit of keeping them, my crew and I comfortably depend upon them to keep our jobs on track and tightly organized. Each detail of construction is effortlessly and automatically noted in a logical place. It does not disappear into our overcrowded memories but is attended to in due course.

The lists—List making for a project starts as soon as I begin negotiating for its construction. I set up a manila folder for the project's paperwork. On the folder's inside flap, I write the phone numbers of the client, the architect, engineer, building inspector and anyone else with whom I will be in constant contact.

Next, I make what I call my "Do" list. I fold a sheet of typewriter paper the long way and clip it to the inside of the folder. At the top of the sheet I write "Do." Underneath, I list the items I must take care of to keep the project tracking smoothly. My first "Do" list includes all the steps of generating an estimate for the project.

The estimate includes all the steps of construction arranged in sequence and serves as a basis for writing the flow chart for the project (chart, next page). With a glance at the flow chart, I can tell exactly when my subcontractors need to begin and end their work, so that we can complete the project on schedule. A corner of the chart serves as a convenient place to

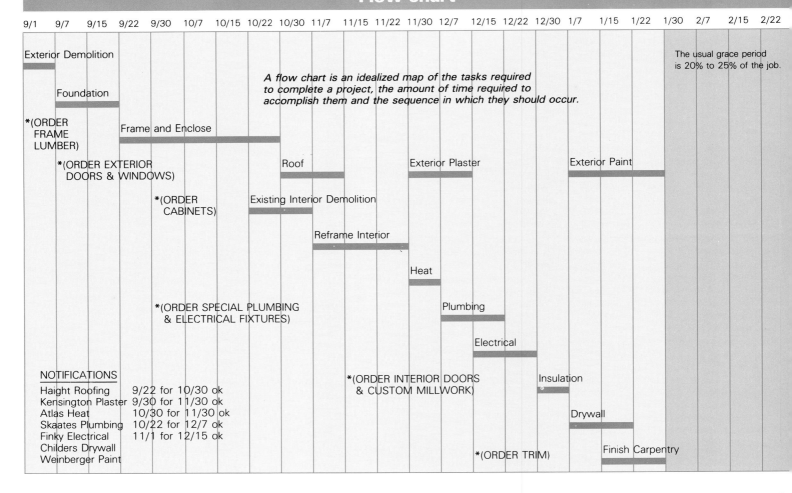

Flow chart

| 9/1 | 9/7 | 9/15 | 9/22 | 9/30 | 10/7 | 10/15 | 10/22 | 10/30 | 11/7 | 11/15 | 11/22 | 11/30 | 12/7 | 12/15 | 12/22 | 12/30 | 1/7 | 1/15 | 1/22 | 1/30 | 2/7 | 2/15 | 2/22 |

Exterior Demolition

Foundation

*(ORDER FRAME LUMBER)

Frame and Enclose

*(ORDER EXTERIOR DOORS & WINDOWS)

Roof

Exterior Plaster

Exterior Paint

*(ORDER CABINETS)

Existing Interior Demolition

Reframe Interior

Heat

*(ORDER SPECIAL PLUMBING & ELECTRICAL FIXTURES)

Plumbing

Electrical

*(ORDER INTERIOR DOORS & CUSTOM MILLWORK)

Insulation

Drywall

*(ORDER TRIM)

Finish Carpentry

The usual grace period is 20% to 25% of the job.

A flow chart is an idealized map of the tasks required to complete a project, the amount of time required to accomplish them and the sequence in which they should occur.

NOTIFICATIONS
Haight Roofing   9/22 for 10/30 ok
Kensington Plaster   9/30 for 11/30 ok
Atlas Heat   10/30 for 11/30 ok
Skaates Plumbing   10/22 for 12/7 ok
Finky Electrical   11/1 for 12/15 ok
Childers Drywall
Weinberger Paint

keep track of notifications to subs. I also use the chart to note deadlines for ordering supplies not readily available at the lumberyard in order to avoid bottlenecks in the job.

Here I've shown a portion of a flow chart for a $200,000 residential remodeling project that included a three-story addition, deck, wine cellar and extensive interior work. The project was organized to minimize disruption of the client's life, so I scheduled the shell of the addition to be completed before we touched the existing interior. Note that the critical elements of the job—namely those which must be completed before others can begin—step down the chart from left to right. Non-critical items (those which could be fitted in at various stages of the job without upsetting overall progress) are placed outside these steps. I also flag items that must be ordered well in advance by bracketing and capitalizing them.

The grace period included at the end of the flow chart is especially useful with contracts that carry a penalty for delayed completion of the project. Nothing takes the satisfaction out of a job or erodes quality like the pressure to rush to completion. A grace period acts as a pressure release valve.

Calculation of a grace period is not guesswork. Instead, all the delays that can occur in a project, such as the plumber arriving to begin rough-in two days later than optimal, are estimated and added up. The total, or some reasonable portion of it, is the grace period. In my experience, grace periods are 20% to 25% of the estimated length of the job.

The flow chart and "Do" list are kept in a folder in my briefcase. A second set of lists comprises what I think of as my "shirt-pocket office." In my shirt pocket I always carry two small notebooks. One is a month-at-a-glance calendar with a day-at-a-glance calendar, made of a sheet of typewriter paper, clipped to it. The other, a small looseleaf binder, contains questions and points of information. It has a page for the major individuals—the client, the foreman, the plumbing sub, the architect and so on—associated with each ongoing job.

At the job site is a third and final set of lists, kept by the foreman. The most important of his lists is the sequence/takeoff list, which records in chronological order each carpentry operation and the materials needed for it.

Rather than make a separate sequence/takeoff list, some builders give their estimates to their foreman, who uses them as a construction guide. My carpentry estimates, however, are done in quite large units—so many board feet of 2x4 for all exterior walls, for example. The foreman needs more precise units—so many 14-ft. and 20-ft. 2x4s for first-floor sills and plates.

Before the job begins, I work from the estimate to list the carpentry operations. On small jobs I list every step in the project. On large jobs I delay finish lists till the rough work is nearing completion. I leave ample room between each item for the foreman and me to make additions

and notes on technique. He completes the lis and does the detailed material takeoffs.

In the past, I did the detailed takeoffs. But th foreman finds the procedure helps him to ac quire the same grip on the project that I got b doing the estimate. Moreover, we have bot learned that material deliveries rarely corre spond exactly to site needs. The foreman ha found he can more readily make field adjust ments when he is the author of the takeoff.

During the workday, the foreman usuall keeps the sequence/takeoff list close at hand i an aluminum forms folder. Along with it h keeps a running list of needs for our on-sit warehouse and a list of questions and observa tions that the crew has for me during my dail visits to the site.

Now, the challenging aspect of our list sys tem: using it.

Linking the lists—One friend who read a early draft of this article told me that she identi fies with the carpenter who refused to keep list. It all sounded dreadfully compulsive. I better illustrate my explanations with cartoons she advised, or be dismissed as a hopeless neu rotic better suited to a career as a statisticial than a builder.

Without denying the charge, I'd like to ob serve that the good builders I've known all shar a certain instinct (compulsion?) for order. Dili gent list making requires that. But it is also tru that once the system and the habit of using it ar

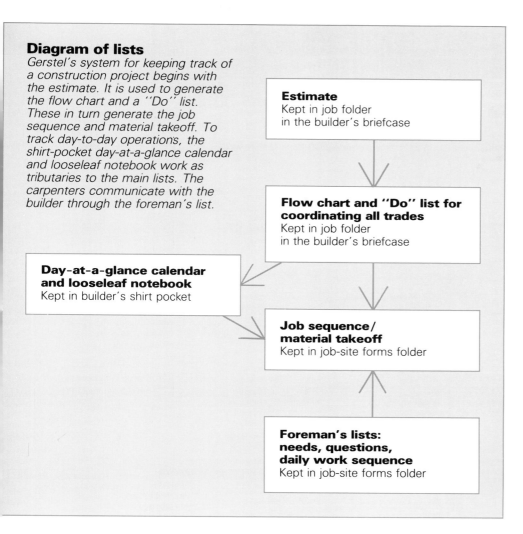

Diagram of lists

Gerstel's system for keeping track of a construction project begins with the estimate. It is used to generate the flow chart and a "Do" list. These in turn generate the job sequence and material takeoff. To track day-to-day operations, the shirt-pocket day-at-a-glance calendar and looseleaf notebook work as tributaries to the main lists. The carpenters communicate with the builder through the foreman's list.

Estimate
Kept in job folder
in the builder's briefcase

Flow chart and "Do" list for coordinating all trades
Kept in job folder
in the builder's briefcase

Day-at-a-glance calendar and looseleaf notebook
Kept in builder's shirt pocket

Job sequence/ material takeoff
Kept in job-site forms folder

Foreman's lists: needs, questions, daily work sequence
Kept in job-site forms folder

established, the lists are used automatically. In fact, they prevent the "oh my God, I forgot to call for an inspection" panics that yank builders out of sound sleep many a night.

Lists must not only be complete but must be used in a systematic relationship to each other. They must form a complete net, not one with gaping holes so that items fall between lists and are forgotten. The relationship of our lists is described in the chart above.

I usually begin my day with a look at my shirt-pocket calendar. Frequently I rewrite it quickly to make sure I have the day's tasks arranged in the most efficient order. Generally I have phone calls to make and appointments to keep in the morning. As each is completed, I scratch it off the list. All devoted list keepers know the great satisfaction of scratching off. One builder I know actually lists items that could be left to memory in anticipation of the fun of putting a line through them when they are done.

By always having the small looseleaf in my shirt pocket along with the calendar, I ensure that I do not lose track of important questions and ideas. My best ones arrive at odd times, like when I'm bellying around in a crawl space or reading the sports page at lunch. With the looseleaf handy, I can jot them down for the appropriate person before they flee from memory.

When the morning's work is complete, I head for the job site and again consult the day-to-day calendar for the items I need to attend to there. I walk about the site, talk with subs and look

over the work. As I do, the looseleaf binder goes in and out of my pocket. I'm checking it for questions that need to be asked or recording additional questions as they come to mind. If I pause to make a phone call to the architect, inspector or a supplier, I open the looseleaf and check it for questions again. Checking my notes saves me those hasty and embarrassing redialings to ask the question I forgot to ask the first time we were talking.

During my visit to the job site, I check my flow chart. A flow chart is, of course, an idealized sketch of the way a job should proceed, and must therefore omit innumerable details. On every project the chart must be fitted to reality. For example, the flow chart here shows roofing work occurring before exterior plaster. In fact, part of the roof work—namely the gutters—could not be completed until the stucco contractor had finished. Such variations from the chart as well as the finer details of the coordination of the subcontractors' tasks are filled out on the "Do" list as the job proceeds. I frequently add to and refine the "Do" list during my daily visit to the site. As I make adjustments during a project, I take care to stay with the original flow-chart pattern of scheduling subs sequentially, not simultaneously. Some years ago, I stuffed plumbing, electrical and heating subs along with carpenters into a 12x15 bedroom/bath remodel. The resulting havoc taught me to spread the subs out.

At the end of my daily visit to the site, I talk

with the foreman. We trade questions and answers from our various lists, and as required we add items and notes on procedure to the sequence/takeoff list. As I leave the site, I consult my calendar for the next task.

The day-to-day calendar is for six days only. I know that if I let it, the construction business will keep me going every waking hour. I do insist on one free day a week.

One project at a time—We work on one project until it's nearly complete before we move to the next, rather than work on many jobs at once. A competitor of mine recently dissolved his company in frustration and bitterness with the building business. Looking back on his career as we stood chatting one day, he thought he had probably made his wrong turn when he expanded to multiple crews in hopes of big money.

The temptation is there, and sometimes I wonder how much income I have sacrificed by staying with one crew on one project at a time. Maybe none. One project run to maximum efficiency can net more than several run poorly. And the chances of a disastrous loss are less. A project that is badly estimated or bogged down because of inadequate attention from a contractor stretched thin over multiple projects can bury a year of earnings.

The rewards of running one project at a time go beyond financial. I enjoy a large measure of the personal freedom that drew me to the life of the builder in the first place. I'm not running about putting out fires and working to exhaustion. I have time to do my builder's work carefully, and I also have time for hobbies and friends. I'm not an office-bound estimator and money watcher, known to the craftspeople only as a name on their paycheck. I stay close to the smell of sawdust and share in the camaraderie of the crew.

Perhaps one day I will want to organize a larger company. If I do, I may have to modify my practice of running one crew on one project at a time. Instead, I'll attempt to keep each of my crews on a single project until it is complete. Morale is damaged when workers are shifted from project to project as if they were utility tools to be shared around the company. If they stay on a project from start to finish, they'll care about it and do their best work.

After all, the ultimate purpose of management is to support good construction. In the portfolio of my own company's work, among the photos of redwood decks, vertical-grain fir trim and cherry cabinets, I have pictures of open forms with the rebar wired in place. When I show them to prospective clients, I point with pride to the accuracy of the work. Our foundation forms are square and straight and plumb to an eighth of an inch or better. That's important because finish work really begins at the foundation. It's not a bad sales pitch, but I should really say that finish work begins even earlier, well before contractor and client meet, with the development of good management practices. □

David Gerstel is a general contractor in the San Francisco Bay Area. He is writing a book on management for small-volume builders.

Backyard Shop

Site-built trusses give a builder clear-span work space, plus an upstairs office

by Charles Miller

Builder Michael Zelver wanted an office and a shop near his house, so he built this redwood-clad outbuilding a few feet behind his Victorian home in Santa Cruz, Calif. Inspired by 19th-century carriage houses, the building has about 600 sq. ft. of usable shop space on the ground floor. When he needs to do paperwork, Zelver climbs a retractable ladder that leads to the upstairs office.

Every builder needs a shop, but sometimes it seems like a lot of other business has to be taken care of before that shop becomes a reality. Before Michael Zelver, a Santa Cruz, Calif., designer and contractor, got to build his shop, he had to rebuild his entire house.

Zelver and his wife Ann Wasserman finished restoring and modernizing their derelict Queen Anne cottage in 1980. By 1982 Zelver finally had the time and money to build something that most builders want but few get: a decent shop a few feet from home.

The only buildable space left on their lot was just behind the back door of the house. There was enough room to accommodate a building with a 20-ft. by 28-ft. footprint. A shop with close to 600 sq. ft. seems like a huge space—until it's filled with a couple of workbenches, tool shelves, hardware bins, a lumber rack and assorted standing power tools, as well as work in progress. Zelver knew the space would seem inadequate soon enough, and he also knew that if his contracting business kept growing, he would eventually have to find a corner in the new building for an office. Since he didn't want an office taking up valuable ground-level shop space, he decided to make the building tall enough to allow for a second floor.

Settling on a design—Zelver's first problem as a designer was to tie the new building to the house—both architecturally and physically. The shop would be a scant 8 ft. from the back door, but he was reluctant to try to mimic the house's Victorian styling. To do so would likely have resulted in a schmaltzy building better suited to an ice-cream parlor on a beach boardwalk.

Instead, Zelver decided to give the workshop a carriage-house appearance. It would have roofs of the same pitch (7 in 12) as the Victorian house, and like the main house they would be finished with cedar shingles. But the similarity would end there. Befitting its role as a workspace in a woodsy backyard, the shop would have unpainted wood siding. Big sliding doors and wood windows with small lites would round out the list of predominant details.

To make the transition between the house and the shop, Zelver filled in the space with a deck built on the same level as the ground floor of the house. A Victorian stairway, complete with newel post and spindle balusters, leads from the deck to the brick driveway and the shop (photo left).

The shop is 23 ft. high, not quite as lofty as

From *Fine Homebuilding* magazine (December 1987) 43:68-71

the roof of the house. While he needed a shop that was tall, he didn't want to overpower the house with a clumsy monolith. So Zelver tapered the building inward, crowning it with a hipped-roof belvedere with glass walls.

Santa Cruz gets a lot of rain in the winter, and although the belvedere is vulnerable to the elements, it takes a pretty stiff gale to get the windows wet. That's because the eaves extend 2 ft. beyond the belvedere wall, and the bottom of the fascia aligns horizontally with the top of the windows. The eaves are quite visible, which gave Zelver an opportunity to dress them up with redwood lath. Tacked to the rafter tails with a pneumatic nail gun, the crisscrossing lath creates a pleasing checkerboard of light and dark in an unexpected place (photo top right).

Pipes in the slab floor—As he contemplated the design of his new shop, Zelver thought about the drawbacks and attributes of other home-based shops that he had worked in. One in particular gave him some ideas on what not to do. While using the bandsaw in a friend's shop, Zelver found the saw's cast-iron table so cold that he had to warm it up with a heat lamp. What's more, the shop had a slab floor and no southern exposure. Between the icy bandsaw and the frigid floor, Zelver could barely work. His feet literally ached from the cold.

Working under such miserable conditions made Zelver resolve to avoid a chilly shop at all costs. When the sliding doors of his new shop are open, the sun shines directly on the slab floor. This direct gain is conserved by a 1-in. thick layer of extruded polystyrene insulation around the perimeter of the slab.

Zelver hoped these simple strategies of direct gain and insulation would raise the temperature of the concrete floor enough to make it tolerable to stand on for long periods. But just in case that wasn't enough, he ran a network of polybutylene tubing on 2-ft. centers throughout the slab for a radiant-heating system. He also installed a woodburning stove.

So far, Zelver hasn't had to hook up the radiant system to get the floor to a comfortable temperature, but he doesn't regret the $100 investment in tubing. It's comforting to know that he could finish the system with relative ease.

A dust-evacuation system for his power tools was another idea Zelver got from visiting the shops of other woodworkers. Before pouring the slab floor, he planned the likely positions of his standing power tools, and assembled a network of 4-in. ABS pipe. Seven pipe stubs come flush to the level of the slab, each at a tool station. The pipes feed into a main line that's connected to a cyclone impeller and a hopper. The cyclone unit separates sawdust from air, allowing the sawdust to fall into the hopper.

Trusses—To maintain the open shop space, unencumbered by bearing walls or columns, Zelver distributed the load of the belvedere and the roof to four trusses (photo bottom right). Two of them, which Zelver calls carrying trusses, bear on posts embedded in the walls. The other two, which he calls connecting trusses, intersect the carrying trusses directly under the corners of

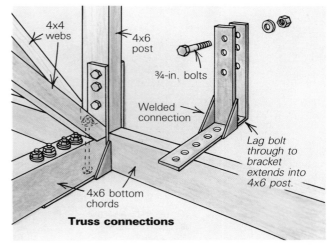

Lath trim and a truss frame. Top, crisscrossing strips of redwood lath create a checkerboard pattern under the wide belvedere eaves. Four trusses carry the weight of the belvedere and its hip roof. The truss on the left in the photo below is one of the carrying trusses; it bears on 4x4 posts embedded in the walls. The two trusses that intersect it are connecting trusses. They are bolted together using metal plates, as shown in the drawing at right. The strap across the bottom of the bracket acts as a tension tie for the bottom chord of the connecting truss. The U-shaped channel at the other end of the bracket secures the corner posts of the belvedere to the carrying trusses.

4x4 webs

4x6 post

¾-in. bolts

Welded connection

Lag bolt through to bracket extends into 4x6 post.

4x6 bottom chords

Truss connections

Michael Zelver

Drawing: Kevin Gunning

The folding staircase to Zelver's office can be retracted when the shop is in use. The office floor is made of 3x6 T&G fir decking, which spans the 9½-ft. width of the office without intermediate supports. The decking bears on angle-iron ledgers nailed to the bottom chords of the trusses.

the belvedere. These heavy-duty connections are accomplished with custom-made hangers of ⅜-in. steel and ¾-in. bolts, as shown in the drawing on the previous page.

Zelver felt confident designing the shape of the building and specifying its common framing details. However, when it came to designing the truss system, he knew he was out of his depth. So he went to a civil engineer for detailed plans.

Not only did Zelver want the trusses to hold up the loft, he also wanted to be able to put a ring bolt on the bottom chords so he could hoist heavy equipment. And since this project was partly for fun, he saw it as a chance to test out some old construction techniques that he'd always wanted to try. One hundred years ago, trusses were assembled with huge bolts and bird's-mouth intersections, and that's how he wanted to put these trusses together.

The engineer thought Zelver's plan too labor-intensive, and suggested it would be much easier to build the trusses using steel plates bolted at the timber intersections. But the side plates would have cost plenty to fabricate, and this was a low-budget project. What Zelver did have to offer was his labor, so he insisted on a design that used web members that were let into the chords. The engineer looked through an old book he had, did the calculations and worked out a design. As it turned out, it was fun to do, and not all that labor intensive.

Zelver went out of his way to find dry fir 4x4s and 4x6s for the trusses. If the trusses had been assembled from wet lumber, they would have been more difficult to lift into place, and wet timber will sometimes sag when it's put in a horizontal position. Once it sags, it stays sagged.

Where the 4x4s that carry the trusses bear on the perimeter footing, Zelver installed extra steel to keep the concrete from cracking. Even though the 4x4s are buried in the wall, he placed additional 4x4s just inside the room for the visual effect.

The trusses got their first real test of strength soon after the building was complete. While muscling his antique jointer into the shop, it fell over. Ordinarily setting a machine upright again is an uncomplicated matter of lifting it. But this jointer weighs over 1,500 lb.

Using a ring bolt for a purchase on the trusses, Zelver hoisted the jointer with a come-along. The building didn't even creak. With the machine still dangling, he called the engineer to let him know that a 1,500-lb. jointer was hanging from one of the trusses.

Office modifications—Once he finished building the shop, it took Zelver nearly two years to move his office into it. He had planned all along to locate the office on a platform built in the belvedere, but even so, he had doubts. With its 20-ft. plus ceiling and multi-lite windows it was just too pretty to cover up. But pragmatism won out, and Zelver designed a floor that would take up as little depth as possible and a staircase that would eat up a minimum of floor space.

The floor of the office is made of double T&G 3x6 fir and spans the entire 9½-ft. width of the platform without any median support. The stock comes predrilled, and when the T&G boards are assembled, they are spiked together sideways. Once common as subflooring and roofing, this material is now fairly difficult to locate. Zelver telephoned a mill in Washington that manufactures the stock and was told to call a number of lumberyards in San Francisco. One yard had it in stock, and had just enough to do the job.

For a bearing surface for the flooring, Zelver had a metal shop cut 1-in. angle iron to length and drill it for 16d nails on 4-in. centers. The ledgers are affixed to the bottom chords of the trusses, and the floorboards drop into place between the ledgers. At least they are supposed to. Zelver's run of 3x6 was warped and twisted, and had to be persuaded into position with pipe clamps and a sledgehammer.

Access to the office (photo right) is by a heavy-duty folding staircase that had to conform to several criteria. It had to be sturdy enough to withstand everyday use and long enough to handle the 10-ft. rise. Also, the stair had to be affordable. Zelver thought about making one himself, conjuring up visions of counterweights and block-and-tackle assemblies. But the effort and expense to make such a staircase persuaded him to check out commercially available stairs first. He looked through the Thomas Register (a multi-volume directory of manufacturers—libraries usually have them) under "Stairs, folding," and wrote to every manufacturer listed there, requesting literature.

Finding a stair with a 10-ft. rise was tough, but sure enough, an outfit in Texas makes one (photo facing page). The Hollywood Disappearing Attic Stair Company (9525 White Rock Trail, Dallas, Tex. 75238) even makes a folding stair that will reach a 12-ft. ceiling. At this writing, the 10-ft. ceiling model retails for $270.

Salvaged parts—Since Zelver was pinching pennies, he frequented salvage yards, looking for potential shop parts. There he found the belvedere windows, fresh from a local Army base, for $5 apiece. The huge sliding doors came from a defunct Forest Service building, and cost $100 per door.

The downstairs portion of the shop is virtually windowless. It's easier to muffle shop sounds with insulated, windowless walls, and the shop is in a quiet, residential neighborhood. Also, Zelver needed wall space for tool and material storage. And the fewer the ground-floor openings, the less risk of burglary.

All that windowless expanse meant that light would be at a premium, especially when the upstairs office became a reality. Zelver is a fanatic about having enough light, so he bought a load of surplus industrial light fixtures for $15 apiece, and hung them 4 ft. apart around the perimeter of the shop.

Zelver had planned to clad the building with board-and-batten siding. But just as he was about to shop for suitable material, a friend called to say that a couple of old redwood water tanks had become available for salvage. All Zelver would have to do was hike down a cliff, dismantle the 16-ft. tall antique structures and pack out the clear, dry first-growth lumber.

Zelver phoned some friends and assembled a work crew. They chainsawed one of the staves

At the top of the stairs, the office looks out on the treetops through the belvedere windows. The slim metal-rod collar ties do not detract from the lofty feeling of the hip roof.

into sections. Then all the other staves loosened up, and they tied a rope to the tank. When they pulled, all the hoops went down, and the entire water tank gracefully spiraled down to the ground into a nice neat coil.

They spent the rest of the day packing out the lumber on their backs. Zelver took his share to a local mill, and had the 2½-in. by 5½-in. staves milled into T&G siding. Each stave was thick

enough to yield three pieces. For the $300 milling charge, he had just enough siding to cover the entire exterior of the shop.

Zelver calculates the total cost of the shop to be about $13,000. All the framing lumber was new material, but the used doors, light fixtures and scrounged siding added up to substantial savings. Of course, this figure reflects no charges for labor. □

Carpentry Texts

Home-building tools like no others

by Tom Law

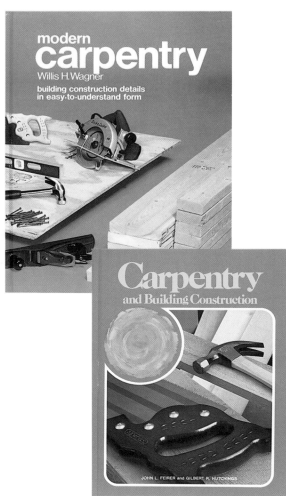

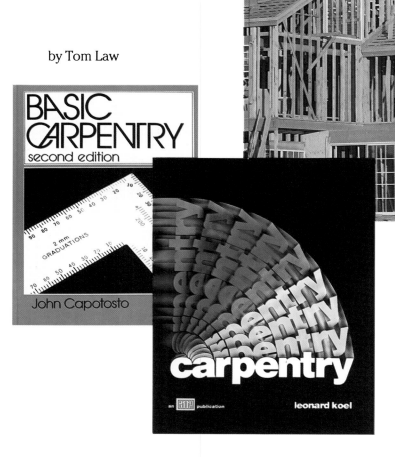

There's a simple rule about learning to be a carpenter: you can't make sawdust without sawing. And you can't lay out a line of rafters or cope a houseful of baseboards simply by reading about how it's done. Carpentry is a trade that is learned in the doing of it, and real skills can be acquired only through job-site sweat and plenty of repetition. But the foundation of any good training program will likely be books of one sort or another. A carpentry text can contain the cumulative knowledge of generations of carpenters, and that's why I took a good look recently at some of the books used in home-building and carpentry training programs.

Exactly what compels me to continue to read about the carpentry trade I'm not quite sure, but I have done it for a long time. During my four-year union carpentry apprenticeship, I worked during the day and went to school at night. I read all of the texts required for the courses I was taking and pored over additional ones when I could. When my apprenticeship was over, I studied architectural drafting and became a certified draftsman. In the years following, I continued to read trade books to satisfy

my curiosity about whether anything new was taking place. I've never thought that I knew it all, and I remain quite convinced of that today. That's why I'm so fond of books.

The carpentry trade is a very old one, and when an author takes on the task of writing a general carpentry text, distinctions must be made between what information is relevant to contemporary readers and what is outdated. But even though some of the traditional techniques aren't used much any more, I like to see them in contemporary texts. I think that a carpentry text should be encyclopedic and infuse readers with the feeling that carpentry is a time-honored craft worthy of all the intelligence and diligence one can muster. That's a lofty ideal but not one without precedent. There was a time when learned gentlemen delighted in calling themselves such things as "Architect and Carpenter."

Each of the books reviewed in this article tries to fill a slightly different niche, and nearly all of them contain at least one block of information that the others don't. The Feirer/Hutchings book is the best at showing dormer framing. Wagner is the only one to mention the use of flitch

beams over wide spans. Reed is exactly right about bay-roof framing. Koel shows accessories that carpenters can build for themselves. Some of the books focus on carpentry, while others step back to take in the whole of home building.

Some of the books, unfortunately, contain far too many mistakes. With all due respect for their authors' prodigious effort, I wish some of them had spent a lot more time coordinating text and graphic material, for this is where many of the problems arise. What follows are my observations on five books on building and carpentry.

Carpentry by Leonard Koel. *American Technical Publishers, Inc., 1155 W. 175th St., Homewood, Ill. 60430, 1985. $25.95 hardcover, $17.95 paperback; 722 pp.*
I got the feeling that *Carpentry* was written for the student in pursuit of carpentry as a career. It covers the trade from residential carpentry to heavy construction, and discusses concrete foundations, metal framing systems, noise control and solar design along the way. Its strong suit, however, is describing techniques used in residential carpentry. The book places particular

From *Fine Homebuilding* magazine (October 1986) 35:68-71

emphasis on the framing of residential floors, walls and roof; the fitting of interior finish work; and the construction of stairways. The section on building stairways is the best of all the texts I reviewed. One of the things I like about the book is its size. It's nearly as big as the telephone book for a small city, suggesting that carpentry is indeed a large subject. But after thoroughly reading its 722 pages, I'm not quite as impressed with *Carpentry* as I was when I first picked it up.

To begin with, I counted a number of errors in labeling drawings and in coordinating them with the text. This might strike you as a relatively minor complaint, but errors of any kind don't do much for my confidence in a book. In the section entitled "Roof Frame Construction," for example, the text says to fasten collar ties to the rafters with four 8d nails at each end. This would be okay if the collar ties were 1x stock, but the drawing referred to by the text shows 2x6 ties—an 8d nail (2½ in. long) won't work.

Another thing that bothers me is Koel's rather authoritarian and condescending language. Instructions frequently begin with the word "always." One of the chief things carpenters need to be able to do is improvise. If you don't have the right tool at hand, use something else, but get the job done. When Koel says, for example, that framed walls should "always" be plumbed with a level and a straightedge, he neglects the fact that a plumb bob can work just as well in a pinch. Koel often uses simple words in place of terms that should be part of a student's new vocabulary—"outside" for exterior and "notching out" for mortising.

The overall organization of the book, however, is good. As the text unfolds in a logical and systematic order, the reader is told what methods and tools have been used in the past and which new ones have been developed and are in current use. Koel's six-page discussion of the use and misuse of the circular saw (Koel calls them "circular electric handsaws") is a good one, but his section on the table saw is inadequate; it's less than a page, and only one-third of that is text.

The 25-page index at the back of the book, along with a helpful table of contents, makes it reasonably easy to find the information you want. Appendices include grade-selector charts, grade descriptions for southern pine, a chart of descriptions of APA plywood panels, and a condensed guide to plywood grades and uses.

Koel was once a journeyman carpenter, and the book shows it. The glossary includes drawings of "Trade Tips," the kind of tricks that every crotchety old carpenter delights in revealing to a new apprentice. There's a tip for straightening bowed studs, another for supporting clear-span joists when you have

to nail them in single-handed, and plenty of others. This feature is unique among the books I've seen, and I like it. Elsewhere, the book shows how to make a sawhorse—a task often assigned by employers to gauge a new carpenter's skill. A real carpenter makes his own accessories.

The best things about Koel's illustrations are that they are numerous, they're sequential and many are in exploded view. Most are in various tones of the same color (cadmium yellow, which ranges in the text from mustard to daffodil). The color adds visual interest to the text, and helps to distinguish various elements of the frequently complex drawings. Incidentally, the hardcover edition of Koel's book is also available from a publishing company that distributes A.T.P. books—they charge $39.95 for it.

Residential Carpentry by Mortimer P. Reed. *John Wiley & Sons, 605 Third Ave., New York, N. Y. 10158, 1985. $17.95 hardcover; 704 pp. Residential Carpentry* deals with specific procedures in the orderly process of building a house from beginning to end, so it's not just about carpentry. Overall, I found the book very frustrating because I kept finding that things I liked about it were offset by things I didn't like. The author uses a conversational tone, and as you read the book his personality comes through clearly. In that style, a textbook becomes less intimidating and easier to read. But after a while, Reed's

wordiness made me impatient—I kept wanting him to get on with things.

Reed's attitude about craftsmanship is good, and he encourages the reader to do the best work possible. Yet he too often discourages the solving of problems, suggesting that the carpenter should get the decisions made by the supervisor, architect or code official. Particularly on small jobs, the carpenter will likely be the one who has to deal with these problems. Throughout the book Reed talks to the reader as "the carpenter" but I really think he could also be saying "the home owner."

Reed often says that as long as individual houses are built by individuals, the methods and results will be different. In that light he shows how unusual situations will be encountered and how to solve them. He makes good points about framing rafters on intersecting roofs with unequal pitches, bay-window roof framing (plenty of details) and full-size layout of winding stairs. He also mentions job-site conditions that actually take place but are seldom seen in textbooks— applying bevel siding from the top down, for example. Another condition that we are all faced with but seldom read about is lumber shrinkage, and Reed brings it up time and again.

In the first half of the book, sections on floor, wall and rafter framing are dealt with, but the building procedures are given without a thorough introduction to the systems involved.

Readers who aren't already well versed in these systems may not be able to follow the directions very easily. Compounding the problem, procedural steps are intermixed to include platform, balloon and braced framing at the same time. It would be better to treat each system separately. Also, many of the methods described are outdated and would not be used by a production carpenter today. For example, Reed devotes nearly a page to trimming floor joists to consistent width, a technique that was more useful in the days when stock varied considerably.

The second half of *Residential Carpentry* deals with the author's strengths—insulation, drywall and cabinets. Each of these sections has an excellent introduction, and Reed's common-sense approach to these subjects makes the procedures he describes easier to follow. Reed includes several helpful appendices at the end of the book, including span tables for structural lumber and a table of R-values for various materials.

In general, I found much of the writing too elementary, and just not technical enough to include all the necessary details. As a book of procedures, this book desperately needs many more illustrations. The illustrations it has are inconsistent: some are excellent, while others look like they belong in a grade-

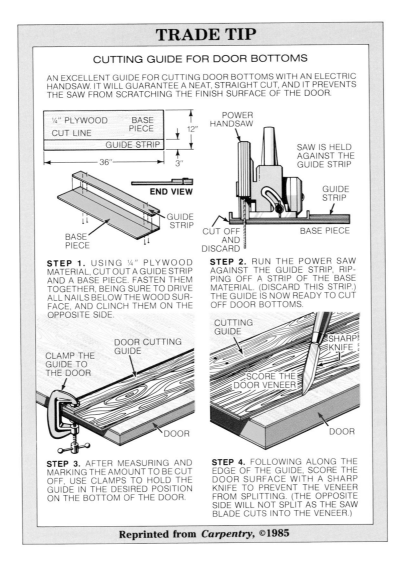

TRADE TIP

CUTTING GUIDE FOR DOOR BOTTOMS

AN EXCELLENT GUIDE FOR CUTTING DOOR BOTTOMS WITH AN ELECTRIC HANDSAW. IT WILL GUARANTEE A NEAT, STRAIGHT CUT, AND IT PREVENTS THE SAW FROM SCRATCHING THE FINISH SURFACE OF THE DOOR.

¼" PLYWOOD
CUT LINE
BASE PIECE
GUIDE STRIP
12"
36"
3"
END VIEW
BASE PIECE
GUIDE STRIP

POWER HANDSAW
SAW IS HELD AGAINST THE GUIDE STRIP
GUIDE STRIP
CUT OFF AND DISCARD
BASE PIECE

STEP 1. USING ¼" PLYWOOD MATERIAL, CUT OUT A GUIDE STRIP AND A BASE PIECE. FASTEN THEM TOGETHER, BEING SURE TO DRIVE ALL NAILS BELOW THE WOOD SURFACE, AND CLINCH THEM ON THE OPPOSITE SIDE.

STEP 2. RUN THE POWER SAW AGAINST THE GUIDE STRIP, RIPPING OFF A STRIP OF THE BASE MATERIAL. (DISCARD THIS STRIP.) THE GUIDE IS NOW READY TO CUT OFF DOOR BOTTOMS.

DOOR CUTTING GUIDE
CLAMP THE GUIDE TO THE DOOR
DOOR

CUTTING GUIDE
SHARP KNIFE
SCORE THE DOOR VENEER
DOOR

STEP 3. AFTER MEASURING AND MARKING THE AMOUNT TO BE CUT OFF, USE CLAMPS TO HOLD THE GUIDE IN THE DESIRED POSITION ON THE BOTTOM OF THE DOOR.

STEP 4. FOLLOWING ALONG THE EDGE OF THE GUIDE, SCORE THE DOOR SURFACE WITH A SHARP KNIFE TO PREVENT THE VENEER FROM SPLITTING. (THE OPPOSITE SIDE WILL NOT SPLIT AS THE SAW BLADE CUTS INTO THE VENEER.)

Reprinted from *Carpentry*, ©1985

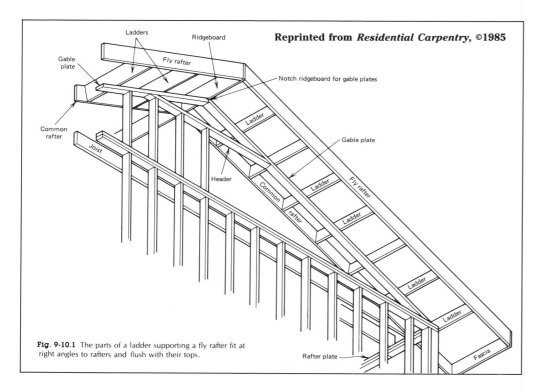

Reprinted from *Residential Carpentry*, ©1985

Ladders
Ridgeboard
Gable plate
Fly rafter
Notch ridgeboard for gable plates
Common rafter
Joist
Gable plate
Header
Ladder
Ladder
Fly rafter
Common rafter
Ladder
Ladder
Ladder
Ladder
Rafter plate
Fascia

Fig. 9-10.1 The parts of a ladder supporting a fly rafter fit at right angles to rafters and flush with their tops.

school book about what carpenters do. Another inconsistency is that the illustrations do not support the text. Rules for safety in dress are given, but a photo of a workman shows him apparently unconcerned about those rules. Elsewhere the text describes a box sill on the foundation wall, and the photo shows second-floor framing. As for the printing itself, I like the new vocabulary set in bold type.

Basic Carpentry by John Capotosto. *Reston Publishing Company, Inc. (a Prentice-Hall Company), 200 Old Tappan Rd., Old Tappan, N. J. 07675, 1980. $27.95 hardcover; 544 pp.*
In his preface, Capotosto claims to "skillfully take the reader step by step through each phase of construction in building a single-family house. Nothing is left to the imagination." That's a pretty big promise for a small book, and one that Capotosto fails to deliver on. This book has too many mistakes—I wonder where the technical reader was before it went to print.

Capotosto's writing style is spare, and his sentences have a clipped cadence that made me long for a few smoothing words now and then. The book is full of inconsistencies. The front cover, for example, features a drawing of a metric framing square, yet the discussion of metrics is quite brief.

The book is clearly intended to accompany classroom instruction: each chapter ends with a glossary, review questions and suggestions for student activities. It also emphasizes tool safety. The longest chapter is on rafters, and many unusual conditions are explained. For example, it describes how to lay out rafters for an unequal-pitch roof with a continuous cornice.

The book is entirely black and white. It looks a little drab, especially when compared to Koel's blazing yellow drawings. The illustrations are not good enough. In the rafter section, roof planes are shown as shaded lines when they should show the rafter locations as a framing

plan does. And the only person who could get away with a drawing like the one on page 388 (a hand holding a circular saw) was H. H. Seigle. The photos are not too bad, though some look like they came from old shop manuals that saw their best years long ago.

Modern Carpentry by Willis H. Wagner. *The Goodheart-Willcox Company, Inc., 123 Taft Dr., South Holland, Ill. 60473, 1984. $21.00 hardcover; 592 pp.*
For years, an old friend has been telling me that the Wagner carpentry book is a good one. But I never really gave it thorough study until recently, and I wish I had taken my friend's advice earlier. For accuracy, coverage, clarity and presentation, *Modern Carpentry* is excellent. It's enough of a carpentry book to cover that subject in detail, enough of a house-building book to show you how to form and pour concrete entrance steps, and enough of a woodworking book to include color photos of 35 different woods so you can learn to identify them.

There are many good color photos, and they help to relieve some of the forbidding quality of a textbook. In fact, I was so surprised to see col-

or photos that I thought at first the book was intended for home owners—books aimed at this group sometimes use splashy color to disguise a lack of content. Wagner's straightforward writing style and the book's clean typeface makes the text easy to read.

Wagner assumes that the reader is wide awake and presents each subject directly. I especially enjoyed his frank discussion of safety. Wagner says that safety is largely a matter of attitude, and that one must be willing to invest time and and put a lot of thought into understanding work processes in order to work safely.

I found only one typographical error and only a few errors in the coordination between text and illustrations, a great contrast with some of the other books I reviewed. I also learned some good tips. One is that using lemon oil to clean your tools will leave an oil film on them for rust prevention. Another tip will change the way I shingle sidewalls. I have always adhered to the "two nails no matter what" rule that applies to nailing wood roof shingles, and assumed that it was also true of nailing wood sidewall shingles. Wagner, however, says to use three nails when shingles are applied as double coursing on sidewalls. This struck me as strange—until I looked it up in the standards put out by the Red Cedar Shingle and Handsplit Shake Bureau and found that he's right.

When someone shows you how to do something more simply and easily, you wonder why you've done it the hard way for so long. When laying wood shingles, I have always run the field first and worked into the valley. This technique is a chore because it calls for a lot of fussy fitting at the valley. But Wagner shows a better way to do it: run the valley first. Eureka! Maybe roofers who work with wood shingles every day know this trick, but for me, this one tip made the whole book worth reading.

Wagner's discussion of framing is excellent. Along with a complete description of floor framing he discusses special problems, like what to do about joists that must be cut to allow plumbing pipes to pass through them. In the section on wall framing, he explains why the 16-in. and 24-in. centers we use for laying out studs are an established practice. This spacing is only to accommodate the sheathing material, and not necessary for structural purposes.

The presentation of rafter framing is also good, but not exhaustive. This is a beginning

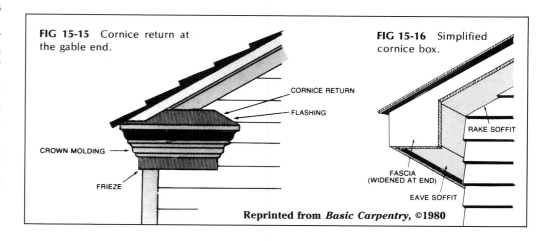

FIG 15-15 Cornice return at the gable end.

CORNICE RETURN
FLASHING
CROWN MOLDING
FRIEZE

FIG 15-16 Simplified cornice box.

RAKE SOFFIT
FASCIA (WIDENED AT END)
EAVE SOFFIT

Reprinted from *Basic Carpentry*, ©1980

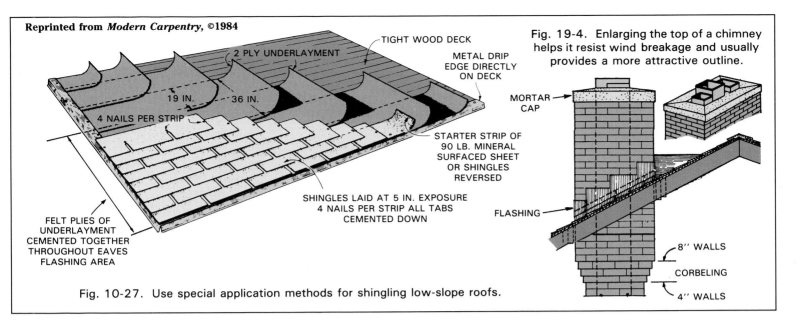

2 PLY UNDERLAYMENT

TIGHT WOOD DECK

METAL DRIP EDGE DIRECTLY ON DECK

19 IN. — 36 IN.

4 NAILS PER STRIP

STARTER STRIP OF 90 LB. MINERAL SURFACED SHEET OR SHINGLES REVERSED

SHINGLES LAID AT 5 IN. EXPOSURE 4 NAILS PER STRIP ALL TABS CEMENTED DOWN

FELT PLIES OF UNDERLAYMENT CEMENTED TOGETHER THROUGHOUT EAVES FLASHING AREA

Fig. 10-27. Use special application methods for shingling low-slope roofs.

Fig. 19-4. Enlarging the top of a chimney helps it resist wind breakage and usually provides a more attractive outline.

MORTAR CAP

FLASHING

8″ WALLS

CORBELING

4″ WALLS

text, I realize, but I kept hoping for a better discussion of unit lengths and the layout of commons, hips and valleys. Wagner's explanation of the common difference in hip and valley jacks is probably the best I've ever read. While it is not hard to put the jacks into place, explaining how to get them started is very difficult.

Modern Carpentry lives up to the first part of its name by including chapters on thermal and sound insulation, prefabrication and solar construction. As with most of these texts, some women are shown doing work that has traditionally been men's. The difference in Wagner's book is that he shows them actually at work and not just modeling. And Wagner points out that the building paper that we have used for so long is not needed where sheet goods like plywood are used, because the sheets don't have the many spaces between them that board sheathing has. Thank you. I haven't used building paper for years on my own work, but have been required to on many architects' jobs. Wagner's appendices provide a wealth of information—span tables, drawings of construction details, fastener specifications and more.

Carpentry and Building Construction by John L. Feirer and Gilbert Hutchings. *Glencoe Publishing Co., Bennett & McKnight Div., 809 W. Detweiller Dr., Peoria, Ill. 61615, 1986. $32.44 hardcover; 1,120 pp.*
Carpentry and Building Construction is full of information on the methods and materials of house building. It's so concerned with house building, in fact, that I think it could easily drop "carpentry" from its title. The tone is matter-of-fact; it's neither authoritarian like the Koel book nor encouraging like Reed's.

This voluminous book strikes a good balance between basic and advanced information, and

MAIN ROOF VALLEY JACK

MAIN ROOF VALLEY JACK

CRIPPLE COMMON RAFTER

DORMER VALLEY JACK

30–29. *Framing a gable dormer with side walls.*

VALLEY RAFTER

DORMER RAFTER PLATE

DORMER SIDE STUD

DORMER CORNER POST

CRIPPLE COMMON RAFTERS

does so with the confidence that comes from the acquisition of vast, assiduously gathered data. Its discussion of plywood grades and construction is particularly good, and it, too, says that building paper can be eliminated under a variety of circumstances. Concerning the discussion of dormer framing, my only complaint is that the text doesn't quite agree with the drawings, which are very accurate.

The book does a better job of compiling information than it does of providing instruction in procedures. Even though it's an excellent book, I'd rate it second to Wagner's—my background is in carpentry, not building, and if I were an apprentice again I'd be looking for the kind of instruction that Wagner provides. If I wanted more information about other aspects of building, however, or if I were in a building trade where product information was important, I'd choose Feirer and Hutchings. For example, I didn't find the chapters concerning termites, moisture problems and ventilation all that use-

ful. I'd rather see these parts boiled down a bit so that the authors could add to the chapters on roof framing and stair building.

A short portion of most chapters is given to estimating, which is another thing I think could be reduced—I guess that's my carpentry bias again. Estimating is difficult to do, particularly when it comes to figuring the labor requirements. In the chapter on building stairs, the authors state that the time requirements given may not be accurate. Indeed that's so, and these estimates could miss by a mile.

The book is easy to read and understand, but I don't much care for the typeface—I found its light weight hard on my eyes after a long read. There are lots of illustrations and black-and-white photos in the text. But I think the book could be improved by increasing the page size from 7 in. by 9 in. to something more like Wagner's 8¼ in. by 11 in., so that illustrations could be closer to the relevant text. As it is, the pages get pretty crowded sometimes and the drawing or photo that corresponds to the text you're reading might be several pages away. I found this awkward.

For Canadian readers, Feirer and Hutchings offer a big advantage over the other books. *Carpentry and Building Construction* is the only book I'm aware of that's available in an SI (Système Internationale) metric edition. Published by Copp Clark Pitman Ltd. (495 Wellington St. West, Toronto, Ont. M5V 1E9, 1982; $44.95 Canadian; 1,034 pp.), the metric edition is based on an earlier edition of the Feirer/Hutchings book. It was adapted by Peter Wilson, and is essentially the same book as the American version but for changes in measurement and building materials sizes. □

Consulting editor Tom Law is a custom builder and carpenter based in Annapolis, Md.

Microcomputers for Builders

A primer on what computers can do for a builder's business

by William Oberschulte

Jay Watson, a custom home builder based in Sandpoint, Idaho, spent two weeks last winter learning how to apply his Macintosh computer and a program called Multiplan to his business. Now that he has the program up and running, business around his office can proceed in the following manner. Watson receives a set of preliminary plans for a new home and is asked to prepare an initial bid to cover foundation and framing work. He knows that these plans will change as the total cost of the project comes into focus, but if he's using his estimating program he needn't be half-hearted in the initial bidding effort because revisions will be easy.

Doing a plan takeoff and estimate can take considerable time, and frequently sections of the estimate can be unintentionally overlooked. Watson has customized his program to include a checklist of critical tasks, so he can be confident that he hasn't left out any important parts of the bid. For instance, his program asks the northerly question, "Does this house have a frostwall?" Since he has his material and labor costs stored on disk, Watson can plug them into the estimate. He has a program that displays the last date a price change was made. If it isn't current, he can change it.

When he finishes his takeoff, Watson prints out a preliminary cost breakdown, like the one on the facing page. It is neat and organized, and all the computations are accurately calculated by the program.

Since the original set of plans was preliminary, Watson knows changes will occur. But instead of a pencil list on a yellow pad that has to be scratched out and recalculated, revisions to the estimate are clean and easy to find. If the subfloor gets changed from ⅝-in. plywood to ¾-in. plywood, he substitutes the appropriate unit price. A keystroke sends the new information rippling through the entire bid, and the new estimate chugs out. This works for one change, or a thousand. With a well-organized cost breakdown, Watson has a detailed listing of all aspects of the project and he can confidently negotiate with his client. If the deal goes through, Watson prints three copies of the breakdown (which averages 30 pages)—one each for Watson, the client and the crew. In it, every stick of lumber is listed as to where it ends up in the building. This ensures that the 16-ft. 2x4s in the greenhouse don't get turned into 8-ft. studs.

When he draws up a contract, Watson recalls that some of his revisions to previous contracts clarified areas of nebulous responsibilities. With the word processor, he can quickly select those paragraphs from contracts stored on disk and insert them into his standard contract form.

During the course of the job, Watson decides to get a new compressor to power the crew's pneumatic framing guns. He puts his database program into his computer and calls his tool-inventory file. Watson enters the date of purchase, serial number and price of the new compressor. This file gives him a record for insurance and tax-depreciation purposes.

As the project progresses, Watson uses his job-costing program to get up-to-date reports on labor and material expenses. By keeping current he can anticipate his money needs and plan his payments to suppliers to take advantage of discounts and avoid penalties for past-due bills.

Watson's crew just about has the frame completed when the client decides to add a pair of French doors to a wall that has already been framed. No problem says Watson. He gets out the word-processing program, calls his change-order file, fills in the data and prints out a tidy change order for his client to sign.

To generate data for his job-costing program, Watson has his employees fill out time cards that list the day in half-hour increments. Each employee notes the time spent for a specific task and the materials that it required. When this kind of information is gathered for an entire project, Watson has a good idea of what it *really* costs to have his crew build a structure, with breakdowns for specific tasks. He can then bid future jobs with less guesswork, and know when he's cutting a bid too close. Watson knows that sometimes the best bid a builder ever makes will be the one he doesn't get.

To compute, or not to compute—Like everybody else in business, builders can't avoid feeling pressured by the media, schools and advertisements to computerize their business operations. Computers are portrayed as magical saviors that create order from chaos and eliminate hours of tedious paperwork. This is partly true, and as Jay Watson can attest, partly false.

Microcomputers are just dumb machines. To do useful work, a knowledgeable operator has to provide them with accurate information. Thinking otherwise is like expecting a table saw to make beautiful cabinets all by itself. Just as the craftsman works wood with the aid of jigs and templates, the computer operator manipulates information with the aid of software.

This article is a look at how builders can use computers to handle the tedious tasks of estimating, scheduling and writing contracts and change orders. If you decide that a computer might help your operation, be forewarned that it is difficult to have a casual relationship with one of these devices. Almost every community has night-school classes in using a computer, and I strongly urge anyone who is thinking about getting a computer to take a beginner's class in computer operation. It takes time to feel comfortable with computers, and every program will deal you some frustrating moments. But if your business needs a stiff dose of organization or if you're curious about new technologies, a computer may be a blessing.

The computer system—Many people hear the phrase "computer system" and think only of computer hardware—the parts you can touch, like the screen and the printer. But a computer system is made up of other parts as well: information and software.

Information exists in two states—raw and processed. Raw data, or input, is the information that gets fed into the computer, and it must be accurate. If your data is inaccurate, the conclusions it leads you to will also be inaccurate. To put it more succinctly: garbage in, garbage out.

The software, along with the computer, organizes raw data into usable relationships and stores it in a specific location in its memory. If you request information, the stored data is again processed by the software with the computer's help and sent to the printer or displayed on the screen. Processed data is called output.

Hardware is the computer and all the things that make it work, such as the monitor, keyboard and circuitry. Hardware is anything that breaks when you drop it.

Software—Before buying a computer, be sure you know what you plan to do with the machine. First identify the tasks you want the computer to perform (sidebar, p. 173), and select the software. Then find a machine that will run it.

Software is a set of programs, procedures and documentation, often stored on a magnetic medium (e.g., a floppy disk). Once in the computer's memory, the software performs certain tasks in a specific order to obtain specific results. Some of these commands are transformed into words on the computer's screen. When the computer asks you for information, you are being guided by the writer of the program to do specific tasks. Generally you can select a particular task from a

From *Fine Homebuilding* magazine (October 1986) 35:64-67

"menu" that is displayed on the computer's screen. The menu is a list of the functions performed by the program. If you accidentally request to see something that isn't on file, a good program will respond with a prompt called an "error message." It will say something like "No such record, check spelling." Through prompts, the programmer directs you to enter the correct data and select the appropriate operations.

If you experience problems with a computer system, the cause is usually software-related. Sometimes poor programming logic causes "bugs" in the software. Generally, the problems arise from confusion caused by indecipherable error messages and poorly explained prompts in the software.

The other principal software problem is the manual. Manuals can be confusing because designers and technical writers make too many assumptions about the user's level of knowledge.

A builder will normally need two types of software—operating-system programs and application programs. Operating-system programs coordinate the respective hardware parts, such as the keyboard, screen, printer, disk drives or other storage devices.

Application software allows you to do a specific business function, such as scheduling jobs or filing information, and must be run along with compatible operating-system software. Once you have the computer running, all the other programs you will use are application software.

Integrated software is the term for application programs that perform different, yet related, tasks. The PFS series by Software Publishing (1901 Landings Drive, Mountain View, Calif. 94043) and Appleworks by Apple Computer Inc. (20525 Mariani Ave., Cupertino, Calif. 95014) are two integrated programs that include word-processing, spreadsheet and database functions. The advantage of these programs is that they can communicate with one another, quickly putting information in one storage file to work in three realms.

Selecting software—Figuring out what functions you want your software to perform is half the battle—selecting it is the other half. Establish some criteria for the system you want, and present them in writing to the software dealer. Don't be taken in by the hard-sell approach. If what the salesperson demonstrates doesn't do what you want it to, go elsewhere.

Always try out a prospective program. Some publishers will provide you with a demo program; other programs have to be tried in the dealer's shop. If you can't try it yourself, don't buy it. If possible, get in touch with others who use the program, and ask them if the software meets their expectations and how easy it was to master (for an account of builders' experiences with various programs, see the sidebar on the next page).

Price is a big consideration in choosing software, but an inexpensive program isn't a good value if you can't understand its manual, if it isn't compatible with your methods or if its error messages are confusing. A good software manual should present topics in a logical and readable manner with a good index, a table of con-

```
                    DEMO DESIGN WORKS, INC.
                 ****************************
                    COST BREAKDOWN/ESTIMATE

     4/7/86                                              Page 1
 ***************************************************************
 PROJECT NAME: DEMO CUSTOM HOME
 PROJECT DESCRIPTION: FOUNDATION AND FRAMING
 ***************************************************************
 PHASE/TASK DESCRIPTION
      TAKEOFF FORMULA          TAKEOFF QTY   UNIT QTY  RATE/UNIT   COST
 --------------------------------------------------------------------
 FOUNDATION-MATERIAL
    1   Back hoe trenching
        1ft*2ft*/27cuft/3cuyds per hr   300Lft    15hrs    40.00    600.00
    2   Concrete 2000 psi
        1ft*2.5ft/27cft per cuyd        300Lft    28cuyd   55.00   1540.00
    3   Rebar 1/2"
        2 bars* 1.05 lap factor         300Lft    630Lft    0.75    472.50
    4   Concrete Piers
        1.5ft*1.5ft*2.0ft/27cft percyd  12each    2cuyd    55.00    110.00
    5   Anchor bolts 1/2" x 12"
        1 bolt/4 ft of footing          300Lft    75pcs     1.25     93.75
        ...........................................................
                          FOUNDATION-MATERIAL  Subtotal  2816.25

 FRAMING-LUMBER
    6   Floor Beams DF  SEL
        6"*10"*10ft/12" to bdft         15pcs     750bdft   1.95   1462.50
    7   Pressure Treated Plate
        2"*6"/12" to bdft               300Lft    300bdft   2.05    615.00
    8   Floor Joists
        2"*8"*14ft/12" to bdft          100pcs   1867bdft   1.85   3453.95
    9   5/8" T&G pl sub floor
        1sht/32 sqft * 1.1 waste fct    2000sqft  69shts   22.50   1552.50
   10   2X4 DF plate
        2"*4"/12"to bdft*3plates to ft  500Lft   1000bdft   1.85   1850.00
   11   92-1/4" Studs DF
        1 stud perft of wall            500Lft    500pcs    0.95    475.00
   12   Door headers
        4"*8"/12" to bdft*6ft span      6ea       96bdft    1.85    177.60
   13   Window headers
        4"*6"/12" to bdft*10'/2hdrs     4ea       40bdft    1.85     74.00
   14   20 ft span Trusses
                                        40ea      40ea    125.00   5000.00
   15   36 ft span trusses
                                        26ea      26ea    195.00   5070.00
        ...........................................................
                          FRAMING-LUMBER     Subtotal  19730.55

 FRAMING LABOR
   16   Layout and plates
        2 men * 8 hrs per day           2days     32hr     17.50    560.00
   17   Set posts and beams for floor
        2 men * 8 hrs per day           2days     32hrs    17.50    560.00
   18   Frame and sheet floor
        2 men * 8 hrs per day           4days     64hrs    17.50   1120.00
   19   Frame exterior walls
        2men * 8hrs per day             3days     48hrs    17.50    840.00
   20   Frame interior walls
        2men *8 hrs per day             3days     48hrs    17.50    840.00
   21   Plumb and line walls
        2men * 8hrs per day             1day      16hrs    17.50    280.00
   22   Set roof trusses
        2men * 8 hrs per day            2days     32hrs    17.50    560.00
   23   Crane rental for trusses
                                        4hrs      4hrs     75.00    300.00
   24   Sheet roof
        2men * 8hrs per day             2days     32hrs    17.50    560.00
   25   Backing/pickup
        2men * 8 hrs per day            3days     48hrs    17.50    840.00
   26   Put up fascia
        2men * 8 hrs per day            2days     32hrs    17.50    560.00
        ...........................................................
                          FRAMING LABOR      Subtotal   7020.00

                               PROJECT COST            29566.80
                          OVERHEAD/SUPERVISION          2956.68
                                     PROFIT             2365.34
                                                      ----------
                          ESTIMATE TOTAL              34888.82
```

Computer estimate sheet. **This sample estimate shows how construction phases can be broken down into their component parts. Material takeoffs are pulled from the building plans and entered under the appropriate heading. Then the computer calculates a unit quantity, depending on the formula you give it. For instance, under framing lumber the entry for six floor beams has the equation 6 in. * 10 in. * 10 ft. / 12 in. to bdft. This is the formula for converting 10-ft. 6x10 beams into a bd.-ft. figure (to a** computer, an asterisk means multiply, a slash means divide). Next to each unit quantity is the unit rate. These two entries are multiplied to get the cost for each item. Once a percentage figure for overhead and profit is given to the computer, a few keystrokes will calculate the cost of all the component parts of the project, the subtotals for the phases and the total cost with figures for overhead and profit. If any of the figures are changed, the computer will recalculate the entire bid to reflect the changes.

tents, an explanation of all screens and reports, and a good general description of the program logic. It should list user commands, and error messages with an explanation of the cause.

Error messages are a good indication of how "user friendly" a program is. In well-designed software, error messages help the new user through the running of the program. In fact, the first thing you should do upon opening a manual is to read the table of contents. If there is no chapter about error messages, go to the index. If there is no mention of error messages in the index, don't waste your time. Go to the next system on your list.

When comparing and selecting a software system, try to find out how long it will take to learn how to get proficient with it. You've got to allocate time and money for training, initial installation, entry of information and sometimes hiring a consultant to customize a program to fit specialized requirements. Good dealers offer training, and the more established software companies offer a period of free telephone support. Generally after a 90-day period you must pay for additional support, which sometimes isn't cheap.

Flexibility and efficiency are important criteria in evaluating software. Can the program be customized to fit your business without any loss in performance? Does the system need a lot of memory for storage? If it approaches the limits of the computer's memory, there won't be room for input, and performance will be sluggish.

Hardware—A computer recognizes positive and negative electrical impulses. Eight such impulses, or bits, compose a byte. Inside the computer, the central processing unit (CPU) furnishes the power to manipulate thousands or millions of bits of data at nearly the speed of light. The CPU drives the parts of the computer and directs the flow and storage of data. An important part of the CPU is the "control processor," which reads the software commands stored on a floppy disk and places them in "main memory," a giant "parking structure" where each spot has a unique identifying number or address.

This addressable memory is called random access memory, or RAM. It's random because a different program may assign different addresses. When a computer is described as having 64k of RAM, its main memory's capacity for active programs and data is 64×1024, or 65,536 bytes of information (k, a constant, is 2^{10}, or 1024). This article, for instance, contains about 28,000 bytes (or characters) of information.

Since program sizes vary, the unused portion of main memory will depend on the number of characters in your program. The unused portion of memory is the space left for you to enter information. Many programs take up a lot of space in main memory, so it's important to select a computer with a large enough RAM to hold the operating system, the applications software and the data. For instance, Version 1 of the spreadsheet program called Lotus 123 takes up approximately 96k. To run it and have room left over to use it you need at least 192k. For most builders working on residential projects, 256k of memory will be enough.

The CPU, along with the operating and applications software, directs the various devices attached to the computer. These attachments are called peripherals, and they include the keyboard, the printer, the CRT (cathode-ray tube, or monitor) and the storage devices (floppy-disk drives, hard-disk drives and tape drives).

Most computers are controlled by typing commands on a keyboard. The computer and the software interact with the user through the monitor or screen. When the computer is ready, a blinking square of light (the "cursor") flashes on the screen. As a command is typed, characters appear and the cursor advances to the right.

You don't have to be an accomplished typist to use the keyboard. If you make a mistake you simply back the cursor over the mistake, strike the erase key, and correct your error. Remember that the machine can do a great amount of work with a simple command, so typing speed is not that important.

Characters displayed on a screen are composed of a pattern of phosphorescent dots called pixels (short for picture elements). The more pixels, the sharper the characters will be. The color of displayed characters is also an important feature. Studies have shown that amber and green characters cause less eyestrain than white characters. Operators must often sit in front of the screen for hours at a time, so don't skimp on the monitor.

Some monitors support color graphics. This is nice, but if your software doesn't use colors, then save yourself the additional expense.

A range of programs and machines

I have spoken with many builders over the years, and the IBM PC (and assorted compatibles) seem to be the most popular microcomputers among builders who have more than a few employees. This is because these machines have more memory capability and a faster operating system than their early competition. As a consequence, most of the various programs aimed at the business community have been written for the PC and its clones.

Dennis Allen, a custom builder in Santa Barbara, Calif., has a crew of around 20, and they are engaged at any one time in eight to ten jobs. Allen says, "I used to spend four to five hours a night running adding-machine tapes to keep track of our time-and-materials jobs." To get out from under this load of paperwork, Allen bought an IBM PC and invested $1,500 in an integrated system from BPI (BPI Systems, 3001 Bee Cave Rd., Austin, Tex. 78746) that combines job costing, estimating, database, payroll and accounting functions. Then came the hard part. Allen says the program was very difficult to learn. He has put hundreds of hours into it now, including professional help to customize the program to suit his business. Now Allen can take care of the evening's work in an hour, and he's teaching his foremen how to bid with the computer.

San Francisco builder Kevin Wallace has a ten-man crew that specializes in remodeling. After reviewing programs designed for builders, he decided that the unit pricing typical of programs written for new construction didn't apply to the vagaries of remodeling. Says Wallace, "In our work, it can cost 65 cents to install a stud, or 65 dollars." Wallace wanted a spreadsheet that he could customize, so he bought the Lotus 123 program and learned how to manipulate it to suit his needs. Like Allen, Wallace's learning period was a time-consuming process that required tutorial help. But now he has a custom program.

Wallace insists that the computer does not replace employees, and he has more paperwork than ever. For many of his bids, the Lotus program is like a fancy adding machine. However, when he and a client start playing "what if?" he can add and subtract the changes to a project at the stroke of a few keys.

While they may not be as fast or have the memory capacity of the IBMs, the Apple II series computers are perfect for some builders. James and Gillian Servais operate a design/build firm in Berkeley, Calif., and they keep track of their business using an integrated program called Appleworks on their Apple IIE with 500k memory. The program, which lists for $250, has a spreadsheet, a word-processing program and a database. Gillian Servais says it's easy to use, and with it she keeps track of billings, correspondence, estimates and payroll for their four employees. She especially likes the checkbook-on-the-screen feature.

In the wings, a challenger awaits the PCs, and its name is Macintosh Plus. The Mac has garnered a loyal following among builders for several good reasons. It is by far the favorite among builders who want some graphics capabilities, there are many programs for it that are easy to use, and the size of its memory makes it faster and more versatile than the other Apple machines.

Craig Savage, a builder in northern Idaho, uses the Mac in his custom home and furniture business. Savage, who confesses to being "drawing impaired," uses the MacDraft program ($239 from Innovative Data Design, 1975 Willow Pass Rd., Concord, Calif. 94520) to generate small shop drawings for his projects. He has the MacWrite program ($125 list price) for word processing, and with it he was producing clean, legible letters in just a few hours. Savage uses Multiplan by Microsoft (10700, Northrop Way, Box 97200, Bellevue, Wash. 98009) to do spreadsheet estimates, and finds them powerful tools for selling clients and getting bank loans. Savage remarks, "When you present an organized-looking bid to a bank on a printout sheet, they tend to believe it."

Savage's biggest problem with the computer is its seductive mystery. "When I'm making up my bid sheets on Multiplan, I feel like I'm at the shallow end of the pool. I want to know what's at the deep end, but I continually have to ask myself, do I really need to know this?"

Not everybody has happy computer stories to tell. Sean Gilligan, a former builder from Santa Fe, N. Mex., was involved in a company developing residential communities. He and his associates tried to put the business on Symphony, an integrated spreadsheet, database and word-processing program, while expanding the company at the same time. "It was a nightmare," says Gilligan. "Symphony is a bear to learn, and we couldn't keep track of where things were because they were changing so fast." Things got out of hand, and the business went bankrupt. Cautions Gilligan, "If you're going to computerize, do it during a slow period."

While some builders I talked with say their computers are unnecessary for small-scale work, every one of them has good things to say about word processing. Dan Rockhill, an architect/builder in Lawrence, Kans., has access to a Mac and the Multiplan program, but he doesn't use it much. For most of his projects, Rockhill gets along fine with a calculator and a legal pad, and he worries that the computer will take some of the craft out of his buildings. "But," he says, "It sure is good for writing letters." —*Charles Miller*

Storing data—When you turn off the computer, all the information stored in main memory disappears. Main memory functions only with power, so a computer requires a storage device. Fortunately, software and data can be saved magnetically, similar to the way a tape recorder saves sound. Today most microcomputers use disk drives to store information.

In microcomputers there are two basic types of disk drives: the floppy-disk drive and the hard-disk drive. The floppy disk is removable. Almost all software a user purchases is stored on floppy disks. Floppies resemble small, limp records that are housed inside square plastic envelopes. They are arranged into sectors that have a specified storage capacity and a unique address. When information is stored on a disk, it is assigned a file name and an address. A directory keeps track of the starting location of the file, and the number of sectors it occupies. When you want to retrieve the information, you call the file, and the CPU displays it on the screen.

Since the floppy is removable, it can be damaged by its environment. Electrical sources, such as telephones or power cords, can generate a magnetic field, and placing a floppy disk near one can disastrously alter the information stored on it. Another hazard is dust. A dust particle on a floppy disk can cause a disk drive to misread information. Any vital information, and all software, should be duplicated on a backup disk and stored in a safe place to avoid costly replacements and lost information.

The hard-disk drive is not easily removed. It is a self-contained, sealed unit that operates much faster than a floppy disk. A floppy disk may store from 180,000 to 1,200,000 bytes of information, but hard disks typically hold anywhere from 5 million to 60 million bytes. This means you don't have to go searching for the right floppy when you need specific information.

But accidents do happen, so the user of a hard-disk system still needs at least one floppy drive. Any important information stored on the hard disk should be regularly copied onto floppies or a tape drive for backup storage. Although hard drives are dropping in price, they do add anywhere from $500 to $1,000 to the initial cost of a basic system. If you expect your business to grow, it's a good idea to buy a computer that can be upgraded to accept a hard disk when the need arises.

The cost to computerize—The cost of computers has steadily declined over the past decade. The IBM PC and the machines made by Apple are the standards in the industry, but the trend seems to be toward the non-brand-name PC clones for best value in a computer. You can now get a PC type with 256k of memory and a monitor for under $1,000. Add about $350 for a printer, $400 for software and $100 for some training and you're in business for less than $2,000. This is the low end of the scale.

The next level up is around $3,000 for the package. The difference is that you've spent $1,000 more to buy a computer with a brand name and history of performance and service.

At the high end you can expect to spend $3,000 for a microcomputer, but it will have a

Software that can help builders

Most builders who are just beginning to apply computers to their business affairs are working on a small scale. They have perhaps five employees, they do two or three major projects per year, and they want to know what functions to concentrate on. The ones below are listed in the order of importance that I think would most benefit such builders.

Estimating—Of all the business-oriented tasks confronting a builder, accurate bidding is most important. Estimates are done either with programs called dedicated software or on spreadsheets. On spreadsheets, you have to fill in the categories and equations that are appropriate, while dedicated software already has categories and equations for a specific application. Both provide the estimator with what amounts to a blackboard-size accountant's worksheet with columns for takeoffs, unit quantities, labor and material rates and the cost to the client. On the screen you look at parts of this worksheet and fill in the pertinent information.

Once the takeoffs, rates and units are filled in, the data can be easily manipulated. For example, a contractor could consider a change to his profit margin on estimates. He can quickly compare the results of different percentages and see how all items in the cost breakdown are affected by the change. If lumber prices change, the new price can be entered in the appropriate equation, and the cost for all related materials will be recalculated. The break-even point can be determined before negotiating with a client.

Job-costing—This is another spreadsheet type of program that lets you track the costs on a job by looking at how much labor and materials go into various tasks. For a job-costing program to be effective, a builder must figure out how much time and material are actually used on a project. This information can then be used to calculate unit costs, which will help determine where a project stands in relation to the budget, and eventually aid in preparing future bids.

Word processing—Anything you can do on a typewriter, you can do on a word processor. The difference is that you don't have to do it as often. You can write a contract for one job, correct any errors on the screen, then print out a perfect copy. The next time you need a contract, you retrieve the one on file, change the names and job description, and print it out again. The same holds for liens, change orders and letters.

Databases—These filing programs allow you to store information and retrieve it in a hurry in a form useful to you. For instance, you ask the computer to give you a list of framing carpenters. It hunts through your subcontractor file and displays all the framers you've listed in there. Your comments under each carpenter would probably include their phone numbers and addresses, how much they charge and how well they performed on past jobs. These listings can be cross referenced so they can be sorted into several different categories without being entered in more than one place.

Accounting—Once your staff gets large enough to need a full-time bookkeeper, you can probably make good use of an accounting program. It will keep track of your cash flow, accounts payable and receivable, payroll and related taxes, and other bookkeeping tasks you assign to it. Running an accounting program will require a large time commitment to train the operator and plug in the data, and to maintain meticulous entries of information.

Critical path—This succinctly named program type is about project management, or scheduling. It defines lead times for the portions of a construction job that have to be finished first because other tasks hinge on their completion. Builders who have large crews working on several projects simultaneously use critical-path schedules to allocate manpower and money.   —*W. O.*

hard disk with a lot of memory. Figure $1,000 each for software, printer and training, and you've got a first-rate setup for around $6,000.

Getting it in writing—When you hook the computer up to a printer you can generate "hard copy"—computerese for data on paper. A builder needs hard copy to generate an estimate, a financial statement or a contract.

In many ways the printer is the workhorse of the system. It endures more operator handling than any device except the keyboard. When you've got a printer and a word-processing program, you no longer need a typewriter. Even an inefficient hunt-and-peck typist can be fast, once the initial document is stored on disk.

Dot-matrix printers are the least expensive, and they are just fine for the needs of most builders. They use a ribbon for an ink supply, and the characters are formed by lightning-fast needles that produce tiny dots in the appropriate pattern. Print quality depends on the density of the dots. Dot-matrix printers work rapidly, which makes them good for tasks that require loads of copy, like accounting reports or estimates. Today many printers offer a "near-letter-quality" mode of printing that closely resembles the type produced by a daisy-wheel impact printer, although it prints more slowly.

Daisy-wheel printers produce crisp type, but

they aren't very fast. If you're primarily interested in making neat, clean letters or very formal reports, then a daisy-wheel printer may be for you.

An 80-column printer, no matter what its printing mechanism, generates a line of type 8 in. long. The next step up is the 132-column printer. It can do a line 14 in. long, which is perfect for spreadsheet applications like estimates. You can expect to pay $300 to $400 more for the larger printer. If you've got the smaller printer, you can still print out your estimates. A command from the computer will condense the 132 columns into an 80-column space. The type is still perfectly legible.

There are various other sophisticated printing devices on the market today. Laser printers use the photocopy principle to create high-quality print. Another type of printer can produce detailed color drawings. For designers, there are dot-matrix printers that can print graphics. For the designer/builder who wants to produce plan-size drawings, there is the plotter-type printer. They use ink-filled styluses to make crisp plans, sections and working drawings up to 3 ft. wide. You can expect to pay at least $4,000 to $6,000 for these printers.

William Oberschulte is a computer consultant who specializes in construction computer systems near San Diego, Calif.

Fine Homebuilding
Editorial Staff, 1981-1988

Mark Alvarez
Fran Arminio
Joanne Kellar Bouknight
Ruth Dobsevage
Mark Feirer
Bruce Greenlaw
Kevin Ireton
Linda Kirk
Kenneth Lelen
Betsy Levine
Michael Litchfield
John Lively
Lori Marden
Lynn Meffert
Charles Miller
Debra Polakoff
Don Raney
Paul Roman
Tim Snyder
Paul Spring

Fine Homebuilding
Art Staff, 1981-1988

Frances Ashforth
Elizabeth Eaton
Deborah Fillion
Lee Hov
Betsy Levine
Chuck Lockhart
Michael Mandarano

Fine Homebuilding
Production Staff, 1981-1988

Claudia Applegate
Barbara Bahr
Lisa Carlson
Mark Coleman
Deborah Cooper
Kathleen Davis
David DeFeo
Dinah George
Barbara Hannah
Annette Hilty
Nancy Knapp
Margot Knorr
Gary Mancini
Robert Marsala
JoAnn Muir
Swapan Nandy
Cynthia Lee Nyitray
Ellen Olmsted
Priscilla Rollins
Thomas Sparano
Austin E. Starbird

Book jacket design:
Jeanne Criscola

Book copy editor:
Kathryn A. de Koster

Manufacturing coordinator:
Peggy Dutton

Production coordinator:
Deborah Fillion

Design director:
Roger Barnes

**Editorial director,
books & videos:**
John Kelsey